Opening Day in Milwaukee

Opening Day in Milwaukee
The Brewers' Season Starters, 1970–2022

Matthew J. Prigge

McFarland & Company, Inc., Publishers
Jefferson, North Carolina

A note on sources: All statistics and transaction information are from baseball-reference.com. Play-by-play information comes from baseball-reference.com and archival game footage. All salary and payroll data, unless noted, is from thebaseballcube.com.

LIBRARY OF CONGRESS CATALOGUING-IN-PUBLICATION DATA

Names: Prigge, Matthew J., author.
Title: Opening day in Milwaukee : the Brewers' season starters, 1970–2022 / Matthew J. Prigge.
Description: Jefferson, North Carolina : McFarland & Company, Inc., Publishers, 2023 | Includes bibliographical references and index.
Identifiers: LCCN 2023002841 | ISBN 9781476689647 (print) ♾
   ISBN 9781476648637 (ebook)
Subjects: LCSH: Milwaukee Brewers (Baseball team)—History. | Baseball players—Wisconsin—Milwaukee—History. | Baseball fans—Wisconsin—Milwaukee. | Baseball teams—Wisconsin—Milwaukee—History. | Baseball—United States—History.
Classification: LCC GV875.M53 P75 2023 | DDC 796.35709775/95—dc23/eng/20230209
LC record available at https://lccn.loc.gov/2023002841

BRITISH LIBRARY CATALOGUING DATA ARE AVAILABLE

ISBN (print) 978-1-4766-8964-7
ISBN (ebook) 978-1-4766-4863-7

© 2023 Matthew J. Prigge. All rights reserved

No part of this book may be reproduced or transmitted in any form or by any means, electronic or mechanical, including photocopying or recording, or by any information storage and retrieval system, without permission in writing from the publisher.

Front cover: Aerial view of Miller Park with the retractable roof open in 2007 (Wikimedia Commons)

Printed in the United States of America

McFarland & Company, Inc., Publishers
  Box 611, Jefferson, North Carolina 28640
    www.mcfarlandpub.com

For Dad

Table of Contents

Acknowledgments   viii
Introduction   1

Chapter One. The Seventies   5
Chapter Two. The Eighties   49
Chapter Three. The Nineties   92
Chapter Four. The Aughts   135
Chapter Five. The Teens   175
Chapter Six. The Twenties   216

Appendix: The Opening Day All-Timers   231
Chapter Notes   233
Bibliography   255
Index   257

Acknowledgments

First off, I'd to acknowledge some people I've never met and who had nothing at all to do with this project. Nonetheless, their own works provided me with essential distraction and inspiration along the brief but intense journey that was creating this volume: Jon Bois, Wet Leg, the Rifftrax gang, Cher, Edi Patterson, Pam Grier, Michael Hobbes and Aubrey Gordon, Jeff Pearlman, the Chapo lads, Lindy West, Stavros Halkias, Kurt and Goldie, Sly and the Family Stone, and Joe Pera.

Closer to home, credit is due for more direct support and encouragement from Jim Cryns, Dennis Degenhardt, Chris Zantow, Liz Kaune, Jason Lebeck, Marc Brubaker, Nick Vossbrink, Jason Jennings, Daniel Mike, Ben Aguirre, Gary Garcia, Kevin Lutes, SABR and the local Ken Keltner chapter, the good citizens of South Milwaukee, and to everyone who's ever shared a moment at Opening Day with me over the years.

A thanks to all those whose photography appears in the book: Joel Dinda, Barrel Man Sammy, Spaluch1, Jeramey Jannene, Stave Paluch, Arturo Pardavila III, Lightburst, Ian D'Andrea, Chris Zantow, Bob Busser, Mark Susina, Steve Schar, Alex Voerman, Jay Seager, C. Beine, and Jessica Burch.

And a special thanks to McFarland, especially Gary Mitchem.

And finally, endless love and thanks to my wife, Erika Gudmundsson, our little beady-eyed babies, my mother Joan Prigge, my sister Angie Yamashita (Rik, Cecila, and Josie, too), and—with a debt of gratitude I cannot ever hope to repay—to my late father, Ed Prigge, without whom none of this would have been even remotely possible.

Introduction

Pop quiz: You need a Milwaukee Brewer to hit a home run in a home opener to save the universe from total destruction. This incredibly unlikely scenario presents you with two options: you can either (a) give Ryan Braun, Gorman Thomas, Prince Fielder, and Cecil Cooper—who combined to hit nearly 1,000 homers for the Brewers—a total of 140 times at bat or you can (b) give backup catcher Gorge Kottaras—who totaled 32 homers over a seven-year Big League career—one time at bat.

Should history repeat itself exactly in this scenario, Kottaras would indeed be your man. In the ninth inning of the 2012 blowout Opening Day loss to St. Louis, Kottaras rocketed a meaningless three-run bomb. Meanwhile Braun, Thomas, Fielder, and Cooper—for all their talent and endless Opening Day ovations—never managed a lid-lifter blast. What's more, if you group Braun and Cooper with Robin Yount and Paul Molitor—forming probably the great quartet of hitters in team history—and you'd find a collective Opening Day stat line of a .202 batting average, a .253 on-base percentage, and a .281 slugging percentage. That roughly equals the offensive output of 2015 Brewer Hector Gomez. Who were the top all-time Opening Day hitters for the Brewers? Among everyone who got at least one plate appearance in a home opener, Kottaras, pitcher Jhoulys Chacin, and outfielder Turner Ward comprise the top three in on base-plus-slugging percentage. Obviously.

How about the greatest single-game opener performance? Remember Glendon Rusch, the lefty who led the NL in losses in 2002 and went 1–12 with a 6.42 ERA in 2003? Well, in the '02 opener, he tossed a complete game gem against the world champion Diamondbacks and slugged a homer. Certainly overall team efforts must be better represented in Opening Day history, right? Well, no. The 10 best teams in Brewers history combined to go just 5–5 in home openers. How about the 10 worst? They also went 5–5 in home openers.

Opening Day—the term I will use throughout this book to refer to the Brewers' home opener—is, ultimately, just one game in the very long season schedule. The 53 Opening Days in team history—the 53 games documented in the pages that follow—represent about three-fifths of 1 percent of the number of games the franchise has played in its history. But I've chosen to use this tiny sample as the framework for this history of the team. The randomness and relative meaninglessness of the games is part of the point. The challenge was to tell the story of Brewers while devoting no more space to a championship season than a last-place campaign. To show Turner Ward excelling where Robin Yount failed. To end the narrative before anything really gets going. Essentially, to carve a path off the well-worn map of heroes and triumphs and tell the year-to-year story of what it means to come back to baseball with an all-too-often naïve hope about what lay ahead.

For all that Opening Day lacks in statistical meaning, it abounds in emotional meaning. It's the one day of the schedule guaranteed to draw a crowd. The one day of the schedule where hope is sure to exist. The day of the season where anyone who even might think of giving a damn is most likely to be paying attention. It's the most democratic day of the season, with every team in the league the same distance from the same prize (at least in theory). But above all, it's about coming back. Back to the ballpark. Back to the summer routine dictated by TV broadcasts and peppered with the background chatter of Bob Uecker on the radio. It's about digging things out—the folding chairs, the portable grill, the cooler—for the semi-hedonistic pleasures of wide-open blacktop and plumes of charcoal smoke. It's about catching up with old friends and family with whom baseball is the pull that keeps you from slipping out of orbit.

The last baseball game I ever watched with my dad was the 2019 opener against the Cardinals. It was the 28th straight year we'd gone together. My most selfish reason for writing this book was the recreate the feeling of being 12 years old, permitted to skip school and riding down to Milwaukee with my dad for the game. Something akin to this is likely, I suspect, the motivation for a majority of the baseball books ever written. The defining feature of Opening Day is not the baseball that will be, but the lack of baseball that was. Those game-less months are filled, of course, with hot stove action: trades, rumors, scandals, and signings. The car ride to the stadium was the time for recounting all that happened, all that had led up to this moment that would become another season of Brewers baseball. The stories that follow are as much about the long winters that proceeded (and something bled into) the opener: half car ride or tailgate prattle or batting practice chatter and half game action. Each story is also proceeded by some non-baseball placesettings: a news item from the day of the game, a movie that was playing in Milwaukee on the day of the game, and a song from the radio top 10 for the week the game was played.

In the ninth inning of that 2019 opener, with the Brewers up by a run and Lady Gaga burning up the airwaves, Josh Hader faced St Louis' Jose Martinez. Hader had faced five batters so far that afternoon and had struck out four of them swinging. No one had even come close to squaring him up. And then, on a 1–0 count, Martinez reached out and caught a fastball with the fat part of the bat. It soared toward the St. Louis bullpen as the breath left 45,000 pairs of lungs. My memory of this moment, corrupted by time and raw emotion, leaves the scene in silence. The only noise are the footsteps of center fielder Lorenzo Cain as he runs at half-speed toward the fence. In reality, it's the din of a collective Milwaukee gasp and the scattered hoots of those damn Cards fans who never miss a chance to travel. Somewhere above that rustle, Dad says to me, "He's got it."

Cain leaps, flicks his wrist, and makes one of the greatest catches I've ever seen in real life. In the outfield, Cain and his teammates jump and shout. In the grandstands, everyone else does the same. Dad and I are in awe, we trade high-fives with the spectators around us and head home happy. It was the exclamation point on a 28-year tradition. A year later, the pandemic came. A year after that, cancer. Sometime after his diagnosis, we were talking baseball and I mentioned that game and that catch. I asked him about his declaration, his casual assessment that Cain would make the game-saving grab. He didn't remember saying anything of the sort. Everything else about the play he could recall with ease. "I was sure it was gone," he said. I've considered the possibility more than once that I simply imagined his whispered reassurance.

That catch was an exclamation point. But it was an ending all the same.

The year after that, 2022, I went to the home opener for the first time without him. I went with some friends and my sister and sat in the cheap seats way up top. And in one of those treasured coincidences baseball often provides, the people who bought the tickets next to us never showed up. Although I certainly noticed it at the time, it didn't dawn on me until the next day what it meant that I had sat next to an empty chair all afternoon. They won that day, but that's not the part that mattered.

CHAPTER ONE

The Seventies

1970

Tuesday, April 7, 1970: Angels 12, Brewers 0 (36,170 attendance)
In the News: A grand jury in Dukes County, Massachusetts, has been empaneled to investigate the death of Mary Jo Kopechne, who drowned last July when a car driven by Senator Edward Kennedy went off a bridge on Chappaquiddick Island.
At the Movies: *Hello, Dolly!* at the Strand Theater
On the Radio: "Easy Come, Easy Go," by Bobby Sherman
For the most part, the players were just glad it was over.
The life of a ballplayer is, by its nature, a semi-transient one. Seven months of the year devoted to travel, all the while serving at the mercy of management. But the plight of the Seattle Pilots during the spring training of 1970 was something rare even in baseball. The entire franchise—its players, coaches, and front office—reported to camp with all the nerves and uncertainty of an on-the-fringe scrub. They had no real idea where they'd be sent once camp was over.
Seattle had been granted a franchise in 1968. Expecting to begin play in 1971, the club was forced into a premature existence when Senator Stuart Symington of Missouri pressured the league to hasten their pace in granting his home state the Kansas City Royals—Seattle's expansion partner and the consolation prize to KC for having lost the Athletics in 1967. The Pilots were forced into a not-ready-for-prime-time Sick's Stadium, a 30-year-old minor league stadium that sat only 25,000 people. The plumbing was so bad the toilets usually quit working by the eighth inning, by which time the cellar-dwelling Pilots were usually out of the game anyway. The season wasn't even over yet before rumors of relocation surfaced.[1]
The drama carried on over the off-season, during which the Pilots went through the motions of preparing for a 1970 season at Sick's. General Manager Marvin Milkes, who needed 53 different players in 1969 to win just 64 games, spent a frantic winter trying to remake his roster. He fired

manager Joe Schultz and replaced him with the 36-year-old Dave Bristol, recently canned by the Cincinnati Reds. When it came time for spring training, the year-old roster was a chaos of no-names and new faces. And even though their uniforms might have read "Seattle," no one was really sure if they should believe it or not.

Meanwhile, fans in Milwaukee had now been four years without a true home team. Having lost Henry Aaron and Eddie Mathews to Atlanta after the 1965 season, Milwaukee was left with Allan H. "Bud" Selig as the principal baseball figure to follow in the sports pages. The 35-year-old headed Milwaukee Brewers Baseball Club, Inc., a front group for local backers who wanted to win a new Major League franchise for the city. They had tried to get an expansion club without luck and suffered through a handful of near-misses in purchasing an existing club to relocate to Milwaukee. They had, however, yielded nothing more tangible for their efforts than a series of Chicago White Sox "home games" staged at County Stadium. As the open of the 1970 season approached, Selig and company threw all they had into buying the moribund Pilots. Selig had been in negotiations with their floundering ownership since September 1969, but he had rivals—both those who wished the team to stay in Seattle and those who wanted to move them to other baseball-starved cities.[2]

A few weeks before the season was set to open, with their ownership's meager resources nearly depleted, the Pilots began bankruptcy proceedings. A deal had been reached early in March to sell the team to Selig's group, but now all was held up in a tangle of courtroom mini-dramas. Waiting on a judge approve the Brewers' $10.8 million offer for the Pilots, club employees working in Arizona (the team had actually lost the lease to their training facility due to non-payment, but had yet to be evicted) loaded up a truck with gear and had it driven to Provo, Utah, to await the final word: either west to Seattle or east to Milwaukee.[3]

Finally, late on the night of March 31, the sale was approved. While it was Selig who broke down in tears, it was the brand new Milwaukee Brewers players who could finally start to figure things out. "It's been tough on them," said Bristol. "You can't tell a man to forget about the home front and worry about your job."[4]

"I'm glad it's over," said third baseman and Ohio resident Rich Rollins. "We've got five children and now it's only a plane ride across the lake. Personally, I was hoping the move would be made."[5]

"I'm sure everybody is happy when you consider the situation they had to go through last year in Seattle," said Ted Kubiak, the team's starting shortstop. "I spent six years in the minors and I wasn't looking forward to going through it all again in that ballpark up there."[6]

But even on a team with a roster as fluid as the Pilots' had been, there were still a handful of players who had been attempting to make a home in Seattle and now found their plans disrupted. Mike Hegan, one of a handful of standouts from the '69 team, had just purchased a house in the city. He still hadn't been able to spend a full day there when he was told to pack for Milwaukee. Second basemen John Donaldson also kept a home in Seattle. "I hope they take care of moving the furniture," he told the *Milwaukee Sentinel*. "It's going to cost a fortune to have it shipped to Milwaukee, $600–$800 probably."[7]

Back home, the city celebrated its return to Big League status and heaped praise on the "Milwaukee 13"—the gang of civic and business leaders who had financed the purchase. There were remembrances of the Braves—who were still just four and a half years removed from Milwaukee—and the old American Association Milwaukee Brewers, the team with which Selig had fallen in love with the game. But as for the new Brewers ... that is, the players everyone was so excited to now call the home team ... expectations were muted.

Seventeen seasons earlier, when the Boston Braves had made a similarly last-minute shift to Milwaukee, they brought with them known players like Johnny Logan, Sid Gordon, and Warren Spahn. The best known of the former Pilots was probably Tommy Harper, who led the American League in steals in 1969. The '53 Braves brought home a popular Wisconsin native in Andy Pakfo, who had starred for a half-decade as one of the nearby Chicago Cubs' best players. The Brewers' resident Wisconsinite was Gene Brabender, hardly a name a casual fan in Milwaukee might recognize. "Nobody in his right mind would even dare to suggest that the new Milwaukee Brewers have the same potential as the Braves, who moved here from Boston in 1953," *Sentinel* scribe Lou Chapman wrote in his less than charitable introduction of the club. "[But the team] doesn't have the ludicrous overtones of the old New York Mets." Per Chapman, Harper was "extraordinary," Rollins was "a pretty good hitter," and Hegan was "a fancy Dan at first base." The pitching staff, Chapman reasoned, "shouldn't disgrace itself."[8]

Turning the Pilots into the Brewers had to be done quickly, which meant that there was no time to put the various prototype uniform sets that the group had prepared into action. When Selig, who had just been named team president, was asked about uniforms in a press conference, he replied, "Very simple. We tear off the 'Pilots' and substitute 'Brewers' and we put an 'M' on the cap in place of an 'S.'"[9]

As for Milwaukee County Stadium, workers rushed to get the 17-year-old ballpark into baseball shape. It had last been used in November for a Packers win over the New York Giants (Don Horn started at QB for the Pack and tossed two TDs), and gallons of green paint were sprayed onto the still-dormant grass in an attempt to hide the football yard markers. Other members of the grounds crew scraped lose paint from the wooden seats while the stadium sound system boomed with "America the Beautiful," "The Mexican Hat Dance," and "Take Me Out to the Ballgame"—ballpark standards prerecorded onto tapes that the Braves had left behind. All the while, potential ticket buyers toured the stadium, allowed to visit seats in person before committing.[10]

Despite some frigid local temperatures during the Brewers' first week of official existence, nature gifted the opener with a sunny spring afternoon. The stadium gates opened at 11:30 a.m., and, once again, local fans had a true home team to watch. Two Milwaukee teenagers greeted the team personally, jumping out of the bleachers while the team was still taking infield practice. Unnoticed in the mishigas of the historic event, no one stopped the two as they walked around shaking hands. The kids took turns sliding into second base before bouncing over the grandstand fence and back into the masses. "We wanted to be the first to welcome the team onto the field and the first to slide into second base," one told the *Sentinel*.[11]

After Milwaukee County Executive John Doyne tossed out the game's ceremonial first ball (it had "nothing on it," remarked the *Sentinel*); righthander Lew Krausse took the hill for the real thing. A decade earlier, an 18-year-old Krausse jumped from high school to the majors and registered one of the most sensational debuts in history, striking out six in a complete-game, three-hit shutout for the Kansas City A's. Having never fulfilled his ace potential, he'd spent the previous years as a middling swingman for the A's. The Pilots picked him up in a trade after the '69 season and a strong spring had convinced Bristol he had the stuff to top the Brewers rotation. His first pitch—a ball—was sent to Cooperstown, and he set down the Angels in order to complete the first half-inning in team history.[12]

The Brewers collected their first hit with one out in the second inning when outfielder Steve Hovley beat out an infield single. But Hovley was stranded and, in the bottom of the frame, the Angels struck. With two on and two out, Bill Voss hit a playable ball to left that Danny Walton misplayed. Voss ended up on third and scored shortly after on a wild pitch. An inning later, with John Gelnar having spelled Krausse, California broke it open. The inning began with center fielder Russ Snyder dropping a pop fly, opening the door for a four-run inning. On the other side of things, Angels ace Andy Messersmith was cruising, keeping the Brewers off balance with a steady mix of fastballs and curves. Hovley's sixth inning double would be the only time a Brewer made it past first base all afternoon.

Still, there was no march for the exits, even when the deficit crept into double digits. The fans in the bleachers, where general seating was just one dollar, took to entertaining themselves. While the shirtsleeve set sat in the grandstands and reminisced about the good old days of the Braves, the bleachers were populated with kids not much older than the stadium itself, long-haired and bearded. The *Milwaukee Journal* transcribed one of the many banners decorating the bleachers in print-friendly terms, "---- the Braves!"[13]

The bleacher kids cat-called and jeered, downed beer, and threw things on their field and at each other. "I hope you get trading stamps on your gas!" one kid yelled at the already well-traveled bullpen cart. They stomped and hollered in an effort to upset Messersmith's rhythm (it did not work) and tried to swipe the regal-looking hats from ballpark ushers (that did work, as several lost their caps and another had his nose broken in a fight trying to retrieve one). The biggest in-game cheer after the first pitch, from the bleachers or anywhere else, came late in the contest when nearly a dozen bleacher kids jumped into the outfield and led ballpark security and police on a chase before being rounded up and arrested.[14]

Messersmith went the distance in the 12–0 Angels rout. True diehards might have been able to recall that the Braves, during their entire 13-year run in Milwaukee, had never lost so badly in a shutout. Once more, the players were just glad it was over. "You wanted a team in the worst way," one fan shouted at Selig as he left the park that afternoon. "And that's what you got!"[15]

But still, Milwaukee had a team.

The Brewers opened the season 5–20 and were already more than 10 games out of first by May. Spending most of the season ahead of only the White Sox, who would lose 106 games, in the American League standings, they closed the season on a 9–5 run and posted their first-ever winning month in September. They finished at 65–97, 33 games out of first.

1971

Saturday, April 10, 1971: Brewers 4, Angels 3 (40,566 attendance)
In the News: The Wisconsin chapter of the ALCU has accused the Journal Company of violating the Civil Rights of three male employees who were recently fired. The suit claims they were dismissed because of their long hair.
At the Movies: *Gimme Shelter* at the Strand Theater
On the Radio: "House of the Rising Son" by Frijid Pink

Marvin Milkes, the general manager who'd built the Pilots and traveled west with them to Milwaukee, was exhausted after the 1970 season. The Brewers managed just a one-game improvement on the dismal 64–98 record posted by the Pilots, and Milkes had worked as hard as any GM in the game for the pleasure. In two seasons, 78 different men had suited up for the Pilots/Brewers (over the same period, the powerhouse Baltimore Orioles had used just 35 players) while Milkes made a flurry of moves to plug the team's many holes. In December 1970, worn out and holed up in Las Vegas to establish residency for his fourth divorce, Milkes resigned his post. His doctor had told him the stress he was under "would have killed any other man."[16]

Enter "Frantic" Frank Lane, a 76-year-old baseball lifer who'd traded over 600 players in four previous GM gigs. He had traded Hall of Famers, local heroes, All-Stars, and even swapped managers as GM of the Indians in 1960. During his introductory press conference in January, he mused about trading Marty Pattin for Frank Robinson, and said that if Atlanta's Orlando Cepeda was the last piece the team needed to clinch a pennant, "we'd make a deal."[17]

But Pattin would not be among the nine members of the 1970 club that Lane jettisoned by Opening Day and the nearest thing to a future Hall of Famer he brought in was catcher Ellie Rodriguez, who would later catch Nolan Ryan's fourth career no-hitter as a member of the Angels. Perhaps no member of the Brewers was as valued as Pattin heading into the 1971 season. The 27-year-old righthander, previously best known for his clubhouse Donald Duck impression, had pitched marvelously in the second half of 1970, posting a 2.60 ERA and winning 10 of 17 starts. During spring training, Pattin had developed a change-up to complement a finesse curve and was tabbed by manager Dave Bristol to start the season opener at Minnesota.[18]

The septuagenarian Lane liked his teams young and hungry, and his first Brewers club would fit well into that mold. The oldest projected regular, Tommy Harper, was just 30 years old, and Ken Sanders, 29, was the graybeard of the pitching staff. Manager Bristol himself was just 38 and two other members of the coaching staff, Wes Stock (37) and Jackie Moore (32), were even younger. Bristol had returned his entire staff from 1970 and added Milwaukee's own Harvey Kuenn, a 10-time All-Star and the 1959 AL batting champ. At the end of spring training he was named the team's first-ever batting instructor and signed on to represent the team on the ceremonial dinner circuit in the off-season.[19]

Once turned loose in the dry Tempe heat, Bristol's young club defied expectations by winning the Cactus League title with a 16–9 record. Officially meaningless (and a notoriously poor predictor of summertime success), the crown was still welcomed by a team that had spent all but a single day of the previous season with a losing record. "We're starting a new era," Lane told the papers after camp broke. "I think we'll have a team that has a lot of pride and one that has a lot more ability than people are willing to grant us." Bristol set a goal for the season of a .500 record and Selig thought the club could improve on 1970s attendance and break the million mark.[20] Skip Lockwood, who'd struggled through a 5–12 season as a rookie in 1970, summed up the team's upbeat attitude with a sticker he pasted on the suitcase he'd packed for the trip north. *It Could Happen Here!* the sticker read.

"That's the way I feel about this year," he told the *Journal*.[21]

In the season opener at Metropolitan Stadium on April 6, the Brewers scored a solid win against the Twins, favorites of the American League West, topping them 7–2 behind a complete game by Pattin and a two-hit, four-RBI performance by left fielder Andy Kosco (an off-season Lane pick-up). The next day, 20-year-old Bert Blyleven shutout the Brewers on just four hits.

Back in Milwaukee, there were expectations that the 1971 home opener could even out-draw 1970's historic but last-minute affair and might even challenge the previous season's baseball bat give-away that set County Stadium's all-time record of 44,387. The field itself looked healthy, with some 9,000 squares of sod having been replaced since the last Packers date in Milwaukee (a 13–10 loss to John Unitas and the Baltimore Colts) and the team reported that every bulb in the scoreboard had been replaced. Behind the scenes, workers prepared two tons of hot dogs and nearly as much bratwurst, while trucks delivered 300 gallons of mustard, 550 barrels of draft beer, and over a quarter million bottles of beer for the opening homestand. The club also boasted a bit more diverse menu for 1971, including Vienna sausages, sauerkraut sandwiches, grilled Italian sausages, and—in a preview of novelty hybrid concoctions to come—an item simply called the "pizzabrat."[22]

Once again, it was the Angels in town for the lid-lifter. The Californians handed the ball to Clyde Wright, a 22-game winner and Cy Young contender in 1970. For the Brewers, it was Lockwood. "It was a long winter," he said before the game, reflecting on his poor showing in 1970. "Now I've got the chance to vindicate myself."[23] It was an odd route to an Opening Day start for Lockwood. A teenage phenom at Norwood High School in Massachusetts, he was signed by the Kansas City A's for a $135,000 bonus and was in the majors at age 18, playing out the 1965 seasons as a reserve third baseman. Stuck behind Sal Bando at third with the A's, he was converted into a pitcher in 1968 and tabbed by the Pilots in the expansion draft the following year.[24] He was "tickled to death" to get the Opening Day start, he told the *Sentinel*, and was eager to match a recent eight-inning gem he'd tossed against California in Arizona.[25]

Before Lockwood got his chance, it would again be Milwaukee

County Executive John Doyne throwing out the first ball. He proclaimed himself in "perfect health [but] overweight" and said he hadn't had a drink since "the morning after St. Patrick's Day."[26]

Both Wright and Lockwood held sway until the fourth inning, when the Angels' first baseman Jim Spencer tagged Lockwood for a solo homer to break a 0–0 tie. In the bottom half of the inning, Wright plunked lead-off man Davey May, who quickly advanced to third on a stolen base attempt and a wild throw. One batter later, left fielder Danny Walton crushed a screwball into the left field bleachers to give the Brewers their first-ever Opening Day lead. Walton, who'd had off-season surgery and was just getting over a bout of influenza, credited his work with Kuenn for a new approach at the plate. "I never felt better, after I hit that home," he said after the game.[27]

Lockwood carried the 2–1 lead into the sixth inning. With two away and Spencer on first, Lockwood walked Ken McMullen to push the tying run into scoring position. Facing catcher Jerry Moses, an All-Star in 1970 with Boston, Lockwood struck him swinging out with a looping curve. But the ball glanced off the corner of home plate and bounced wildly away from catcher Ellie Rodriguez toward the California dugout. Spencer had a good jump from second and came all the way around to tie the game. "It was the kind of thing that maybe happens once a season," Rodriguez later said.[28]

In the bottom of the seventh, 34-year-old Roberto Pena, who had unexpectedly beaten out rookie Rich Auerbach for the starting shortstop job, laced a one-out double over center fielder Ken Berry and scored minutes later on a base hit by Rodriguez. In the top of the eighth, a gassed Lockwood, now over 120 pitches, surrendered a double to Tony Conigliaro. Marcelino Lopez, in to relieve Lockwood, set down the Angels in order, but a stolen base and sacrifice fly once again tied the score, 3–3.

Wright also ran into trouble in the eighth. Harper walked to open the frame and outfielder Bernie Smith beat out an infield single to set up a Dave May sacrifice bunt that moved both runners up. Wright intentionally walked Kosco before giving way to righthander Mel Queen. After Bill Voss fanned, Pena came to bat with a chance to play hero once more. "I was going to swing at anything over the plate," he later said, but Queen took a surprisingly cautious approach to a batter with a career on base percentage of .291. Nibbling at the edges, Queen walked him to force in Harper and put the Brewers on top, 4–3. The crowd was still buzzing when the Brewers carried their lead into the top of the ninth. Lopez fanned two straight before Sandy Alomar grounded to Pena, who scooped and tossed to first to secure the win.[29]

After the game, in the upbeat clubhouse, Bristol praised his shortstop. "Pena just has the right kind of heart."[30]

Despite a four game improvement on their record from 1970, the '71 club posted a losing record each month of the season and suffered through a brutal early-summer stretch in which they lost 15 of 17. The opener was the only time all season they drew more than 29,000 fans and they topped 20,000 in just four other games.

1972

Saturday, April 22, 1972: Tigers 8, Brewers 2 (8,968 attendance)

In the News: The home of a federal judge in Memphis is being guarded by armed federal marshals. The judge recently issued a desegregation order for local schools and has been the victim of numerous death threats.

At the Movies: *Frogs* ("a tidal wave of slithering, slimy, horror") at the Centre Theater

On the Radio: "In the Rain" by The Dramatics

Despite Frank Lane remaking his roster as frantically as ever, the Brewers of 1971 found themselves no more a contender than they had been in 1970. The most significant of his 11 in-season swaps was a late April deal with the Phillies that brought outfielder John Briggs, who ended up pacing the team in homers, on-base percentage, and slugging percentage. Lane didn't even wait until the off-season proper to pull the trigger on the biggest deal in franchise history—all he needed was a rainy night in Baltimore. As game two of the World Series between the Orioles and Pirates was washed out, Lane announced a 10-player blockbuster deal with the Boston Red Sox. Principal in the package to Boston were All-Stars Tommy Harper and

George "Boomer" Scott arrived in Milwaukee and became the city's biggest baseball star since the Braves left town. A Gold Glove regular at first base, he actually played third base during his first Milwaukee home opener in 1972 (1976 SSPC #237).

Marty Pattin. Headlining the return was former Cy Young Award winner Jim Lonborg and slugging first baseman George Scott.

The consensus around the game following the trade was that the Brewers had won big. One scout told the *Sentinel* that the team had pulled off "baseball's greatest deal in ten years."[31] Lane boasted that the trade "might make us a contender for the division title." Scott was expected to anchor the lineup and pair with Briggs as one of the more potent 3–4 lineup tandems in the American League (where the Brewers would now reside in Eastern Division, after two years holding Seattle's old spot in the West) while Lonborg added experience to a raw but talented crop of starting pitchers.[32]

Twenty-eight years old, Scott was a three-time Gold Glove winner and had received MVP votes in 1971, but he'd gained a reputation in Boston as a trouble-maker, clashing with managers and once being benched because of what the team considered to be an unacceptable weight gain. But whatever of that reputation had been just, it was nowhere to be found when Scott arrived at Brewers camp in Tempe. He'd gotten into shape over the winter and reported early to spring training to get in extra work with his new team. As a boy in Greenville, Mississippi, he'd idolized Henry Aaron and was eager to try out the power alleys in Aaron's old home park (he even still used an Aaron model bat). "It gives me a little extra incentive to know that the Milwaukee organization and the people there are depending on me," he told the *Sentinel* at the opening of camp, looking trim and having shaved off his intimidating Fu Manchu mustache. "I don't see any reason we shouldn't be fighting for the pennant. Anyway, we should beat out Boston."[33]

Sentinel reporter Lou Chapman noted that "the only trouble [Scott] has caused so far is being too downright cooperative."[34]

But the optimistic feelings from a contented George Scott and a full season of John Briggs were overshadowed in the last weeks of camp by a matter that was still mostly foreign to baseball fans: labor troubles. Major League Baseball players had officially unionized six years prior. Tense negations in 1969 had resulted in the signing of a basic agreement with the owners, but that deal was set to expire in 1972. The only concession the players wanted in a new agreement was an increase in the pension plan to match inflation. The owners, confident the players would never strike over such a small matter, refused. As spring training drew to a close, union head Marvin Miller proposed that the matter be settled by arbitration—an offer that the owners quickly turned down. Meanwhile, the players were voting team by team whether or not to authorize a strike. On March 30, just after tossing seven innings in a 5–1 victory over Cleveland, Brewers team representative Jim Lonborg oversaw the ballots as the Brewers voted

26–2 to approve a possible strike. The next day, Lonborg and pitcher Jim Colburn, another off-season pickup and the team's alternate player rep, flew to Dallas for a final vote. In a move that stunned the sporting world, the player reps voted unanimously to strike.[35]

Opening Day in Milwaukee was still tentatively scheduled for Friday, April 7, against the Cleveland Indians. Back in Arizona, team president Bud Selig shut down camp as the players refused to show up for a morning workout. The owners canceled the remainder of the spring's exhibition games. Barred from team facilities, the players were left to their own devices to make it back home.[36]

Most did just that, leaving just a handful of players—most of whom had homes in the area—left behind in Tempe. The players expressed hope that the strike would be settled quickly. Most said they did not want to strike, but felt they had no choice. "All we're asking for is what is ours," Lonborg said. "I think if they could resolve that one issue, the rest of the strike could be settled."[37]

Perhaps not expecting the players to actually hold their ground into the regular season, the Milwaukee sporting press was less than enthusiastic about any real analysis of what had led to the strike. Case in point was the *Sentinel*'s account of "Homer Plate," a fictitious Brewers fan said to the be the team's most loyal backer. In the story, Homer heads to the stadium to watch the home opener, but is stunned to find the players picketing instead (evidently the superfan hadn't read a sports page in the past few weeks). Poor Homer wanders through the empty stadium, finding everyone ready to play ball except for the players. He weeps, the author sarcastically notes, at the thought of them having to survive on a pension of "only" $1,500 a month and encounters a ragamuffin youngster heartbroken at the canceled game who can only ask what a pension is. "The realization of it all left him numb," the paper wrote of their protagonist. "Opening Day, 1972, was not to be." Homer's crocodile tears for the players were just about the most sympathetic thing that the papers would publish on their behalf.[38]

When April 7 finally came, Homer's Opening Day dreams would have been dashed anyway. An afternoon of snow and bitingly cold winds shut down any outdoor activity in the city. Regardless of the weather, Selig held out hopes that a settlement could be reached by the weekend. The players had mostly made their way back to Milwaukee, working out in the days before at facilities at the University of Wisconsin–Milwaukee, playing basketball and volleyball to keep in game shape. On the scheduled day of the opener, a handful of players hung around the stadium. Pitcher Jim Slaton sat in the grandstand with his dog, Shane, watching the snow fall. Outfielder Joe Lahoud hung out in the clubhouse, playing gin rummy with former Braves catcher Bob Uecker, the newest addition to the Brewers TV broadcast crew.[39]

Despite the optimism from Selig—no doubt driven by the belief among the owners that the players would quickly fold—there would be no baseball that weekend in Milwaukee or anywhere else. The players held tight for five more days before the owners, now at risk of losing more in game revenue than the pension concession would cost them, gave in. On April 15, the Brewers opened the season in Cleveland, looking sharp in a 5–1 win.[40]

After dropping two and losing a game to rain in New York, the Brewers finally returned to Milwaukee as an active unit. Five hundred fans greeted the team at Mitchell Field, many eager to get a look at George Scott. "The fans are expecting so much of me. The organization is expecting so much of me and I'm expecting so much of myself," he said upon arriving in Milwaukee, admitting that his one-for-12 to start the season might have been caused by the pressure he was putting on himself. Bill Parsons, a lanky righthander who had been the AL's top rookie pitcher in 1971, would get the start, matched behind the plate with 20-year-old Darrell Porter, the Brewers' first-ever first round draft pick.[41]

And then, after three weeks of uncertainty, there was some more. With the re-jiggered schedule, the Brewers' first home game would fall on Friday, April 21—which was slated to be a night game with Detroit. "Who Ever Heard of Opening Night?" the *Journal* complained, and the Brewers agreed. The Brewers initially announced that the game would be shifted to the afternoon, but the Tigers objected, citing a rule that permitted a visiting club to veto a game time change if it would result in playing a day game following a night game. The Tigers were set to play in Baltimore the evening before and, in yet another team vote, were unanimous against the change. The Brewers asked the Orioles if they would change the time of the Thursday game, but the team refused. Opening Night it would be.[42]

But then came the rain: A cold and steady downpour that seemed the only appropriate way to usher in the season that just wouldn't start. Things were reset for a Saturday afternoon opener on the 21st. John Doyne was back for the first pitch and a pregame ceremony honored former Milwaukee Brave Bill Bruton, who smacked a walk-off homer in the first-ever game at the Stadium in 1953.[43]

Just over 8,000 fans were on hand and not even Bud Selig was willing to watch the game in the damp 40-degree elements—he watched a television feed with Frank Lane in Lane's office. The field was in what the *Journal* called the worst condition it ever had been for baseball, with muddy patches and standing water dotting the outfield.[44]

As it turned out, the umpire's long-awaited call of "Play ball!" was the high point of the afternoon for the Milwaukee faithful. The first five Detroit batters reached base and scored and Parsons was chased in the second inning. Meanwhile, 25-year-old Tigers starter Joe Coleman was twirling a gem. With an 8–0 lead heading into the bottom of the seventh, he had yet to allow a hit and had faced only two over the minimum. The only well-struck ball the Brewers had managed was a fifth inning Billy Conigliaro drive that right fielder Willie Horton snagged with a fantastic running grab. Leading off the inning, Briggs hit a ground ball that shortstop Ed Brinkman backhanded, but his throw pulled Norm Cash off the base. The judgment call went against Coleman and Briggs was awarded a hit. Joe Lahoud provided Milwaukee's only highlight a few batters later when he stroked a homer to set the 8–2 final score.[45]

"It was hardly worth the waiting," wrote the *Journal*.[46]

Dave Bristol was fired just 30 games into the 1972 campaign as the Brewers opened 10–20. The team fell into last place in the AL East on May 13 and stayed there for the rest of the season. They didn't draw more than 27,000 to any home game that season.

1973

Friday, April 13, 1973: Brewers 2, Orioles 0 (13,883 attendance)

In the News: Harold Lipset, a private eye hired to lead the Senate Watergate investigation, has resigned after it emerged that he pleaded guilty in 1966 to charges of illegally bugging hotel suites in aid of cooperate espionage.

At the Movies: *The Poseidon Adventure* at the Mill Road Multiplex

On the Radio: "The Night the Lights Went Out in Georgia," Vicki Lawrence

In the metaphorical sense, the dreary weather that cast a pall on the 1972 opener never lifted. The Brewers started out 3–10 and Dave Bristol was fired before the end of May. The team drew more than 20,000 fans just three times all season and a crowd of 26,735 for a Sunday afternoon tilt with Kansas City was the year's biggest. Their overall attendance of 600,440 was the worst in the majors and their 65–91 record earned them yet another last-place finish.

After three seasons in Milwaukee, the $10.8 million that the Brewers' ownership group had paid for the club looked like an act of civic charity than a wise business investment. In February 1973, Edmund B. Fitzgerald, one of the team's biggest shareholders, said that owners had poured another $3 million into the team since the purchase. In the same breath, Fitzgerald and Selig were forced to deny a *Sentinel* inquiry about whether there had been any consideration of selling or relocating the club.⁴⁷

Leading into the '73 season, the club conducted what Selig called an "in-depth market survey" about fan expectations of the ball park experience. In an effort to brand the stadium as such, and perhaps move past the expectations set by the Braves, the words "HOME OF THE BREWERS" were added to the exterior of County Stadium in tall, illuminated letters, offset by a pair of 16-foot-tall Brewers "barrel man" characters. The Brewers insignia was added to the dugout roofs (such efforts were also aimed at preparing the park for the 1975 MLB All-Star game, which had been awarded to Milwaukee in November). Attempts were also made to connect the franchise to the city and its German heritage. A four-piece Bavarian band was hired to stroll the parking lots and grandstand and the grounds crew would be outfitted in matching German costumes.⁴⁸

The highest-profile of the new additions at the stadium was the return of Bernie Brewer. The moniker of retiree superfan Milt Mason—who spent 40 days living atop the County Stadium scoreboard in 1970, vowing not to come down until the team sold out a game (he had to settle for a crowd of 40,000)—was now bestowed on a full-time club mascot. Bernie would

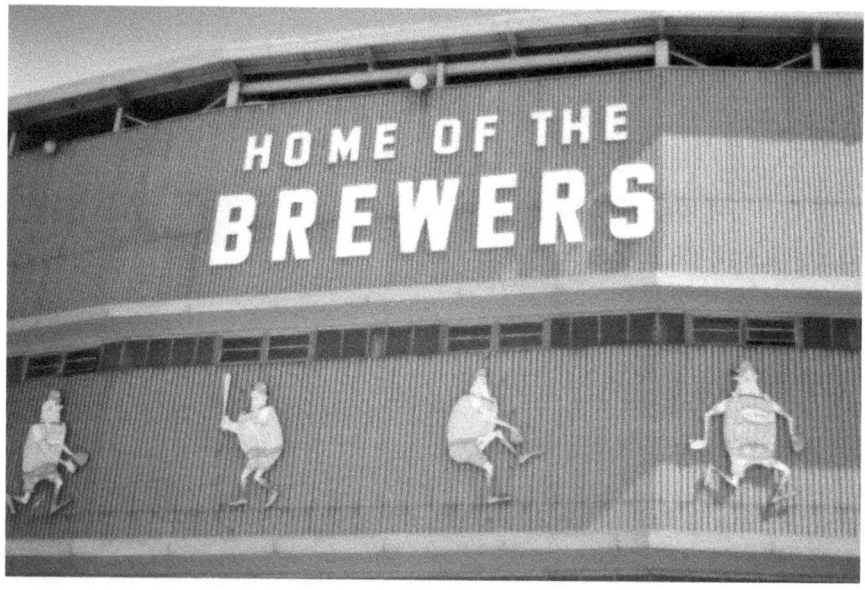

The Brewers added this signage to County Stadium for the 1973 season, part of an effort to help the team forge its own identity as they struggled to post a winning record—something the Braves had never failed to do in 13 seasons in Milwaukee (Bob Busser).

"live" in a center field chalet, connected to an oversized beer mug via a 24-foot slide. Bernie would celebrate each Brewers home run by taking a slide into the mug, with "booms and sirens" accompanying him.[49]

And for the second year in a row, the Brewers had made a big October trade in the hopes of jump-starting their offense. It was the first big move in the tenure of new GM Jim Wilson, who replaced Frank Lane after the end of the '72 season. The Brewers sent four pitchers to the Phillies, including Jim Longborg and relief ace Ken Sanders, in exchange for three-player package headlined by Don Money—a slick-fielding third basemen with a live bat. Del Crandall, the former Braves All-Star who had taken over for Bristol as manager, was thrilled with the trade, calling Money a "guy who can contribute to a ballclub for ten years." Money, who was bringing a career slash line (AVG/OBP/SLG) of just .241/.302/.371 to Milwaukee, wasted no time in blaming his former club for his struggles. "I can help the Brewers," he told the *Sentinel* after the trade. "But I've got to be left alone [and] hit my own way. That was my main trouble in Philadelphia: overcoaching."[50]

But before anyone could get down to business in 1973, the owners wanted to reassert themselves a bit. If the successful 1972 players strike was a home run for labor, the 1973 lockout was a follow-up brush-back pitch from management. In February, the owners canceled the first two weeks of spring training, barring the players from team facilities until a new collective bargaining agreement was signed. The dispute, in short, was that the players wanted the right to go to arbitration with salary disputes and the owners did not. After a two-week stalemate, the players got their way and camps opened.[51]

Having moved their Arizona camp from Tempe to Sun City, the Brewers featured a number of new faces to match their new home. Money was the new man at third base and rookies Gorman Thomas and Pedro Garcia won spots in the starting lineup at right field and shortstop, respectively. "Boy," Garcia had mused during camp, "they got a lot of old people in Arizona." The same could not be said of the Brewers, who broke camp with a lineup featuring four of the starting nine under age 25 and no regular or starting pitcher north of 30.[52]

From Sun City, the team traveled to Baltimore for a three-game set before they would return home to open against Boston on April 10. They got in two games against the Orioles (both losses) before Mother Nature once again intervened. After a day of rain in Baltimore, Milwaukee was pounded with its worst April snowstorm in 50 years. The Tuesday opener against Boston was canceled early on Monday—with a new date (Wednesday) that no one held out much hope for either. By that afternoon, a blanket of snow covered County Stadium. The Red Sox hadn't even yet bothered to fly to Milwaukee.[53]

The storm paralyzed huge parts of the state, stranding hundreds of motorists—including Bud Selig, who spent part of Tuesday stuck on Highway 100. Jim Wilson and other members of the front office were snowed in at County Stadium and forced to spend the night there. The only baseball event that went on as usual was the annual "Play Ball" luncheon at the Marc Plaza Hotel in downtown. The guests of honor were all players who were staying at the hotel and had nowhere else to go.[54]

For two members of the team, the snow was not just an inconvenience, but a whole new experience. "When I woke up this morning, I check out my window and saw little pieces of ice coming down. I said, 'What's going on?'" the *Journal* quoted Garcia, a resident of Guayama, Puerto Rico, who had never seen a snowstorm.[55]

Ollie Brown, an Alabama native and a California resident, was similarly surprised. "This is the first time I've been in falling snow. You can tell by my wardrobe. I didn't bring clothes for it," Brown said. "I always wondered what would happen in weather like this. I thought everything would close up. I see people slow down a bit, but they still go about their business."[56]

By Tuesday night, nearly a foot of snow sat atop the County Stadium turf and a call was put out for 150 locals to help shovel out the grandstands. The field, which was still covered by a tarp, could not be cleared using mechanical equipment and would need to be emptied of snow by hand. The club knew of no reasonable way to fully clear the outfield without ruining the playing surface. Their best bet was to clear what they could and wait for the rest to melt. As it became obvious that the entire opening series against Boston would be lost, the team hoped to be able to play by the weekend. Whenever they opened, the team would not sell any tickets in the upper seating bowl—the prospect of a drunken rabble in the cheap seats launching snowballs all afternoon was too realistic to ignore.[57]

It wouldn't be until Thursday evening that the last of the snow was removed from the field. With helicopters—rented for $90 per hour by the team—hovering over the playing surface to dry out the turf, a Friday afternoon matchup against the Orioles was finally confirmed. For the second straight year, Bill Parsons was tasked with starting the lid-lifter. His 1972 start had been a disaster, and with a spring training shoulder injury and three days' delay due to weather—not to mention a Baltimore offense projected to be one of the league's best—his chances in 1973 didn't look much better. He took the hill in the damp and chilly weather hoping he could make it through five innings.[58]

Parsons had trouble finding his groove, but the Orioles had more trouble finding a way to square up on him. Through three innings, he'd walked three but allowed nothing harder hit than a few outfield flyouts. In the bottom of the third, Pedro Garcia—now feeling at home in the snow and choking up on his 36-ounce bat—popped a 2-2 Mike Cuellar fastball just inside the left field foul pole for the game's first hit. Two innings later, Ollie Brown—who had vowed to make do with his springtime wardrobe—slugged a 370-foot homer. The homers gave Bernie Brewer his first trips ever down his slide. Mr. Brewer, whose real identity the club was keeping secret, showed perhaps more early season rust than anyone on the team. "He hardly resembled a tobogganist on his balky trips down the chute," the *Journal* noted.[59]

Meanwhile, Parsons continued to, by his own estimation, "struggle" on the mound. "My fastball wasn't sharp.... I couldn't put the ball where I wanted it," he said later. Now down two, the O's went 1-2-3 in the sixth and, to open the seventh, Parsons worked a groundout from Don Baylor and a fly ball from Brooks Robinson to leave him just seven outs from one of the most unlikely no-hitters in recent memory. But with two away, Paul Blair got just enough of a Parsons slider to dump it into center field. Parsons could only shrug. He finished the inning and got the first two outs of the eighth before being lifted for Jerry Bell—who closed it out for a clean 2-0 victory.[60]

After the game, Blair admitted that his hit—the only one the O's managed—was "lucky." But Parsons deflected. "Oh, I knew I had a no-hitter going," he said. "But that was really a secondary consideration. It was amazing that I got as far as I did with the stuff I was throwing up there.... They were just hitting the ball right at people."[61]

After a sluggish start, the Brewers caught fire in June, winning 15 of the month's first 16 games to briefly take over first place in the East. After falling back, they had a .500 record as late as August 15, but ended up at 74–88, their best record to date.

1974

Friday, April 5, 1974: Red Sox 9, Brewers 8 (32,761 attendance)
In the News: A speech by the leader of American Nazi Party at the Holiday Inn Midtown in Milwaukee has been cancelled for reasons not yet announced.
At the Movies: Double feature of *The Big Doll House* and *Detroit 9000* at the Apollo Theater
On the Radio: "Come and Get Your Love," Redbone

The 1973 Brewers had, for five months, anyway, shown remarkable new life under the leadership of Del Crandall. And much to the delight of Bud Selig, they had finally hit the magic mark of 1,000,000 for yearly attendance. Slugger George Scott, who led the AL in total bases and claimed his third straight Gold Glove in 1973, met his magic mark in December, when he signed a one-year contract worth between $110,000 and $120,000. He became the first Milwaukee baseball player to top the century mark in annual pay and would enter 1974 as one of the American League's best-paid players.[62]

So it was little surprise that the media centered its early spring coverage on the man they called "The Boomer." They were not so interested now in the money he was making, but the money he was spending. The kid who had worn rags picking cotton in Mississippi for two cents a pound arrived in Sun City in a white double-knit suit with blue trim and a polka-dotted silk lining worn over a blue turtleneck that showcased his gold crawfish medallion necklace. He spent $250 each on his custom-tailored suits and dropped about $15,000 annually on his wardrobe, which he refreshed every 12 months. His bulging bankroll was kept in a gold money clip inscribed with "$100,000"—a gift from his wife, Lucky. His gold-plated Cadillac had cost $14,000 and he was considering buying a $75,000 home in Brown Deer. "I've always had steak and eggs for breakfast," he told reporters. "Now I order fillet mignon with my eggs."[63]

Bucking the Frantic Frank Lane model of favoring youth, second-year GM Jim Wilson had opted to add more experienced talent following the '73 season. His major move was a swap with California that shipped Ollie Brown, Skip Lockwood, Ellie Rodriguez and two others west for a package headlined by a trio of former All-Stars—Clyde Wright, Ken Berry, and Steve Barber—each on the wrong side of 30. The other notable winter addition was the 38-year-old Felipe Alou.

Shortstop was going to be an issue in 1974. The Brewers had proven a fairly effective offensive unit in '73. Darrell Porter, Don Money, and John Briggs had all impressed with solid numbers while George Scott and Dave May both made the All-Star team and received MVP votes. But the shortstop position was a black hole for offensive production. Rookie Tim Johnson was given 125 starts at short that year, one of just 13 shortstops in the league to see more than 500 plate appearances. Among those 13—a group itself mostly devoid of offensive threats—Johnson ranked dead last in batting average, on-base percentage, slugging percentage, hits, and extra-base hits. Robin Yount—the third overall choice in the previous year's amateur draft and a kid less than a year out of high school—had been invited to camp as a non-roster player, but wasted no time in making himself the talk of Sun City. Just a few weeks into camp, Yount emerged as the top candidate for the starting job at short. By mid–March, he was leading the team with a .412 average. Batting coach Harvey Kuenn said that there was "no reason" that Yount couldn't hold the job.[64]

The *Sentinel*'s Lou Chapman, perhaps aware that no position player had been a regular at age 18 since Phil Cavarretta was the Cubs' everyday first baseman in 1935, asked the kid directly if he could handle the starting shortstop job. "His eyes," Chapman wrote, "under a thicket of hair, didn't blink as he calmly replied, 'I think I can.'"65

Indeed, calmness and steady hitting became Yount's trademarks during that first spring. Near the end of the exhibition schedule—with Yount's average settled around .300, but still leading the club—Crandall informed him that he would be the Brewers' starting shortstop. "I told him yesterday he had made the team," Crandall told the *Sentinel*. "He broke out in a grin. That was the first emotion I've seen him display."66

Just 18 years old, Robin Yount brought a quiet cockiness with him to spring training in 1974 and won the starting shortstop job by swinging the team's hottest spring bat (1976 SSPC #238).

The decision to keep Yount was one of the easier calls that Crandall had to make. He told reporters that there were about 33 players on the roster he'd like to take north, joking that in 1973, there were only "about eight." Among his newly prized assets was righthander Jim Colborn, who had broken out in 1973 with the franchise's first-ever 20-win season. The Brewers picked up Colborn in a little-noticed swap with the Cubs prior to the '72 season and he had served as a swingman before injuries forced him into the rotation early in '73. By mid-season, he was an AL All-Star and one of the loop's top pitchers. For 1974, Crandall was counting on him to be the team's ace and penciled him in as the starting pitcher for the April 5 opener against Boston at County Stadium.67

There was still snow on the ground when the gates opened that Friday, but in a rare Opening Day weather break for the team, the snowstorm that was predicted to strike that afternoon failed to develop.68 Still, the rookie Yount—who'd grown up and still lived in Southern California—arrived at the stadium in long underwear. "I've never played in this kind of weather," he told the *Sentinel*, "but I'm not thinking about that." He admitted that nerves kept him up most of the night before but he didn't exactly seem to be overwhelmed mentally. A reporter asked him what he knew about the Red Sox. "Zero," he replied. And what about Boston ace Luis Tiant, whom he'd be facing that afternoon? "Nothing."[69]

Whatever John Briggs knew about Tiant, it hadn't done him much good. When he came to the plate in the bottom of the second with two on and two out, he'd managed just three hits off Tiant in 18 tries. But he caught a mistake from the big Cuban and rocketed it into the right field corner for a three-run homer that sent the 30,000 in attendance into a frenzy. But a half-inning later, Boston's Bob Montgomery tagged Colborn for a two-run blast. In the bottom half, the Brewers got one back when Don Money's sacrifice fly (following up on Yount's career-opening bases on balls) scored Pedro Garcia and extended the Brewer lead to 4–2.

In the top of the third, Colburn, who didn't feel comfortable all afternoon, walked a pair before getting Carl Yastrzemski to ground into what could have been an inning-ending double play. But Yount, after taking the shovel from Garcia, got crossed up at second base. Boston's Cecil Cooper slid in hard and caught Yount's shin with his cleats and sent the rookie's throw skipping into the dirt and past Scott at first. With Yount bloodied and two men on, Rico Petrocelli and Montgomery laced run-scoring singles around a Bernie Carbo walk to tie the game and chase Colborn. Jerry Bell came on in relief and promptly surrendered a bases-clearing double to Doug Griffin to make it 7–4 Boston.[70]

Mid-game, Tiant and Bell both settled in, trading scoreless innings as the crowd looked elsewhere for inspiration. A chant of "Go, Brewers, Go!" turned into a zeitgeisty cry of "Streak! Streak! Streak!" as a gaggle of young men along the third base line took off their shirts and threatened to vault onto the field. A tall man, dressed, jumped the fence mid-inning and tried to make his way around the bases backward before being tackled by security at second. A group in the upper deck performed an impromptu "cowbell concert" while another man—proving that the most engaging entertainment is often the simplest—drew an ovation by marching through the aisles with a beer in each hand and a pair of hot dogs in his mouth.[71]

The Brewers regained the spotlight in the bottom of the sixth when, with one out, a gassed Tiant walked Porter and Bob Coluccio to load the bases. Tiant, unable to find the plate, then walked Pedro Garcia to force in a run and make it 7–5 Boston. Yount was due next, but—despite having made up for his blunder in the third with a snap throw to catch a Boston runner breaking for home during a run-down in the top of the inning—was lifted for Felipe Alou. Alou struck out, but a passed ball from Diego Seguí—in for Tiant—scored another run. A wild pitch and then a walk to

Don Money allowed two more to score and—despite just one hit and never getting the ball out of the infield—the Brewers had tallied four to take an 8–7 lead.

But the Milwaukee faithful barely had time to make sense of the mess on their scorecards before Boston struck back. With one away in the bottom of the seventh, Cooper singled and Yastrzemski crushed a Kevin Kobel fastball into the right field bleachers to put Boston on top for good. The only big cheer the rest of the afternoon came in the bottom of the ninth when a 22-year-old Milwaukee man jumped down from the bleachers wearing a hooded sweatshirt—and only a hooded sweatshirt. Pursued by a half-dozen of Milwaukee's finest, he made it as far as center field before being tackled and covered in a trash bag. "I figured one would show up sometime," said Briggs after the game. "It was just a question of when he was going to appear. He almost waited too long."[72]

Postgame, warming up in the locker room, Crandall stated the obvious. "This wasn't a well-played ball game by either side." Yount, with his leg freshly taped, admitted that he'd made a mistake on the double play ball that had opened the door for five Boston runs, but Crandall was still impressed with the way the kid had handled himself. "Robin is going to learn. He will learn from that play when he got hurt," he said. "Sometimes that is the best way to learn."[73]

Overall, Yount finished 0–1 with a walk, three assists in the field, and at least one hard lesson learned. He had game one out of the way and now he could get down to the business of being a big leaguer. As he was dressing at this locker, a reporter asked him what he planned to do that night. Yount shrugged. "I don't know."[74]

The Brewers fought and scrapped in '74, once again holding first place for part of June and holding at the .500 mark well into the second half of the season. But a 12–18 August deflated the team and they once again placed in the second division with a 76–86 mark.

1975

Friday, April 11, 1975: Brewers 6, Indians 2 (48,160 attendance)
In the News: The Department of Transportation has proposed that current automaker regulations that require either airbags or seatbelts with a buzzer notification system be extended through the end of 1976.
At the Movies: *Tommy*, "In Quadraphonic Sound," at the Southtown 1
On the Radio: "Lady Marmalade (Voulez-Vous Coucher Avec Moi)" by LaBelle

It was, in the words of one reporter, "the worst kept secret since Watergate." Henry Aaron, who just six months prior had been perhaps the most closely-scrutinized American aside from Richard Nixon, was coming home. Having finally broken the career home run record and mostly shed the media and fan attention that made Aaron as miserable as he was famous, Aaron wanted out of Atlanta, where his relationship with the Braves had soured beyond repair.

It was widely assumed that Aaron would simply retire at the end of the 1974 season. His final tour of National League stadiums had acted as a de-facto farewell tour and his contract with the Braves was about to expire. At an end-of-the-season press conference at which it was thought Aaron would announce his retirement, he instead told those assembled that he had played his last game as a Brave. He was "50-50" on returning for 1975, but made it clear that he only had one destination in mind if he did return. "I don't want to go any other place but Milwaukee." By mid–October, with the Braves' permission, Aaron began negotiating a contract with the Brewers.[75]

As they had the year before, the Brewers showed some fire in the early part of 1974. They were around the .500 mark and just a few games out of first through the end of July, but faded in the second half for yet another losing season and second-division finish. Aaron would be 41 in 1975 and his '74 season, while still All-Star quality, had been his least productive since his rookie campaign. But a switch to the AL would allow him to move into a designated hitter role and a twilight season in Milwaukee would be miles removed from the

Bringing home run king Henry Aaron back to Milwaukee in 1975 was easily the boldest move the young Brewers franchise had yet made. He nearly hit one out during this first game back at County Stadium (1976 SSPC #239).

pressure and bother of his chase of the homer record. The Brewers made clear they did not just want him as a novelty to juice attendance. They wanted a hitter.

Finally, in early November, the deal was done. Outfielder Dave May would go to Atlanta and Aaron's rights would go to Milwaukee, where he'd already agreed in principle to a two-year contract worth about $480,000. The pact would make him the highest-paid player in baseball for 1975 and '76. At a press conference at the Hotel Pfister, Aaron was all smiles. He said he'd struggled last year because of all the attention. He predicted he would hit 30–35 homers and said his only goal was to win a World Series. "This was a city that showed me respect when I was growing up as a young kid," he said. "I want to end my career here."[76]

Although the Brewers had, in one move, made the biggest trade and handed out the biggest contract of the off-season, it was not an indicator that they were about to remake their roster—or, as Darrell Porter would learn, take a more open approach to player pay. Porter was perhaps the best prospect the franchise had yet developed. The fourth overall pick in the 1970 draft, Porter made the All-Star team in 1974 and was probably the top catcher in the AL not named Fisk or Munson. As training camp approached, Porter had not yet signed his contract for 1975. He told the papers that there was "no way" he'd sign for what the Brewers offered. Brewers GM Jim Baumer, in his first months on the job, called Porter's demands "out of line." Porter said that if he didn't get his money, he wouldn't sign and play the 1975 season without a contract, becoming the first "test case" in the effort by the player's union to challenge the reserve clause.[77]

Porter would eventually sign and Baumer made it clear that the Brewers would not budge on player threats. "If you give in now, you'll go through the same thing next year."[78]

With Porter in the fold, the Brewers headed to Arizona with mostly the same roster they'd had in 1974. Their only other significant moves were to dump two pieces of the big trade they'd made with the Angels in 1973, releasing Ken Berry and trading Clyde Wright to Texas for righty starter Pete Broberg. If the Brewers were to shine in 1975, they'd need to rely on the continued development of their young core, some surprises on the pitching staff, and a rejuvenated Henry Aaron.

Unfortunately, the Brewers were playing from behind on this plan before they even came north for the summer. Jim Colborn, having struggled with the injury during his disappointing 1974 season, was sidelined indefinitely with a groin pull and young fireballer Kevin Kobel—expected to be in the starting rotation—was shut down with shoulder pain. Ed Sprague and Eduardo Rodriguez—both key parts of a bullpen that was expected to excel—were each suffering from arm ailments. Meanwhile, Henry Aaron was batting in the low .200s and couldn't muster his first home run until early April.[79]

"I was happy to hit one out," Aaron told the press after the game—one of the last of the spring. "I had to practice my trot."[80]

Robin Yount, who hadn't even been born when Aaron debuted with the Milwaukee Braves in 1954, couldn't resist a chance to needle his teammate. "That home run doesn't count," he told the *Journal*.[81]

But sore arms and unofficial homers hardly mattered to Milwaukee baseball fans, for Henry was coming home. As the team broke camp, more than 48,000 tickets had been sold for the home opener and the team expected that more than 50,000 would be on hand for the game. As County Stadium was prepped for the Friday afternoon tilt with Cleveland, crews were working on expansions to the upper and lower decks along the left field line, which would add nearly 8,000 new seats in time for Milwaukee to host the 1975 All-Star Game. For Aaron's return, a few thousand folding chairs were added to the just-set concrete of the lower bowl.[82]

For the first time ever, coverage of the home opener began in the parking lot as the *Journal* made note of the numerous tailgate parties that brought a little early warmth to fans on the 37-degree day. Tailgating—a tradition that can be traced back to civilians picnicking and drinking wine before watching battles during the Civil War—had long been a staple of college and professional sports fandom. But in Milwaukee, Brewers fans already seemed to be taking it to a different level. "I've never seen anything like it anywhere I've worked," remarked Brewers radio announcer Merle Harmon in 1974. "People tailgate other places too … but this is something else." With smoking grills making the parking lots look something not unlike a Civil War battlefield, music blasting, brats crackling, kegs tapped, and a dozen balls of all sorts being tossed about, the pregame had all the energy of a rock concert or a revival meeting.[83]

Once inside the stadium (the start of the game was delayed by 10 minutes to allow everyone to get to their seats), there was no doubt as to the idol of the masses. When Henry Aaron stepped out of the dugout in his white Brewers uniform trimmed in blue and gold, 48,000 people broke into song, singing "Welcome Home, Henry" to the tune of "Hello, Dolly," followed by a two-minute standing ovation. Making his way through yet another media scrum, Aaron was handed a microphone to address the crowd. "It's a great thrill for me to be back here in Milwaukee," he said before trotting over to join his teammates along the first base line.[84]

Also warmly greeted during introductions was Cleveland player-manager Frank Robinson. Fourth on the all-time home run leaderboard with 574, Robinson was making his own history that season as the first

African American manager in big league history. The fans had less love for baseball commissioner Bowie Kuhn, still reviled for his role in allowing the Braves to leave Milwaukee, who was loudly booed as he took his seat near the Brewers dugout.[85]

Another long ovation greeted Aaron during his first time at bat, drawing a walk against Jim Perry after fouling off seven pitches. Two innings later, he grounded into a fielder's choice to drive in Bob Coluccio from third to open the scoring. A few pitches later he was out easily on the most unlikely of stolen base attempts. "We thought we'd surprise them," said Crandall sheepishly after the game, who had called for Aaron to steal.[86]

With a steady performance by tall righthander Bill Champion, the Brewers went into the bottom of the sixth locked in 1–1 tie. Leading off against Perry, John Briggs smashed a homer into the open space between the right field grandstand and bleachers. Aaron followed up by crushing a pitch toward the foul pole in left. Aaron later said that the roar from the crowd made it sound like "the roof fell in," but the roar quickly subsided as the ball curved foul. A few pitches later, Aaron connected again, rifling a single to left for his first American League hit.[87]

After Aaron advanced to second on a fielder's choice and Don Money popped out, Robinson Perry intentionally walk Darrell Porter to bring up 21-year-old rookie Sixto Lezcano. With AAA Sacramento in 1974, Lezcano had abused Pacific Coast League pitching, batting .325 with 34 homers. But Robinson, who had managed against him in the Puerto Rican League, always liked his chances against the slender outfielder. "[In Puerto Rico], I think he walked the batter in front of me five times," Lezcano said after the game. "It's a custom with him."[88]

Lezcano broke tradition by lining a base hit to center, scoring Aaron and chasing Perry. Dick Bosman came in for Cleveland and allowed a double to Pedro Garcia to score two before Robin Yount reached on an error to plate another. Riding that five-run frame, the Brewers coasted to a 6–2 victory.

In the Brewers locker room after the game, it was, once again, all about Henry for the media. Aaron smiled politely while answering their questions—mostly the same questions he'd been answering all week—before trying to shoo them away. "Why don't you interview Briggs? Briggs is the one that hit the home run," he said. "And Champion pitched very well. Look, this is a fine, young team. The enthusiasm is great. I just want to be a part of it."[89]

At John Briggs' locker, George Scott held an invisible microphone under the outfielder's chin. "Say, John, how'd it feel to hit that home run?" When the press got to him—after asking him about how it felt to hit in front of Aaron—he finally had a moment to talk about his homer. "You know, I told my daughter I'd probably hit a home run today because she fixed dinner for me last night," he said, beaming. "Fried chicken with rice and gravy.... She's a good little girl."[90]

Aaron, thinking he was finally done with all the questions, was walking toward the showers, worn out in more ways than one, when one last reporter asked him about how he felt about the reception he'd received. "This is the 15th time I've answered it," he said before giving a monotone response. "Great. Tremendous. It was great that we won. It was just great all the way around. I can't put it into words."[91]

In what was becoming a familiar theme, the 1975 Brewers flirted with contention in the early going, played like a .500 team for the first 100 games or so, and then collapsed in the dog days of summer. A game under even at the end of July, they went just 16–41 the rest of the way to finish at 68–94.

1976

Thursday, April 8, 1976: Brewers 5, Yankees 0 (44,868 attendance)

In the News: The owner of Victor's Cocktail Longue on North Van Buren Street has been charged with violating a city ordinance against racial discrimination based on complaints that black patrons were required to show an ID while white patrons were not.

At the Movies: Double feature of *Deep Throat* & *The Devil in Miss Jones* at the Towne Art Theatre

On the Radio: "Right Back Where We Started From" by Maxine Nightingale

Things can fall apart pretty quickly in baseball. The Brewers found that out over the long, hot summer of 1975. On July 4, they were a franchise-best eight games over .500, tied for first place, and looking forward to hosting the All-Star Game. Two months later, they were 23 games back and the team was in disarray. During the slide, team president Bud Selig had approached Henry Aaron—in the midst of the worst season of his career—about taking over Del Crandall's job as manager. Aaron, who never really wanted to manage and certainly didn't want to be party to the dismissal of his old teammate and dear friend, declined. Crandall made it to the last weekend of the season before he was finally canned. After improving on their record for three straight seasons, inching ever nearer to the modest goal of a .500 season, the 1975 squad finished eight games behind where they had been in 1974.

In November, the Brewers hired Alex Grammas as the fourth manager in franchise history. Grammas had played for 10 years in the majors as a hard-edged infielder but made his name as Sparky Anderson's third base coach in Cincinnati, winning three NL flags and the 1975 World Series. Grammas lacked the "nice guy" reputation of Crandall that some in the organization felt contributed to the club's second-half lag in '75. He also lacked Crandall's optimism. "Let's face it," he told reporters that winter, "Boston came within a few outs [of winning the World Series] last year. Baltimore's going to be tough. So are the Yankees. Cleveland's improved. We'd have to have all of our players have their best years and be injury-free. But even then, I couldn't say we'd be in contention all year."[92]

Coming off such a disappointing campaign, it was widely expected that the Brewers would have an active off-season. And indeed, at the 1975 winter meetings, rumors involving the Brewers abounded: *Don Money to the Yankees for Rudy May and Sparky Lyle ... or perhaps to Boston for Cecil Cooper.... Charlie Moore and George Scott were on the block.... Mickey Rivers was headed to Milwaukee.... Jim Gantner was ready to take over for Money ... teams were asking about the previously untouchable Robin Yount....*[93]

But all that came from the winter meetings were a fistful of speculative newspaper columns. And in the months that followed, the team made just a single move—signing 37-year-old Vada Pinson, who was coming off a season in which he posted an anemic slash line of .223/.248/.335. He would not make the team. Indeed, the only new look for the 1976 version of the Brewers would be the result of Grammas' new "clean-shave" policy that forbid long hair and beards. Darrell Porter got his shaggy hair cut and beard shaved at a Mitchell Street barber shop—and sent the bill to Bud Selig.[94]

But management had bigger concerns than sloppy hair as spring training '76 drew near. In December, independent arbitrator Peter Seitz sided with the players in a dispute over whether players could become "free agents" after playing a season for which they had not signed a contract. While a federal appeal to the decision was being considered (it would be upheld in early March), the owners closed their training camps, locking the players out in an effort to pressure them into a compromise. Selig quickly established himself as a leading advocate for ownership. He told the *Sentinel* that baseball would be courting financial disaster if they gave up on the reserve system that bound a player for life to the team that drafted him. He also cited a number of clubs—San Francisco, Minnesota, and Cleveland—that could be pushed over a financial brink if free agency were permitted league-wide.[95]

Meanwhile, the Brewers renewed the contracts of six unsigned players. Among the six was Robin Yount—who had established himself as one of the AL's best shortstops despite having just turned 20 years old. Yount and the other five players all received a 20 percent pay cut—the maximum amount a team was allowed to cut a player's pay in a contract renewal. If the pay cuts were a message, Yount had one of his own. "I want to play where I can make the most money," he told the *Sentinel* in an interview in which he said he was seriously considering playing out his option. "I would just as soon stay in Milwaukee, but everyone likes to make the best deal for himself." Baseball insiders speculated that he could command as much as $500,000 a season on the open market—twice what the Brewers were paying Henry Aaron.[96]

While the lockout lingered, a report appeared in the *Sentinel* that several Brewers were currently—and had been in years prior—receiving unemployment checks from the state of Wisconsin. As seasonal workers, players not under multi-year contracts were eligible for unemployment benefits, which totaled about $117 a week for the 34 weeks of the off-season. Sportswriters and fans came down hard on the players. *Journal* scribe Bill Dwyre devoted an entire column to trashing the "poor, oppressed Major League players" for claiming unemployment and Selig himself jumped in, claiming that the club had always opposed the practice.[97]

Even Yount, still disgruntled over this pay cut, took heat in the newspapers. "Is he forgetting how much he owes to Milwaukee? I've read so much about Robin Yount being so mature, I think it's all hogwash ... it make[s] no difference to me if [Yount] play[s] in Milwaukee, Oakland, Seattle, or Mud Creek," one fan wrote.[98]

Finally, in mid–March, with a deal between the owners and players to establish a form of staggered free agency in which players would be eligible after six Major League seasons, teams opened their camps. The Brewers stumbled through a 14-game spring schedule and headed north, like nearly every other team in the league, still trying to shake off the rust from an extended off-season.

The Brewers were set to open against the New York Yankees, early favorite for the AL East crown. "About the only thing the Yankees and Brewers have in common is short hair," wrote the *Sentinel*'s Paul Levy. Catfish Hunter was tabbed to start for the Yanks, while Jim Slaton—who had been using a set of courses on cassette tape to improve "poise and confidence" throughout the spring to help him get past a poor 1975 showing—was given the ball for the Brewers.[99]

Despite the ill feelings from spring and temperatures in the mid–40s, Opening Day '76 was as much a party as the opener had ever been. Young people, in particular, seemed drawn to the free-flowing beer and barbeque of the County Stadium parking lot. Hours before game time, the place already had the feel of a rock festival—with loud music blasting from any number of cars outfitted with makeshift stereo systems in their trunks or on their roofs. The party continued inside the stadium, as young people roamed the concourses, downing beers, laughing and flirting. It wasn't yet noon before the first people were admitted to the nurses' station for having too much to drink, and at one point in the afternoon, every cot in the room was occupied with someone unable to stand.[100]

Don Money started at four different positions in 10 home openers over his 11 years with the Brewers. Only Paul Molitor had a more diverse Opening Day record.

Those who weren't in their seats for the one o'clock first pitch missed most of the action. In the bottom of the first, Yankees ace Hunter labored mightily. After retiring lead-off man Charlie Moore, Don Money laced a double and George Scott and Porter drew walks to load the bases for Aaron. The home run king had recently said that if he hadn't signed a two-year contract with the Brewers, he would have walked away from the game after the 1975 collapse, but he opened the '76 season with a flourish, lacing a full-count pitch from Hunter over shortstop Jim Mason to score two runs. Sixto Lezcano followed with another single before Bill Sharp chopped a bouncer that Mason booted to score Porter. An inning later, Porter and Aaron cracked back-to-back run-scoring hits that set the final score of 5–0 before most of the 44,000 ticket holders even had a chance to settle in.[101]

Hunter later admitted that he did not have his best stuff and was feeling the effects of the cold weather. But he also felt that the County Stadium playing surface was offering too much of a home field advantage to the Brewers, namely, the pitcher's mound. "It was too flat," Hunter said. He claimed that the low grade of the mound was causing his foot to hit the dirt too early and throwing off his rhythm.[102]

Yankee skipper Billy Martin, never shy about airing his grievances, backed his pitcher. "It was like he was throwing uphill," Martin said. "The next time, if my pitcher complains about the mound when he warms up, I'm going to go out to the ump, call time out and make them get the ground crew out there with shovels and fix it properly." Martin filed an official protest over the issue with the league office after the game.[103]

The slope didn't seem to bother Jim Slaton in the least. The righthander went the distance, tossing a four-hit shutout despite recording just one strikeout and not being able to get a good bend on his curveball. Grammas dismissed Martin's protest, saying, "If our guys start to complain, I'll do something about it. But I'm not going to build a mound for someone else." Meanwhile, Hunter told reporters that he was going to bring a shovel with him on the next trip to Milwaukee so he could grade the mound himself.[104]

After a 10–5 start, the Brewers hit a 1–10 skid that sent them into a tailspin from which they would not recover. A brutal four-game sweep in Detroit in late May that included three walk-off losses dropped them into last place for good. They finished at 66–95.

1977

Thursday, April 12, 1977: Orioles 1, Brewers 0 (55,120 attendance)
In the News: President Carter commuted the 20-year prison sentence

for Watergate mastermind G. Gordon Liddy, making him eligible for parole in July after having served 50 months.

At the Movies: *Andy Warhol's Frankenstein in 3D* at Points Cinema
On the Radio: "Dancing Queen" by Abba

Hope died early for the 1976 Brewers. A 9–3 April was followed with a 1–9 open to May and the team never recovered, stumbling to their fifth 90-loss season in seven tries. But the labor agitation from that spring had inaugurated a new era in baseball and, for the first time since the roster-poaching age of the 1910s, veteran players had earned a degree of autonomy over their futures.

The players and owners had agreed to a free agency system in which eligible players would enter a "draft," allowing teams, choosing in reverse order of the previous year's standings, to put a claim on the rights to negotiate with a free agent player. A player could be drafted by up to 13 clubs and a club could draft as many as 12 players. Once this negotiation matrix was settled, a team was permitted to sign two players. For the first-ever free agent draft in November 1976, Reggie Jackson, late of the Baltimore Orioles, was the marquee attraction, but a trio of former Oakland Athletics—third baseman Sal Bando, outfielder Joe Rudi, and first baseman Gene Tenace—were also considered game-changing talents. The Brewers drafted all three.[105]

Even with the concept of free agency still brand new, it did seem a bit audacious for a team that had never even threatened the .500 mark to be considered major players for buying up the heart of the three-time champion A's. But Brewers president Bud Selig was dead serious about making big additions and had the money to make it happen, saying he was willing and able to spend about $3 million that off-season. He'd been talking with Bando since well before the draft, hosting him in Milwaukee just after the '76 World Series. Rumor had it that the Brewers were also the favorites to land Tenace, Bando's close friend and long-time Oakland roommate. The pair had both received MVP votes in 1976 and had combined to hit nearly 50 homers.[106]

The Brewers already had a top-tier first baseman in George Scott, but the marriage between the slugger and the Brewers had been damaged beyond repair. He saw the team quit on themselves late in the season, but felt that he was getting the blame for the club not winning. He clashed repeatedly with manager Alex Grammas, the first-year skipper who even rescinded the team captain assignment that Scott had been given by Del Crandall. After the Brewers made their intentions known with Tenace, Scott asked to be traded.[107]

Just before Thanksgiving, the Brewers and Bando made it official. The Brewers gave the four-time All-Star a deal worth $1.5 million over five seasons. Although Bando would be 33 years old in 1977, his leadership—he had been team captain in Oakland and was widely seen as a future manager—was an asset Selig prized most for turning around the Brewers. At an introductory press conference at the Hotel Pfister, Bando ate a few slices of pizza while sipping a Pabst Blue Ribbon beer. "I feel right at home here," he told the assembled media. Taking a shot at the lackluster attendance of the A's, he added, "I'm used to playing in front of crowds of this size." Asked if leaving the Athletics—whose ownership he had repeatedly clashed with during their three-title run—was difficult, he replied, "Was it difficult leaving the Titanic?"[108]

Two weeks later, with Tenace nearing a deal with San Diego, the Brewers made two major trades involving a trio of discontented players. They returned George Scott and Bernie Carbo, who was also unhappy in Milwaukee, to the Red Sox for a slick-hitting 26-year-old named Cecil Cooper. They then sent former All-Stars Jim Colburn and Darrell Porter to Kansas City for infielder Jamie Quirk and outfielder Jim Wohlford. Like Scott, Porter was supremely talented, but the Brewers felt they were not getting enough from him. Like Scott, Porter strained under the rule of Alex Grammas. Both Scott and Porter told the press they were glad to be out of the organization.[109]

The calendar year 1977 opened under a dark cloud for the Brewers. On New Year's Day, relief pitcher Danny Frisella, who had led the team in saves and ERA in 1976, was killed when a dune buggy he was riding in crashed on a desert road just outside of Phoenix. Frisella had recently moved to the city with his pregnant wife and three-year-old son. Frisella had been acquired mid-way through the 1976 season, but quickly became a central part of the team. "There would be times that I did bad and he would pat me on the back or say something and make me feel better," pitcher Jerry Augustine said of Frisella. "And it just seemed like he had everything going for him, too. He was so happy go lucky, just an easy going guy." When the team opened training camp two and a half months later, a black band of mourning was added to their uniform sleeves.[110]

A new attitude prevailed once the spring schedule started, with new players emerging in leadership positions. Bando was named team captain and several players—whether openly or by omission—made it clear that George Scott was not going to be missed. "He's Boston's problem now," said pitcher Billy Travers. Cecil Cooper was as soft-spoken as Scott was garrulous. The youngest of 13 children, Cooper came from a baseball family—his father Roy had played in the Negro Leagues and two of his brothers played with the all-black Indianapolis Clowns barnstorming team. Cooper joined the Red Sox in 1971 and spent the next six seasons mostly as a part-time player, stuck behind Carl Yastrzemski at first base. He announced his presence in the first intersquad game of the spring with two homers—including a grand slam. "This is the first time in six years that we've had a first baseman who knew the meaning of the word 'we,'" GM Jim Baumer told the newspapers.[111]

The Brewers ran through the Cactus League schedule to finish with a league-best 16–8 record. The *Journal* said the camp brought about "one of the most amazing changes in attitude ever chronicled." Longtime *New York Daily News* sportswriter Dick Young even picked the Brewers to win the highly-competitive AL East.[112]

"We used to come into Milwaukee in July and August and those guys looked dead," said Cooper. "This is a lot different. Now we've got some rah-rah here."[113]

"This club is like the A's of 1968, our first year in Oakland," Bando said. "These are all really good young guys. I don't think it's going to take this club as long to become a contender as it took the A's."[114]

The feel-good Brewers opened the season in New York, taking two games of three from the defending AL champ Yankees. They returned home to a city abuzz. A run on tickets would continue right up until the first pitch, and by 7 a.m., the parking lots had already begun to fill and backups were forming on all roads to County Stadium. With the temperature topping 80 degrees, there was a noted uptick in the tailgating festivities from recent years, with roaming polka bands and party spreads including lawn furniture and long, buffet-style tables. Young men without a party—or wishing to visit as many as possible—walked the lots with six packs of beer, not ready to find their seats until each can was empty.[115]

Inside the stadium, lefty Bill Travers faced off against the Orioles and reigning Cy Young winner Jim Palmer. Travers had been a bright spot for a beleaguered Brewers staff in '76, posting a 2.81 ERA over 240 innings and making the AL All-Star team. But he'd tough-lucked his way to a 15–16 record. The Brewers had been shut out in his last three starts, including the season opener in New York. Travers watched the cars flow into the parking lots from the clubhouse window before the game and bounced around the locker room trying to work off his excited energy.[116]

His first goal for the afternoon was to open with a strike to shake off the nerves. Just past 1 p.m., with more than 55,000 either cheering him on or making their way inside, he delivered one to Al Bumbry. He got Bumbry on a lineout and worked around a walk for a scoreless first. He did the same with an error in the second and got the O's 1-2-3 in the third. On the other side, Palmer matched him, allowing only two baserunners through three innings. While Travers kept the Orioles off balance, Palmer began to dominate. After a walk to Jamie Quirk in the third, he set down 18 in a row to send the game into the ninth inning locked in a scoreless tie.[117]

Jay Saeger and some friends snuck out of classes at Cudahy High School on a whim to attend the first-ever Brewers home opener in 1970. Fifty-some years later, he is a part of the small group of fans who have been to every Opening Day in franchise history open to attendees. Saeger (in the cap) is seen here before the 1979 opener with (back row, left to right) Barb Karlson, Vicki Hassi, Lauren Faulkner, Lori Gieske and (kneeling) James Livingston (courtesy Jay Saeger).

Rookie Eddie Murray opened the ninth with a single to center field and Lee May bunted him to second to bring catcher Rick Dempsey—1 for 13 on the season—to the plate. With a base open, Travers tried to get him to chase and Dempsey worked a 3–0 count. With Brooks Robinson—40 years old and beginning his 23rd and final Big League season—on deck, Grammas considered having Travers put Dempsey on, but decided against it. Given the green light, Dempsey was looking for a fastball. Travers gave him one and Dempsey laced it back up the middle to score Murray to put Baltimore up, 1–0. A minute later, Robinson gave Travers the groundball he'd been looking for and the Brewers rolled up an inning-ending double play.[118]

Jim Wohlford led off the bottom of the ninth with a clean single and the crowd came back to life. Charlie Moore, who'd taken over catching duties from Darrell Porter, tried to bunt Wohlford over, but the ball took an odd hop in front of home plate, ricocheting back to Dempsey, who fired to second to start the double play. Von Joshua was up next and popped out on the infield to end the heartbreaker of a game.[119]

But the mood afterward was still upbeat. It had been the largest crowd to ever see a sporting event in Milwaukee. "It was very exciting. I'm grateful to know that Milwaukee is behind us that much," Bando said after the game. "From I saw today, this might be the best town in baseball."[120]

Once again, the Brewers started at 10–5—even advancing to 14–7 while holding first place—before tumbling into the cellar. They finished at 67–95. In their first eight seasons of existence, the Brewers post–All-Star break winning percentage (.398) was more than 50 points lower than their first half winning percentage (.451).

1978

Friday, April 7, 1978: Brewers 11, Orioles 3 (attendance: 47,824)

In the News: The usual damage from rabbits at the Summerfest grounds is minimal this year, owing to a family of foxes that has taken up residence underneath the main stage.

At the Movies: *Close Encounters of the Third Kind* at the Movies Northridge

On the Radio: "Stayin' Alive" by the Bee Gees

It had become so terribly familiar. The 1977 Brewers, full of promise and potential, had a terrific April, a mediocre May, and then lingered until the dog days when they completely fell apart and finished miles out of contention with 90-some losses. "I can't say I've enjoyed baseball that much," Robin Yount told the *Journal* that September, near the end of his fourth season as the Brewers' regular shortstop. "I haven't gotten anything out of it."[121]

While the face of the franchise grew introspective about his career, team president Bud Selig executed an overhaul of the club's leadership. Manager Alex Grammas, GM Jim Baumer, Director of Player Development Al Widmer, and coaches Jimmy Bragan and Hal Smith were all fired. The new man in charge would be Harry Dalton, whom Selig had lured away from the California Angels, where he had been vice president and general manager since 1971, following up a run as Baltimore Orioles GM in which he'd built the team into a World Series winner. But he had been unable to replicate that success in California and team ownership had recently marginalized his authority. In Milwaukee, Selig gave Dalton total control over personnel moves and left it to him to hire a new manager.[122]

In the midst of all this, the Brewers finalized their second major free agent signing in as many years. Looking to jump-start a lineup that had featured Jim Wohlford and Von Joshua—who combined for 11 home runs and a sub-.300 on base percentage—as regular outfielders in 1977, the Brewers made Larry Hisle their top off-season target. With the Twins in '77, Hisle had led the AL in RBI and slugged 27 homers with 20 steals to cement his reputation as one of the league's top-hitting outfielders. Encouraged by what Sal Bando and Cecil Cooper had to say about the organization, Hisle agreed to a six-year pact with about $3 million. The Yankees—reigning world champions—had also gone hard after Hisle, but he had no desire to play in New York. "I'm the kind of person who likes to make himself a part of community life. I'm not a big city type," he said at his introductory press conference.[123]

Dalton had told the press that he was in no rush to name a new manager and, as fall gave way to winter, it was clear he was serious. Many considered Frank Howard to be the leading candidate. A Wisconsin native and author of nearly 400 Big League homers, "Hondo" had joined the Brewers coaching staff before the '77 season and was well-regarded enough to survive the post-season purge. The leading outside candidate was thought to be Frank Robinson, recently departed from the Cleveland Indians.[124]

While the club waited on its new field leader, Dalton made a splash by dealing away ace Jim Slaton. The All-Star had made no secret of his displeasure with the bottom-feeding Brewers and had only a year left on his contract. In return, Dalton got 29-year-old Ben Oglivie, a lefty slugger he had long coveted. Dalton had also tried to work a deal for Padres outfielder Dave Winfield, but balked at the asking price.[125]

Finally, in late January, Dalton found his skipper, ending what the *Journal* called "one of the longest searches since Columbus went sailing." Dalton settled on an old friend from Baltimore, Orioles pitching coach George Bamberger. The plain-spoken Staten Islander had overseen a staff that produced four Cy Young Award trophies and 18 20-game winners and helped the O's to three pennants and a world title. Bamberger was blunt about the Milwaukee team that had been. "We felt they did not care," he said of Orioles-Brewers match-ups in 1977. "[They] didn't think they could win, so they would just put in their nine innings and lose." But he also saw something in what remained of that listless bunch. With Oglivie and Hisle, he saw an offense that could take on the Yankees, Red Sox, and Orioles. "The only thing they have that we don't have is their pitchers have been around longer."[126]

Dalton would make one more significant roster move before spring training, re-acquiring outfielder Gorman Thomas from the Rangers. Thomas had been a first round draft choice of the Seattle Pilots and had lingered for years as a talented-yet-flaky fringe man on the Brewers roster. The Brewers had banished him to the minors for 1977 and Thomas got the wake-up they were hoping for. He punished Pacific Coast League pitchers, batting .322 and slugging .640 with 36 homers and 114 RBI. It was something of a surprise, then, that Thomas was traded just after the season, completing a meaningless swap the Brewers and Rangers had made a few months earlier. The whole thing was a set-up, with the Rangers needing to clear a roster spot and the Brewers wanting to protect the out-of-options Thomas from being claimed by another team. He was returned to Milwaukee for an undisclosed sum.[127]

For those who believed in omens, it might have seemed that the Brewers' 1978 season was doomed before it even began. Just days into training camp, flooding in Sun City washed out the Brewers' spring playing field and destroyed the team's clubhouse, ruining thousands of dollars in gear and equipment. After the roof of the building collapsed, Bamberger and Dalton waded into the hip-deep water and—in an action as rich in metaphor as any in team history—salvaged what they could from the wreckage.[128]

Robin Yount reported to camp wrecked in his own way. He was once again without a contract and just a year away from free agency. He had been worn down by the losing and seemed to just be going through the motions. A lingering foot injury and sore elbow contributed to his malaise. He played in just 10 spring games, batting .212 with four errors, before he asked for some time away from the team and was placed on the disabled list.[129]

Meanwhile, another young Brewers shortstop was having an outstanding time in the Arizona sun. Paul Molitor, drafted by the Brewers just nine months earlier from the University of Minnesota, was impressing the Big League brass both in the field and at the plate. With Yount gone, he saw some action in spring games and quickly pushed his batting average well over .300—where it would remain until the end of camp. But even with Yount unsigned, Molitor prepared for a second season in the minors.[130]

PAUL MOLITOR   INFIELDER   MILWAUKEE BREWERS

Paul Molitor expected to open the 1978 season in the low minors. But when Robin Yount became so disillusioned with losing that he was considering leaving the game, Molitor was named the Brewers' starting shortstop.

Yount's holdout—and the floods—were the rare blemishes in an otherwise upbeat camp. Players who had chaffed under Grammas now felt encouraged and the team's vibe was impressing even the veterans. Sal Bando, still the team captain, spoke about Bamberger's openness and his willingness to work with the younger players. And Larry Hisle—whose biggest purchase since signing his $3 million deal had been a camera—was looking every bit the superstar the Brewers had hyped him as, batting over .400 on the spring and leading the club in home runs.[131]

As the team was packing up to head north, it was clear that Robin Yount would not be part of their immediate future. Molitor was sitting in Jim Gantner's car outside the team training facility in Sun City, waiting to be driven over to the minor league camp when a staffer came and told him to prepare for Milwaukee instead. He was the new starting shortstop and lead-off hitter.[132]

The Brewers were set to open against the Orioles on April 6, but a string of rain showers drenched the field until early afternoon, while frost on the ground kept the drainage system from working properly and pushed festivities back a day. The delay seemed to calm the team, with the usual opening act jitters amplified in players like Hisle and Molitor, who were both eager to prove themselves to the hometown fans. By April 7, the team was ready and loose, looking sharp in their new pinstripe uniform set (although the new ball-and-glove insignia on their caps was "confusing" in the eyes of the *Journal*).[133]

Only about 36,000 of the 47,000 ticket holders made it to the rescheduled game, but the 63-degree first-pitch temperature kept everyone happy. The tailgating had started early on 6th, and many fans kept the party going even after the game had been called, with a hearty few even camping out to get an early start the next day. Coach Hank Raymonds and forward Ulice Payne of the 1977 Marquette National title–winning basketball team threw out the first pitches while Wisconsin native Jerry Augustine took honors for the Brewers.[134]

The afternoon's first big debut came in the bottom of the first, when Hisle came to bat with two men and one out. After a nice welcome from the crowd, Hisle—feeling the nerves—grounded into a double play to end the inning. Molitor—whom the *Journal* described as being "pale-faced" with stress—got his first chance in the field on a sharp grounder up the middle with one on. He made a clean scoop and tapped second for the out, but slipped on the throw and sent what he described as a "balloon ball" to Cooper at first. "I was lucky it didn't go into the bleachers," he said later. "Cooper had to run under it like it was a touchdown pass."[135]

In the bottom of the second, the new-look Brewers woke up. With Sixto Lezcano on, Lenn Sakata singled to set up a two-run double by Andy

Etchebarren. Molitor followed with a line-drive single to put the Brewers up by three. The next inning, Hisle said hello with a ringing double and scored on a Cooper base hit. Perhaps bolstered by the early 4–0 lead, a banner soon appeared in the bleachers that read, "Yount Tees Us Off," a reference to the rumor that the missing shortstop was threatening to abandon baseball for a golf career. Yount was a surprise guest at the game, making his own way to Milwaukee after the team briefly lost contact with him following his exit from training camp. When asked by a reporter when he planned to rejoin the team, he threw his arms up in an exaggerated shrug.[136]

Two innings later, with Sal Bando on, Hisle slashed a Tim Stoddard pitch into the left field bleachers to set the margin at six. Skipping out of the box, Hisle clapped his hands—a remarkable show of emotion for the usually reserved slugger. Meanwhile, the lefty Augustine kept the Orioles off balance, junk-balling his way to a spree of ground balls and weak pop flies. And in the bottom of the seventh, the Brewers went in for the kill. Don Money reached on an error, Bando walked, and Hisle took one in the ribs to load the bases for Lezcano. Still just 24 years old, Lezcano was already in his fifth season with the Brewers. He'd clashed with manager Del Crandall and was even briefly suspended by the team in 1975 for insubordination. But he'd made efforts to mature since, and in 1977 he was one of the team's steadiest hitters despite missing nearly two months with a broken hand. And stepping in that afternoon, following up on a lousy spring and three hitless trips to the plate, he was just hoping to make contact. Stoddard offered him a low fastball, trying to coax a double play, but Lezcano got under it and drove it high into the steady easterly wind and

Sixto Lezcano did not have an easy road to stardom in Milwaukee, but he came to deliver some of the Brewers' most memorable Opening Day moments (1976 SSPC #241).

watched with surprise as it dropped into the left field bleachers for his first career grand slam. County Stadium shook as he rounded the bases with the Brewers up 10–0.[137]

Augustine came within two outs of tossing a shutout before Eddie Murray ripped a ninth-inning homer. The O's slopped across a couple more runs before Terry Crowley popped out to Bando to end the biggest Opening Day win in Brewers history. Perhaps no one in the building was as relieved at the last out as Bamberger, who had felt none of the rain-delay relief of his players. He was so stressed for his debut—against the Orioles and his old mentor Earl Weaver, no less—that he'd been unable to eat all day. The first thing he did after the post-game handshakes was to ask for a glass of milk.[138]

Augustine, having just thrown the best game of his career, spoke of it as a turning point for the franchise. "You can feel it," he said. "You don't have to worry now about runs. You can tell by the way they're swinging the bat."[139]

Molitor, who'd collected a hit and was robbed of another and was impressive in the field, said he felt capable of playing shortstop all season. Yount was in the clubhouse afterward. "Good game," was all he said to Molitor.[140]

"It's kind of a funny feeling," Molitor said of the situation. "I wonder what's going on in his mind, but I'm in no position to ask."[141]

The Brewers were 12–12 when Yount returned to the team on May 6 and they'd continue on a .500 pace until early June, when they won 13 of 14 to start a hot streak that would last all summer. Finally pairing a strong start with a collapse-free second half, they won 93 games in 1978, but only in mid-September were they able to get within four games of first place.

1979

Friday, April 10, 1979: Brewers 3, Red Sox 0 (54,392 attendance)
In the News: The U.S. Senate has approved a measure to restore prayer in public schools, but an attached amendment by opponents has effectively guaranteed the bill will not be adopted.
At the Movies: *Richard Prior: Live in Concert* at the Riverside Theater
On the Radio: "Sultans of Swing" by Dire Straits

It finally happened on September 9, 1978. The Brewers beat the Twins 3–0 in Bloomington for their 82nd win of the season, guaranteeing Milwaukee's first winning baseball season since the Braves had left for Atlanta. The Brewers finished the year with 93 wins, but with the Yankees and Red Sox both on a 99-win pace, the upstart Brewers mostly spent the year as fringe contenders. But it was no matter to Milwaukee fans, who'd finally accepted the club as a true substitute for the Braves. Cecil Cooper, Paul Molitor, and Gorman Thomas had all taken star turns while Larry Hisle delivered on every cent of his contract, placing third in AL MVP voting. Mike Caldwell won 22 games and placed second in AL Cy Young voting. George Bamberger quickly emerged as a beloved figure, occasionally visiting tailgating parties in stadium parking lots after games. And Robin Yount, who seemed as though he might never return to baseball, returned to the club in April and turned in his best season to date. A franchise-record 1.6 million tickets were sold in 1978 and Milwaukee fell in love with the bunch they called "Bambi's Bombers."

Things had taken such a turn that Jim Slaton, traded away as a discontent before the '78 season, was drafted and signed on for five more years in Milwaukee in late November. Ben Oglivie, whom the Brewers had gotten in return for Slaton from Detroit, parlayed his 18-homer, .303 season into a long-term deal of his own. Paul Molitor, who was literally waiting for a ride to the minor league side of training camp when he learned he would be starting for the Brewers in '78, was also ready for the long haul in Milwaukee and spent the off-season condo-shopping in the city. He even felt comfortable enough to joke about Robin Yount's 1978 holdout—the one that opened the door for him to make the team, but also put him in the incredibly awkward spot of replacing the Brewers' franchise player. "I sent Robin a tennis outfit for Christmas," he said in a nod to the rumors that Yount was ditching baseball for pro golf.[142]

A small measure of fame even came to the previously unknown Brewers. Bamberger became a popular guest on the off-season "rubber chicken circuit" of honorary dinners. But the homebody Bamberger didn't take naturally to the practice. "If I didn't get this award, I wouldn't be here tonight," he told one group. "And I wouldn't have been in Kansas City last weekend. I wouldn't have been a lot of places." He also filmed an ad for a television maker, but called the finished product the "worst commercial I ever saw" and declared an end to his pitchman career. In the spring of '79, Bamberger—along with Sal Bando and Larry Hisle—appeared on *Sports Challenge*, a game show hosted by Dick Enberg. The Brewers bunch made it to the final round of the tournament-style jock quiz program before losing to a trio from the Dallas Cowboys.[143]

By the time spring training rolled around, the roster was so deep that all but a few spots on the final squad were settled. Former Reds star Clay Carroll was in camp competing for the final spot in the bullpen with a few prospects and the last reserve infielder job was down to Lenn Sakata, Jim Gantner, and Tim Nordbrook. In comparison with the desperate urgency of years past, spring training 1979 was, the in words of the *Sentinel*'s Lou Chapman, a "crushing bore."[144]

But there was nothing boring about the bunch who had already staked their place on the 1979 Brewers. The group that arrived in Sun City that spring had the swagger and camaraderie that winning breeds and they were easily the loosest and most fun-loving bunch that the team had ever put together. Gorman Thomas—who had finally broken out in 1978 with a 32-homer season—was usually at the center of the revelry. He stole teammate's clothes after games, snuck into the County Stadium scoreboard to put messages on the Fan-O-Gram, commandeered courtesy wheelchairs in airports for joy-riding, and once hid a frog in Sal Bando's jockstrap. He also predicted the Brewers would win 104 games in 1979 and declared that he deserved the Gold Glove award for his all-out play in center field. "Nobody went into the wall 15 times last year as I did.... I'll go through a wall if I have to."[145]

Thomas was also the team's leading "ripper"—master of the insults that members of the club traded freely. The most prominent examples of this (and most suitable for print in the newspapers) were the nicknames he handed out. Cecil Cooper and his bald spot were known as "Divot Head"; Jerry Augustine was "Boo-Boo" for his resemblance to Yogi Bear's sidekick; Don Money was "Volkie" because, per Thomas, his ears made him look like a Volkswagen with the doors open; Robin Yount was "Lucan" for his resemblance to the long-haired man-child raised by wolves in the TV series of the same name. Charlie Moore was "Fifi Lamour" ("He looks like a little, sweet Frenchman with a wing on," Thomas said) and Sal Bando was "Troll" ("Because as his off-season occupation, he hides under bridges and waits for kids to go to school. They have to give him potato chips before he lets them pass"). And finally Jim Gantner, still just a fringe player fighting for a roster spot, was dubbed "Gumby." "He's like a rubber doll," Thomas explained. "No fingers, no toes—just arms and legs."[146]

For the record, Thomas' own nickname was "Spike," given to him by coach Frank Howard, whose huge stature had earned him the nickname "the Washington Monument" during his time with the Senators. "You ask me why?" Thomas said. "When the man [Howard] is 6 foot 8 and weighs 320 pounds, you don't ask why."[147]

The Brewers opened the season in New York against the world champion Yankees. The Brewers had made no bones that the Yankees would be their biggest rival in '79. Despite finishing 6.5 games behind them in standings, the Brewers had owned the Yanks in '78, winning 10 of 15 matchups. Reggie Jackson said that the Brewers would be the Yankees' toughest opponent in 1979. Bud Selig, perhaps emboldened by a record pace for ticket sales, said that "people all over the country" were pulling for Milwaukee to dethrone the Yankees.[148]

The Brewers spoiled the Yankees' opener with a 5–1 win as Caldwell continued his dominance of the Pinstripers (he'd held them to a 0.99 ERA over 45 innings in 1978) and took the opening series two games to one. Caldwell also got the call for the home opener against the Red Sox. Perhaps no one on the Brewers' roster exemplified the team's upstart, rough-around-the-edges, chip-on-the-shoulder attitude as much as the man they called "Mr. Warmth." He'd been a non-prospect who'd bounced around the first half of his career, often clashing with management and possessing a sour disposition that earned him his nickname. He landed in Milwaukee in the middle of the 1977 season in a trade that impressed few observers, but in 1978—backed by a manager who believed in his talents (and who also was alleged to have taught him to throw the spitball)—he was finally able to prove his detractors wrong.[149]

As excited as the home crowd—which was the second-largest in County Stadium history at 54,392—was to greet the Brewers, they were almost as eager to let George Scott know how little he was missed in Milwaukee. He was booed loudly during pregame introductions and was jittery all afternoon. In the bottom of the first, Yount laced a lead-off single, stole second, and moved to third on a fly ball out. Cooper then hit a bouncer to Scott at first, where the big man hesitated for a moment as Yount sprinted home. He rushed a throw that bounced in front of the plate, allowing Yount to slide in safely. It was all Caldwell would need.[150]

It was hardly a day made for offense anyway, with a stiff easterly wind making the high–30s temperatures bite even harder, but Caldwell and Boston's Dennis Eckersley didn't need much help as they traded zeros into the bottom of the fifth. With one away, Yount sliced an Eckersley fastball into the right field corner. The ball stayed under the winds and zipped over the fence to make it 2–0. The Sox threatened in the top of the sixth, putting two on with one out for the heart of their order. But Caldwell fanned Carl Yastrzemski and barehanded a sharp come-backer from Scott to end the inning. It was Scott's third ground-out to Caldwell in as many at-bats. The home crowd roared in approval.[151]

Aside from Scott, the biggest target for the fans was the crew of umpires. The Major League umpire's union was out on strike, leaving the game to be called by a single league-assigned replacement ump and a trio of locals who had been selected by the Brewers from a pool of just 12 applicants. Drawn from the college and semi-pro ranks, the crew had trouble all afternoon. In the bottom of the sixth, Larry Hisle was called out trying to tag up from third on a Sixto Lezcano fly ball. Hisle had clearly beaten the throw, but was alleged to have missed the plate. Bamberger and Bando protested loudly, but the soft-spoken Hisle just shook his head and sighed, "If that's what he thinks...."[152]

The Brewers tacked on another run in the seventh—aided by another Scott misplay in the field—to give Caldwell a 3–0 lead. But it did nothing to take the edge off of Mr. Warmth. With two away in the eighth, Fred Lynn worked a bases-on-balls. Caldwell felt that Lynn had been crowding the plate and gave the outfielder an earful as he jogged to first. Lynn chirped back. Caldwell then, in the words of the *Journal*, "allegedly told Lynn to perform some sort of unnatural act with his Louisville Slugger." He was the last Boston baserunner of the afternoon.[153]

After the game, as Hisle jokingly searched the wiry Yount's arms for the muscles required to homer on a day when he and the other Milwaukee big men couldn't reach the warning track, Lary Sorensen talked up Caldwell the way a wrestling promoter might hype his most gruesome attraction. "The guy's just not a friendly man," he told reporters. "He eats nails and glass. He likes to swallow toads live. About two or three days before he's supposed to pitch, he starts to get nasty. That means ... he's a nasty, rotten human being somewhere between 60 and 80% of the time."[154]

The Brewers were even better in 1979, winning 95 games, but with the AL East led by the 102-win Orioles, they again spent the summer without really threatening for the division crown. From August 1 onward, they could get no closer than six games behind Baltimore. Had they still been in the AL West, they would have easily won their second straight division title.

Chapter Two

The Eighties

1980

Thursday, April 10, 1980: Brewers 9, Red Sox 5 (53,313 attendance)
In the News: Television producer Norman Lear has donated $500,000 to a fund to support passage of the Equal Rights Amendment in "memory" of Edith Bunker, an *All in the Family* character who, it has been announced, will die sometime in the upcoming season.
At the Movies: *Fist of Fury Part II* (Savage Fury! Deadly Action!) at the Centre Twin
On the Radio: "Call Me" by Blondie

Only two teams in baseball won more games than the Brewers did in 1979. Unfortunately, one was the Baltimore Orioles, who outpaced the Crew in the AL East by eight games and went on to win the pennant. The Brewers were the only team to win 93 games or more in both 1978 and 1979, but had never really been within striking distance of first in either season. The years of bad baseball and bad breaks had finally given way to a true powerhouse team, but it was one of many in a stacked American League East.

If the Brewers had a weakness in 1979, it was the bullpen. No Brewer finished with more than six saves and Jerry Augustine's 3.47 was the team's lowest ERA among relievers who'd pitched 50 or more innings. After several years of trying to get their own Goose Gossage-type pitcher, it briefly appeared as though the real thing might be headed to Milwaukee. During the Orioles-Pirates World Series broadcast, ABC's Howard Cosell mentioned that a trade sending Gossage to the Brewers in exchange for a package headlined by outfielder Sixto Lezcano was imminent.[1]

But there was nothing to the rumor and, indeed, it would have taken more than Gossage to wrest Lezcano from the Brewers. At 25 years old, the outfielder had broken out in 1979, batting .321 with 28 homers and winning a Gold Glove Award. He became a national hero in his native Puerto Rico and spent the off-season giving clinics in his homeland and gifting kids with baseball gear. He had been the subject of trade rumors in the past, and a number of teams asked about the slugger following the '79 season. By the open of training camp, knowing how much the Brewers valued the outfielder, teams were no longer even bothering to put together an offer.[2]

With no reliever in baseball meeting their asking price for Lezcano, the Brewers once again looked to the free agent draft for help. With their top pick, they tabbed Angels fireballer Nolan Ryan. The team made a serious approach to Ryan and manager George Bamberger said publicly that he considered Ryan a possible centerpiece of the bullpen, but Ryan had his heart set on playing in his native Texas and ended up with the Houston Astros, having never seriously considered Milwaukee.[3]

Even if the Brewers opened camp with lingering questions in the bullpen, the team brimmed with confidence. Young arms like Dave LaPoint, Rickey "Buster" Keeton, and Willie Mueller looked to break into the already-strong starting rotation and Charlie Moore and Larry Hisle looked strong in their return from injuries. Shortstop Robin Yount, whose offensive numbers had slid a bit after his 1978 star-turn, reported to camp with a new physique—his slender frame now stacked with muscles after he had taken up weight training in the off-season. Gorman Thomas arrived with his usual flourish, walking through the locker room with his bags, insulting each of his teammates as he passed by. Coming up to Rene Quinones, a minor league pitcher whom he'd never met, he politely nodded and said hello before continuing on his vulgar way. "It's nice to see the guys," he said. "It's like a big, happy family. We're a happy-go-lucky bunch of guys who like playing together."[4]

But like most families, the worries with the Brewers centered on finances and health. The financial trouble again centered on the strained relationship between the players and ownership. Players were unable to come to an agreement with owners on the issue of compensation to teams losing free agents, and the Brewers voted to authorize a strike date of April 1. The health problems, however, hit the team in a way that went beyond baseball. In February, hitting coach Harvey Kuenn endured five agonizing operations in a single week to try to correct a blood clot problem in his right leg. The final procedure was an amputation. Despite it all, Kuenn was upbeat, joking as he watched early camp workouts from a wheelchair. "They always said I hit off my front foot anyway. What the hell do I need the back one for?"[5]

On March 6, George Bamberger was taken to a nearby hospital after complaining of chest and back pain during morning drills. A few days later, it was learned that he'd suffered a minor heart attack. He was told to get some bed rest and third base coach Bob "Buck" Rodgers was put in charge of the team. But mid-way into camp, it was clear that Bamberger needed more than just rest. On March 26, he underwent an eight-hour coronary bypass surgery and was given a recovery time of at least two months.⁶

Both Bamberger and Kuenn were beloved by their players. Mike Caldwell, whose career Bamberger had resurrected, admitted that there was a "kind of an aura, or a cloud, hanging over [the team]." And it was more than just Bamberger and Kuenn. Two days after Bamberger's surgery, the Brewers voted to strike and, on April 1, the players left camp a week early. They agreed to report for the opening of the season, but set May 22 as a possible date for an in-season stoppage. The owners were insisting on changing the compensation for a lost free agent from a draft choice to a major league player. The players said this would roll back the freedoms they had already won.⁷

But nothing could dampen Milwaukee's Opening Day optimism. The Brewers were one of the favorites in the American League and the baseball part of spring training had been mostly good news, as both Robin Yount and Paul Molitor batted over .400 with Yount flashing some newfound power. The Opening Day rematch against Dennis Eckersley and the Red Sox had been sold out since late February and, despite temperatures in

Craig Counsell was just 10 years old when he attended his first Brewers home opener. The son of longtime team employee, Counsell grew up in Whitefish Bay and would return for home openers as a player (both with the Brewers and Diamondbacks), executive, and manager (Arturo Pardavila III).

the low 40s and gray skies, the tailgaters arrived early and got loud quickly. One group of more than 100 had already tapped three quarter-barrels of beer and had a full pig roasting on a spit by the time most people were reporting to work.[8]

After the pregame ceremonies, which included the now-traditional players' parade around the field in pickup trucks, the crowd was directed to the brand-new right field scoreboard. The new state-of-the-art board had replaced the original board inaugurated by the Braves in 1953 and used 30,000 low-wattage light bulbs to create an early version of a video screen. And the team had the perfect guest for its debut video presentation: George Bamberger, who had been released from the hospital just the day before. "I'd like to thank the fans," Bamberger said to the silent crowd. "I'd like to wish the ball players much success. We've got very capable coaches who know their business. So sit back, enjoy the game, and have a beer on me."[9]

The crowd went wild, eventually breaking into a chant of "Bambi! Bambi!"[10]

The Red Sox struck first, getting to lefty Jim Slaton in the second for a run and tagging him with two more in the third. With two on and one out, Rodgers had an arm ready in the bullpen when Slaton coaxed Tony Perez into a 5-4-3 double play. The twin-killing allowed Slaton to catch his breath and settle in. Against Butch Hobson leading off the top of the fourth, he dropped his arm a bit and got him to ground out. It felt better and he kept with it. Carl Yastrzemski and the rest of the Red Sox noticed the change. "He looked like he picked up five miles an hour on his fastball," said Yaz. The Sox would not have another hit until the ninth inning.[11]

It was the first County Stadium opener for outfielder Ben Oglivie. The wiry Panamanian would eventually enroll in courses at UW–Milwaukee, as a matter of curiosity rather than in pursuit of a degree. Oglivie read constantly, everything from philosophy to electronics manuals. He was even known to read while driving. When he stepped up against Eckersley in the bottom of the fourth, he got an excellent read on a fluttering fastball and drove it into the right field bleachers.

Thomas followed with a walk and Sixto Lezcano—now being introduced as "Sixtooooooo Lezcanoooooo" by PA announcer Bob Betts—crushed a two-run homer to tie the game, 3–3.[12]

General Manager Harry Dalton called Bamberger, who was at home in Florida, to update him on the score. By the way, Dalton told Bamberger, "you owe us $57,000."

"Why?" asked Bamberger.

"Because everyone is having a beer on you. They're all signing your name to the tab."[13]

An inning later, Molitor cracked another home run off Eckersley to give the Brewers the lead, and in the sixth, Don Money got one up into the wind off Steve Renko to make it 5–3. And that's the way it stayed until Slaton took the mound for the ninth. Yastrzemski led off for Boston, waiting on that fastball that no one seemed able to catch. When he finally got one, Slaton left it over the plate and Yaz crushed it to make the score 5–4. One batter later, Butch Hobson tattooed another Slaton mistake to tie the game. Reggie Cleveland came in and secured the final outs of the inning, but the damage had been done.[14]

"Tell those guys to bust their butts," Bamberger was reported to have told Dalton, who was now giving the manager the play by play over the phone. While it is unlikely that Bamberger, who came from Staten Island and had the vocabulary to show it, said exactly *that*, the players got the gist of it. Molitor led off the ninth with a single off Dick Drago. He was bunted to second by Cecil Cooper and, after a foul out by Dick Davis, Drago intentionally walked Oglivie to bring up Thomas with two out and two on. The grisly-tempered Thomas, who famously swung from the heels and took no shame in striking out, took the first two pitches for balls. He took a hack at the third offering and popped it down the left field line. Third baseman Hobson and shortstop Rick Burleson both gave chase and both seemed to have a bead on the ball, but it landed just out of reach, even with Burleson diving over the tarp to try to end the inning and send the game to extras. After another strike, with the crowd fully back into the game, Thomas started to toy with Drago, stepping out twice as the pitcher came set. After a quick mound visit, Drago threw one in on Thomas and sent the slugger backpedaling from the box. Two more foul balls and the stadium buzzed with tension. Drago's final, exhausted pitch of the at-bat was in the dirt and Thomas took first to load the bases for Lezcano.

The crowd never even had a chance to catch their breath. Knowing Drago wouldn't want to waste a pitch after the battle with Thomas, Lezcano swung at the first offering and drove it into the Brewers' bullpen for a game-winning grand slam. As Lezcano raised his arms rounding first, Bamberger couldn't even hear Dalton's voice over the phone. But the reaction of the crowd told him everything he needed to know.[15]

In the locker room after the game, Lezcano breathlessly recounted the moment as Thomas teased the mild-mannered Don Money, who was giving his own interview. "Hey, Mon. Are you gonna get us some beer or are you going to run for office?"

A case of beer was procured and Lezcano grabbed a Pabst Blue Ribbon and took a sip. "This is for Bambi. He told us to have a beer on him, so I'm having it," Lezcano told a reporter. "I miss him a lot. He's like a father to me."[16]

The Brewers were just 3.5 games out when Bamberger came back on June 6, but the team struggled after his return and Bamberger resigned after three months, handing the club back over to Rodgers. They ended up at 86–76 in 1980—the fourth-best record in the AL—but 17 games behind the Yankees. The players had backed off their plan to strike, but the labor situation was far from resolved.

1981

Thursday, April 16, 1980: Indians 1, Brewers 0 (54,296 attendance)
In the News: President Reagan has announced a pardon of two former FBI officials after they were convicted of approving illegal break-ins targeted at anti-war activists in the early 1970s. The pardon was signed three weeks ago, but action was delayed after Reagan was shot on March 30.
At the Movies: *11* ("As good as a '10' but does so much more!") at the Parkway Theater
On the Radio: "Morning Train (Nine to Five)" by Sheena Easton

Nineteen-eighty had been a step backward for the Brewers. Bamberger returned in early June and took over a team just 3.5 games out of first place. Three months of .500 baseball later, he stepped down with the team hopelessly out of the race, officially beginning the Buck Rodgers era. The move, Bamberger insisted, had nothing to do with his health.[17]

The Brewers had a lineup as fearsome as any in baseball. They'd led the league in homers in 1980 with 203, including a stunning 23 from bulked-up shortstop Robin Yount. Only six other teams in AL history had ever hit 200 or more homers in a single season. Although Bob McClure had emerged a steady back-end reliever, the team was still determined to add a true star to the bullpen. Meanwhile, the San Diego Padres—already mediocre and about to lose Dave Winfield to free agency—were looking to unload Rollie Fingers, who'd been one of baseball's best stoppers for nearly a decade and had won the Rolaids Relief Man of the Year award in three of the past four seasons. Working with excessive offensive talent, the Brewers quietly began shopping outfielder Gorman Thomas, trying to work a deal with San Diego for Fingers and with the Cubs for Bruce Sutter.[18]

By the opening days of the winter meetings in Dallas, however, that work was all for naught when the Cardinals pulled deals for both pitchers in a two-day span. As things devolved, Fingers was the clear odd man out in St. Louis and Dalton entered into frantic negotiations that included the ace reliever and starting pitcher Pete Vuckovich, both of whom would be free agents after the 1981 season. St. Louis had also just signed the former Brewer Darrell Porter, who would now be their starting catcher. The incumbent, Ted Simmons, had no desire to switch positions and was now demanding a trade.[19]

During a 24-hour marathon of phone calls and whispered conversations, Dalton and the Cardinals were close on a deal that would send Fingers, Vuckovich, and Simmons to Milwaukee for pitchers Lary Sorensen and Dave LaPoint, outfielder Sixto Lezcano—who followed up his breakout '79 campaign with a largely underwhelming 1980—and 19-year-old outfielder David Green, who was considered one of the best prospects in baseball. Sensing perfect timing to exercise the power of his no-trade rights, Simmons told the Brewers he would not agree to the trade without reworking the final three years of his contract. Dalton, well aware that it had taken 100 wins or more to win the AL East in each of the past four seasons, agreed and promised Simmons an extra $250,000 per season. The trade was announced on December 12. "Fifteen minutes ago we were a non-contender," Rodgers told a reporter. "Now we're a contender."[20]

The deal was undoubtedly a risky one, especially given the contract status of Fingers and Vuckovich and David Green's high ceiling. But no one doubted the awesome potential of the new Brewers lineup. Molitor would now move to center field, pushing Thomas into right. Jim Gantner, who'd hit .282 as a utility man in 1980, would play second base. Don Money and Roy Howell, an All-Star in 1978 signed away from the Blue Jays, would split time at third. Charlie Moore, Larry Hisle, and Mark Brouhard, all of whom would be starting on any other team, would make up one of the deepest benches in the league. The home opener against Cleveland sold out in January, the earliest in team history, and by the open of training camp, some were calling the Brewers' lineup the best since the 1961 New York Yankees.[21]

Vuckovich, the least heralded of the three pickups, made it clear that he was the best fit on a team whose personality was defined by the oddball antics of Gorman Thomas. Known in St. Louis for his off-putting mound antics—crossing his eyes, snapping his head back and forth between third and first bases while checking on runners, and wearing mis-matched socks or shoes ("Sometime, the batter thinks, 'What is this guy? Some kind of idiot?'" Simmons had said of catching Vuckovich, "It can't hurt, you know"). Vuckovich was asked by Brewers PR man Tom Skibosh early in camp what was the first thing that came into his mind when he thought of Opening Day. "Dead bugs on the grill of a vehicle," he replied immediately. Skibosh was confused. "That's the first thing that popped into my mind," Vuckovich explained.[22]

But as the new-look Crew pounded their way through the spring schedule, labor troubles—the still-unresolved matter of compensation for lost free agents—were once again at the forefront. After the owners unilaterally implemented a new compensation system that would permit a team losing a free agent to select a man from a list of 13 "unprotected" players from the signing team's big league roster, the players voted to authorize a late–May strike date for the second consecutive year. This time, it was reported that both sides had ample reserve funds of cash to ride out a significant work stoppage.[23]

The Brewers opened the '81 season with a pair of wins in Cleveland (Fingers recorded a multi-inning save in the first and Simmons hit a two-run homer in the second) and a pair of losses in Chicago (with Fingers and Vuckovich each taking a loss). All the while, newsstands in Milwaukee and across the nation sold the latest issue of the *Sporting News*, which featured Simmons, Oglivie, Cooper, Thomas, and Yount on the cover, each posed with icy glares under the banner headline "MURDERERS ROW."

The hometown fans were so eager to welcome the club home, they were lined up outside the parking lots gates at 8 a.m. the day of the opener. The first group in was a carload of kids from Watertown. They talked to a *Journal* reporter, but would not give their names. "We had to lie to get here," one said. "You know, we're all sick or on family vacations."[24]

Another group arrived in a caravan that included an Andecker beer truck and a hearse. Another wore matching shirts that read "Party 'Til You Puke." "I'm here getting ripped," said one tailgater. He was on a sick day, he told the reporter. "I'll be sick by about 5 p.m." One man, who gave his name as "Liquor Johnny," walked the parking lots in a tuxedo jacket, ruffled shirt, paisley shorts, and a cowboy hat. "This is the big one!" he whooped.[25]

Inside, Marine Sgt. Kevin Hermening of Oak Creek, one of the 52 American hostages recently freed from Iran, threw out the game's first ball. County Executive John O'Donnell, per tradition, threw out a ceremonial ball as well.[26]

Mike Caldwell, who'd been gifted a custom t-shirt by the team that read "Mr. Fucking Warmth," took the hill for the Brewers and had no trouble getting warm in the mid–40s chill. After a clean first inning, a walk and a Bo Diaz looping fly that just eluded Molitor's glove in center gave Cleveland what would be their only run of the afternoon. Meanwhile, Cleveland's Wayne Garland, in the fifth year of a huge 10-year free agent contract with the Indians that was universally regarded as a disaster for the team, found some of his old magic. He set down the first 10 Brewers he faced, keeping the mighty lineup off balance with screwballs and curves.[27]

Caldwell ran into trouble in the fifth, allowing three straight one-out singles, but got DH Miguel Dilone to pop out to Cooper and then froze outfielder Rick Manning for a called strike three. The Brewers followed with their own threat in the bottom half, with back-to-back hits from Simmons and Thomas. With two on and one out, Don Money hit a rocket to center, but right at Manning. Jim Gantner followed with a bloop behind first, but Mike Hargrove snagged and made a throw from his knees to get Gantner by a half step.[28]

The score held at 1–0 heading into the ninth. After Hargrove led off with a single, Rodgers called for Fingers. Pinch-hitter Jerry Dybzinski tried to bunt Hargrove to second, but the ball got to Fingers too quickly and he spun and fired to Yount covering second. The throw appeared to pull Yount off the bag, but Hargrove was called out. The testy Hargrove leapt up and threw his helmet in protest, earning him an ejection. Fingers ended the threat three batters later.[29]

With thousands dressed in colorful satin tavern jackets, hunched over in the cold and without much to stand for, *Journal* reporter Barbara Dembski noted that the stadium looked like a giant Easter basket. But in the bottom of the ninth, Cooper led off with a single and stole second on a busted hit-and-run play to bring the crowd back into the game. When Oglivie grounded out to move Cooper to third, things reached a pitch. Larry Hisle, hitless on the afternoon, came up with a chance to play hero. He smoked Garland's first pitch deep down the left field line, but it arched foul. He had the timing of Garland's next pitch, another slider, but fouled it back. Then Garland offered a big, looping screwball that Hisle hacked at and missed. Ted Simmons was next. He got a pitch he liked and drilled it down the right field line, but—like Hisle—was just a tick too fast as the ball arched outside the foul pole. The last pitch of the game was another screwball. Simmons saw it all the way and made good contact but lined it on a bounce to Dybzinski at second base, who tossed to first to end the game.[30]

"If you'd told me we were going to get shut out 1–0 on Opening Day, I would have called you a damn liar," Rodgers said after the game.[31] The players could do little else but shrug. Larry Hisle sat in front of his locker with his head in his hands.

"As far as I'm concerned, when I do bad, I let the team down," he said, still replaying his near-homer in the ninth.[32]

Ted Simmons had just as much to sulk about, but couldn't help but focus on the positive. "This is the first time in my whole career I've had a crowd that size react that way and be on my side," he said. "St. Louis is a different kind of place, not necessarily bad, but not as close and not as loud."[33]

The players went on strike on June 12, with the Brewers at 31–25 and three games out of first. Two months later, when the season resumed, the standings were reset as the league adopted a "split-season" format. The Brewers clinched a playoff berth on the second-to-last day of the season, but lost the first-ever "Divisional Series" to the Yankees three games to two. The format kept the Brewers out of the ALCS which, based on overall records, would have featured the Brewers versus the Oakland A's.

1982

Thursday, April 16, 1982: Rangers 4, Brewers 1 (49,887 attendance)
In the News: State officials are eyeing a site in the Menomonee Valley near Milwaukee County Stadium, formerly the grounds of a cement factory, as the location of a new state prison.
At the Movies: *Silent Rage* at the Centre Twin
On the Radio: "Call Me" by Blondie

Nineteen eighty-one could have been the coming out for the Brewers, but instead it felt like an incomplete honor. The players, as long threatened, went on strike in mid–June and more than 50 game dates were lost before the labor peace was restored. With the standings reset when play resumed, the Brewers rushed to the top of the AL East, clinching a playoff berth on the second-to-last day of the season. But just 28,000 were on hand to see the Brewers celebrate and tens of thousands of seats were empty for each of the two divisional series games at County Stadium against the Yankees. Despite having the division's best overall record (the Yankees would have finished tied for third), the Brewers dropped the series 3–2 and were left without even a proper title flag to fly over the bleachers.

The Brewers were still one of the teams to beat in the American League. They'd signed Pete Vuckovich and Rollie Fingers to contract extensions prior to the strike, and each responded with a career year. Vuckovich led the league in wins and winning percentage and Fingers won both the AL Cy Young and MVP awards—the first reliever to win the latter in more than 30 years. But there was a feeling among baseball people the team had underperformed in 1981. For many players, the cause of this was obvious. And, just days after the team was eliminated by the Yankees, this "cause" had his contract renewed.[34]

Bob Rodgers once said that taking over for George Bamberger was like trying to replace Santa Claus. Bamberger had not only made the Brewers into a winner, but he was an easy-going "player's manager." And, in return, his players loved him for it. Rodgers was the taskmaster, playing the numbers and stressing strategy. His players—a naturally loose bunch—saw him as cold and aloof, micromanaging where they needed someone to get behind their swing-from-the-heels type of play. Into the final month of the season, chasing a playoff berth, the team held two players-only meetings. Sal Bando, urged back to play in '81 even though he'd planned to retire, worked to keep the club focused. A few unnamed players spoke to the media about animosity and Rodgers began to count enemies on the team. Vuckovich outed himself as one, and Ted Simmons and Gorman Thomas made their dislike of this style known. Mike Caldwell, "Mr.

Fucking Warmth" per a t-shirt the team had given him, hated Rodgers and Rodgers hated him right back. After he signed his extension, only a handful of players would even comment on the situation.[35]

But overall, Harry Dalton felt pretty good with the status quo. The only off-season roster move of note was an October trade with Houston that netted reliever Pete Ladd—whose shoe size (15) still outpaced his career innings total (12.1). With Bando's retirement and the underwhelming performance of Roy Howell, Paul Molitor would take over at third base, permitting Gorman Thomas to move back to center and opening a spot for Charlie Moore—who had requested a trade after the '81 season due to his lack of playing time. Don Money, entering his age 35 season, would then take on a super-utility role. With a team so loaded with offensive talent, it wasn't much of a surprise when Dalton turned down a trade offer from the Phillies for Caldwell. The centerpiece of their offer was a 21-year-old infielder named Ryne Sandberg.[36]

The Brewers were heading into spring training with confidence, depth, and playoff experience. Their biggest goal for training camp was to stay healthy. Still, no one thought much of it when some pitchers were horsing around after a storm had drenched their Sun City practice field. A few guys got shoved into puddles and Rollie Fingers, generally known as a man who took little seriously, started to literally sling mud. Randy Lerch, slated for the back end of the starting rotation, ducked a Fingers toss and playfully grabbed hold of the reining MVP's leg. Fingers rolled over and landed on his shoulder. He heard it pop, and a moment later, the pain came. "It was like someone stuck a knife there," Fingers said. "I turned about eight shades of white." Fingers was diagnosed with a separated shoulder and missed the next two weeks of camp. Rodgers told the press he would speak to the team about "fooling around."[37]

Fingers was ready to go by the time the team headed north for their Tuesday, April 6, opener against Cleveland, but the weather was not. It snowed all day that Monday as temperatures struggled to reach 30 degrees. The opener was pushed back to Wednesday, but by Tuesday, with the snow still flying, it was clear that the entire opening series would be lost. Games all across the Midwest and East Coast were similarly canceled due to weather. The Brewers, without a place to practice, tried to reserve Minneapolis's brand-new Metrodome, but the Blue Jays and White Sox had already laid claim to it. So the team was forced to rent a van and haul their gear to the Astrodome in Houston. Meanwhile, the Indians were stranded in Milwaukee, left to work out in the ballroom at the Eagle's Club on Wisconsin Avenue.[38]

It would be 10 days before the Brewers would be back in Milwaukee for the April 16 opener against the Rangers, sitting on a 3–3 record after visits to Toronto and Cleveland. The snow had melted, but it was cold and rainy. The only effect the weather had on the parking lot revelry was that the party lasted a little bit longer, with the start of the game delayed by 30 minutes. After the tarp was pulled off the field and the team was paraded around the soggy diamond in Chevy trucks, the players walked a special, blue and gold carpet out from the dugout during pregame introductions. Rollie Fingers got the biggest cheer, during which Gorman Thomas dropped to his knees and bowed to the MVP. The first pitch was delivered by six-year-old Jim Dean, chosen from the crowd at random for the honor.[39]

Moose Haas started for the Brewers. He was in his seventh season with the Brewers, one of the handful on the roster left over from the pre–Bamberger era. Haas had been trained as a locksmith by his father (just in case his baseball career didn't work out) and had trained in karate (he'd just earned his black belt) and practiced magic tricks in the off-season. But he'd also had Reggie Jackson on his mind all winter. In the decisive game five of the divisional series against Yankees, with the Brewers up 2–0 in the fourth inning, Haas hung a curveball that Jackson crushed to tie the game. He rode out the rain delay smoking a cigar in the locker room, trying to calm his nerves. He needed to redeem himself.[40]

Haas opened big, allowing only one of the first 12 he faced to reach. Dave Schmidt, spot-starting for Texas after Doc Medich came down with the flu, matched Haas until the bottom of the fourth. Paul Molitor led off with a single and, when Charlie Moore hit a come-backer on a hit and run, raced straight through to third base, sliding in just under first baseman Pat Putnam's throw. He scored on a Cecil Cooper groundout a batter later. The Rangers got the run back in the fifth when a pair of weak singles and a Mark Wagner double tied the score, 1–1. It would be the only hard-hit ball Haas would allow.[41]

The game still tied in the ninth, Fingers trotted in to a roaring ovation. He worked around a lead-off single to set the Brewers up to win it in the bottom half. Ed Romero—starting at shortstop in place of Robin Yount and his aching hamstring—opened with a base hit, but Molitor popped up a sac bunt attempt before Danny Darwin dispatched Kevin Bass—in for Charlie Moore, who had tweaked his groin—and Cooper to send the game to extras.[42]

This was exactly why the Brewers had gotten Fingers and a big part of why he'd been so honored in 1981. Just three days earlier, he'd gone three and a third innings, holding off Cleveland in a tie game to set up a tenth-inning Brewers win. But Fingers felt "sluggish" in the damp and cold. His fastball was dull and his breaking ball lacked its usual snap. He gave up back-to-back singles to open the tenth to bring up Bill Stein, a light-hitting infielder. Anticipating a bunt, Cooper rushed in but Fingers hung his slider and Stein slapped it for a run-scoring double. A Lee Mazzilli single and a sac fly from Leon Roberts pushed two more across before the inning ended. In the bottom of the tenth, Ted Simmons opened with a walk, but the faint hope among the stunned home fans was doused when Ben Oglivie bounced into a double play. Gorman Thomas ended it—just two and a half hours after it had started—with a weak pop-out in foul ground.[43]

It was certainly a letdown for a game a week and a half in the making, but Cecil Cooper, warming himself in the clubhouse afterward, wasn't about to read too much into it. "One game doesn't make a season," he said.[44]

After starting the season 23–24, Rodgers was fired and Harvey Kuenn took over as interim manager. The team quickly found its groove and bashed their way to the AL East title. Down 2–0 in the ALCS, they stunned the California Angels with three straight wins to clinch the AL pennant before falling in the World Series to the underdog Cardinals in seven games.

Harvey Kuenn spent more than a decade on the Brewers' coaching staff before leading the Crew to the 1982 World Series. He lost his only opener as manager (1986 TCMA All-Time Brewers #12).

1983

Friday, April 15, 1982: Royals 4, Brewers 3 (54,0497 attendance)

In the News: Milwaukee was recently the subject of a feature article in *The Advocate*, a magazine geared to the gay community. The article presented Milwaukee as a relatively friendly city for gay adults and cited a survey in which 76 percent of gay Milwaukeeans asked rated the city as a "great" place to live.

At the Movies: *Flashdance* at the Northtown Cinema
On the Radio: "Do You Really Want to Hurt Me?" by Culture Club
Eleven outs.

After Pete Vuckovich got Tom Herr to ground to third in the bottom of the sixth inning in Game Seven of the 1982 World Series, the Brewers leading 3–1, they were 11 outs away from winning the World Series.

They never got those 11 outs. Vuckovich allowed a couple of hits and Bob McClure, coming on in a situation in which Rollie Fingers—out with a torn muscle in his forearm—had dominated all year. But McClure gave up the lead and an hour later it was all over.

But they returned to Milwaukee as the people's champions, feted with a downtown parade and County Stadium celebration that felt more like a rally for 1983 than the culmination of 1982. Days after their return from St. Louis, manager Harvey Kuenn was given a one-year contract to return for '83 season. Kuenn, the team's long-time hitting coach who still lived in the little apartment behind the blue collar bar that his wife, Audrey, owned and operated, had been named interim manager after Bob Rodgers was fired in June. The Brewers, who had been sluggish under the little-appreciated Rodgers, sprang to life and ran to the pennant. Although Harry Dalton had decided late in the 1982 season not to bring Kuenn back as manager, the World Series trip and outright love felt for him by players and fans made such a move untenable. The players, mostly silent a year prior when Rodgers had been extended, now offered nothing but praise.[45]

Once again, the Brewers swept the AL MVP and Cy Young awards, with Robin Yount easily taking the MVP title and Pete Vuckovich, with a league-best win-loss mark of 18–6, winning the Cy Young. When he was called at his home in Arizona and told he was about to be named MVP, Yount, just returned from grocery shopping, replied, "OK. Do I have time to bring in the rest of the groceries first?" Cecil Cooper, Gorman Thomas, and Paul Molitor also placed in the top 12 in MVP voting, a righteous showing for an offense that slugged 216 homers—the sixth highest team total in baseball history.[46]

For the first time since the days of the Braves, Milwaukee's baseball fever did not fade with the first snowfall. The *Journal* reported that John Counsell, in charge of the team's speaker's bureau (and father of future Brewer Craig Counsell), was one of the busiest men in town as he tried to keep up with all the requests for player appearances and engagements. Dozens of banquets wanted Brewers as their guests of honor. Cecil Cooper was in demand for radio and TV ads. Paul Molitor was wanted for a national soap ad campaign. Robin Yount, as unassuming as ever, turned down nearly everything he was offered. Vuckovich, trailing far behind his teammates in invites, quipped, "I'm not your classic dinner guest."[47]

The *Journal* reported that Brewers baseball was the topic of discussion at taverns and bars across the city, with fans chatting about hot stove rumors even while Green Bay Packers games played on the TV. Stores couldn't keep Brewers gear in stock in the run-up to Christmas and the home opener—set for April 15 against the Royals—sold out in just four days.[48]

Except for the retirement of Larry Hisle, who had played in no more than 27 games in any of the final four years of his five-year contract, the Brewers would return pretty much the entire 1982 team for 1983. Dalton admitted that he didn't have much of an agenda for the off-season, despite a lineup that was projected to feature five regulars 32 years or older. Further complicating matters was Fingers' torn muscle, which was not healing as quickly as the team had hoped. But by the time training camp opened, optimism abounded for the Brewers. Paul Molitor, set to be a free agent after the season, had signed a five-year extension. Fingers was able to throw without pain in early workouts. The team won eight of their first nine spring training games and the *Sporting News* picked the Brewers to repeat as AL champions.[49]

But in mid–March, the team took a gut-punch when Pete Vuckovich was diagnosed with a torn rotator cuff. It was an injury that, for a pitcher, was a career death sentence. He had been pitching with pain since the '82 pennant stretch, but it had finally become too much for him. The usually effervescent Vuckovich wore a grim expression after telling reporters of the injury. He began to talk about death, how he'd faced it many times in his short life—born with the umbilical cord wrapped around his neck, peritonitis at one and a half, a brain tumor a year after that, rolling his car while going 105 miles an hour at age 21, nearly being electrocuted while installing a 15,000-volt reactor shortly after that—"I've been on a death bed before, which is worse than a rotator, a hell of a lot worse. I came out of that alive."[50]

"They say no one ever came back from it," he said. "This could be the first, you never know."[51]

Shortly after Vuckovich was shut down, the team announced that Fingers would open the season on the disabled list. But nothing could dampen the optimism of the Milwaukee faithful. A poll by the *Sentinel* just before the season showed that 48 percent of respondents thought the Brewers would win the World Series and nearly three-quarters picked them to return to the postseason. A separate poll found that Robin Yount was the Brewer fans would most like to invite to a barbeque (although men had a strong bias toward Gorman Thomas) and Paul Molitor was the Brewer women would most like to date.[52]

The Brewers went .500 on an eight-game road trip to open the season before returning home to Milwaukee to face the Royals in a Friday afternoon opener. Once again, the ceremonies got no help from the weather, as temperatures lingered in the high 30s and the early morning tailgaters were met with light snow flurries. Reserve outfielder Bob Skube, who'd grown up in California and had played sparingly with the Brewers in '82, said it was the coldest weather he'd ever seen in his life. When the flurries started, he assumed it was ash from a nearby bonfire.[53]

As was becoming the annual tradition, the tailgaters started at it earlier than ever in 1983, with grills going and beers cracked as early as 7:30 a.m.—early enough for coverage of the revelry to make it into that evening's *Journal*. "On Opening Day, no partying can start too early," one tailgater told the paper. Inside the stadium, where crews had just finished sweeping out the 1,200 tons of sand used to sandblast and repaint the girders and railings, Gorman Thomas and a few teammates were getting in an early game of "flip" before batting practice. Flip was one of the staples of '82 team, a game in which players stood in a circle and used their gloves or bodies to "flip" a baseball to each other and anyone who allowed the ball to drop was eliminated.[54]

For the first time since 1958, Milwaukee got to welcome a pennant-winner for the 1983 home opener. A flag honoring the 1982 AL championship was raised before the game (Mark Susina).

American League president Lee McPhail was on hand for a pregame ceremony in which he presented the club with the AL championship trophy and presided over the unfurling of a blue and gold championship flag in center field. But the biggest ovation of the afternoon was saved for Harvey Kuenn as he took his place along the baseline during pregame introductions. Robin Yount's greeting was, per the *Sentinel*, a "distant" second. Kansas City's Willie Wilson, who had taken off the final game of the '82 season to preserve his lead in the AL batting race over Yount, was loudly booed. Hank Raymonds, who had just retired as Marquette University's men's basketball coach, threw out the first pitch.[55]

Bob McClure took the hill for Milwaukee and Larry Gura, who had already beaten the Brewers in '83, started for Kansas City. The action was muted until the bottom of the third when Don Money opened with a grounder to third that George Brett airmailed into the seats behind first base for a two-base error. Charlie Moore followed with a bloop double and a groundout by Jim Gantner and sac fly by Molitor gave the Brewers a 2–0 lead—their first multiple-run Opening Day lead since Sixto Lezcano's grand slam in 1980.[56]

Heading into the fourth, McClure had the lead but lost the feel on his sinker. With U.L. Washington on first, he mishandled a Brett come-backer and a double play ball turned into a fielder's choice. After walking the bases full, right fielder Jerry Martin smoked a hanging sinker for a two-run single to tie the game.[57]

Ben Oglivie put the Brewers back on top with a fourth inning sacrifice fly, but McClure kept pitching himself in and out of trouble. He finally got burned in the sixth, when, after a Hal McRae single, Frank White hit one up into the wind stream that carried into deep right center, landing between Thomas and Charlie Moore and rolling to the wall. McRae scored and White scooted to third. Martin followed with a sac fly to put the Royals on top, 4–3.[58]

Tom Tellmann, a tall right-hander picked up in a little-noticed trade just after the World Series, came in for McClure and kept the Royals off balance enough with a mix of pitches and the manic enthusiasm of someone playing in their first home opener. Tellmann stalked around the mound between hitters, applauded his fielders, and sprinted off the rubber between innings.[59]

But the Brewers were just as stifled by Gura and the 4–3 score carried into the bottom of the eighth. Now facing side-armed relief ace Dan Quisenberry, Thomas and Oglivie stroked back-to-back one-out singles to put runners on the corners. DH Don Money was due, but Kuenn pinch hit Skube, a left-handed batter, to face the righty Quisenberry. The crowd of 54,000-plus came back to life but Skube, freezing and standing in for just his ninth major league at-bat, grounded to White at second for a tailor-made double play.[60]

Tellman and Quisenberry each tossed perfect frames in the ninth and the Royals held on for a 4–3 win. "The key word is frustration," Molitor said of Gura's performance after the game. "I look forward to facing a guy like that, but when the game's over, I wonder why I looked forward to it in the first place."[61]

After a slow start, the Brewers caught fire in July and August, going 40–21 to take over first place in a highly competitive AL East. But a brutal 1–12 stretch in early September sealed their fate. They finished 87–75—their sixth straight winning season—but fell to fifth place, 11 games behind the Orioles.

1984

Tuesday, April 17, 1984: Brewers 7, White Sox 3 (53,038 attendance)

In the News: General Motors has introduced a new program that will pay $10,000 to the family of any driver of a GM car who is killed in a crash while wearing a safety belt. The offer will only be valid for the first year after a new car purchase.

At the Movies: Ingmar Bergman's *8 1/2* at the Oriental Theater

On the Radio: "Footloose" by Kenny Loggins

The 1983 Brewers held first place in the AL East as late as August 25, but three nightmare weeks later, they had fallen to fifth place, 10.5 games behind the eventual world champion Orioles. The offense, by most measures, was still productive, but lacked the fearsome clout of years prior. Following up on a 216-homer season by the 1982 club, the '83 Brewers managed just 132. Gorman Thomas, for years the competitive heart of the Brewers, hit just five before being sent to Cleveland in a June trade that the fans hated. The pitching staff ranked both as one of the oldest and least effective in the American League. In another blow to the spiritual center of the team, manager Harvey Kuenn was fired after the final game of the season. It had been obvious for weeks that Kuenn would not return for 1984.

Harry Dalton only had one name in mind for Kuenn's replacement. Rene Lachemann did not have the typical resume for the lone candidate for a top-level managing gig. In 10 seasons as a manager in professional baseball, he'd had just two winning seasons and never placed a team higher than second place. But he moved up the chain fast enough to take over the Seattle Mariners at age 36. The M's fired him halfway through the 1982 season after opening with a 26–47 record. But his players loved him and he was considered a forward-thinking man for his time. The only thing his teams had lacked, in Dalton's estimation, was talent.[62]

But despite the step backward in '83, Dalton entered the off-season with a relatively short to-do list. "The fan waiting over the winter thinking 'show me a stronger team' is probably going to be frustrated," he admitted. After Ted Simmons filed for free agency, Dalton worked a deal with the Texas Rangers for Jim Sundberg, who was considered among the top defensive catchers in baseball, but was also about to be 33 and coming off the worst offensive season of his career. The same day, the Brewers sent Jim Slaton—who had been with the Brewers for 12 of the past 13 seasons—to the Angels for outfielder Bobby Clark. A month later, they released Don Money after 11 years in Milwaukee.[63]

But Dalton was not about to cut ties completely with his postseason core. Rollie Fingers, who didn't pitch at all in 1983, was recovering from surgery and looked to contribute in 1984. Pete Vuckovich, thought to be finished after tearing his rotator cuff, had actually started three games in '83 and had been throwing all winter. By the spring, he was throwing without pain, but refused to consider himself optimistic for his future. "I'm calling it curiosity," he said. "I'm curious, if anything, to see what lies ahead. The stigma of the injury still lies in my subconscious, so to speak. I'm curious as to the workload my shoulder can take."[64]

Ted Simmons would also return to the Brewers in 1984, although under much different circumstances. He'd been one of the few Brewers to have a better season in '83 than in '82, but he still found few takers for his services on the free agent market. He was thought to be done behind the plate and held out little hope for coming back to the Brewers. But after the Brewers declined to seriously participate in free agency for the second straight year, they offered Simmons a three-year pact to return to Milwaukee as the team's primary designated hitter.[65]

Rollie Fingers, in the biggest offer of relief he'd given in a year and half, finally managed to throw pain-free innings in live action that spring. He was pounded, but that was of little concern. In late March, it was announced that he would be on the Opening Day roster. Pete Vuckovich, however, would not be. Just a few sessions into his spring workouts, the pain returned and he underwent surgery to remove bone spurs. Doctors told him it would be three to four months before he'd be able to throw again.[66]

But the big blow came when Paul Molitor's elbow began to ache. Molitor had been destroying Cactus League pitching at the time, batting over .500 and eager to make up for a sluggish 1983. He was diagnosed with a tear of his MCL and ordered to rest the arm, limiting him to the designating hitter role and displacing Simmons. Even with Molitor still active, the team that went north in 1984 featured nine players who were not on the team in 1983.⁶⁷

When the Brewers opened the season in Oakland on April 3, it was hailed as the beginning of a new era in franchise history, for reasons that had nothing to do with the action on the field. The game was the first live event carried on Sportsvue, a pay cable channel launched by a partnership between the Brewers and the Milwaukee Bucks. The network would carry Brewers and Bucks as the feature attractions in a lineup of Wisconsin sports action. The Brewers had seen a spike in revenues over the past two years, but they had also been among baseball's freest spending clubs and team president Bud Selig saw cable television as a way for the Brewers to keep pace with the league's larger market teams. The channel's debut game was a bomb—the Brewers blew a three-run lead in the bottom of the ninth, with three of Oakland's runs charged to Fingers—but only about 4,000 people were

Launched for the 1984 season, SportsVue was supposed to give Milwaukee sports its own superstation. But the channel was as a big of a bust as the Brewers were in '84.

watching anyway, as the network had thus far sold only about 1/10 of the subscriptions they had needed to reach a break-even point.⁶⁸

The loss was the start of five-game skid for the Brewers, and by the time they arrived back home for the April 17 opener against the White Sox, they sat at 3–7 and were already six games behind the front-running (and undefeated) Tigers. The conditions on game day matched the ugly open to the Brewers' season. The temperature hovered just above freezing as the first tailgaters got set up in the parking lots and a cold drizzle persisted for most of the day. Inside the stadium, a tarp covered the infield and the grounds crew readied hundreds of bags of Diamond Dust—a drying agent—to be used on the dirt throughout the game.⁶⁹

As reliable as it was for the weather to be lousy on Opening Day was the determination of the hometown fans to ignore it. Open flames were used as much for warmth as for grilling, but some fans showed a little more creativity in their Opening Day spreads. Suckling pigs had become a minor trend outside the stadium and barbeque chicken had become a more common alternative to hot dogs and bratwursts. Some tailgaters were even (almost) up to the musical times, as one group had a disco dance party with a $3,000 stereo set-up and another group of 12 danced through the parking lots in full-on Michael Jackson costuming.⁷⁰

Paul Molitor, a dismal 2–15 on the season, had lobbied Lachemann to let him start at third for the opener in spite of his aching elbow. Lachemann considered it, but Dr. Frank Jobe, the specialist working on Molitor's elbow, would not sign off. Rookie Randy Ready, who had twice hit over .370 in full minor league seasons, took his place in the field and atop the lineup.⁷¹

Brewers starting pitcher Moose Haas, the trained locksmith and amateur magician, had gotten more serious about his hobby over the winter. For Christmas, his wife Diana had gotten him a straitjacket from which he could practice escapes. He already had one, the *Sporting News* had noted in January, but this was an "improved" model. Haas might have needed it for warmth on this afternoon, which he'd later say was the coldest weather he'd ever felt. Lachemann could sympathize. He settled into the dugout wearing three pairs of long johns, a stocking cap, and ski gloves.⁷²

Ready led off the game with a booming double and, after a Yount base hit, scampered home on a wild pitch by Tom Seaver, who was making just his second American League start. Third baseman Vance Law tagged Haas for a solo homer an inning later. In the third, as the Brewers and Sox traded sloppy, scoreless frames, it began to gently snow. Dirt and Diamond Dust clotted on the players' spikes and sharp winds cut through their damp uniforms. The stadiums lights were turned on, giving the field a ghostly glow. At one point, Seaver tumbled over as he went into his windup. All involved expected that, if the tie was broken, play would be ended after the five inning minimum for an official game to be reached.[73]

In the top of the fifth, with two on and two out, Haas finally needed to use those escape techniques he'd been practicing all winter. But Scott Fletcher, a slap-hitting shortstop, beat him for a run-scoring single. Expecting that he'd just given up the potential game-clinching hit, Haas cursed and kicked the mud. In the bottom of the inning, Sundberg led off with a single and Charlie Moore, playing as though it were the bottom of the ninth, tried to bunt Sundberg over. But the ball died as soon as it landed in the soggy dirt and Sundberg was out easily at second.[74]

But as the rain had turned to snow, conditions on the field began to stabilize. The umpires took no action after the end of the fifth and Haas struck out the side with numb hands. In the bottom half, Cecil Cooper led off with a single and Ted Simmons drew a walk to chase Seaver. Reliever Juan Agosta came in and walked Ben Oglivie to load the bases and the crowd—which numbered far less in person than the official tally of 53,000-plus—came to life. Jim Gantner laced a run-scoring single and Sundberg followed with a two-run hit. Two batters later, Ready came up with two outs and two on. Out in the Brewers' bullpen, Jerry Augustine and his pen mates were trying to start a fire in a steel trashcan. They couldn't even get a match to light. But Ready found his spark when Salomoe Barojas—in for Agosto—left a 1-1 slider up in the zone. Ready did not miss. The ball arched high in the air down the left field line and dropped just over the wall for a three-run homer to extend the Brewers' lead to 7–2. As Ready floated around the bases, Sox outfielder Ron Kittle, stunned the ball had carried out, stood and stared at the spot where it had cleared the wall.[75]

Pete Ladd took over in the seventh and permitted just one run over the next three as he closed out the game to the joy of the scattered thousands still left in the stands. In the locker room afterward, Lachemann cracked open a beer and lit a cigar. "The weather was more conducive to the Packers, but I'll take it," he said.[76]

Lachemann might have earned his cigar, but all the post-game buzz was for the rookie Ready. He was considered one of the team's top prospects, and his Opening Day break-out seemed like the start of something big. He'd found out only early in the day that he'd be starting. "I just come prepared," Ready told the *Journal* after the game. "An at-bat is an at-bat, and that's it."[77]

Already seven games out of first by the second week of the season, the 1984 Brewers peaked at 17–16, the only time all season they boasted a winning record. They finished in last place, 36.5 games behind the Tigers. Sportsvue fell far short of its subscriber goal and folded after the 1984 season.

1985

Thursday, April 9, 1985: White Sox 4, Brewers 2 (53,027 attendance)

In the News: Amy Carter, the 17-year-old daughter of former president Jimmy Carter, was arrested at an anti–Apartheid protest in front of the South African embassy in Washington, D.C.

At the Movies: *Revenge of the Nerds* at the Villa Theater

On the Radio: "We Are the World" by USA for Africa

If 1983 had been a let-down for the Brewers, 1984 was an outright disaster. Out of the AL East race in late May, the team tumbled to a 67–94 record—their first losing record in seven seasons. Ted Simmons, Cecil Cooper, and Ben Oglivie—all now on the wrong side of 34 years old—each put up their worst numbers in years. Randy Ready, a Rookie of the Year candidate early in the season, finished with a .185 batting average. Paul Molitor, a previously unblemished face of the franchise, not only missed all but 13 games with an elbow injury but was also named in an investigation into cocaine trafficking in Milwaukee. Ugly details of Molitor's early 1980s drug use—along with teammates Dick Davis and Mike Caldwell—emerged in the probe but the commissioner's office decided that no disciplinary action would be taken.[78]

Skipper Rene Lachemann, Dalton's only candidate for the job just a year earlier, was fired on the last weekend of the season. Brewers officials felt that Lachemann was "mentally intimidated" by the veteran players on the team, the players being too resigned to mediocrity and Lachemann being too laid back to challenge them.[79]

Taking over for Lachemann was fan and player favorite George Bamberger. Bamberger had come out of retirement to take the Mets' managerial post in 1982, but was fired mid-way through the '83 season. Rumors about his return to Milwaukee had been percolating for months. "Believe me," Bamberger told the media, "if it wasn't Milwaukee, I wouldn't be back." Once again, Dalton and company needed Bamberger to right the ship.[80]

Despite everything, Dalton was hesitant to entirely make over the aging roster. He sent 39-year-old Don Sutton, picked up during the stretch run in 1982, to Oakland for 34-year-old Ray Burris, who'd ranked ninth in the AL in ERA in 1984 to upgrade a rotation spot. He traded Jim Sundberg in a three-way deal that netted pitchers Danny Darwin and Tim Leary—the latter a favorite of Bamberger's in New York. But Dalton still found a place for Pete Vuckovich and Rollie Fingers, both of whom he brought back on short-term deals. Mike Caldwell, caught up in the drug scandal and coming off his worst season as a Brewer, was released. Jerry Augustine and Roy Howell, also members of the 1982 pennant winner, were similarly cut loose.

The chatter around the Brewers as they opened camp in Arizona was mostly focused on the up and coming. Dion James had a stand-out rookie season in 1984, but lost his chance to open the season as the starting center fielder when he dislocated his shoulder during the camp's second full workout. But Bill Schroeder, who'd contributed from behind the plate in '84, was still on target to take over the starting spot there and outfielders Mike Felder and Doug Loman—as well as Ready—were all expected to compete for regular playing time. Meanwhile, Brian Giles, an infielder acquired in the Rule 5 draft that winter, quickly found a big fan in Bamberger. Giles, who had earned the nickname "Iceman," had a shot at opening the season at shortstop.[81]

Robin Yount, the Brewers' man at short for more than a decade, had closed out the 1984 season with shoulder pain and underwent surgery to smooth jagged bone growth and repair some tendons. Both Yount and Molitor—recovered from what would eventually become known as "Tommy John" surgery—were back in the Brewers lineup early on during the spring schedule. But while Molitor was back to manning third base, Yount's place in the field remained unclear. The plan was to eventually return him to shortstop, but his throwing arm was still too weak. Yount himself seemed unconcerned about the shift, even though his lifetime experience in the outfield amounted to a single exhibition game in 1979. His biggest worry about the new position? "There's no one to talk to," he said. "You're all alone. I can't get on Gumby [Jim Gantner]."[82]

But perhaps the most intriguing story line of the spring involved a player who wouldn't even make the big league team. Yutaka Enatsu was a baseball legend in Japan. He'd been one of the Japanese League's most dominant starting pitchers, winning two MVP awards before moving to the bullpen and setting the league record for career saves. But he also had a reputation as a hard-to-manage player and, after being suspended by the Seibu Lions, his Japanese career was effectively over. The Brewers had made another international signing just the year before (pitcher Theodoro Higuera of Mexico, who did end up making the team in 1985), so they took a flyer and offered Enatsu a chance to become the first Japanese-born Major Leaguer since 1965. He impressed early in camp, working with finesse and a looping, 60-mph change-up, but struggled once the team tried to stretch for multiple-inning appearances. He finished camp with a 4.91 ERA in 11 appearances and was released. He retired shortly thereafter.[83]

By the admission of the Brewers' own marketing department, County Stadium in 1984 had a "funeral parlor" feel. With a familiar face at the helm and a fresh attitude among the players, the Brewers wanted to spice things up at the ballyard. They introduced a new team theme song, "Come See What's Brewing," added regular live music to the stadium experience, and increased the number of promotions and giveaways. They replaced the bleacher seating, which dated back to 1961, and constructed a new sound tower in the center field seating area. The tower necessitated the removal of Bernie Brewer's "chalet" home, in place since 1973.[84]

Despite the struggles of 1984, fans rang in the 1985 season with their usual upbeat (and well-lubricated) enthusiasm. The April 7 opener versus the White Sox had sold out in 24 hours and, as always, fans turned out early to welcome back baseball. The game lined up with spring break week for most area high schools and colleges and the *Sentinel* noted a younger bend to the '85 crowd. The new vibe at the stadium came with a new effort to ensure an environment that was more family friendly. Vendors were ordered to refuse service to "rowdy" fans and beer cups now carried the message "Sobriety Is No Accident." Per the *Journal*, that attitude had not yet extended to the parking lots. In an interview of one group of fans dressed in foam TNT costumes as "Bambi's Bombers," one of the bombers—already quite bombed—explained himself by asking, "Would you wear this thing if you were sober?"[85]

Another pair of fans wore striped prison costumes. An on-going issue for the Brewers was the new state prison that was slated to be built in the Menomonee Valley—within sight of County Stadium. Team president Bud Selig was adamantly opposed to the project, certain that it would drive down attendance and harm the financial stability of the ballclub. Baseball commissioner Peter Ueberroth was on hand for the opener and had meetings planned with Governor Tony Earl about the situation.[86]

The ceremonial first pitches that afternoon were also tied into Brewers political intrigue. The tosses came from Jim Fitzgerald, Herb Kohl, and Lloyd and Jane Pettit. Fitzgerald had just sold the Milwaukee Bucks to Kohl, a local businessman (and also a childhood friend of Selig) who had pledged to keep the

By the early 1980s, Opening Day in Milwaukee had become an unofficial city holiday and restaurants, bars, breweries, and radio stations all sponsored pre-game party tents at County Stadium. Saz's operated one of the first bus shuttles to carry its customers to and from the stadium (Matthew J. Prigge).

team—whom many thought was bound for a new home—in Milwaukee. Just days after the sale, the Pettits had pledged $40 million to build a new, state-of-the-art home for the team. The Pettits wanted the new arena to be located next to the stadium. Selig, although silent on the matter so far, harbored deep concerns about a next-door arena. Selig would indeed help kill an arena site near the stadium. It would eventually be built downtown.[87]

It would be another Tom Seaver–Moose Haas matchup for the opener. Haas ran into trouble right out of the gate when Cecil Cooper and Jim Gantner flubbed a Vance Law pop-up for a two-base error. Harold Baines followed with a walk and Greg Walker singled home Law. Ron Kittle followed with a ground ball that could have been an inning-ending double play, but Gantner's relay throw to first was wide, allowing another run to score. Luis Salazar followed with another easy roller that Gantner bungled before a Daryl Boston foul pop ended the inning. Gantner, one of the best-fielding second baseman in the league, could only shake his head.[88]

After Seaver set down the Brewers, officially breaking Walter Johnson's career record with his 15th Opening Day start, the Brewers game of infield hot potato continued. Cecil Cooper mishandled an Ozzie Guillen grounder and, in the next at-bat, Paul Molitor airmailed a throw to first. Haas got out of the inning unscathed, but the Brewers had already tallied four errors in a season that was only two innings old.

The Sox got another run in the fourth when Boston hit a bloop double and scored after a pair of sacrifices. Haas now trailed 3–0 despite allowing only two weak hits. Meanwhile, Tom Seaver was looking every bit like a future Hall of Famer. The Brewers had trouble making solid contact and, heading into the bottom of the seventh, they had only managed one runner as far as second base. Seaver set down Cooper and Ben Oglivie to open the frame before Ted Simmons singled to bring up 26-year-old Doug Loman, who was playing in just his 24th career game. Loman stroked a double to bring the tying run to the plate in catcher Bill Schroeder. It was Schroeder's first Opening Day start and the young slugger was looking for something from tiring Seaver that he could drive. But Seaver suddenly lost the plate and sent two pitches skipping past catcher Marc Hill to score Simmons and then Loman to cut the Sox lead to 3–2. Schroeder drew a walk, but was stranded when Gantner grounded out.

The Brewers defensive yips were not over yet. With two out in the eighth, Salazar tried to bunt for a hit, but Haas threw the ball away and Salazar reached second on the Brewers' fifth error of the afternoon. Boston followed with a base hit that scored Salazar to set the final score of 4–2. Simmons reached with a double in the bottom of the ninth to bring up Loman as the tying run, but the rookie rolled harmlessly to first to end it.

Afterward, there wasn't much to say from the Brewers' side of things. "What the heck?" Bamberger said of the five errors, per the *Journal*. Although it seemed doubtful that Bambi was in the kind of mood to say "heck."[89]

The *Journal* caught up with one fan who'd watched the game from the bleachers. "They play like I did when I was in that over-40 [softball] league last summer," said the man, who was playing hooky from his job at a local dairy. "But it still beats a day on the farm."[90]

The 1985 Brewers flirted with the .500 mark for two months, and then fell apart. They would end up 71–90, outplaying only the moribund Texas Rangers and Cleveland Indians for the AL's third-worst record.

1986

Monday, April 14, 1986: Rangers 10, Brewers 1 (52,487 attendance)

In the News: Former Philippine First Lady Imelda Marcos has claimed that the vast and expensive collection of clothing she left behind after fleeing the country were going to be gifts for others and denied that she and her husband embezzled billions in aid money.

At the Movies: *Back to the Future* at the Modjeska Theater

On the Radio: "West End Girls" by Pet Shop Boys

There would be no going home again for George Bamberger in 1985. Energized as the fan base was, his team was an ill mix of aging or ailing World Series vets and unproven youngsters. They managed .500 ball for the first two months, and then slid steadily until bottoming out with an 8–21 September to seal another second-division finish. That November, the team cut ties with Rollie Fingers, Pete Ladd, and Mark Brouhard—all key figures in their 1982 pennant winner. They also gave Japan's Seibu Lions permission to negotiate a contract with Ben Oglivie, who—along with fellow '82ers Ted Simmons and Charlie Moore—was rumored to be very near to end of his time with the Brewers.[91]

For the first time since 1980, the Brewers were not the first team to sell out its home opener. For years, the game had sold out within days of tickets going on sale, but the Brewers' post–World Series struggles had finally thrown a little water on the fans' hot stove enthusiasm.[92]

Indeed, it was the type of off-season not seen in Milwaukee in more than a decade. With bad money blotting the payroll, the Brewers were forced to get creative. They brought back David Green, the key piece of the 1980 deal with St. Louis that netted Fingers, Vuckovich, and Simmons. Green had since struggled on the field and off—he'd sought treatment for alcohol abuse in 1984, but was still reportedly dealing with the issue—but the Brewers still saw him as a high-ceiling guy. They picked up reliever Mark Clear from Boston, an All-Star in 1982, to take over for Fingers at the back end of the bullpen. And in a little-heralded swap with the Giants, they added an outfielder who had shown tremendous power in the minors, but was considered a non-prospect because of a low batting average and Herculean strikeout totals. He was, like Green and Clear, a project player, but in the *Sporting News*, Peter Gammons wrote that the Brewers thought they might have "a young Gorman Thomas" in 25-year-old Rob Deer.[93]

On the free agent front, the Brewers were once again quiet. They made no real effort to re-sign Danny Darwin, despite a respectable '85 season, and said that Darwin was probably the only free agent they would even consider. "I don't think there are too many people out there who will excite us," said GM Harry Dalton. Nor was any other club in baseball excited about free agency that winter. Led by stars Kirk Gibson and Carlton Fisk, the 62 players who had filed for free agency after the 1985 season received a total of zero contract offers from rival teams.[94]

The Brewers still hadn't sold out the opener by the time players began reporting to training camp in Arizona. During the annual Diamond Dinner ceremony at the Hotel Pfister just before camps opened, Bamberger had caused a minor kerfuffle by blankly stating his opinion of the team's prospects for '86. "We aren't going to win the pennant this year," he said. "We're on the right track, but I can't say we're going to win the pennant, it's just not realistic." It wasn't that anyone disagreed, they just thought he was being a bit too blunt.[95]

The Brewers had a new Arizona home for the 1986 season, finally having escaped Sun City—a locale defined by acres of blacktopping and citrus trees with rotting oranges—for the comparative oasis of Chandler, where a brand-new facility was just being completed. On February 27, about a week before the opening of the spring schedule, workers were attending to a malfunctioning heater when a gas line ignited and a massive ball of flames erupted into the coaches' locker room. Pitching coach Larry Haney's arm caught fire and Bamberger helped to extinguish him and one of the stadium workers who had staggered out of the smoke with his clothes on fire. Third base coach Tony Muser was caught in the middle of the blast and suffered burns to nearly half his body. He had to be airlifted to a nearby burn center and nearly died. Nine players and coaches in total were injured in the explosion.[96]

A week later, with the shaken team back to the business of baseball, the Brewers parted with another member of the '82 team when they traded Ted Simmons to Atlanta for catcher Rick Cerone. Despite two All-Star appearances, Simmons had never really clicked with the fans in Milwaukee. Since his arrival in Milwaukee, he was the only Brewer to regularly be booed at home. He was seen by too many as overpaid and underproductive. It wasn't fair, but it was what it was. Simmons didn't hang around the still-damaged clubhouse after being told of the trade. He left quickly and avoided what would have certainly been many emotional goodbyes. "There's a lot of things we could have talked about, but I'll say one more time for emphasis, it wouldn't have made it any easier or better," he told the *Journal* after reporting to the Braves. "I'll miss all those people. Charlie. Mac. Vuke," he said, referring to '82 teammates Charlie Moore, Bob McClure, and Pete Vuckovich, who was in camp as a non-roster invitee. "Oh, God, I'll miss Vuke."[97]

The Brewers opened on the road in Chicago with a surprise sweep of the White Sox before moving to the Bronx where they dropped three straight to the Yankees. Robin Yount opened the year as baseball's hottest hitter, collecting 13 hits in the first week and posting a .520 batting average. When "Bambi's Babies" finally came home for the April 13 opener against Texas, their starting lineup included three rookies (of the six total on the roster) and featured only two players (Yount and Paul Molitor) who had played in the 1985 opener.[98]

As youthful nervousness bubbled in the Brewers locker room, the playing field and parking lots were a dreary mess. Morning tailgaters were greeted by a cold mist that turned into a downpour that washed out batting practice. But, as was becoming the Opening Day norm, the real fun was to be had before the first pitch. "Are they going to cancel the game?" some asked above the din of music and laughter. "Who cares?" answered one man waving a bottle.[99]

The most common tailgating fashion that afternoon was the classic inverted trash bag with arm and head holes added, but the most unique look came from a group that bused in from the Wooley Boys tavern in Pewaukee. They dressed in bee costumes, basing the look on the logic that so-called "Killer Bees" had been discovered in Mexico the year before and that the Mexicans had defeated the Texas Rangers at the Alamo. "Out to the sting the Texas Rangers," one of the bees told the *Journal*. "Get it?"[100]

Meanwhile, it kept on raining until mid-afternoon. By the time the stadium gates opened, parts of the parking lot were covered in ankle-deep water, but there was little movement toward the stadium until word spread that a start time of 3:30 had been announced. Inside, a grim mood permeated the half-empty ballpark. Bob McClure, who was perceived as being overpaid, and Rick Manning, traded to Milwaukee for the beloved Gorman Thomas, were both loudly booed during pregame introductions.[101]

Things didn't get much better once the game finally got underway. The Brewers had trouble making solid contact off 19-year-old Ed Correa, who was making just his third career start, while Tim Leary, starting for

In 31 home openers at Milwaukee County Stadium, the Brewers posted a 15–16 record (Joel Dinda).

Milwaukee, was missing on everything. Former Brewer Darrell Porter, MVP of the 1982 World Series as a Cardinal, slugged a fat Leary offering for a home run in the second and, after the third opened with a walk and two singles, a pair of sacrifices made it 3–0 Texas. The Brewers didn't get a baserunner as far as third until the bottom of the sixth, by which time an Oddibe McDowell homer off Leary had made it 4–0.

Danny Darwin, who had spelled Leary in the fifth, put up a pair of ugly-but-scoreless frames before Bamberger called in rookie lefty Dan Plesac in the top of the eighth. Plesac had been the Brewers' top draft pick in 1983 and had made his Big League debut just three days earlier. He got Larry Parrish and Porter before Steve Buechele, pinch-hitting for Geno Petralli, drilled the Rangers' third solo homer of the afternoon to make it 5–0.

The Brewers finally showed life in the bottom of the inning as Paul Molitor drew a walk off the tiring Correa and a badly spiked wild pitch moved him all the way to third. Billy Jo Robidoux, the sturdy rookie who had been designated as the successor to the injured Cecil Cooper at first base, then poked one down the first base line that took a bad hop and evaded Texas' Pete O'Brien, trickling into right field while Molitor scored and Robidoux scampered to second for his second double of the afternoon. The crowd finally came alive after Paul Householder drew a two-out walk to put runners on the corners for Deer, who'd impressed enough in spring training to be named the team's starting right fielder. A small Deer fan club, camped out in the bleachers under a sign that read "Deer X-ing," led the cheers as the slugger dug in. Deer had homered off Tom Seaver in his first at-bat as a Brewer, but had struck out 10 times in 23 tries since. With a shot to bring the tying run to the plate, Deer offered a few mighty but futile hacks and struck out to end the inning. The fan club packed up their banner and joined the stream for the exits.[102]

What had been a lousy game turned into an outright laugher in the ninth. Plesac opened with a walk, then surrendered a triple and a base hit to make it 7–0. Lefty Ray Searage took over and allowed another single to set the stage for Larry Parrish to crush a three-run homer. After a couple of knock-down pitches, a warning to both sides, and some on field chattering between the teams, the game came to a chilly end with a 10–1 final score. It was the worst opening loss for the Brewers since the franchise's very first game.[103]

"That's the worst game we've played all spring," Bamberger told reporters in the locker room. "We would have been better off if we'd been rained out."[104]

Over .500 as late as August 24, the Brewers once again faded late and finished with a 77–84 mark, their third straight losing season. Bamberger stepped down with nine games left on the schedule and Tom Trebelhorn, who had replaced Muser as third base coach, was named interim manager.

1987

Monday, April 6, 1987: Brewers 5, Red Sox 1 (52,585 attendance)

In the News: Tensions are high in schools near the St. Croix Reservation in northwestern Wisconsin after a court ruling has allowed tribal members to spearfish and hunt off the reservation on lands that their peoples once occupied. Tribal children are reporting bullying and verbal abuse from classmates.

At the Movies: *Over the Top* at the Highway 100 Budget Cinemas

On the Radio: "Nothing's Gonna Stop Us Now" by Starship

Tom Trebelhorn had expected to spend 1986 in Canada. He'd first joined the Brewers in 1984 as Rene Lachmann's third base coach. When Lachmann was fired after the season, the Brewers assigned him to manage the AAA team in Vancouver. He led the team to a Pacific Coast League title and was slated to be back in '86. But after the near-tragic explosion at the Brewers' spring training facility put third base coach Tony Muser out of commission for three months, Trebelhorn was called back to the majors. And when George Bamberger stepped down with a week and half to go in the season, it was "Treb" who got the call as interim manager. He led the Brewers to a 6–3 finish and, on October 1, was named Bamberger's permanent replacement.[105]

A substitute teacher in the off-season, Trebelhorn took a nuanced approach to the game. He planned more base stealing and hit and run plays. He wanted a fast outfield and talked up young talent like Glenn Braggs and Mike Felder—who'd swiped 16 bases in 18 tries in just 44 games in 1986. He envisioned a younger club for '87, and was especially high on 22-year-old catcher B.J. Surhoff, whom the Brewers had taken with the #1 overall pick in the 1985 amateur draft. Surhoff had jumped to AAA in just his second pro season, batting .308 with a sharp eye at the plate.[106]

Meanwhile, the Brewers continued to part ways with members of World Series team. Ben Oglivie was not offered a contract and left to play in Japan. Charlie Moore, now the longest-tenured player in team history, turned down Milwaukee's offer of a 30 percent pay cut and signed with Toronto. Gorman Thomas, signed by the Brewers in mid–July after being released by Cleveland, was released shortly after the season. "If this is the end of the road, which it looks like it is, what the hell," Thomas said. "I was very fortunate to play here because this is the greatest place in the world."[107]

The major trade of the off-season was a swap with the Dodgers that returned first baseman Greg Brock. Brock had two 20-plus homer seasons for the Dodgers and gave the Brewers the power-hitting lefty they'd long coveted. The trade pushed another veteran star to the periphery as Cecil Cooper, the team's starting first-sacker since 1978, would now primarily DH. But aside from Brock, the team would look from within to improve for 1987. They expressed no interest in any of the 82 players who filed for free agency that winter. And, curiously, neither did any of the other 25 teams in the league. For the second straight year, no free agents were offered contracts by new teams.[108]

As the Brewers headed to spring training—and as the players' union was filing a grievance accusing ownership of collusion—the best player the team had developed since Paul Molitor was refusing to leave home. Signed out of the Mexican League in 1983, Ted Higuera debuted in 1985 and placed second in the AL Rookie of the Year voting with his 15–8 record and 3.90 ERA. But in 1986, Higuera emerged as one of the league's best pitchers. He won 20 games, struck out 207 batters, and recorded a 2.79 ERA. He made the All-Star team and finished second in AL Cy Young voting to Roger Clemens.[109]

Higuera made just $140,000 in base pay for the season. For 1987, the Brewers were offering Higuera about $300,000. He wanted half a million.

The holdout lasted into the second week of camp before he finally settled for an amount slightly higher than the team's original offer. He made no secret of his disappointment in the deal, but was ready to move on. "Today's the last time you'll hear about it," he said upon his arrival in camp. "I'm here to play baseball."[110]

With Higuera now in line as the team's ace, attention turned to a battle for a spot at the end of the rotation, where Pete Vuckovich was hoping to catch on for one last shot in the big leagues. In the four years since Vuckovich won the AL Cy Young Award, he'd pitched just 31 games. He'd thought his career was over after an injury-scuttled spring in 1986, but by mid-season he found himself finally throwing pain-free. He made six starts over the last month of the season for the Brewers, posting a solid 3.06 ERA.[111]

But Vuke was sidelined early in camp by a painful condition—what the *Sentinel* called a "boil on his backside" and the *Sporting News* a "rectal cyst"—and was never able to find his rhythm. After a pair of awful outings, Vuckovich announced his retirement. "I just don't feel in my mind, physically or mentally, I have what it takes to be a consistent winner in the

County Stadium awaits the open of the 1987 season. It would be another year of transition for the team, with World Series heroes Charlie Moore, Ben Oglivie, Gorman Thomas, and Pete Vuckovich having departed over the winter and manager Tom Trebelhorn about to start his first full campaign (Bob Busser).

Major Leagues," he said. "So that's that. I can live with it. It wasn't that tough of a decision."[112]

The Brewers headed north with six rookies on the roster and an average player age of just under 27—down from nearly 30 in 1986. Every national baseball publication had picked the Brewers to finish in either sixth or seventh place in AL East and only 5 percent of Brewers fans survey by the *Journal* predicted a division title. Only 20 percent could positively ID Trebelhorn as team manager.[113]

The 1987 season opened at home, with the Brewers hosting the defending AL champion Red Sox. The skies were blue and bright and the temperatures held in the mid-50s. Most notable among the parking lot fashions were a group of fans dressed in detergent box costumes printed with slogans like "All Temperature Deer" and "Whiten the Sox with Brock." Dawn Schroeder, wife of Brewers' catcher Bill, was taken with the entire spectacle. "What are all these people doing here at 8 a.m., drinking beer and eating brats?" she told the *Sentinel*. "You just don't get tired of Opening Day. It's a different feeling every time."[114]

Newly-elected governor Tommy Thompson had declared it "Tom Trebelhorn Day" in Wisconsin and Thompson and Marquette University athletic director Hank Raymonds threw out the ceremonial first pitches. Higuera got the call for the Brewers and the Red Sox, with Clemens having just ended a holdout of his own, tabbed Bob Stanley. Stanley had been on the mound for the Mets' walk-off win against the Sox in game six of the 1986 World Series and the issue of *Sport* magazine currently on newsstands feature a story titled "Bob Stanley's Offseason in Hell."[115]

The Brewers put Stanley's attempt to redeem himself on hold as Paul Molitor laced his fourth pitch of the game into the right-center field gap for a triple. Robin Yount, who was rumored to have been considering retirement over the winter, lined the next pitch back up the middle for a run-scoring single. "I was jacked," said Molitor after the game. "It was a good way to start the season."[116]

The Brewers managed three hits off Stanley in the second, but could not score. Higuera, who had not pitched well in his abbreviated spring, kept Boston off balance through three despite not having great command of his fastball. But after Bill Buckner singled to open the fourth, Jim Rice laced one down the right field line. Buckner was running with the pitch, but as perhaps the slowest man in the league, it was a surprise to all involved when Red Sox third base coach Joe Morgan waved him home. In right, Braggs played the ball off the wall, turned and fired to Brock, who spun for a perfect relay to Schroeder at the plate to nail Buckner. "Anybody else and it's a run," Schroeder said after the game. "But hats off to him for even being out there. The guy can barely walk."[117]

The Brewers showed some more flash on defense an inning later. After catcher Marc Sullivan led off with a single, Spike Owen muffed a bunt attempt, popping the ball toward Brock at first. Brock charged in, but with Sullivan moving back toward first, he let the ball drop. It was a play that Trebelhorn had his infielders practice endlessly in spring training. Brock's smooth deception forced Sullivan to break for second while he tossed to Jim Gantner, who stepped on first and fired a dart to shortstop Dale Sveum, who applied the tag for a rally-killing double play. "[Brings] tears to a fundamentalist's eyes when things like that happen," Trebelhorn said later.[118]

The Brewers chased Stanley in the bottom half. Gantner opened with a single and scored three batters later on a double by Yount. Braggs followed with a base hit to score Yount. In the bottom of the sixth, now facing Steve Crawford, Gantner and Molitor each tallied run-scoring hits to set the score at 5–0 Brewers. As the Brewers had won just one of their last six openers, the mood at County Stadium was as bright as the midday sunshine. The team had scrapped the between-inning organ music for canned rock and pop songs blasted through the stadium's new sound system and the bleachers rocked along with classics like "Mony, Mony," "Shout!" and "Louie, Louie."[119]

After Higuera worked around a couple of base runners in the seventh, his afternoon was finished. Mark Clear worked the eighth and Dan Plesac—the lanky southpaw who'd established himself as the Brewers ninth-inning man in '86—worked around an unearned run to close it out.

"I could have pitched the whole game. But this is the first time I've gone seven innings this year," Higuera told reporters after the game, with Juan Nieves serving as interpreter. "I'll just take it day by day. Now, my goal is to win the second one."[120]

Trebelhorn, upbeat as always and beaming, was also looking forward to the second one. "It was an emotional day, exciting stuff," he told reporters. "We're 1–0. That means we're at least tied for first, doesn't it?"[121]

The Brewers won the second one and the 11 after that on their way to a 20–3 start that stunned the sports world. But they lost 18 of their next 20 and were little more than a curiosity in the AL East race through the rest of the season. Nonetheless, their 91–71 record was their best since 1982.

1988

Monday, April 15, 1988: Yankees 7, Brewers 1 (55,887 attendance)
In the News: Milwaukee police have arrested three 12-year-old boys who brought a gun to Mitchell Elementary School on North 23rd Street.

The gun accidentally discharged while the boys were playing with it in class. They said they found it in some bushes on the way to school.

At the Movies: *Good Morning, Vietnam* at the Prospect Mall Cinemas

On the Radio: "Get Outta My Dreams, Get Into My Car" by Billy Ocean

Nineteen eighty-seven had shown the great promise of Tom Trebelhorn's Brewers. Sure, they were a team given to cold streaks and had more questions than answers on the pitching staff, but they were a hungry and resilient bunch. They had an impossibly good April and a May that nearly gave it all back. But they held strong and ended up as just the fourth team in franchise history to win more than 90 games. Young talent like B.J. Surhoff, Dale Sveum, and Glenn Braggs established themselves as strong everyday players while Dan Plesac and Chuck Crim emerged as the core of the bullpen. Meanwhile, the team had high hopes for up-and-comers like Bill Wegman, Juan Nieves, and Chris Bosio. Perhaps at no point in franchise history had the Brewers possessed so much burgeoning talent.

Greg Brock had also had a stand-out year in '87. Playing every day for the first time in his career, he batted .299 and drove in 85 runs and got on base at a .371 clip. His performance erased any hope Cecil Cooper had of seeing regular time at first base and the veteran was miserable in the designated hitter role. Batting just .248 and hitting for little power, he was bumped from his DH spot when Paul Molitor returned from the disabled list. From the All-Star break through the end of the season, Cooper was on the active roster, but never saw game action. For 76 straight games, he sat. The Brewers waived him in January, paying out the final year of his contract with little fanfare.[122]

GM Harry Dalton entered the off-season looking to add a pitcher, both in the rotation and the pen. He dangled Bill Schroeder, whose starting catcher job had been taken over by Surhoff, but took a stingy approach and ended up making no moves. The Brewers were also once again silent in the free agent market. While a handful of free agents would change teams over the winter of 1987–88, the owners continued to act in concert by sharing information about offers they had made to players. After Paul Molitor, who had batted .353 in 1987 while capturing national attention with his 39-game hitting streak, filed for free agency that fall, the only offer he received was from the Brewers.[123]

While Molitor had to settle for a raise of less than $150,000, Ted Higuera—not yet eligible for free agency, but able to file for salary arbitration—was due for a much bigger pay bump. Coming off an 18-win season in which he set a team record with 240 strikeouts, Higuera agreed on a one-year pact with the Brewers that pushed his base pay from $300,000 to more than $1 million, with another $750,000 possible in incentives. He reported to spring training on time and happy.[124]

But spring came to the Milwaukee Brewers somberly in 1988. On February 28, Harvey Kuenn died in Arizona, where he was preparing to spend the next six weeks working for the Brewers as an advanced scout. Back in Milwaukee, an impromptu wake formed at Cesar's Inn, the low-key tavern owned by Kuenn and his wife, Audrey. Pete Vuckovich sat on a barstool, beer and shot in front of him, talking with a reporter. "The man told the worst jokes in the world," he said. "But he was probably the best man who ever lived to tell a joke to." Many of the players from Kuenn's 1982 team regarded him as a father figure. Several served as pallbearers at his funeral, where Bob Uecker delivered the eulogy. "Over the last several years, Harvey was kind of working with a 3–2 count," Uecker said to the bleary-eyed room. "Each time they tried to slip one past Harvey on the outside corner, he fouled it off. To get one [past] Harvey looking, He must have wanted him pretty bad."[125]

| 49 | **Ted Higuera** | P |

The Milwaukee Police Department Stadia Athletic Shoes and WTMJ Radio present the 1988
Milwaukee Brewers

Teddy Higuera, for reasons good and bad, was the center of conversation for many hot stove seasons. His first home opener start was a gem against the Red Sox.

The Brewers opened the season on with an East Coast swing, sporting an H/K memorial patch that the team would wear throughout the season. They started with two wins in Baltimore, including a 12–0 pounding in the opener. But in New York, they lost three in a row to the Yankees and then did the same in Boston to the Red Sox. They limped home sitting at 2–6 and already 5.5 back of the red-hot Yankees, who were waiting for them in Milwaukee.

The opener had sold out just a few weeks before the game and a handful of standing room tickets were still available the day of. But if that indicated a lull in excitement, there was no evidence of it at 7:29 that morning, when the *Journal* reported the first tailgate keg had been tapped, officially opening another season of Brewers baseball in Milwaukee. By 11 a.m., the parking lots were filled and the sizzling bratwursts—not to mention the racks of ribs and one group of fans roasting 20 whole chickens on spits—took a bit of the chill out of the sub-30-degree weather.[126]

One surprisingly welcome group of guests during the tailgating festivities were agents from the local IRS office. With the opener falling on Tax Day, the IRS chartered a red, white, and blue bus for the game, staffing it with three agents who helped fans check over their returns and provided free filing and copy services. They reported processing about 50 returns before the game, with most filers coming in with a drink in one hand and their forms in the other.[127]

The pregame ceremonies inside the stadium were a tribute to Harvey Kuenn. With the center field flag at half-mast, a short memorial honored Harvey, while his widow Audrey—and countless others in the park—openly wept. Audrey threw out a ceremonial first pitch, along with John Norquist and Dale Schultz (Milwaukee's mayor-elect and county executive-elect, respectively) and West Allis native and Olympic speed skater Dan Jansen.[128]

But whatever feelings were brought on by the pregame ceremonies, they left the building quickly once the game got underway. After Higuera was a late scratch with a tweaked back, Mike Birkbeck, who had missed most of 1987 with an injury, had his turn moved up a day and was given the heady task of making his first start in nearly a year in front of a sell-out crowd. He called it a "dream come true." That feeling would not last.[129]

Rickey Henderson bunted Birkbeck's first pitch down the third base line. Birkbeck fielded it cleanly, but threw wide to first, pulling Brock off the base. Henderson, blazing down the line, made what appeared to be a slight turn toward second after passing the base. Brock saw this and applied a tag. Safe, called the first base umpire. That drew Trebelhorn out of the dugout. He made a futile argument that Henderson should have been called out.[130]

Two pitches later, with Willie Randolph at bat, Birkbeck was called for a balk and Henderson was sent to second base. Over the off-season, the league had clarified a portion of the rule surrounding the balk—easily baseball's most enigmatic bit of regulation—stating clearly that a pitcher must come to a complete stop with both feet on the ground before starting his delivery from the stretch position. And no team in baseball had struggled as much with the redefined rule as the Brewers. In their first eight games of 1988, they had already been called for seven balks. The call on Birkbeck made it eight—equaling their team total from all of 1987.[131]

Trebelhorn again came out of the dugout for clarification. Randolph walked and, two batters later, Jack Clark singled in a run. Then Mike Pagliarulo singled to load the bases. Another walk and a base hit scored two runs before Birkbeck, facing catcher Don Slaught, was called for another balk. Birkbeck exploded, arguing nose to nose with umpire Tim McClelland before Trebelhorn came out again to argue and defend his pitcher. It was 4–0 Yankees, with two balks, three Tom Trebelhorn arguments, and one out recorded. The thousands of fans still making their way inside heard the chorus of boos and could only image what was going on.[132]

The Yankees tacked on another run before the end of the inning to make it 5–0 before the Brewers ever had a chance at bat. The Brewers went quietly in the first against 45-year-old junkballer Tommy John before the Yankees hit Birkbeck for another run—and another balk—in the top of second. Birkbeck recorded just one out in the inning before being pulled. In the bottom half, Glenn Braggs belted a laser beam of a solo homer into the left field bleachers that accounted for all of the Brewers scoring. During the few instances in which the Brewers got men on base, the crowd chanted, "Balk, balk, balk" at every movement the New York pitcher made on the mound. It did no good, although Brewers reliever Dave Stapleton was nailed for one more balk in the third.[133]

42   **Tom Trebelhorn**   Mgr.
The Milwaukee Police Department
Stadia Athletic Shoes and WTMJ Radio
present the 1988
Milwaukee Brewers

Tom Trebelhorn began his tenure as Brewers manager on a 26–6 run, but he'd only win one home opener during his five years at the team's helm.

And so the biggest home opener crowd in Brewers history was left to mostly entertain itself as the Brewers dropped their seventh straight. The mood in the clubhouse after the game was one of dumbfounded frustration. "To me, this whole balk situation is destroying the game," pitching coach Chuck Hartenstein said. "I'm about ready to turn in my damn uniform."[134]

Trebelhorn was a bit more diplomatic. "56,000 people figured somebody better argue with the umpires, so I did," he told reporters. "But they have set the ground rules, and I have no complaint. We're just not doing a good job of handling this."135

Birkbeck summed the afternoon up as total loss. "Everything I needed to get done, I didn't do," he said. "There was all kinds of havoc out there. It was a nightmare."136

The Brewers had a .500 record as late as August 29 in 1988, but a late-season surge (and an usually weak AL East) thrust them into a surprise pennant chase in September. They finished the season 87–75, just two games behind the division champion Red Sox.

1989

Monday, April 10, 1989: Rangers 6, Brewers 4 (10 innings) (54,301 attendance)

In the News: Arsons at two Florida abortion clinics, one of which burned to the ground, are believed to be in response to an abortion rights march in Washington, D.C., that drew more than 300,000 people.

At the Movies: *Major League* at the Prospect Mall Cinemas

On the Radio: "Like a Prayer" by Madonna

For two seasons, Tom Trebelhorn's Brewers had existed on the cusp of something big. In 1988, their pitching staff emerged as one of the best in baseball, anchored by Ted Higuera, who just missed an AL ERA title with a 2.45 mark. But a cold start and an offense too reliant on Paul Molitor (who was healthy for his first full season since 1983) and Robin Yount held them back in an AL East in which the top five teams were separated by just 3.5 games.

And for the second time in franchise history, the Brewers' fortunes were tied to a teenage shortstop. After putting up some monster numbers at El Paso and Denver (.327 average, 28 homers, .395 OBP), 19-year-old Gary Sheffield was summoned to Milwaukee for the Brewers' '88 stretch run, hitting four homers in 24 games and showing a poise at the plate that belied his status as the league's youngest player. Although there was already talk about him being "trouble"—he had been arrested twice during his time in the Brewers' organization—the team was convinced his problems were behind him. With Sheffield preparing for a full season with the Brewers, the *Sporting News* mentioned the Brewers as one of the early favorites in AL East for 1989.137

With depth and an abundance of young talent, Harry Dalton chose to mostly stand pat over the off-season. The only moves Dalton made were to re-sign Jim Gantner and trade catcher Bill Schroeder—out of a job with

B.J. Surhoff set to assume full-time duties behind the plate—to California. Dalton made inquiries with free agent pitcher Nolan Ryan, but made no formal offer. "We have not been active in the free agent market for the last eight years," Dalton said. "And I don't see us changing that now."[138]

Ryan ended up signing with Texas, one of a handful of impact players that changed teams via free agency that winter in the first truly open market since 1984. Prior to the 1988 season, an independent arbiter had ruled the owners had illegally colluded in refusing to sign free agents following the 1985 season. Cases were pending on the following two seasons. After player salaries had stagnated during the collusion period, the 1988–89 market once again drove up player pay. The average team payroll climbed from $10.2 million in 1988 to nearly $13.5 million for 1989.

Indeed, finances were front and center in that winter's hot stove chatter. The New York Yankees had just signed a new cable television broadcast deal worth $500 million over 12 years. The Brewers earned just $3 million per season for the TV broadcast rights for their games. Early on in the 1988 season, the Brewers had made it official that they wanted to build a new stadium. They considered County Stadium to be "economically obsolete" and pledged to finance the new ballpark if the county and state would cover the infrastructure costs associated with the project. "The stadium issue is intertwined with all the issues we are talking about here," Bud Selig said in reference to the economics of the post-collusion era. "If we have a new stadium, if we have the new revenue sources we could generate on that score, then we can remain competitive." Selig hoped the new park would be ready for the 1994 season.[139]

Just before spring training, the Brewers were hit with a pair of health scares. The first was disheartening—Ted Higuera would need back surgery and would open the season on the DL. The second hit much closer to home. While in Los Angeles filming for *Mr. Belvedere*, Bob Uecker suffered a mild heart attack. With the Brewers since 1971, "Mr. Baseball" had become a national celebrity by the late 1980s. A regular on the *Tonight Show* with Johnny Carson and a fixture of a long-running Miller Lite TV ad campaign, Uecker landed the lead role on *Mr. Belvedere* in 1985. He had just finished a marathon week in LA, recording an episode of *Mr. Belvedere*, a *Tonight Show* appearance, and a syndicated sports highlight program before checking into the hospital. The 54-year-old said he would take about a month off in order to ready for the open of the baseball season.[140]

As usual, Uecker handled the situation with humor. "I'd like to thank the fans for the letters and flowers," he said after being discharged. "I woke up one morning in kind of a fog. I saw all these flowers, but I couldn't hear any music. I thought my wife had bought me a real cheap funeral." His recovery work included long walks and daily swimming. He also discussed a better diet with his doctor. "I said, 'I've been eating a lot of chicken,' and the doctor says, 'Now try eating it without the feathers.'"[141]

But while Uecker was on the mend, Higuera had company on the disabled list. Dale Sveum, still recovering from a broken leg suffered in a collision with outfielder Darryl Hamilton, and Juan Nieves would miss the entire 1989 season. Paul Molitor would miss the first week after tearing a ligament in his finger during spring training horseplay. And so as the Brewers went to Cleveland for the season opener, they did so with players like Gus Polidor, Terry Francona, and Dave Engle expected to see playing time. Still, the *Sporting News* and a handful of other national publications picked them to win the AL East.[142]

The Brewers arrived in Milwaukee after splitting four games with the Indians and Tigers and one game called in Detroit due to cold. It wasn't much warmer in Milwaukee, with temperatures sitting below freezing and a light snowfall as the parking lots began to fill at 7 a.m. Cups of coffee were nearly as common as cans of beer in the early going, and snowmobile wear outmatched Brewers gear, but the cold was once again no match for baseball fever. One item of note was the first documented appearance of a "beer bong" (although the *Sentinel* did not use the term). "This is fun!" one Opening Day regular told the paper. "This is classic Milwaukee."[143]

Milwaukee Bucks owner and newly-minted U.S. Senator Herb Kohl threw out the first pitch to his lifelong friend Bud Selig, who had to dive out from the behind the plate to make the catch. Also on hand was Bart Giamatti, just 10 days into his term as baseball's seventh commissioner. He advocated for a new stadium in Milwaukee and promoted the idea of a salary cap as a cure for the game's money imbalance.[144]

Burly righthander Chris Bosio got the start for the Brewers, and the Rangers wasted no time in putting a kink in his Opening Day plans. With one out, Scott Fletcher singled and Rafael Palmeiro poked a fly ball homer to right. It stayed 2–0 until the bottom of the second when the Brewers got to Texas knuckleballer Charlie Hough. The 41-year-old Hough had long struggled against the Brewers and, after a clean first, his control left him. Rob Deer led off and tagged a Hough knuckler for a home run to left. After two walks, Jim Gantner singled through the middle to score Braggs and, after another walk, Surhoff came through with a hit of his own to score a pair and make it 4–2 Milwaukee. Hough, on a short leash with the cold conditions, was pulled for righty Brad Arnsberg, making just his second appearance since having what was now being referred to as "Tommy John" surgery.

Arnsberg quieted the Brewers, tossing scoreless frames in the fourth and fifth. He did so as the only player on the field—and maybe the only person in the stadium—not wearing long sleeves. But this was not

Chapter Two. The Eighties 91

a show of machismo. "I've kind of got a fetish about that," he said after the game. "The sleeve rubs on the top of my [surgery] scar and irritates it. It's a bad omen for me." While Arnsberg pitched sleeveless, another wardrobe-related item of note occurred in the outfield. Giving in to the Opening Day trend of fans running onto the field during play, one man attempted to jump from the bleachers onto the warning track. But he evidently had second thoughts and had his friends pull him back. He ended up stuck halfway, fans pulling on one end while security guards yanked on the other. After nearly losing his pants, he was taken into custody.[145]

The Rangers tied it up in the top of the sixth when Pete Incaviglia destroyed a 2–2 Bosio fastball for a two-run homer. Bosio had tried to keep the ball away, but with the cold air deadening his grip, it drifted too close to the plate and "Inky"—Texas' own version of Rob Deer—sent it halfway up the left field bleachers to make it 4–4.[146]

The Brewers had a chance to break the tie in the bottom of the seventh, when Bill Spiers looped a single into right-center for his first career hit and Mike Felder followed with a walk. After Surhoff struck out, Cecilio Guante came on for the Rangers to face Yount, who laced one into the gap in center—where the burly Incaviglia ran it down to end the inning.

After Chuck Crim, coming off a season in which he'd led the AL in appearances and logged a 2.91 ERA, got Julio Franco to line out and end a Rangers threat in the top of the ninth, the Brewers again got two men on to set the stage for Yount. With Surhoff on first and Gantner just 90 feet away from a walk-off win, Texas summoned their All-Star closer Jeff Russell. After taking a ball, Russell fanned Yount on three straight fastballs.[147]

Going to extras, the Brewers faltered quickly. After a walk to Palmerio, Ruben Sierra sliced a tie-breaking double off the left-center field wall. After another walk by Crim, Cecil Espy banged a single to score Sierra. The Brewers went in order against Russell in the bottom half for a 6–4 final score.[148]

After the game, Yount, who twice missed his chance to play hero, summed up his thoughts. "It's a pretty basic game," he said. "It's not that tough. You either do it or you don't."[149]

Yount did it in 1989, batting .318 with 21 homers to win the 1989 AL MVP award, but the Brewers didn't, hovering around .500 for most of the year and finishing at 81–81. The phenom Sheffield also failed to deliver, struggling with injuries and publicly criticizing the team.

Chapter Three

The Nineties

1990

Monday, April 10, 1990: White Sox 5, Brewers 3 (50,294 attendance)
In the News: Radio Doctors record stores in Milwaukee have pulled all copies of 2 Live Crew's *As Nasty as They Wanna Be* from their shelves following court rulings in Tennessee and Florida was that it was obscene.
At the Movies: *Teenage Mutant Ninja Turtles* at the Times Cinema
On the Radio: "I Wanna Be Rich" by Calloway

They had an MVP in Robin Yount, a healthy Paul Molitor, an emerging second ace in Chris Bosio, and one of the best bullpens in baseball—but the 1989 Brewers were still a messy underachiever. Batting coach Tony Muser and pitching coach Chuck Hartenstein were fired after the season and rumors about problems with "chemistry" in the clubhouse littered every post-season write-up. "I think some changes are in order," said Molitor. "I don't see a good blend with the veterans and the young guys."[1]

And then there were the money matters. The Brewers had settled on a site just past the center field bleachers for their new stadium, which they now hoped could be open as soon as 1993. They insisted that they would be able to pay for the park, as long as the county and state could cover the demolition and replacement of the freeway that presently ran through the site. But any payday from a new facility was still years off and the Brewers had bills coming due much sooner than that—substantial ones.[2]

MVP and face of the franchise Yount filed for free agency on November 10 and figured to be among the top players available. Molitor, Dan Plesac, and Ted Higuera were all eligible for salary arbitration and all figured to earn significant raises. And—while Harry Dalton again dismissed the idea of the Brewers signing a free agent, saying, "It taxes your imagination how we would do it"—Yount made it clear he wanted to return to the World Series and that the Brewers needed to add pieces to make that a reality.[3]

While rumors abounded about where Yount might land, the Brewers taxed their imaginations and signed former MVP and two-time NL batting champ Dave Parker to a two-year deal worth $3 million. The Brewers, wrote the *Sporting News*, were desperate to show Yount that they were serious about winning in 1990 and soothing the clubhouse gulfs that irked Yount late in 1989. Parker had a reputation as an excellent veteran locker room presence and, as the team had never had a designated hitter with more than 12 homers or 56 RBI in a single season, the first impact DH in club history.[4]

With the California Angels reportedly offering Yount more than $3 million per year—and agreeing to work out a deal to repay the $5 million-plus that Yount still owed on the loans the Brewers had helped him secure during this last contract negotiation—the consensus in baseball was that Yount was as good as gone. Shortly after signing Parker, Selig visited Yount at his home in Arizona and spent the day talking with the center fielder. "It was an emotional day," Selig said. "What was said is between the two of us, but it got emotional in the end." By the end of the visit, Yount had agreed in principle to a three-year deal that would—briefly—make him the highest-paid player in baseball.[5]

But with Molitor, Selig took a different approach. The rules of the time only allowed a player to file for free agency every five years. Molitor—having just finished a three-year contract—was unsigned, but could not negotiate with other teams. According to Ron Simon, Molitor's agent, Selig opened talks by unloading on Molitor. He called Molitor and Yount "wimps" and "greedy ballplayers" and said they'd offered no leadership in 1989 as the team floundered. Simon accused Selig of playing Yount and Molitor against each other in negotiations, obscuring offers to each in order to drive down the price of the other. After he signed a three-year deal for $9 million—about $600,000 less than what Yount had gotten—Molitor made no comment on the deal to the media.[6]

After Plesac and Higuera got their raises, the Brewers' 1990 payroll topped $20 million—nearly double what it had been in 1989 and the ninth highest in all of baseball. And rulings on the three years of collusion continued to go against the owners, with the total damages now topping $100 million. What's more, the basic agreement between the owners and players signed in 1984 had expired at the end of 1989, and after months of unsuccessful negotiations—including an attempt by the owners to implement a salary cap—ownership refused to open training camps in mid–February, starting a 32-day lockout of the players. With the cap issue a non-starter, the conflict mostly boiled down to reconfiguration of the arbitration system. In the end, the players won increased arbitration eligibility, an increased minimum salary, and an agreement from the owners to fill all 25 spots on the active roster, ending the three-year-old tactic of every team playing a man short. The owners were allowed to study revenue sharing.[7]

After a truncated spring training, the Brewers pushed back their opener from April 6 against Texas to April 10, hosting the White Sox as a part of a two-game home-and-home series. The logic that a shorter camp would leave less time for injuries did not hold out. Over the short schedule, Molitor sprained his thumb and Gary Sheffield injured his wrist, while Jim Gantner and Bill Spiers were still hobbled by injuries from '89.[8]

Sheffield recovered in time for the season opener in Chicago. The Brewers were ready to move past 1989 and still considered Sheffield a big part of their future. They'd brought in another former MVP in Don Baylor to replace Muser as the hitting coach and stationed Parker's locker next door to Sheffield's, hoping that the pair could better connect with the young star than Trebelhorn and other white coaches had. While fans partied in the parking lot, this year with 10 different radio stations broadcasting live, three rocks bands performing, and a contingent of the UW marching band parading through the grills and kegs, Parker stuck close to Sheffield in the locker room. "Guys like Sheff were defensive because no one ever wanted to know the person inside him," Parker later wrote. "I wanted to know everything about him, his town, his boys, his family. I wanted the kid to make the very best of himself, in all ways."[9]

After Packers head coach Lindy Infante threw out the first pitch to a huge ovation (he had just led the Packers to their first 10-win season since 1972), Ted Higuera tossed a perfect opening frame and Sheffield lined a clean single through the hole to right field. He sped to third when B.J. Surhoff singled and scored when Yount smoked a base hit to center. The home crowd, who had been relentless in their booing of Sheffield in 1989, cheered wildly.[10]

But just as quickly as they'd struck, the Brewer bats went quiet against the Sox righty Eric King. After Yount's hit, he set down 11 in a row while Higuera worked in and out of trouble. In the top of the fifth, he finally got burned. A lead-off walk to Robin Ventura was followed with Lance Johnson reaching on a bunt and a Higuera misplay. Higuera got Ozzie Guillen and Sammy Sosa before walking Scott Fletcher. Ivan Calderon followed with a booming double that scored two before Fletcher was thrown out at home. By this time, things had gotten so rowdy in the bleachers that all bleacher beer sales were cut off. More than a few of 130 arrests made at the game stemmed from bleacher fistfights between Brewers fans and Sox loyalists.[11]

In the bottom half, still 2–1, Greg Brock led off with a walk, but was pulled for pinch-runner Mike Felder. It was a bold move so early in the game, but Trebelhorn wanted to "change the tempo" of the game by inserting the team's fastest man in a running situation. But Felder never got the chance as Glenn Braggs followed with a double that scored Felder easily. Edgar Diaz then reached on an error and, in another attempt to make

Chapter Three. The Nineties 95

something happen, Trebelhorn pinch hit rookie slugger Greg Vaughn for weak-hitting second baseman Bill Bates. Vaughn, who'd hit as many as 33 homers a year in the minors, worked reliever Scott Radinsky like a seasoned vet, drawing a six-pitch walk to load the bases for Sheffield. Sheffield swung at the first pitch and skied it to center, deep enough to score Braggs and give the Brewers a 3–2 lead.[12]

Still threatening and with just one out, Surhoff came to bat looking to break the game open. Ahead 2–0 in the count, he popped one down the third base line that caught in the heavy wind and drifted right into the path of Ventura, who chased it down for out number two. Hearing third base coach Duffy Dyer shout for Diaz to tag from third, Ventura spun and fired a perfect, no-look throw to Carlton Fisk who took the ball on three hops and tagged Diaz out to end the inning.[13]

The momentum had swung. A Fisk single and a pair of walks loaded the bases for the Sox in the sixth and a Johnson base hit and a Guillen sac fly brought them all around to make it 5–3 Chicago. The Brewers threatened in the bottom half and again in the eighth, when they loaded the bases with one out, but the Sox lead held into the bottom of the ninth. Facing closer Bobby Thigpen, Dale Sveum—playing in his first game since he broke his leg in an outfield collision in September 1988—poked a hit past the first baseman and, a batter later, Surhoff lined a single to center. And for the second straight home opener, Yount came to bat with a chance to win the game. With the count 0–2, Thigpen left a pitch over the plate and Yount crushed it to deep left field. The ball arched high in the air and then, hitting the 30 mph winds that had kept the home crowd chilly all afternoon, it died and dropped into the glove of Dave Gallagher, his back nearly against the wall.[14]

With just one hit with runners in scoring position and 9 walks issued—their most in a single game since 1986—the Brewers had plenty to dwell on after the game. "We generally had the right guys up there in certain situations. We just squandered too many opportunities," Trebelhorn said after. "It's time to knock that baloney off."[15]

The Brewer were quick out of the gate in 1990, leading the AL East into the last week of May, but injuries to Molitor and Bosio, as well as a mediocre season by Yount, doomed the team by mid-summer. Parker and Sheffield were among the club's few standouts.

1991

Monday, April 15, 1991: Orioles 7, Brewers 2 (50,058 attendance)
In the News: President Bush has ordered a rapid withdrawal of forces from southern Iraq, despite some 40,000 refugees still left in the region.

At the Movies: *Goodfellas* at the Mill Road Theaters
On the Radio: "Rico Suave" by Gerardo

After two seasons as up-and-comers, Tom Trebelhorn's Brewers spent 1989 and 1990 as highly-touted disappointments. And for the second straight year, the Brewers' mediocrity on the field was paired with a dour locker room atmosphere. The *Sporting News* wrote that Milwaukee's clubhouse lacked leadership and "barely seemed to have a pulse." Players spoke of clubhouse cliques and resentment from some players that others were too focused on money.[16]

As expected, the team's underwhelming play led to rumors about Trebelhorn's job security. He was always regarded a player's manager; the popular question now was whether Trebelhorn was "too nice." Questions swirled around GM Harry Dalton as well. Word had it that he was too heavy-handed with Trebelhorn and he undermined his coaching staff. Players complained that no one seemed to know their roles and that no one had their backs when they weren't meeting expectations.[17]

And then there was Ted Higuera, who filed for free agency in early November. Despite missing time for the second straight season with injuries, Higuera was among the game's top pitchers—and possibly the best left-hander—since he debuted in 1985. He'd fallen off a bit in 1990, his second sub-standard performance since being truly dominant in 1988, but he projected to be the second-most highly sought-after free agent pitcher behind reigning AL Cy Young Award winner Bob Welch. While Welch was expected to re-sign with Oakland, Higuera had already turned down a three-year extension from the Brewers and—with as many as 12 teams expressing interest in his services—was not expected to return to Milwaukee. Some players wondered if the loss of Higuera would essentially push the team into a rebuilding mode.[18]

But for the second straight year, the Brewers surprised the baseball world by retaining a home-grown talent. In mid–December, Higuera agreed to return for a four-year, $12.4 million deal. On the same day, the Brewers announced the signing of first baseman Franklin Stubbs, formerly of the Astros, to a two-year pact for $4 million. Stubbs was coming off a 23-homer season in the cavernous Astrodome, and it was hoped that Stubbs could boost those numbers in Milwaukee.[19]

Meanwhile, the bill had finally come due for the owners on collusion. In a final settlement with the players' union, the owners agreed to pay a total of $280 million in damages for the wage suppression that resulted from the three-year moratorium on free agent signings. The Brewers' share of this would be about $11 million. Bud Selig continued to press publicly for both revenue sharing within the game and a new stadium for the

Brewers. "We can't survive with our current revenue stream," Selig told the *Journal*. "It can't be done."[20]

While Selig began to openly question the resolve of the local politicians to support the stadium plan, the portion of its overall cost that would need to be publicly funded continued to climb. And city officials, including Mayor John Norquist, kept asking the club to consider a downtown site for the stadium. For the first time, Selig began to talk about relocation.[21]

Whatever optimism fans felt at the opening of training camp was doused in mid-March when Higuera was shut down with a sore shoulder. While early reports indicated he could be back in six weeks, an examination revealed a partially torn rotator cuff—an injury from which pitchers rarely fully recovered. A day later, the Brewers made a surprise trade, sending Dave Parker—an All-Star and a Silver Slugger winner in 1990—to the Angels for outfielder Dante Bichette.[22]

The trade was meant to open a spot for Molitor as the full-time DH, but the loss of Parker hit the team hard. "He was like a father away from home for me," said Greg Vaughn, who refused any further comment on the trade. "I miss him already," said Jim Gantner. "It's a quiet place around here [without him]." "I don't know how you figure this team is going to get better without Parker," said Gary Sheffield. "We're just that much worse."[23]

Sheffield, who'd batted .294 with 25 steals and more walks than strikeouts in 1990 under Parker's watch, stewed about the trade all spring. Finally, during the last week of camp, he unloaded in an interview with the *Wisconsin State Journal*. He said Dalton was "ruining the team" and he had no respect for him and "just enough" for Trebelhorn. "If I'm going to be a scapegoat, then I'm going to tell you how I feel."[24]

With Higuera on the DL, Mark Knudson got the start in the season opener and beat Nolan Ryan and the Rangers. After taking another win in Texas and dropping three of four in Toronto, the Brewers arrived home in Milwaukee for a tax day match-up with the Orioles. Chris Bosio, who'd tossed eight shutout innings in Texas, got the ball for the Brewers. Eager to make up for his 1989 home opener loss, Bosio woke up at 5:30 on game day. After burning off some nervous energy on a stationary bike at his apartment, he left early for the stadium and was the first player to arrive. On a normal opener, he might have been arriving just as the first grills were being lit. But it was a rainy morning, the steady showers putting a damper on an otherwise mild spring day.[25]

With the charcoal hard to light, many tailgaters opted for the party tent sponsored by WMTJ Radio, where the station was giving away 6,200 free bratwursts and other assorted treats. And, with another April 15 opener, the Milwaukee IRS office was once again stationed in the parking lot, offering free tax consultations and filings.[26]

The exterior of Milwaukee County Stadium as it appeared in the early 1990s (barrelmansammy).

With combat in the Gulf War having ended about six weeks earlier, there was a distinct theme of militarism to the pregame festivities. Every fan was given a small American flag as they entered the stadium and the first pitches were thrown by five Wisconsin veterans, each from a different war. The U.S. Army dance band played before the game and "The Star-Spangled Banner" was accompanied by a C-130 fly-over.[27]

During pregame introductions, Gary Sheffield—batting third and playing third base—heard a mix of cheers and boos. It was a bit of a surprise for the man who was regularly portrayed in the newspapers as the Brewers' most disagreeable player. But after two uninspiring seasons and with their latest high-dollar player out with an injury before he'd even received the first check from his new contract, there might have been a significant part of the fanbase who shared his dim view of Harry Dalton. The boobirds saved their true venom for Dan Plesac, whose ERA had ballooned in 1990. He was set to earn nearly $4 million over the next two years.[28]

Scoring got underway in the second inning, when Orioles first baseman Glenn Davis crushed a 3–1 fastball into the back half of the left field bleachers. But Bosio held focus and didn't allow another base runner until the top of the fourth when he walked Randy Milligan on four pitches. With the Brewers yet to get a man as far as second base against Jose Mesa, Cal Ripken squared another fluttering Bosio fastball for a two-run shot to left to make it 3–0. The next man up was Davis and, either in retaliation for his own homer or Ripken's, Bosio planted his second pitch in Davis's back.[29]

In the bottom half, Sheffield laced a one-out triple into the right-center field gap and scored when Greg Brock—starting in place of a banged-up Stubbs—rolled a hit through the infield. The score held at 3–1 Orioles until the bottom of the sixth when Sheffield again got things started by lining one past third base and legging out a double. After a walk to Brock, Dante

Bichette said hello to his new home fans with his own line-drive double to score Sheffield and cut the Orioles lead to 3–2.

Bosio finished out a clean seventh inning before giving way to Chuck Crim. Although still trailing, Bosio had gutted through with sub-par stuff to give the Brewers a chance to win it late. Crim got his first two hitters without problem, but then suffered through three long at-bats that yielded singles to Davis and Ripken and a walk to veteran Dwight Evens. Crim gave way to righthander Edwin Nunez. Signed in a little-noticed move in December, Nunez had a fine season pitching from the bullpen for the Tigers in 1990. Also warming in the pen had been lefty Mark Lee, who was similarly sharp for the Brewers the year prior. Although Lee would have been the better matchup against Sam Horn, the left-hander due up, it probably would have forced O's skipper Frank Robinson to counter by pinch-hitting Leo Gomez, who was hitting .429 on the young season. Trebelhorn preferred to face Horn, 1–13 on the season with nine strikeouts. He had the matchup he wanted, but Nunez slipped on his third pitch and served up a hanging splitter that Horn obliterated. When the ball finally landed, it was 7–2 Baltimore and fans began streaming for the exits.[30]

The game was already a lost cause in the bottom of the ninth when second baseman Willie Randolph, picked up just before the season began, beat out a roller to the shortstop for his 2,000th career hit. Those still on hand gave the six-time All-Star a standing ovation before B.J. Surhoff bounced into a double play to end the game.

After the game, Sheffield—who'd scored the Brewers' only runs and accounted for five of their 12 total bases—ruminated on his mixed reaction. "Some fans supported me and some didn't. I kind of expected that. It bothers you to get booed in your own home park. I don't know if they want me to do good here." Sheffield thought for a moment and stepped back from another headline-grabbing harangue. "If I do good, I'll get cheered, so I guess I better do good."[31]

After hanging around the .500 mark for the first three months of the season, the Brewers bottomed out in July and were 43–60 in early August. But from there, they unexpectedly caught fire and finished the season on a 40–19 run to clinch their first winning season since 1988. Sheffield did not do much to earn cheers and was lost for the season shortly before the team's late-season success.

1992

Monday, April 6, 1992: Twins 4, Brewers 2 (52,470 attendance)
In the News: Campaigning in Wisconsin ahead of the April 7

Republican presidential primary vote, Pat Buchanan toured the factory floor of the headphone manufacturer Koss Corporation in Milwaukee.

At the Movies: *Wayne's World* at the South Shore Marcus

On the Radio: "Bohemian Rhapsody" by Queen

It was hard to pin a reason on how the 1991 Brewers, who were 43–60 heading into their August 4 game against the Rangers, having lost the first two games of their three-game set by a combined score of 29–6, suddenly became baseball's hottest team and finished out the last two months of the season with a .678 winning percentage. But whoever was due the credit for those months of fantastic baseball, it would not be Tom Trebelhorn or Harry Dalton. Two days after the season ended, Trebelhorn was fired and Dalton was reassigned to another job in the organization. "I think we're just adjusting to the times," Bud Selig told the media.[32]

Sal Bando, veteran of five seasons in Milwaukee and a special assistant to Dalton since 1981, was named Dalton's replacement. Bando had been one of a number of people in the organization who felt that Trebelhorn had been too lenient with his players. In their post-mortems on the season, the newspapers again brought up the "too-nice" tag that had dogged Trebelhorn since his teams had stopped contending. "I feel like a guy in an open casket at his own funeral," Trebelhorn said. "Everyone walks by and says what a good guy you were. But it doesn't do you any good. You're still dead."[33]

From a group of candidates that included Tony Muser, Gene Tenace, and batting coach Don Baylor, the Brewers tabbed Astros third base coach Phil Garner as their next manager. A three-time All-Star and former teammate of Bando's, Garner had a hard-nosed reputation that earned him the nickname "Scrap Iron." But he also possessed a sly sense of humor and was open-minded enough to have once posed for *Playgirl* magazine (his mustache, the magazine wrote, "sways in the breeze like the ghost of a little girl looking for her mother in the middle of an abandoned carnival"). He hadn't been among the top initial choices of Bando's, but won the position with a sterling interview. "In all honesty, I didn't expect him to be that good," said Bando announcing the hire.[34]

No player had been more key to the Brewers' late-season run in 1991 than Bill Wegman. A big right-hander from Cincinnati, Wegman had been mostly underwhelming during his five-plus years with the Brewers. But something had clicked in '91 and he went 9–1 with a 2.23 ERA in his final 12 starts. After another lost season from Ted Higuera, the Brewers were desperate to shore up the top part of their rotation. With Wegman about to become a free agent, they signed him to a four-year deal worth $9.5 million. The consensus around baseball was that the deal was one of the worst of the off-season.[35]

The Brewers' payroll now projected to more than $30 million for 1992, a three-fold increase from 1989. Meanwhile, the plans for a new stadium inched forward. The state had agreed to loan the team $35 million for construction costs, but money from the county and city for infrastructure work had yet to be secured. Polling showed that public funding for the project was opposed by a two-to-one margin. And the Brewers had still not articulated exactly how they planned to raise their $100 million-plus commitment to the project. "Listen, nobody has more deep and sentimental attachment to this building than I do," Selig told the *Journal*. "But I'm telling you, you will go bankrupt in the mid–1990s trying to play in this economic environment. That's a fact." The target for opening the new stadium was now 1995.[36]

Gary Sheffield's 1991 season ended in late July—just before the Brewers took off. All the fun and success of 1990 had been lost for him in '91. He hit .194 with no power and was nagged by injuries, paranoia, and distrust. His grandmother passed away just as camp opened, and when he was finally able to report, his aches and pains returned. In mid–March, he again trashed the team over their handling of his injuries. "I'll never be comfortable here," he told the *Sentinel*. "I wish it was different, but it's not. It's been four years and things haven't changed. All the talking in the world can't solve the problems."[37]

Two weeks later, the Brewers traded the greatest prospect the team had ever developed to San Diego for outfielder Matt Mieske, shortstop Jose Valentin, and pitcher Rickey Bones. The reaction in the clubhouse seemed to be one of mixed regret. Paul Molitor said the situation had been a failure of a "collective" responsibility among all involved. "Here was a guy who was labeled as a superstar before he hit the clubhouse," he said. "It's disappointing that it didn't work out better for him in the organization."[38]

Attendance in 1991 had fallen for the second straight year and the season total of 1.48 million was the team's lowest since 1986. Seeking to build momentum for the new stadium drive, the Brewers bumped their advertising budget by 20 percent for '92. Central to their campaign would be Robin Yount and his pursuit of 3,000 career hits. Yount needed 122 hits to become just the 17th player in baseball history to reach the milestone. They also introduced new features at County Stadium, including the "Brewers Boardwalk" on the third base concourse where fans could get their picture custom-printed on Donruss baseball cards or take swings in a batting cage with video screens that made it seem like you were standing in against Brewers pitchers. They also planned to debut "Skybox One," a model of a luxury suite that would be used to secure deposits for box space in the new stadium.[39]

The Brewers opened the season at home on April 6, hosting the reigning champion Minnesota Twins. With temperatures reaching the low 60s, there was an unusual number of calls to the Brewers ticket office for last-minute seats. However, a glitch on the team's switchboards had those calls accidentally re-routed to the phone in Phil Garner's office, which was ringing non-stop during his pregame talk with reporters. "No wonder they're giving me all of these dollars," he said. "I've got to sell tickets too. If they ask me to drag the infield, I'm in trouble."[40]

Nineteen ninety-two was an election year and, with Wisconsin's swing-state status and President George H.W. Bush's approval ratings under 40 percent nationally, Vice President Dan Quayle had been dispatched to Milwaukee to throw out the game's first pitch. After mingling with tailgaters before the game (someone threw a plastic football at him), he greeted players in the locker room. While talking with the Brewers, Quayle mentioned that Bush was throwing out the first pitch in Baltimore that same day and—evidently unaware which league the Brewers were in—told the team how wonderful it would be if the Brewers and Orioles met in the World Series. "That was the best," an anonymous Brewer told the *Journal*. "I couldn't believe it."[41]

Quayle was met with more boos than cheers and his pitch to B.J. Surhoff sailed high and outside. Wegman took the ball for the Brewers and worked around a couple of baserunners for a scoreless first and second while Scott Erickson—a 20-game winner for the champs in '91—similarly shut down the Brewers. In the third, Chuck Knoblauch slapped a single and stole second before Kirby Puckett teed up a hanging curveball from Wegman for a long home run to left.[42]

In the bottom of the fifth, still 2–0 Twins, Greg Vaughn, who'd broken out with a 27-homer season in 1991, looped a base hit to left. Yount then smoked a double down the left field line for career hit number 2,879 to put runners on second and third, the first time all afternoon the Brewers had been in scoring position. Franklin Stubbs followed with a walk to load the bases for third baseman Kevin Seitzer, who had been signed just the day before. It had been a long and troubled road to Milwaukee for Seitzer. After a sensational rookie season with Kansas City in 1987, Seitzer struggled mightily off the field. He had troubles with alcohol and contemplated suicide. He became a born-again Christian in 1988 and managed to turn his life around, but was never able meet the expectations his '87 season had set. After a poor 1991 and a worse spring in 1992, the Royals released him at the end of camp. On a 1–0 pitch, Seitzer bounced into a double play that scored Vaughn to make it 2–1 Minnesota.[43]

Erickson and Wegman traded scoreless frames until the bottom of the seventh, when Vaughn again opened with a single and Yount followed with a walk. With Stubbs batting, Erickson uncorked a wild pitch that moved both runners up. With a chance to tie the game, Stubbs—who'd batted just .150 with runners in scoring position in 1991—dropped down a surprise bunt to first baseman Gene Larkin, who was playing too deep for a play at home. Vaughn streaked home to tie the game. Seitzer followed with another chance to put the Brewers on top, but he grounded to third and Yount, running on contact, was thrown out at home.[44]

Wegman got into trouble in the top of the eighth, walking Chili Davis and giving up a double to Larkin to put runners on second and third. After he walked pinch-hitter Randy Bush to load the bases, the light-hitting Scott Leius worked a 3-1 count and then smoked two line drives just outside of the left field foul line. On Wegman's last pitch of the afternoon, Leius again hit it right on the screws, but Scott Fletcher—signed over the winter to fill in at shortstop while Bill Spiers recovered from back surgery—made a lunging stop to start a 6-4-3 double play.[45]

After Carl Willis shut down the Brewers in the top of the eighth, Garner called on Edwin Nunez, who was eager to make up for the grand slam he'd given up in the 1991 opener. Although he'd struggled in '91, an impressive camp cemented him as Garner's setup man for closer Doug Henry. Greg Gagne led off with a single and moved to second on a ground out to set things up for Chuck Knoblauch to strike again. He ripped one into center field for his fourth hit of the game and Gagne sped home. Puckett followed with a double to chase Nunez and a sac fly off Jim Austin made the score 4–2 Twins.

Facing Twins closer Rick Aguilera in the last of the ninth, Yount laced a one-out single to give Stubbs a chance to play hero. After Larkin muffed a pop-up in foul ground that would have been the second out, Stubbs hung tough, fouling off three more pitches. With the crowd on its feet, Stubbs hit one high and deep to right, but the wind kept it in the park for a warning-track out. "I hit that ball good enough to get out of here on a normal day," Stubbs said after the game. "If there's no wind, that ball's a homer."[46]

It had been a 10-pitch at-bat for Stubbs, to put Aguilera at 31 for the inning. Tired, but still crafty, he battled Kevin Seitzer for six more pitches before Seitzer continued his hard-luck day and popped out to the catcher to end the game.

"I was trying to do too much," Seitzer said later. "I got too excited and didn't give myself much of a chance. I was just careless up there."[47]

The 1992 Brewers exceeded expectations, hanging on the periphery of the AL East race until mid–September, when they won 17 of 20 to pull within two games of the Blue Jays. They finished at 92–70, four games behind the eventual world champions. It was their best finish since 1982.

1993

Monday, April 12, 1993: Angels 12, Brewers 2 (53,621 attendance)
In the News: Los Angeles is bracing as the federal case against four LAPD officers caught beating motorist Rodney King on videotape has gone to the jury. In 1992, a not-guilty verdict in the state trial against the officers led to a week of riots.
At the Movies: *The Bodyguard* at the Avalon Theater
On the Radio: "Two Princes" by Spin Doctors

Nineteen ninety-two felt like a revival for Brewers baseball. They posted the team's best record in a decade and—with a pennant race that lasted until the last weekend of the season and Robin Yount chasing his 3,000th hit (he got it on September 9 in front of 47,000 at County Stadium), attendance increased by 25 percent. Shortstop Pat Listach came out of the nowhere to win the AL Rookie of the Year award and Paul Molitor, healthy for the second straight season, batted .320 with 31 steals. Cal Eldred, a big 24-year-old from Iowa, joined the rotation in mid–July and went 11-2 with a sensational 1.79 ERA while earning ROY votes of his own.

But the season had barely ended before cold water hit the hot stove. Word leaked that the Brewers—whose $30 million payroll ranked in the middle of the league for 1992—would need to scale back by as much at 25 percent for 1993. Kevin Seitzer, Chris Bosio, Scott Fletcher, and Dan Plesac had all been significant contributors in 1992. But each filed for free agency after the end of the season with no real hopes that the Brewers would bring them back. Robin Yount also filed that fall, after declining an option year on this contract. This was little more than a favor to the club. The National League was adding two teams for 1993—the Florida Marlins and Colorado Rockies—and with Yount off the roster, the Brewers would not have to protect him from the expansion draft. The only decision Yount was going to make that winter was whether or not he wanted to play in 1993.[48]

Paul Molitor also filed for free agency that fall. Molitor wanted very much to remain in Milwaukee, and GM Sal Bando said publicly that keeping Molitor was his top goal of the off-season. But for more than a month after Molitor filed, the team had almost no contact with him. In late November, Bando told the *Journal* that the team was going to adjust Molitor's value based as his role as a designated hitter—that is, as someone less valuable than a full-time position player. A week later, the team made its first official offer to Molitor: a one-year deal with a pay cut.[49]

Mostly absent from the process was Bud Selig. He had been appointed baseball's acting commissioner in 1992 and was devoting the bulk of his time to that role as well as the drive for a new stadium. Once targeted for '93, the opening date for a new park was now projected for 1996. But things had still been moving forward. The state, county, and city had committed nearly $70 million in infrastructure money and, during the 1992 season, the Brewers unveiled renderings of an Ebbets Field–style stadium with a brick façade that would seat 48,000 for baseball and 60,000 for football. But the Brewers' part of the financing package had yet to be secured.[50]

Selig jumped into the Molitor talks at the last moment, but he was still unable to put together any kind of offer that Molitor considered reasonable. On December 7, Molitor signed with the Toronto Blue Jays for $13 million over three years. In what was easily the highest-profile Milwaukee baseball departure since the Braves left for Atlanta, the hometown sentiment was decidedly against the Brewers. "If all the fans are upset," Bando told a reporter, "where were they the last 15 years when we had him?"[51]

Back in Arizona, Robin Yount was still undecided. "[Retirement] was a thought," he'd say later. "That was a pretty good season and it would be nice to end your career on an up note." He'd also later admit that the loss of Molitor nudged him a bit closer to walking away. But with a standing offer of $3.5 million and a team option for 1994, he couldn't say no. Although any mention of Yount's personal finances were always dismissed, often angrily, by his brother and agent, Larry, the *Sentinel* wrote that with his money still tied up in various real estate deals, the two-time MVP needed the cash.[52]

Heading into spring training, little was expected from baseball's surprise team of just a year earlier. Having lost four regular position players, a top starting pitcher, and their leader in bullpen innings pitched, the Brewers added low-rent veterans like Tom Brunansky, Bill Doran, and Dickie Thon. And bad money deals still populated their books. They paid Franklin Stubbs $1.4 million to buy out the last year of his dreadful contract. Ron Robinson, released after a handful of awful spring innings, was owed $1.2 million. And Ted Higuera, who missed all of 1992 and had only pitched in seven games since 1990, had nearly $7 million left on his pact. He entered camp competing for the fifth spot in the rotation, until he was shut down with a shoulder strain.[53]

The team slogan for 1993 was "Rounding second and headed for first." It was a play on their second-place finish in 1992. It made it sound as though they were running the bases backward.[54]

The Brewers opened the season with a five-game West Coast trip, with the home opener set for April 12 against the Angels. As the Brewers broke camp and headed west, something was going terribly wrong back home. Almost overnight, thousands of city residents were experiencing vomiting, cramps, and diarrhea and emergency rooms were overwhelmed with patients. The source of the outbreak was quickly traced to the city's water supply and on April 7—as the Brewers beat the Angels 3–2—the city was ordered to boil all tap water before it was used. By the time the Brewers moved on to Oakland, a parasite known as cryptosporidium had been detected in the city's water. The boil order was still in effect when the Brewers returned home, sitting on a 2–3 record, for the opener.⁵⁵

The U.S. Army Reserves set up in the parking lots before the Opening Day tilt with the Angels, on hand to pass out 800 gallons of water to tailgaters. Given the obvious beverage of choice for pregame revelry, there were few takers for the clean water, although the California Angels took 40 gallons for use in the locker room and dugout.⁵⁶

With the loss of Molitor, left fielder Darryl Hamilton was plugged into the lead-off spot. Yount, with his 3,000th hit secured now and a virtual lock for the Hall of Fame, played first base. Jim Gantner, who was still recovering from off-season rotator cuff surgery, was in uniform, but not officially a member of the team or coaching staff. He hit grounders during batting practice, but declined to be a part of pregame introductions. "No," he said. "They know me."⁵⁷

A bug had gone around the Brewers clubhouse—unrelated to the water—that kept John Jaha out of the lineup. With Yount covering for him at first, Alex Diaz, a speedy Brooklyn native, got the start in center. Reigning Rookie of the Year Listach was held out with a strained groin and Greg Vaughn was relegated to designating hitting with a pair of sore hamstrings. Cal Eldred, coming off a brilliant eight-inning, three-hitter against the Angels six days earlier, was given the start.⁵⁸

Eldred hardly had time to settle in before California

A trio of ticket stubs from the author's 28 consecutive home openers (author's collection).

struck. With two outs in the first, he clipped J.T. Snow with a pitch and Chili Davis followed by working a full count before crushing a two-run homer to right field. But the Brewers came back quickly. Hamilton, batting well over .400 on the young season, led off with a hit and Yount added another a batter later. With men at the corners, Vaughn laced a run-scoring single, followed by a Tom Brunansky walk and a Dickie Thon base hit to even the score. Angels starter Chuck Finley was rattled and, with the bases loaded, he walked B.J. Surhoff on four straight to give the Brewers a 3–2 lead.

In the bottom of the second, Hamilton ripped another base hit, stole second, and was brought around to score on a Yount single to make it 4–2. But Eldred found his own troubles in the top of the third. Feeling good despite the mid-40s temperatures, Eldred opened the inning by allowing four straight singles to tie the score at 4–4 and then walked Tim Salmon to put California on top. With the advantage, Finely settled in and got the Brewers in order in the bottom half, but the Angels got to Eldred again in the fourth. A lead-off double by Gary Disarcina was followed up with a Chad Curtis single that made it 6–4 Angels and chased Eldred. It was easily the worst outing of the young phenom's career.

Graeme Lloyd, who had become the first native Australian pitcher in MLB history the day prior when he debuted against Oakland, came on and traded zeroes with Finley for two innings. In the bottom of the sixth, Joe Kmak, who'd opened the season as the primary catcher with Dave Nilsson on the DL, led off with a single followed by a Hamilton walk. Garner, trying to get something going, then pinch hit Listach for Spiers, hoping the aching youngster could find a gap. Listach flew out, but it moved Kmak to third and the rookie scored two pitches later when Yount grounded out.[59]

In the seventh and eighth innings, the Brewers threatened against reliever Julio Valera, each time putting two runners on with one out. But each inning ended with a room service double play grounder—one by Diaz and the other by Yount. The Brewers were knocking on the door, getting good licks on an Angels bullpen that was one of the weaker in the American League. To hold the line in the top of the ninth, Garner handed the ball to Doug Henry, a righthander who'd gotten Rookie of the Year votes in '91 and saved 29 games in '92. But he'd gotten off to a rough start in '93, allowing runs in each of his early outings. He got his first batter, but walked Curtis and allowed a run-scoring hit to Snow. He then fanned Chili Davis, but walked Salmon to set up a two-run single by catcher Greg Meyers. Now trailing 9–5, he walked Gonzales and served up a first-pitch pumpkin to spindly second baseman Damion Easley, who hit a laser-beam three-run homer to left. As three Angels trotted home, those in attendance who hadn't already left for the exits booed loudly. After the game, Henry would call it his worst outing since A ball. Valera set down the Brewers in the ninth to seal a 12–5 thrashing. It was the Brewers' sixth straight Opening Day loss. They had won just two openers since 1981.[60]

As Paul Molitor helped the Blue Jays to their second straight World Series win, the 1993 Brewers sank to the bottom of the AL East. In dead last place from June 27 on, they finished at 69–93. The city's boil order was lifted on April 14, but not before 400,000 more people were sickened. Sixty-nine people died from the contagion, nearly all of them AIDS patients.

1994

Tuesday, April 5, 1994: Brewers 11, Athletics 7 (52,012 attendance)
In the News: Domino's Pizza has settled in a lawsuit brought by a woman who sustained spinal and head injuries after she was broadsided by one of the chain's delivery drivers. The incident caused the company to drop their promise of delivery in 30 minutes or the pizza is free.
At the Movies: *What's Eating Gilbert Grape* at the Oriental Theater
On the Radio: "Whatta Man" by Salt-N-Pepa featuring En Vogue

It was not difficult to find the parallels between the story of the 1993 Brewers and that year's off-the-field stadium drama. There were frustrations and money troubles, and the only movement seemed to be leaping steps backward. After years of insisting the new stadium would be privately funded, the team broached the possibility of needing public assistance in May as the already committed share of public financing for infrastructure costs inched upward. Meanwhile, city politicians saw this as an opening to again advocate for a downtown stadium, something Bud Selig was still very much opposed to.[61]

Shortly after the season, with the team again expected to cut the payroll, the Brewers announced a salary freeze among non-uniform employees. In announcing the move, Selig told his employees that it was going to be an uphill battle to keep the team in Milwaukee and claimed $8 million in losses for 1993. Losses in the millions had become an annual claim for the team, dating back to the collusion settlement.[62]

Selig had more than just a local mess to deal with. In a *Sporting News* article titled "An Awful Offseason," it was reported that—despite Selig's insistences he did not want the job—there was still no clear plan to find a permanent commissioner. Both league presidents wanted to quit. A half dozen teams were rumored to be for sale with nearly as many struggling to finance new stadiums. With CBS having no interest in renewing their broadcast deal with baseball, the league had formed the Baseball Network, a collective broadcast deal that would keep the game on TV but generate far less revenue. And there was no movement to be found in negotiations with the players over the now-expired collective bargaining agreement.[63]

Back in Arizona, Robin Yount was at home, undecided if he would return for a 21st season. Nineteen ninety-three had been taxing for Yount. He'd played in just 127 games and posted perhaps the worst statistics of his career. While some rumors had the Blue Jays interested in bringing him north to join Molitor, Yount insisted he would either play for the Brewers or retire. The team announced that a deal for 1994 with Yount had been agreed upon, pending Yount's decision to return. "Everything's in place," Yount said in a rare off-season statement to the press. "It's just a matter of me making up my mind."[64]

As Yount pondered, the team held off on other transactions. The $3 million-plus he would get was essentially their entire off-season budget. But the team found other ways to make news. In November, they unveiled a plan to sell advertising space on the outfield wall at County Stadium, the most intrusive of a planned boost of in-stadium advertising that was hoped to generate as much as $3 million annually. "The old-time charm of County Stadium will be dramatically enhanced with this new advertising," said a team spokesperson. The Brewers would be the only team in Major League Baseball with pole-to-pole outfield wall advertising. Critics were quick to point out the decidedly bush league aesthetic the new ads would bring to the stadium.[65]

But it would be more than just the outfield fences that would have a new look in 1994. Near the end of the 1993 season, the Brewers announced that the long-familiar "ball and glove" logo and accompanying uniform set would be retired and replaced with a brand-new look for what they were promoting as their "25th anniversary" season (although 1994 would actually be their 25th season, not their 25th anniversary). The new look debuted in January, with the bright blue and yellow color scheme replaced with deep navy, metallic gold, and hunter green. The friendly curves of the script wordmark and clever ball-and-glove combo morphed into a Germanic font with hard angles and an interlocking M and B cap logo. A crossed-bats 25th anniversary sleeve patch was also included in the rebrand, as well the franchise's first-ever alternate jersey top. "These colors are extremely hot right now," one team official gushed.[66]

With spring training just a few weeks away, Robin Yount finally made up his mind. On February 10, sitting at a small table in the dingy County Stadium press room beside his wife, Michelle, Bud Selig, and Sal Bando, Yount announced his retirement. "There's not going to be any emotional speeches or anything," he said. "I think I'm going to wait to get home to do that." He still wanted to prove that he could play at a top level and atone for his poor 1993 season, but he no longer had the drive to be an everyday player. He said that his decision had been based partially on conversations he'd had with Michael Jordan, an off-season golf partner who had retired from the NBA the year before. A reporter asked if Jordan's recent entry into professional baseball changed his mind in any way. "I don't know," Yount answered. "In a week or so I might go to the Bucks and see if I can get a tryout."[67]

It took five weeks to get County Stadium ready for the season opener on April 5 against the Athletics. Thousands of gallons of paint were needed to repaint the entire mezzanine level and every instance of the old logo and team colors needed to be covered over. A crew of five plumbers was needed to fix the various leaks in the 42-year-old system of drains and pipes and 3,000 lower box seats were to be replaced with padded models to create the stadium's new Diamond Box section—where fans would be able to get food delivered to their seats as an effort to cater to a more "upscale" portion of the fan base.[68]

Crews got to work at 5 a.m. on game day to remove the inch and a half of snow that fallen overnight and the tailgaters got started a few hours later. The only line longer than that for the porta-potties was the line at the WKLH radio tent, where Morganna the Kissing Bandit was signing photos

Featuring the team's brand-new logo, the seats nearest to the field behind home plate were fitted with padding and rebranded in 1994 as the Diamond Box section in an effort to maximize revenues at the old ballpark (barrelmansammy).

for $5 each. The 30-degree weather was a paired with a sharp wind that put the wind chill near zero. A reporter touring the parking lots found that the idea of a retractable roof for the new stadium—the latest alteration to the plan now being floated by the Brewers—was a welcome one. "As long as we don't have to pay for it," one fan noted.[69]

Inside the stadium, Phil Garner got to debut the new Harley-Davidson bullpen motorcycle—a sidecar model that was meant to bring pitchers from the bullpen to the pitcher's mound. Garner gave reliever Jesse Orosco a ride around the warning track before dropping him off and peeling out. In the locker room, Greg Vaughn handed out custom-printed t-shirts that read, "Don't Believe the Hype: Giant Killers."[70]

After Dave Bristol, who'd managed the Brewers for their inaugural season in 1970, threw out the first pitch, the A's set to work on Cal Eldred, making it look like another Opening Day dud for the Brewers. Rickey Henderson led off with a double, moved up on a groundball, and scored on a sac fly to put the Brewers in a quick hole. Mark McGwire followed with a double and Eldred, unable to get a decent grip on the ball, walked two to load the bases for Terry Steinbach. Eldred worked him full, but Steinbach battled, fouling off two before crushing Eldred's 35th pitch of the inning into the bleachers. It was 5–0 and the home fans were booing before the Brewers even had a chance at bat.[71]

The Brewers got one back in their half on a Greg Vaughn sac fly, but Eldred again worked into trouble in the second. Two walks and a Stan Javier single loaded the bases for Ruben Sierra. Hearing more boos, Eldred got Sierra to bounce to John Jaha, who stepped on first and fired home to Nilsson, who applied the tag to a sliding Mike Bordick to complete a momentum-shifting double play.

As Eldred settled in, the Brewers kept chipping away. They got a run in the second on a Darryl Hamilton sac fly and then loaded the bases against a laboring Bobby Witt in the third. After Bill Spiers worked a five-pitch walk to make it 5–3 Oakland, Alex Diaz ripped one up the middle that glanced off second baseman Brent Gates' glove and dribbled into center field for a two-run double to tie it 5–5.[72]

Eldred finished five innings before giving way to Mark Kiefer, who had locked himself in the bullpen bathroom to warm up before coming in. Troy Neel, Oakland's rookie DH, greeted Kiefer with a high fly that caught the wind and dropped just over the fence for a tie-breaking homer. Kiefer bent but didn't break and worked around a walk to end the inning.[73]

In the bottom of the sixth, Vaughn laced a two-out single off Steve Ontiveros and Jaha followed with a hit-by-pitch. With the crowd getting into things, Nilsson roped a single to right that Sierra bobbled, allowing

Vaughn and Jaha to score and put the Brewers on top, 7–6. Then Tony LaRussa walked to the mound and called to the pen for Ed Nunez.[74]

The Brewers had been itching to face Nunez. Not because, as a Brewer in 1991 and 1992, he'd turned in two wretched Opening Day outings, but because of a bench-clearing brawl between the A's and Brewers in August of '93, where Nunez sucker-punched B.J. Surhoff, who was being restrained at the time, sending the Brewers catcher to the hospital for stitches. As the agitated home crowd let Nunez hear it, Jody Reed—an off-season pickup—smoked a 3–1 pitch into the left field corner for a run-scoring double. Bill Spiers followed with a single that scored Reed. And Alex Diaz turned the dagger with a triple that made it 10–6. The old ballpark shook with noise.[75]

After trading runs with Oakland on a couple of sac flies, Mike Fetters set down the A's in the ninth, getting Gates to roll to Reed who relayed to Seitzer at first to close out the Brewers' first Opening Day win since 1987. "That's the way we're going to play this year," said Nilsson, who collected four hits on the afternoon, after the game. "We're not going to give up."[76]

Grit and hustle kept the 1994 Brewers above .500 for a month, but a franchise record 14-game losing streak in May dropped the team into last place in the brand-new AL Central Division. That's where they remained on August 11, when the players' strike ended the season.

1995

Wednesday, April 26, 1995: Brewers 12, White Sox 3 (31,426 attendance)

In the News: Milwaukee retailers cannot keep Michael Jordan #45 jerseys in stock. Jordan's new Bulls gear has been selling out daily since his return to the NBA.

At the Movies: *Friday* (featuring a bonus presentation of Dr. Dre's new video, "Keep Their Heads Ringin'") at the Grand Cinemas

On the Radio: "Big Poppa/Warning" by Notorious B.I.G.

Unwilling to cede to ownership's demands of a salary cap and with the owners withholding nearly $8 million in payments in the players' pension fund, the players walked off the job on August 12, 1994. A month later, the remainder of the season—along with the playoffs and World Series—was officially canceled. As the stalemate dragged on, the hot stove went cold and the only baseball talk of the winter was the vitriol hurled at both sides in the dispute. Whatever enthusiasm for the new stadium had existed before the work stoppage soured as the anticipated cost of the project, which now included a retractable roof, continued to balloon. In late October, the Packers announced that they would not return to Milwaukee for home games in 1995. The Brewers, having dropped their efforts to fund the stadium privately, were now pressing for a statewide lottery to raise the nearly $200 million needed to build the facility. After the state legislature approved the issue, it was slated to go the voters in April 1995. Polls showed it could be a tough sell, especially if the strike dragged on.[77]

In December, the owners unilaterally implemented a salary cap and a form of restricted free agency for players with four to five years of service time. The owners said that if the players maintained their strike, they would move ahead with a plan to use replacement players and whatever union players would cross the line. Kevin Seitzer, the Brewers' team representative for the union, expressed frustration. "The players did everything we could possibly do except sell the farm, and they've thrown it back in our faces," he said. "Now they'll go through with this replacement junk."[78]

As the owners began to plan for spring training with replacement rosters, Brewers manager Phil Garner, who'd been active in the union as a player, felt pressure—along with the rest of the league's managers and coaches—not to report to spring training in an act of solidarity. He expressed sympathy for the players' stance, but packed for Arizona nonetheless. "I'd probably get fired," he said. "I'm contractually bound to be there."[79]

County Stadium sits empty during the 1994 players' strike. The dark clouds forming over the old ballpark were an apt metaphor for the future of baseball in the city (Bob Busser).

In January, the Brewers held open tryouts in California, Arizona, and Texas. Ads appeared in local newspapers asking for players to report with their own gear, ready to run drills. Pro experience was preferred, but not required. From these masses, the Brewers tabbed 160 players to report to spring training and, after a few weeks of often brutal intersquad action, a group of 40 graduated to the spring roster and began to play exhibition games as the Brewers.[80]

Only a handful of these players had any Major League experience. Catcher Robby Wine, who'd seen action in 20 games and was most recently the Brewers bullpen catcher, was the most seasoned veteran of the bunch. Bob Kappesser left his job as an elevator repairman to join the team. Tim Dell, selected for the starting rotation, managed a restaurant in Canada. Ron Rantz, another pitcher, hadn't played competitive baseball since college. Bobby Cuff, a reliever, hadn't played since 1987. Nearly a third of the roster hadn't played pro ball of any kind in 1994.

After playing to a .500 record in Arizona, the Brewers finalized their 32-man roster for the regular season (25 active players plus a seven-man taxi squad) and prepared for the strangest of Opening Days on April 4 in California. But just two days before the Mets and Marlins were set to open the replacement season, federal appeals judge Sonia Sotomayor issued an injunction against the owners and ordered both sides to be bound to the rules of the expired labor contract.

The strike was officially over, but the ill feelings it fostered were far from gone. Just as the players were getting back to work—with the Brewers now set to open the season at home against the White Sox on April 26—the sports lottery measure was crushed at polls, with 64 percent of voters rejecting the plan. Governor Tommy Thompson, perhaps the state's loudest backer for a publicly-funded stadium plan, vowed to fight on. "We are going to build a stadium," he said after the loss. "I don't know how yet."[81]

Meanwhile, the union Brewers sped through a brief spring training and headed north to face an uncertain reception from the home fans. The roster was mostly leftovers from the mediocre '94 club, with a few prospects and fringe additions. With Ted Higuera, Jaime Navarro, Jesse Orosco, and Brian Harper off the books, the payroll for 1995 was projected at about $16 million. That was about half of what it had been in 1992 and the second-lowest in all of baseball.[82]

Even with mid–50s temperatures in the forecast, the team expected a crowd of only about 30,000 for the opener. Even with the general sense of anger surrounding the game, not to mention the overcast skies and light rains that hung in the sky that afternoon, there were still plenty of Brewers fans glad to have baseball back. A few local restaurants even chartered busses to ferry fans to and from the stadium. WTMJ saw steady action at their "World's Largest Tailgate" tent, where they were again giving away 6,200 free brats. And as proof that the weird energy of the home opener had not been entirely lost, a pair of fans in full KISS shock rock costuming roamed the lots before the game.[83]

Well aware of the potential for an ugly initial reaction from the fans, the Brewers took efforts to keep the mood up. Nearly every player signed autographs before the game. The honor of the ceremonial first pitch was given to 60 Little Leaguers, with every member of the Brewers and White Sox catching. Robin Yount was even brought back, in uniform, as an honorary member of the coaching staff and was the first to be greeted by the crowd during pregame introductions, after which every member of the Brewers tossed their caps into the crowd.[84]

But the boo-birds had their say. A group of fans unfurled a 30-foot banner reading "DI$APPOINTED" in the lower grandstand and Rickey Bones—coming off an All-Star season in 1994—heard boos after walking two and allowing a run in the first. But Sox starter Alex Fernandez had even more trouble knocking off the rust and allowed singles to Pat Listach and Seitzer before walking Derrick May—an off-season pickup and son of former Brewer Davey May. John Jaha followed. Not trying to do too much, he was just looking to make contact when Fernandez hung a 0–2 slider that Jaha swatted into the bullpen for a grand slam. As he rounded the bases, the Milwaukee faithful roared like old times.[85]

In the second, Jose Valentin, who'd gotten a handful of Rookie of the Year votes in 1994, led off with a walk, and Pat Listach, who'd been shifted to second base to make room for Valentin, saw a sacrifice bunt attempt turn into a two-base run-scoring play when Fernandez threw wildly to first. After Sox right fielder Mike Devereaux dropped a Darryl Hamilton fly ball on the warning track and Seitzer drew a walk, slugger Vaughn came up with a chance to break the game wide open. He rolled into a double play, but Listach was able to score to make it 6–1 Brewers. An inning later, Listach got to Fernandez again with men on base, when he rolled one through past the shortstop for a two-run single. Fernandez left with his team in an 8–1 hole.[86]

The rout was on and, back in the bleachers, Sox fans and Brewers backers kept up with the rowdy tradition of picking fights and throwing beers. Devereaux, participating in his first Brewers-Sox game, was taken with the spectacle. "They were trying to throw beer on me," he said after the game. "It was crazy out there. I guess it's a Milwaukee-Chicago thing."[87]

The Brewers scored twice more in the fifth after the Sox reliever walked a pair—two of 14 overall bases on balls on the afternoon—and

Listach and Hamilton came through with back-to-back run-scoring singles. An inning later, Turner Ward belted a two-run homer to make it 12–2. The only remaining suspense was over who would win the first-ever on-field Opening Day Sausage Race (it was the Polish by a nose).[88]

The Sox managed one more run before Mark Kiefer set them down in order in the ninth to end it. It was their second straight Opening Day win, the team's first lid-lifter winning streak since 1978–1980. "We're a better team than people think," said Garner after the game. "We'll surprise a lot of people."[89]

For the first four months of the abbreviated season, Garner was absolutely right. Hanging right around .500 most of the year, the Brewers jumped into the playoff race with a late-August hot streak. On August 27, they were just a half game out of the AL Wild Card spot—a creation of the new three-division format. But a putrid 6–21 September sealed their fate. Opening Day was one of just two games all season in which the Brewers drew a crowd of more than 30,000.

Presented by: Waukesha Police Department
Waukesha Sports Cards and
Delzer Lithograph Company

John Jaha recorded just three hits in 20 tries in home openers, but his first-inning grand slam during the 1995 lid-lifter did much to welcome back diehard fans still angry about the players' strike.

1996

Tuesday, April 9, 1996: Brewers 10, Athletics 4 (42,090 attendance)

In the News: Names of several of the Unabomber's victims were found among the paperwork in the remote Montana cabin of Theodore Kaczynski. Police now believe they have enough evidence to charge the former math professor in the crimes.

At the Movies: *Mr. Holland's Opus* at Loomis Road Theater

On the Radio: "Ironic" by Alanis Morissette

After the crushing defeat of the lottery plan, the Brewers had staked all of their new stadium hopes on a regional sales tax plan that would fund the $250 million publicly-financed part of the $340 million project. As the Brewers dropped 10 of their last 12 games of the 1995 campaign, the bill appeared to have the necessary support in the state legislature. But just days after the season ended, the bill hit a brick wall in the state senate. Governor Tommy Thompson said that if the bill did not pass, the Brewers would not be playing in Milwaukee in 1996. Finally, in the early morning hours of October 7—just 10 days before the Brewers' lease at County Stadium was set to expire—a marathon session of voting and backroom pleading pushed the stadium bill through by a single vote.[90]

In the midst of the stadium drama, the Brewers announced that their payroll—27th in the 28-team league in 1995—would not be increased. Outfielder B.J. Surhoff, who had finally fulfilled his potential in '95 with a .320 batting average and 13 homers, was a free agent and expected to sign elsewhere, as was Darryl Hamilton, who'd performed ably as Robin Yount's replacement in center field, and third baseman Kevin Seitzer, Milwaukee's lone 1995 All-Star.[91]

But after the stadium financing package was finalized, the Brewers loosened their purse strings for the first time in almost five years. They made a bid for Paul Molitor, a free agent again after playing out his deal with the Blue Jays. They managed to put together a "creative" package to retain Seitzer and made serious attempts at signing pitchers Bobby Witt, Kevin Tapani, and Tom Gordon.[92]

It would have been hard to imagine a more soothing development for a haggard Brewers fanbase than a reunion with Molitor. A two-year pact would have him in Brewers blue for his 3,000th hit and leave him primed to move into the front office or a coaching role after his retirement. Well aware his absence in the 1993 contract negotiations had miffed Molitor, team president Bud Selig played an active role in these talks, even hosting the DH in Milwaukee and showing him models of the new, convertible-roof stadium. The Brewers' offer to Molitor was for $4 million over two years, with another $1 million due for post-career work for the team.[93]

But in the end, Molitor's heart led him back home to Minnesota, where he signed a slightly smaller deal with the Twins. "I thought about trying to recreate something after you've been removed from it," he said of a possible return to Milwaukee, "and I wasn't sure how it was going to be."[94]

Losing out on Molitor was a blow for obvious reasons, but it also highlighted the grim reality that the Brewers, with a bit of money to spend for the first time in years, were having a hard time finding anyone to take it. Hamilton, after signing with the Texas Rangers, unloaded on the team and revealed that he'd recently made a settlement with the club after filing a grievance with the players union accusing the team of purposely keeping him out of the lineup late in 1995 to prevent him from accruing enough playing to time to activate an incentive clause in his contract. "Milwaukee has such a bad rep now with free agents. Guys who left have bad things to say," he said. "Look at Bobby Witt. He was offered more money to go there, but stayed with Texas."[95]

But in late January, Sal Bando and company finally landed a big money player. Ben McDonald had been one of the most hyped pitching prospects of all-time when he debuted in the Orioles starting rotation in 1990. Just 22 years old, he was an Olympic gold medalist with a $2 million contract and a galaxy's worth of expectations. But he had been slow to mature as a pitcher and, despite ranking among the AL's better pitchers between 1993 and 1995, was non-tendered by Baltimore in late December. He was a late entry into the free agent market, and the Brewers went after him hard. After a week of rumors and speculation, the team announced him as the recipient of the biggest free agent contract in franchise history: $6 million guaranteed for two years with incentives that would push it as rich as $13 million over three.[96]

McDonald was easily the highest-profile addition to the Brewers since Dave Parker. And like Parker, he brought some much-needed color to the team. Six-foot-seven with hands so large he could hold seven baseballs in each, McDonald hunted alligators as a hobby in his youth. He didn't use weapons, however; he waded into Louisiana swamps and grabbed them around the neck. By the time the Orioles made him give up gator-wrestling, he estimated he'd caught 100 in his lifetime. He caught one fishing shortly after being drafted and smuggled it into a teammate's bathtub as a prank. With the news of gator-hunting, word spread in Milwaukee that he ate a can of mustard sardines for good luck before every start. He later corrected the narrative, saying that he'd actually given up the habit as a minor leaguer when his roommate complained about the smell.[97]

Despite their brief playoff push in '95 and the addition of a top-of-the-line starter, the Brewers were once again a near-universal pick for last place in the AL Central. And then, in February, trouble once again emerged on the stadium front. Word leaked the Brewers had yet been unable to secure their part of the funding package. Work on the project was stopped and the stadium board voted to suspend collection of the regional sales tax unless the Brewers came up with their share. The stadium's groundbreaking, scheduled for March 18, was called off. Despite the most expansive marketing push in franchise history, ticket sales slowed and—less than two weeks out—only 35,000 seats had been sold for home opener. After a 2–4 road trip to open the season, the Brewers arrived back in Milwaukee to see their pre-opener workout at the stadium canceled due to snow. And the team had a week to come up with $90 million or risk tanking the entire stadium deal.[98]

As the parking lots began to slowly fill on April 9, the skies were gray and temperatures hovered in the mid–40s. It was a bland day and the mood among the tailgaters was predictably anxious. Bud Selig walked through the parking lots before the game and received well wishes, hugs, and lots of encouragement as he explained the situation over and over again. He had met with Governor Thompson the day before and came from the meeting optimistic enough to cancel a meeting of baseball's executive council that had been scheduled for the 11th. It was widely expected that at that meeting the council would endorse a possible relocation of the franchise.[99]

After the Packers' Robert Brooks threw out the ceremonial first ball (a football), Ben McDonald took the hill against the Oakland Athletics. McDonald, who'd thrown six scoreless innings in the season opener at California, was sharp from the start. He struck out the side in the first, working around a couple of Oakland singles on defensive miscues by the Brewers that drew early boos from the home crowd. He needed just 10 pitches to set down the A's in the second before outfielder Turner Ward, who was having trouble seeing due to issues with his contact lenses, saw

In one of many attempts to boost revenues, the Brewers added pole-to-pole outfield wall advertising for the 1994 opener. It was derided as "bush league" at the time, but nearly every other team would eventually follow suit (barrelmansammy).

enough of a Todd Van Poppel offering to punch a two-run homer to center that just avoided the glove of Ernie Young. As the ball rattled around in the bleachers, the 42,000-plus on hand came to life.[100]

After another clean inning from McDonald, Fernando Vina, the undersized but gutsy second baseman who'd played his way into the lead-off spot, singled, and a batter later, Kevin Seitzer rocketed a homer to left-center field to make it 4–0. In the bottom of the fourth, it was Vina again. Batting with two on and two out, Vina scorched a base hit to left to score two and scampered into second on the throw home. After Tony LaRussa brought in righty Steve Montgomery to spell Van Poppel, shortstop Jose Valentin joined the fun with a long homer down the right field line. It was 8–0 Brewers and the sun—literally—finally began to shine.[101]

Oakland got on the board in the fifth with an RBI single by Young, but the Brewers took it right back in the bottom half on a Jeff Cirillo RBI double. After a 1-2-3 sixth, McDonald left to a rousing ovation and the good times kept on rolling. A couple of fans drew cheers for continuing the Opening Day tradition of running onto the field and a few of the heartier men in the crowd doffed their shirts and danced in a way that made it clear they felt none of that afternoon's cold air. The Athletics, who had no answers for McDonald, fared the same against Cris Carpenter and the lanky Australian Graeme Lloyd—who'd seen snow in person for the first time in his life the day before—as each set down the A's in order.[102]

Ward's eyesight cost the Brewers a meaningless run in the ninth when he misplayed a Jason Giambi pop-up that was followed by a two-run homer by Geronimo Berroa off closer Mike Fetters. Reserve catcher George Williams followed up with a solo shot, but Fetters worked through to secure the 10–4 win and give the Brewers at least one last chance to bask in the glow of a (nearly) full house.[103]

"I don't mind telling you," Selig said after the game, "with everything that's gone on, when Turner Ward hit that home run, I almost started to cry." He went on about all of the positivity he'd witnessed that afternoon, contrasting it to the acrimony of the political process and the unnamed enemies of his agenda. "When he hit that home run, people were so excited that all of the sudden all that other crap—pardon my language—but all that other crap doesn't really seem important."[104]

The 1996 Brewers were a surprise offensive power, setting a franchise record for runs scored that still stands. Their 80–82 record was their best output since 1992. In late June, after an effort by the city to move the project to a downtown location, the Brewers secured enough low-interest loans to meet their financial obligations and restart the stadium project.

1997

Monday, April 7, 1997: Brewers 5, Rangers 3 (42,893 attendance)
In the News: Microsoft has purchased WebTV for nearly half a billion dollars. The service, which allowed users to surf the Internet from their home television sets, had launched just seven months ago.
At the Movies: *Private Parts* at Marcus Westown Cinemas
On the Radio: "Wannabe" by the Spice Girls

The 1996 Brewers should have provided a feel-good summer for Milwaukee. They bashed their way to a franchise record in runs scored and, behind the steady lead of Ben McDonald, surprised everyone with an 80–82 record—their best since 1992. But the drawn-out drama over the funding of Miller Park hung a cloud over everything. Even after a deal was finally reached in late June—officially re-starting the stalled project—the club was forced to jettison talent to save money. Greg Vaughn, who'd established himself among the AL's most feared sluggers with 31 homers and 95 RBI over the first four months of the season, was sent to San Diego at the end of July. He'd asked the Brewers for a three-year extension worth $18 million, an amount that GM Sal Bando insisted was beyond the team's capabilities. A few weeks later, former mainstays Pat Listach, Graeme Lloyd, and Rickey Bones were sent to the Yankees and a week later they shipped third baseman Kevin Seitzer, batting .316, to Cleveland. He was due to make more than $1.2 million in 1997. It was the first mid-season fire sale of pricey talent in team history.

That fall, just after ground was finally broken for Miller Park, Bando announced that the Brewers' roster was unlikely to change much before Opening Day. "We made most of our moves during the season," Bando said. "We like the team we have."[105]

Bando had insisted that his in-season moves were not an indicator of giving up on 1996 or 1997. Instead of adding prospects, the Brewers had added young players with big league experience. For Vaughn, they got a package headlined by former first-round draft choice Marc Newfield, who took over right field for the Brewers and batted .307 over the season's final months. For Lloyd and company, they'd received Wisconsin native Bob Wickman, a relief pitcher with a nasty sinker. And for Seitzer, they got a power-hitting outfielder named Jeromy Burnitz, who had been lost in Cleveland's historically-deep mid–90s outfield. While the Brewers might have been happy with what they had, the national media was—once again—unimpressed. They were universally regarded as one of the AL's weakest clubs.

While the Brewers idled, the players and owners signed a new four-year labor contract, their first active agreement in the two-plus years since the strike. The deal implemented both revenue-sharing and a luxury tax on the league's highest payrolls and also allowed for interleague play. Bud Selig, now four years into his term as acting commissioner, had vowed to step aside and return full-time to running the Brewers as soon as the deal was completed. But, closing in on the 1997 season, he made no moves to extract himself from the position. The game, he insisted, still needed him.[106]

But even with labor peace, a team with potential, and a hole in the center field parking lots that would soon give rise to Miller Park, fans remained wary of their Brewers. As the team opened the season by splitting a four-game opening road swing, tickets sales were up about 18 percent over 1996, but still lagged badly behind pre-strike levels. The home opener, set for April 7 against the Rangers, had about 15,000 unsold seats. It was expected that the lid-lifter, for a decade and a half a guaranteed sell-out, would again draw about 40,000. "We still feel we're in the initial stages of a healing process," said Bob Voight, team VP for ticket sales. "We're doing everything we can to embrace our fans." That included $1 tickets and free parking for the week of games following the opener.[107]

As dawn broke on Opening Day, 1997, it had never been clearer why the team had pressed so hard for Miller Park's retractable roof. The 30-degree temperatures were cut to sub-zero with the wind chill, and the huge gusts of frigid air wrought havoc on anyone trying to set up a tent or start a grill. The wind even tore a huge piece of insulation off the County Stadium roof and sent it soaring into the air before crashing down in a thankfully-unoccupied part of the parking lot.[108]

As the fans slowly streamed into the stadium, each was gifted a magnetic schedule—an Opening Day give-away staple since 1992—and a free baseball commemorating the Brewers' 1987 opener and the 12-game winning streak that it started. The baseballs were part of a league-wide promotion sponsored by True Value Hardware. The first big cheer of the afternoon was for Aaron Taylor, starting left guard for the world champion Green Bay Packers, who threw out the game's first pitch. But after Taylor had taken his bows and the pregame introductions had ended, a few stray baseballs were tossed from the crowd onto the field. A few more flew as the Brewers took the field and Cal Eldred—back after missing the entire second half of the 1996 season with an elbow injury—took his warm-up throws. Action on the field was halted while the grounds crew gathered up the balls and dropped them into five-gallon buckets.[109]

Eldred opened, showing some rust. Mark McLemore led off with a wind-aided double and moved to third on a wild pitch. He would score on a groundout, but Eldred managed to work around a pair of walks with no further damage. In the bottom half, the Brewers managed nothing more than a Dave Nilsson walk and Eldred followed with a scoreless top of the second.[110]

As Newfield led off the bottom half for Milwaukee, the crowd buzzed with weird energy. Despite the sunshine, it was among the coldest openers in team history. Minutes earlier, a pipe had burst beneath the upper deck along the first base side, spraying water across section 17 in the lower grandstand and displacing about 80 fans. Patrons still filed in from the parking lots, chilled rooters who'd each had an extra half hour to slop beer and eye-opener cocktails. Each of whom was handed a free baseball at the gate. Newfield was still in the middle of his at-bat when the balls began to fly. One or two at first, greeted by a mix of cheers and boos. Then two or three more. When play was halted so the balls could be cleared, a couple more were thrown onto the field. Newfield stepped out and the boos came louder. After Texas left fielder Rusty Greer felt a ball buzz past his ear, Rangers manager Johnny Oates stomped out of the dugout and pulled his team off the field.[111]

Oates made an official protest with the umpires and it was 14 minutes before the Rangers retook the field. Settling back in as police officers made

The notorious give-away baseball from the nearly-forfeited 1997 home opener. Two delays were required during the game because of balls being thrown onto the field. This ball is part of the author's collection and proof that he took his father's warning that he would "leave [his] butt at the stadium if [he] throw[s] that thing" very seriously (Matthew J. Prigge).

their way through the crowd, Newfield fanned and Burnitz followed with a walk. With the crowd trying to work itself up to counter the bad vibes of the delay, shortstop Jose Valentin beat out an infield single and center fielder Gerald Williams laced a base hit to left to load the bases. There was likely no one in the Brewers lineup that Texas pitcher Ken Hill was happier to see in such a situation as catcher Mike Matheny. Since Matheny had joined the Brewers in 1994, there was exactly one player across baseball (Minnesota's Matt Walbeck) who had seen as much playing with as little offensive production. Hill got him to two strikes and then went for the kill with his forkball. But in the cold air, Hill's pitch fluttered and hung so far over the plate that not even Matheny could miss. He pounded it high down the left field line, where the twisting winds held it just inside the foul pole for a grand slam.[112]

The more rational portion of the home crowd was still celebrating when the balls resumed bouncing across the outfield grass. With the Brewers leading 4–1, crew chief Jim McKean waved the Rangers back into the dugout. In a huddle with the managers, McKean said that one more delay would result in a forfeit for the Brewers. The microphone usually reserved for pregame honorariums was hooked up and Garner, after taking a moment to suppress his growing rage over the situation, took to the field to plead with the crowd. "We urge you," he said, "for the safety of the players, the umpires, and your fellow fans, don't throw the balls." Meanwhile, sheriff's deputies working the game made an emergency call for 35 more officers as those on the scene lined the field, ready should the game be forfeited and a riot break out.[113]

As a message flashed on the scoreboard warning of a forfeit, McKean also spoke. "Please folks, let us play baseball," he begged. "We have a beautiful day here. There are kids here. Let us play." As a few stray baseballs were launched onto the field, Eldred hustled out to the bullpen to keep his arm loose during the increasingly long half-inning. He would later admit he felt certain the game was going to be ended early.[114]

With nothing else to comment on in the broadcast booth, the usually chipper Bob Uecker let loose. "This is a bad day in baseball for Milwaukee, I'll guarantee you that," he told his listeners. "This has been a friendly ballpark, but that is not true today."[115]

After a delay of 16 minutes, the Rangers again returned to the field. Hill needed just three pitches to end the frame, but the crowd applauded cautiously anyway.[116]

As it was, the worst of it was over. Texas got a run back in the top of the third as Eldred, stiff from the long layoff, labored through a seven-batter inning. Despite sloppy play on both sides, the score held until the fifth, when McLemore muffed a Burnitz grounder to permit a two-out run. The next inning, Jose Mercedes, having taken over for Eldred, allowed a solo shot to DH Mickey Tettleton. Despite a stray ball or two being launched fieldward, the crowd mostly behaved itself for rest of the afternoon. The seventh-inning Sausage Race, now a staple of home games, was nonetheless canceled. The team claimed it was because of the high winds. McKean said he'd ordered it called off. For obvious reasons.[117]

At 4:45 that afternoon, when closer Doug Jones got Rodriguez swinging to end the game, the Brewers felt more like survivors than victors. The team had already decided that, moving forward, any promotional item that could go airborne would be handed out after the game.[118]

Thanks to a surprisingly weak AL Central, the 1997 Brewers were just 2.5 games out of first place as late as September 2. But the team slipped under .500 a week later and finished at 78–83, their fifth straight losing season.

1998

Tuesday, April 7, 1998: Brewers 6, Expos 4 (51,408 attendance)

In the News: The "Mars Face," a mysterious shape on Mars that appeared to resemble a human face in a photo taken by the Viking Probe in the 1970s, has been revealed to be nothing more than a jagged rock formation. Scientists say the "face" image was a coincidental trick of light and shadow.

At the Movies: *Mouse Hunt* at the Avalon Theater

On the Radio: "Gone Till November" by Wyclef Jean

Despite running their losing record streak to five seasons—the longest since the Brewers had their first winning year in 1978—a few things had gone right in 1997. They had hung in the AL Central race until early September. The back end of their bullpen was one of the best in baseball, anchored by the under-the-radar additions of Bob Wickman and 40-year-old Doug Jones—who collected a few stray MVP votes for his 36-save, 2.02 ERA campaign. And outfielder Jeromy Burnitz, picked up in a similarly unheralded deal, slugged 27 homers with 20 steals and a .281 batting average over his first full-time season.

But even with work progressing on Miller Park and a brief pennant chase, the buzz for the Brewers remained minimal. Only twice in 1997 did they draw more than 40,000 people and they lingered near the bottom of the league in overall attendance. But just after the end of the World Series, it was officially announced that the Brewers would become the first franchise in Major League history to switch leagues. The move was necessary to accompany the expansion Arizona Diamondbacks and Tampa Bay

Devil Rays—who were assigned to the National and American leagues, respectively—assuring an even number of teams in each loop.

Bud Selig, still running the Brewers while serving as acting commissioner, had wished to see as many as 15 teams change leagues, but mass resistance among the owners for the plan whittled it back to just a single shift. The offer to jump leagues was first given to the Kansas City Royals, whose management split on the concept and declined. Selig loathed to appear to be offering undue preference to his own team, but after the owners backed him, he agreed to allow the Brewers to make the jump. While his fellow owners claimed that no other team wanted to change leagues, his detractors saw it as yet another pitfall in permitting the leader of the game to own one of its clubs.[119]

Banking on a bounce from the league shift and looking to build momentum with just two years before opening Miller Park, it was reported that the Brewers could push their 1998 payroll past $30 million, roughly a 40 percent increase over 1997. And, improbably, the team had their sights set on that off-season's biggest free agent prize: four-time All-Star center fielder Kenny Lofton. With Atlanta in 1997, Lofton had hit .333 with 27 steals while topping a Braves lineup that reached the NLCS. In late November Lofton had lunch with GM Sal Bando at Miss Katie's Diner in Milwaukee, and a week later, the Brewers made him an offer reportedly worth $45 million over five years. But Lofton's heart remained in Cleveland, where he'd spent five seasons and blossomed into a star. Days after the Brewers made their pitch, he signed with the Indians for $24 million over three years.[120]

While the move dashed the Brewers' big-time hopes, it also made Cleveland's incumbent center fielder, speedster Marquis Grissom, expendable. A week after they lost out on Lofton, the Brewers landed Grissom for a package of pitchers including Ben McDonald, Mike Fetters, and Ron Villone. It was a week before Grissom spoke to the press about the trade. Having played in the last three World Series, he was forced to deny rumors that he didn't want to go to Milwaukee and said he relished being an underdog. "That's what my career is all about," he told a reporter.[121]

With Grissom about to begin a five-year extension he had signed while with Cleveland—and having just inked Burnitz to a four-year extension of his own—the Brewers now had a core of eight players who would be under contract when the new stadium opened: Grissom, Burnitz, the entire infield of Dave Nilsson, Fernando Vina, Jose Valentin, and Jeff Cirillo, and pitchers Cal Eldred and Scott Karl. Entering training camp, the team projected a record-high payroll of $32.3 million, which, despite the team's new financial attitude, ranked them second to last in all of baseball.[122]

But hope sprung in Arizona for the Brewers that year, even as they dropped 12 of their first 15 spring games. They were on pace to break the franchise record for season ticket sales and national prognosticators had sweetened a bit on their chances in the wide-open National League Central. And rising beyond the center field bleachers of County Stadium was the steel framework of Miller Park, which the Brewers insisted would be ready for Opening Day, 2000—despite reports that work was behind schedule.[123]

The Brewers opened with a six-game road swing and entered the National League with a bang. After dropping a 2–1 heartbreaker in Atlanta to open the year, the Brewers beat the Braves in extras two days later and then swept four from the world champion Marlins, outscoring the mostly-dismantled title-holders 26–10. They landed back in Milwaukee in first place to face the Montreal Expos for the first NL game in Milwaukee since 1965.

With sunshine and temperatures in the 50s, it was the most celebratory opener—and perhaps the highest-energy home game—since the strike. For the first time since the stoppage, the Brewers expected a crowd of more than 50,000. The parking lots buzzed as thousands streamed past the Miller Park site. Most of the subterranean work on the project was already completed and the concrete horseshoe that would be the field-level seating slab was poured and set. One group of tailgaters arrived in a limousine. Another erected a red-and-white tent dubbed "Uncle Paul's Funhouse" and served up roast chicken, tenderloin sandwiches, and a variety of sausages. Local musicians like Pat McCurdy and the Love Monkeys played free shows at radio station–sponsored party tents. "I'm excited for the first time since the strike," one tailgater, a bartender by trade, told a reporter before the game. His opinion seemed to be a common one.[124]

To commemorate Milwaukee's return to the National League, Henry Aaron threw out the game's first pitch. Southpaw Scott Karl took the ball for the Brewers. After a scoreless first, the Expos stuck in the top of the second with some help from the always-troublesome Opening Day winds. After a two-out Brad Fulmer double, left fielder F.P. Santangelo looped one into center. Marquis Grissom closed in on the ball, but the wind drove it into the turf as it eluded the diving Grissom. Fulmer trotted home to make it 1–0. The wind saved Montreal again in the bottom half when, with two away, Mike Matheny crushed an 0–2 offering from Dustin Hermanson that looked certain to be Matheny's second-straight Opening Day homer. But once again, the wind got on top of it, holding the catcher to a double. He ended up stranded at second.[125]

Hermanson and Karl traded zeroes until the bottom of the fifth. After a one-out single from Jeff Cirillo, John Jaha and his aching back came to bat. A sore muscle near his neck had somewhat limited Jaha's range at the plate and he took a far more cautious approach against Hermanson than he would have at full health, resulting in a five-pitch walk. Jeromy Burnitz followed, batting .380 on the season. In two times at bat on the afternoon, he'd see only two strikes and he had laced one of them for a single. Hermanson challenged him with his first pitch, a fastball up in the zone, and Burnitz drew back and unleashed a vicious hack that rocketed the ball into the right field bleachers to put the Brewers up, 3–1. It was his fourth blast of the year, tying him with Mark McGwire for the NL lead. A batter later, shortstop Jose Valentin joined them atop the leader board with his fourth of the year, a liner into the right field gap. County Stadium roared like it hadn't in years.[126]

The Expos got one back in the top of the sixth on a Rondell White solo homer, but the Brewers took it right back in the bottom half. Matheny led off with another double and moved to third on a picture-perfect sacrifice bunt from Karl, who was still getting cheers over the novelty of a Brewers pitcher batting. After Eric Owens pinch-ran for Matheny, Fernando Vina slapped a single past a drawn-in infield to score the run and make it 5–2 Milwaukee. It was classic station-to-station National League baseball.[127]

The beauty of the Brewers sixth was muddied a bit by sloppy play in the seventh. Karl permitted a pair of one-out singles before leaving the game with tightness in his shoulder. Garner called on Chad Fox and the sinker-baller worked a ground ball from pinch-hitter Scott Livingstone, but Jaha muffed the double-play chance and the Expos loaded the bases. Fox lost the plate and walked in two—drawing boos from the otherwise high-spirited crowd—before getting another grounder to end the inning, the Brewers clinging to a 5–4 lead.[128]

The Brewers got an insurance run in the eighth on a Vina single, packaged in between scoreless innings from the Brewers' one-two punch of Wickman and Jones. Jones coaxed Jose Vidro into a towering pop to center field, where Grissom made the squeeze to secure the 6–4 win and push the Brewers into first place in NL Central.

After the game, Karl marveled at County Stadium's newfound energy. Admitting he'd actually preferred pitching on the road last season because of the limp atmosphere at home, things in Milwaukee felt totally renewed for 1998. "There was a buzz going through here," Garner raved in the locker room. "[They] sounded like a European soccer crowd."[129]

The Brewers were one of the NL's hottest teams through April, going 16–9 on the month, and had a winning record as late as mid-July. But they faded badly after the All-Star break to finish at 74–88. Including the opener, they drew more than 50,000 six times, thanks in large part to a late-season homestand that brought Mark McGwire and Sammy Sosa to town in the midst of their assault on Roger Maris's single-season home run record.

1999

Friday, April 16, 1999: Cubs 9, Brewers 4 (55,770 attendance)
In the News: The *Milwaukee Journal Sentinel* is offering live, pitch-by-pitch overage of the home opener on their website, along with navigable, 360-degree images of County Stadium and a live Miller Park webcam.
At the Movies: *Cookie's Fortune* at Oriental Theater
On the Radio: "No Scrubs" by TLC

When Bud Selig took charge of baseball's executive council in 1992 after commissioner Fay Vincent was forced out by the owners, he said he expected to hold the position for no more than four months and insisted he had no interest in becoming baseball's ninth commissioner. Nearly six years later, Selig finally accepted the crown. In doing so, he finally had to officially cut ties with the Brewers. Just after the 1998 All-Star break, he placed the one-third of the team he owned into a blind trust and the Brewers board of directors voted Wendy Selig-Prieb, his daughter, as the team's second-ever CEO and president.[130]

Selig-Prieb had been with Brewers in an official capacity since the late 1990s and had been handling most of the day-to-day operations of the club during Selig's term as acting commissioner. And, like her father, her connection to the club ran far deeper than a mere business relationship. But those who might have hoped for a shift in course with the change in leadership were quickly shut down. "I can tell you, I'm not going to be anything different," Selig-Prieb said of taking over for her father.[131]

The Brewers turned in a sixth straight losing season in 1998, their second-longest stretch of futility since Selig had brought the team to Milwaukee. While the payroll would balloon for 1999—up to $42 million—it was almost entirely the result of raises to the existing roster. The Brewers added only two players of any significance via free agency: pitcher Jim Abbott and first baseman Sean Berry. Berry was coming off a season in which he'd batted .314 and was expected to start at first base, pushing Dave Nilsson back behind the plate (the move also cleared the way for Opening Day hero Mike Matheny to be non-tendered). Abbott had not been an effective pitcher in nearly four years, but he'd once been a top-of-the-rotation starter despite his having been born with just one hand. The Brewers cited his "leadership," "influence," and "character" when announcing the signing.[132]

Elsewhere on the roster, the Brewers once again found themselves priced out of the market for one of their own All-Stars. Fernando Vina, picked up from the Mets for deposed closer Doug Henry after the 1994 season, emerged as a sparkplug at the top of the Brewers' lineup in 1998. He batted .311 with 22 steals while walking more often than he struck

The Brewers planned a series of farewell events to County Stadium during the 1999 stadium, including debuting this patch in the '99 opener against the Cubs. A tragic crane collapse at the Miller Park site, however, would extend the old ballpark's life by a year (Matthew J. Prigge).

out. Although he was still under contract for 1999 and 2000, the Brewers offered him a four-year extension worth about $13 million. Vina was unmoved. "Why should I take a contract that isn't market value now and take it two years from now?" he said of the offer. "That's stupid."[133]

With Ron Belliard, who projected as a Vina-type hitter with more power, seemingly ready to take over at second base, the Brewers shopped Vina all winter, but held tight to their high asking price of a top-of-the-line starter. Among the names heard in rumors were Kevin Millwood and Denny Neagle of the Braves and Matt Morris of the Cardinals.[134]

And then there was another round of Paul Molitor drama. Molitor was again a free agent after the 1998 season and the Brewers made one last bid to lure the franchise icon back to Milwaukee. The team left him with an open offer to join the team as a coach or an executive or to continue on as active player. The possibility of having Molitor in uniform led to speculation that—if the team didn't compete in 1999—he would be in line to replace Phil Garner as manager. But, in a third straight rebuff, Molitor announced his retirement in December and had plans to join the Twins' TV broadcast crew.[135]

Instead, the Brewers made plans to retire Molitor's #4, although it had been worn since by Pat Listach, as a tribute to Molitor, and had briefly been worn by minor leaguer Wes Weger during spring training in 1996—a move seen by some as a slight to Molitor after he declined to return to Milwaukee as a free agent.[136]

As the Brewers opened camp in Arizona—where Garner, feeling the burn of the hot seat, promised a more demanding spring to cut down on mental errors—it was revealed that work on the roof was about a month behind schedule. Bad weather had delayed work and the first roof panel to be lifted into place did not fit properly. "It would be misleading to say we're comfortable. We're not at that point yet," said the head of the stadium board.[137]

Nonetheless, fans were buying season tickets—and thus securing priority seating at Miller Park—at a record clip and County Stadium's final home opener, set for April 16 against the Cubs, sold out well in advance. The club expected a near-record crowd for the game, which would kick off a "year-long" tribute to the old ballyard. The marketing slogan for 1999 was "Bringin' Down the House."[138]

The Brewers opened the season in St. Louis, where negotiations with Cardinals for a possible Vina trade went right up until game time with no success. They dropped two of three in St. Louis and scuffled to a 4–5 mark on the nine-game opening road swing. But back in Milwaukee, the Brewers faithful could care less about the standings. The mood in the parking lots before the game was as warm and optimistic as it had been in a decade. Fans traded memories and recounted Opening Days past as they prepared for one last lid-lifter out in the cold. And while the mid–40s chill was tolerable, the cutting 35 mile per hour winds kept everyone huddled close to their grills.[139]

But in the dank and cramped Brewers locker room, there was less love to be found for their old home park. "I'm not a very nostalgic person. It's just old," said slugger Jeromy Burnitz, who was expected to be the centerpiece of the Brewers offense at Miller Park. "Getting a new stadium is bitchin'."[140]

Warren Spahn, the 78-year-old Hall of Famer who'd thrown the first official pitch at County Stadium in 1953, threw out the first ball.

"Walking from the dugout to the mound is a hell of a lot farther than it used to be," he noted. After a moment of silence for long-time County Stadium PA announcer Bob Betts, who'd passed away that winter, and a less-than-enthusiastic welcome when manager Garner was announced in the pregame introductions ("I thought they were saying, 'Garrrr!'" the skipper joked after the game), Bill Pulsipher took the hill for the Brewers with the façade of Miller Park looming beyond the center field bleachers.[141]

The lefty—years removed from his status as a can't-miss prospect with Mets—ran into trouble right away. With one out, a trio of singles loaded the bases—including one by home run hero Sammy Sosa, who'd blistered Brewers pitching in '98 for a .378 average and 12 homers. But Pulsipher limited the damage to a single RBI groundout.

In the bottom half, Fernando Vina showed that the off-season turmoil had done nothing to change his gritty style of play. On a grounder to first, Mark Grace booted the ball and, as it kicked away, Vina tore off for second base, diving in just ahead of the throw. But he was stranded at third after a sacrifice and strikeouts from Jeff Cirillo and Burnitz.

A Gary Gaetti homer in the next half made it 2-0 and, in the top of the third, the Cubs broke the game open. After setting down the first two Cubs batters, Pulsipher walked Sosa and Glenallen Hill to bring up veteran catcher Benito Santiago, who was batting just .120 on the year. Pulsipher's first offering to Santiago was a lifeless change-up, the same pitch Gaetti had teed up, and Santiago made similarly damaging contact. The ball soared over left fielder Geoff Jenkins for a three-run homer to give the Cubs an early five-run advantage.

In the bottom of the fourth, the Brewers threatened, loading the bases with one out. But the rookie Jenkins followed with a harmless fly ball and Rich Becker, pinch hitting in the pitcher's spot, fanned on a 3-2 pitch well outside the zone to end the threat. In the top of fifth, Sosa gave the many Cubs fan in attendance exactly what they'd been waiting for when he swatted a 3-0 Al Reyes offering into the left field bleachers. Sosa bounced around the bases to make it 6-0 Chicago.[142]

But in the bottom half, the Brewers set off some fireworks of their own. After a Vina walk and a single by Cirillo, Jeromy Burnitz lashed the second pitch he saw for a three-run blast—his second straight Opening Day blast. Three batters later, a Mark Loretta double scored Nilsson to cut the Chicago lead to 6-4. After a scoreless sixth, Brewers reliever Eric Plunk found quick trouble in the top of the seventh when Sosa and Hill stroked back-to-back singles. With Santiago at the plate, the Brewers played for a double play, with first baseman Sean Berry creeping in to defend against a bunt. On an 0-1 pitch, Santiago missed a bunt signal and sent a hard bouncer to Cirillo at third. Cirillo scooped, kicked third, and fired to Vina at second. With Hill bearing down, Vina had to stretch to his right to make the play, but held onto the base and turned for a quick throw to Berry, who had scampered back to first. The ball came in a step ahead of Santiago to complete just the third triple play in franchise history.[143]

With the momentum swung in the Brewers' favor, Cirillo led off the bottom half with a sharp single to bring the tying run to the plate in Burnitz. The old stadium buzzed and Cirillo, pumping his fist on first base, felt that the Brewers were going to pull it out. But the heart of the Brewers lineup froze and, a pair of foul-outs and a whiff later, the last threat the Brewers would mount that afternoon was over.[144]

Chicago tacked on a run in the eighth and two more in ninth off the Brewers already-taxed bullpen. The 9–4 loss made five times in 10 games that the Brewers had allowed five or more runs, a situation dire enough that Garner and his coaches held a post-game meeting on what the *Journal Sentinel* called "the pitching mess."[145]

In the parking lot, after the game, there were a number of groups of fans not quite ready to go home. Despite the chill and the lopsided loss, they wanted this opener to last just a little bit longer. "Why leave when

The crane known as "Big Blue" lays over the wreckage of Miller Park in the summer of 1999, just after the accident that killed three ironworkers. It was later determined that work was being done in unsafe conditions in an effort to keep the project on schedule (Matthew J. Prigge).

you're having fun?" one tailgater told the *Journal Sentinel*. "We might just fire up the grill again."[146]

It was another season of mediocrity for the Brewers, who would neither catch fire nor fall apart. Their 74–87 record, however, would not define the season. In July, hurrying to keep the project on schedule, a crane collapsed at the Miller Park site, killing three men and setting the project back a full year. A month later, Garner was fired and GM Sal Bando was reassigned within the organization.

Chapter Four

The Aughts

2000

Monday, April 10, 2000: Brewers 4, Marlins 3 (53,509 attendance)

In the News: Juan Gonzalez, father of six-year-old Elian Gonzalez, will remain in the U.S. while an appeals court rules on the custody of his son. The boy was the only survivor when a raft traveling from Cuba to the U.S. capsized on Thanksgiving Day, 1999.

At the Movies: *The Sixth Sense* at Avalon Theater

On the Radio: "Thong Song" by Sisqo

It had now been nearly a decade since Bud Selig had announced his intention to build a new, privately-financed stadium for the Milwaukee Brewers. And improbably, after the project survived nearly every imaginable obstacle, the Brewers looked ahead to the 2000 season needing yet again to rebuild.

While the Miller Park site was still being cleared of debris from the crane disaster, general manager Sal Bando recommended to Wendy Selig-Prieb that he should fire manager Phil Garner and then step down as GM. A week later, the plan was executed. "I've got to call it justified," Garner said. "We didn't play up to my expectations or their expectations."[1]

In late September, Selig introduced Dean Taylor as the new GM. Taylor had been the right-hand man of John Schuerholz for nearly 20 years as he built championship clubs in Kansas City and Atlanta. He was praised by colleagues as a workaholic and a stickler for details. Selig-Prieb left it to him to hire the new manager.[2]

After interviewing a pool of candidates that included Ken Griffey, Sr., Grady Little, and Willie Randolph, Taylor settled on Don Baylor—the former Brewers batting coach who'd led the Rockies to three winning seasons and a wild card berth. But Baylor was also being wooed by the Cubs and the Northsiders—with a bigger budget and more ready-to-go talent—got their man. With Baylor gone, Taylor settled on Padres first base coach and four-time All-Star Davey Lopes. Lopes was a gamer, hard-edged

Opening Day in Milwaukee

County Stadium hosting its final homestand. Despite another losing record, the Brewers had a fantastic closing run at the stadium, winning eight of 10 and stoking enthusiasm for the 2001 season (barrelmansammy).

and old-school. He didn't shy away from acknowledging that Milwaukee was lacking in talent and said plainly that the Brewers he'd seen in 1999 from the San Diego dugout did not play with the kind of passion he would expect from his team. "I believe I can get the job done," he said in his introduction as the Brewers' skipper. "How long it will take, I don't know. But I guarantee it will happen."[3]

Meanwhile, Taylor got busy making over the roster. In mid–December, he swung a blockbuster three-team deal with the Rockies and Athletics. The centerpiece of the deal was Jeff Cirillo, the Brewers' most reliable hitter for the past half-decade. Cirillo and lefty Scott Karl—both due $7 million in 2000 and both free agents after the season—were sent to Colorado for a return package that included starting pitchers Jamey Wright and Jimmy Haynes and catcher Henry Blanco. It was a money-saving deal that took a bet on Wright and Haynes, both of whom had lousy seasons in 1999 but both of whom had significant upsides. Taylor then turned some of the savings from that deal into a three-year contract for free agent infielder Jose Hernandez worth about $10 million. A rangy defender with power, Hernandez was to take over at third for Cirillo.[4]

A week later, Fernando Vina, also a year away from free agency, was also traded away. After they held out for a sky-high asking price a year earlier, the Brewers were left to dump him—he'd missed all but 37 games with a leg injury in 1999—on the Cardinals in exchange for Juan Acevedo, a former closer who projected as a back-of-the-rotation starter.[5]

That November, in a move planned well before the Miller Park accident, the Brewers unveiled a new logo and uniform set. Replacing the never-beloved Germanic block-letter get-up was a more contemporary look: a sweeping, script letter wordmark and a dashing "M" cap emblem accented with a barley sprig that looked suspiciously like the "M" in the Miller Brewing wordmark. The makeover was supposed to coincide with the move to Miller Park, but the team decided to go ahead anyway.[6]

In January, after the project received a $100 million insurance settlement, roof panel lifts were resumed at Miller Park. Moving forward, the lifts would be smaller and—with three firms involved in the project having been found negligent and fined for their roles in the accident—done under much stricter safety conditions.[7]

As work resumed on Miller Park's roof, the Brewers made one more trade of note, sending Cal Eldred and Jose Valentin to the White Sox for former Brewer Jaime Navarro and pitcher John Snyder. Both Eldred and Navarro had pitched terribly in 1999, and both had had promising careers repeatedly interrupted with injuries. With Valentin, who'd lost his shortstop job to Mark Loretta, thrown in, it was a swap of two sets of bad contracts in the hope that new scenery could help.

The Brewers made a handful of other moves during spring training that—like the trade with the Sox—were more notable for their narrative than their impact on the field. That spring, the Brewers released Antone Williamson—the fourth overall pick in the 1994 draft—and Bobby Hughes and Brian Banks—both second round picks. The Brewers had gotten virtually nothing from this trio of top draft choices. Indeed, only five players drafted and developed by the Brewers figured to be on the roster to open 2000 and only left fielder Geoff Jenkins had been drafted in either of the first two rounds. *Baseball America* rated the Brewers farm system as the worst in baseball and counted just one Brewers prospect—1999 first-round choice Ben Sheets—among the top 100 in the game.[8]

After opening the season with the ever-rare weather-shortened tie in Cincinnati, the Brewers managed to go 3–3 on the opening road trip despite a pair of blow-up performances from the pitching staff in St. Louis. Back in Milwaukee, crews had been busy getting County Stadium back into shape for one more season. With the rebrand, hundreds of team insignias had to be replaced all over the park and every broken seat in the stadium was replaced. Forecasts had called for up to three inches of snow for the opener, but luck broke in the Brewers' favor and the 2000 edition of Milwaukee County Stadium's last Opening Day dawned with near-freezing temperatures but no precipitation.[9]

After the crane collapse, it was decided not to try to recreate the "year-long celebration" of 1999. Aside from the final homestand, it would be a year of muted reverence for the old ballpark and little more. The first tailgating of the new millennium was a little less sentimental than it had been in '99. While people still streamed past the Miller Park site, the buzz in the lots that morning had nothing to do with baseball and everything to do with Packers tight end Mark Chmura, who had just been arrested for sexual assault on a complaint filed by 17-year-old girl who had been at a post-prom party that the 31-year-old had "crashed."[10]

Bob Uecker threw out the first pitch while the UW-Madison men's basketball team, which had just completed a surprise run to the Final Four, was honored in a pregame ceremony. With space-heaters running at full-tilt in each dugout, the game opened with clean frames from Jimmy Haynes and the Marlins' Vladimir Nunez. With two on and two out in the top of the second, Nunez hit a soft grounder down the first base line that Kevin Barker, a fringe prospect who'd taken over at first base after Dave Nilsson opted to retire and return to Australia, let go right between his legs. The first boos of the season rained down as Mike Lowell scored from second.[11]

The Brewers got the run back in the bottom half when Jenkins, who'd hit 21 homers in '99 to establish himself as the team's clean-up hitter, golfed a hanging curve ball into the gap between the right field bleachers and the lower grandstand. The Brewers struck again an inning later when Nunez lost his command in the chilly air and walked Henry Blanco, Marquis Grissom, and Mark Loretta to load the bases with one out for Burnitz. Coming off a 33-homer season and a start in the All-Star Game, Burnitz worked Nunez to a 3–1 count before ripping one just past Kevin Millar at first to score two. Jenkins followed with a sac fly to make it 4–1 Milwaukee.

Milwaukee's County Stadium hosts one last Opening Day with work on Miller Park progressing just past the bleachers. After a spree of honors and celebrations for the old ball park during the 1999 season, the 2000 campaign was played with less fanfare (Matthew J. Prigge).

In the top of the fifth, the Marlins struck back. Haynes walked Luis Castillo to open the frame. Rattled by the lead-off free pass, Haynes began to press for a ground ball, but he couldn't find a good grip on his breaking ball and Mark Kotsay and Brant Brown both squared him up for back-to-back singles to score Castillo. After moving to third on a ground-out, Kotsay scored on a sac fly before Haynes got Millar to end the inning.[12]

The Brewers threatened in the fifth and again in the seventh, when they put men on second and third for Jenkins with two away, but could not score. Meanwhile, the Marlins had no better luck against Brewers relievers Matt Williams and David Weathers. The biggest cheer came in the seventh, when a trio of fans ran onto the field, including one woman—whom the long-timers in the press box speculated might have been the first woman to run onto the County Stadium turf during a game since Morganna the Kissing Bandit.[13]

In the top of the ninth, facing closer Bob Wickman (the Wisconsin native was one of the few players not wearing long sleeves), Castillo (also sleeveless) hit a bouncer to third for an infield hit. Castillo had swiped 50 bases in 1999 and Wickman was prone to allow steals, but the point was moot when Kotsay bounced the first pitch he saw to Ronnie Belliard, who flipped to Loretta for the force at second. Loretta later said that his hands were so cold, he couldn't even feel the ball and this sensory confusion caused him to double-clutch on the relay to first, which was still in time to finish the double play. A minute later, Wickman fanned Derrick Lee to seal the 4–3 win.

One week into the season, the Brewers—almost universally regarded as a last-place team by the national media—were playing winning baseball. "Everybody else is surprised," Lopes said as he warmed up in the locker room, "but I believe in these guys."[14]

The 2000 Brewers dropped under .500 in mid–April and never regained their footing. Although they finished at 73–89, they managed to close out County Stadium in style, winning 21 of their last 32 home games, capped by an 8–2 closing homestand that included four walk-off wins.

2001

Friday, April 6, 2001: Brewers 5, Reds 4 (42,024 attendance)

In the News: The two oldest children of the late Milwaukee organized crime boss Frank Balistrieri are headed to court in a bitter dispute over their father's estate. A court order had halted the sale of the family home and other personal items.

At the Movies: *Crouching Tiger, Hidden Dragon* at Mayfair Mall 18

On the Radio: "Jaded" by Aerosmith

For the last two-plus months of 2000, Davey Lopes' Brewers were a winning team. Kick-started by the late July trade that sent pitchers Jason Bere, Steve Woodard, and Bob Wickman to Cleveland for lanky slugger Richie Sexson—like Burntiz, another talented player with no place in Cleveland's loaded lineup—the Brewers spent the second half as a respectable up-and-comer. And in between innings of the final game ever at County Stadium, 21-year-old Ben Sheets—fresh off a flight from Australia, where he'd just won the gold medal-clinching game for Team USA at the Summer Olympics—bounced out of the dugout, medal around his neck, and waved to a crowd that couldn't wait for the 2001 season to begin.

Topping GM Dean Taylor's off-season wish list was an established lead-off hitter. Neither Marquis Grissom nor Ronnie Belliard had shown much as the primary lead-off men in 2000. After trade talks that would have swapped Kansas City's Johnny Damon for Jeromy Burnitz, Taylor and company dipped into the long-promised wealth of Miller Park and gave Jeffrey Hammonds the richest contract in franchise history: $22 million over three years. Once one of the game's most-hyped prospects, Hammonds was coming off a break-out season with the Rockies where he'd batted .335 with 20 homers and 106 RBI. Although those numbers were inflated by Denver's thin air (his road batting average, on base percentage, and slugging percentage were much more in line with a mediocre hitter than an All-Star) and he had a long history of injuries (a total of seven trips to the disabled list in his career), the Brewers were convinced that they'd landed their man. "A lot of people might think it was an aberration last years," Lopes said at the press conference announcing the deal. "But I feel that his better baseball is yet to come."[15]

Meanwhile, the Brewers continued to shop Burnitz. The slugger would be a free agent after the 2001 season and made it clear he wanted a deal worth at least $10 million per season. A deal was in place with San Diego, swapping the outfielder for third baseman Phil Nevin, but fell apart when Burnitz refused San Diego's under-market extension offer. As much a free-speaker as he was a free-swinger, Burnitz had taken no pause in the past in criticizing the Brewers for not doing enough to field a winning team. But as he arrived in Arizona to open spring camp, he vowed not to speak against the club, even after his frustrating and uncertain off-season. He did, however, say that he expected 2001 to be his last year as a Brewer.[16]

But in early March, the team reached a surprise extension agreement with Burnitz, adding two years and $20 million to his existing deal. The deal was part of a four-day spending spree that included extensions with Geoff Jenkins ($18 million over four years) and Sexson ($17.5 million over four years), and solidified the heart of a lineup that had managed to do some real damage in the second half of 2000. The trio was even profiled in *Sports Illustrated*, dubbed the "Bleach Boys" as each had added blond highlights to their hair. They were the core of the loose and fun-loving clubhouse, one that was young and not shy about showing some swagger. "The attitude is totally different here now," Burnitz said. "It's time for us to make some noise. I'm not saying we'll win the World Series, but we need to show people we can contend."[17]

Meanwhile, the hype around Ben Sheets had been thrown into overdrive. Now rated as *Baseball America*'s fifth best prospect in baseball, Sheets was easily the team's most promising rookie since Gary Sheffield. As Sheets impressed in spring, registering a 3.16 ERA over six starts, he got a feature article of his own in the *Sporting News*. In it, the 21-year-old admitted that he was afraid of the dark, and had been his whole life. "[I'm] afraid of everything," he said with a laugh. "It's a good thing those mounds are well-lit." The mound, it seemed, was the one of the few places he felt no fear. The magazine named him their preseason pick for NL Rookie of the Year.[18]

Despite the big head of steam, the Brewers opened the 2001 season flat, dropping all four games of a season-opening road trip. But come Friday, April 6, it made no difference to Milwaukee. Opening at night for the first time in team history, the Brewers had the attention of the baseball world in way not seen since the 1982 World Series. Miller Park, finally ready for baseball, was polished and gleaming, with a roster of baseball and political dignitaries on hand to help inaugurate what the Brewers promised would be the next great cathedral of sport.

With a 7:15 start time, traffic around the stadium had snarled to a halt by 4:30 as fans slowly streamed into the reformatted parking lots. The tailgating atmosphere was more reserved than in years past, with no one willing to miss the opening festivities for an extra brat or beer or two or three. One group, unwilling to waste time in line for the restrooms, brought their own porta-potty, strapped down to a flatbed trailer. Meanwhile, as fans lingered past the rugged patch of dirt where County Stadium no longer stood, ticket scalpers were overseeing the biggest boom market for Brewers tickets ever, flipping $10 seats for $100 or more.[19]

Bob Uecker emceed the pregame ceremonies, quipping, "Isn't it nice you can tell what's up there?" after a video played on the massive (and fully functional) center field scoreboard. Robin Yount spoke and said the new stadium was so breath-taking that he'd had an inkling to put his old uniform back on. Bud Selig followed with a short but emotional speech. "After all of these years and all the struggles," he said, "it's hard for me to articulate for one of the few times in my life how I feel today." Selig took the mound for the stadium's first regular-season pitch, getting it to Davey Lopes on the fly as the crowd showed its appreciation. Following Selig, to a mix of cheers and boos, was President George W. Bush, just two and a half months into the job. Bush's one-hopper was the first presidential first pitch since Bill Clinton's in 1996. During the National Anthem, a bald eagle named Challenger swooped in from the center field concourse and landed on his trainer's hand as he stood on the pitcher's mound. And finally, after 11 years, it was time to play ball.[20]

At 7:17, in windless, 60-degree comfort, Jeff D'Amico wound up and delivered a first-pitch strike to Cincinnati shortstop Barry Larkin. D'Amico had been one of the surprises of the 2000 season, nearly winning the NL ERA after missing almost all of the two previous seasons to injury. The big righty set the Reds down in order in the first before allowing a lead-off single to Sean Casey to open the second—the first hit in Miller Park history. Casey was erased on a double play and D'Amico finished the third having faced the minimum. In the bottom half, shortstop Jose Hernandez hit a gapper and cruised into second base for the first Brewers hit in the new park. But the Reds' Rob Bell set down the next three in order to strand Hernandez.

In the top of the fourth, Larkin opened with a single and center fielder Michael Tucker, who had hit the last home run in County Stadium history, turned on an inside change-up and drilled it into the bleachers above the visiting bullpen. Goaded by his bleacher mates, the fan who caught the ball threw it back.[21]

But the Reds' 2–0 lead was short-lived. In the bottom of the fourth, third baseman Tyler Houston opened with a base hit and after Sexson and Jenkins struck out, Burnitz and Hammonds—who Lopes had eventually designated as his #6 hitter—drew back-to-back walks to load the bases for Hernandez. Despite a disappointing 2000, Hernandez had been lethal with the bases loaded, batting over .500 with two grand slams. On an 0–1 breaking ball from Bell, Hernandez laced it into the right field gap, one-hopping the wall and clearing the bases to give the Brewers a 3–2 lead.[22]

With D'Amico settled in, the score held until the bottom of the sixth when Burnitz came to bat with one away. Facing Cincinnati side-armer Scott Sullivan, Burnitz took a defensive swing at 2–1 pitch and popped it foul while the bat flew out of his hands and 15 rows deep into the field-level seats behind the Milwaukee dugout. A creature of habit, Burnitz wanted the bat back. The fan who'd ended up with it obliged, swapping it out for another piece of lumber. Preferred bat back in hand, Burnitz crushed the next pitch for a high, looping homer to right. In left field, Bernie Brewer took his first official home run trip down the winding, yellow slide that had replaced his old center field beer mug.[23]

But once again, the lead would not hold. Dmitri Young led off the seventh with a solo homer into the Milwaukee bullpen and Casey followed with a base hit. After Mike DeJean came in for D'Amico, Aaron Boone stroked a run-scoring single to tie the game. It was still tied up in the bottom of the eighth, when Jenkins led off against lefty Dennys Reyes with a towering fly to center that Tucker caught a step in from the wall. He'd hit it to the deepest part of the park and just missed it. Richie Sexson followed and, on a 2–2 fastball, did not miss. Knowing he'd gotten it right off the bat, Sexson strode out of the batter's box with a broad smile and pointed to the Brewers' dugout while the ball landed deep in the second deck in left.

David Weathers came on for the save in the top of ninth, working two harmless fly balls to Hammonds in center while, outside in the chilly spring darkness, a steady rain began to fall. He got catcher Kelly Stinnett to a full count and, with 42,000-plus on their feet, fanned him swinging to clinch the win. "We needed this one bad," Weathers said after the game.[24]

While the rain kept falling, the roof was opened in a post-game ceremony, the rain and rush of cold air doing little to dampen the spirits of the fans who remained in their seats.

On paper, the new Miller Park era felt a lot like the darkest days at County Stadium. After flirting with contention in April and May, the team tapered off and fell apart completely in the second half. They finished at 68–94 record, their worst since 1984. They drew 2.8 million fans, a new team record, but well short of the three million they expected.

2002

Friday, April 5, 2002: Brewers 6, Diamondbacks 2 (43,005 attendance)

In the News: Prime Minister Tony Blair will spend the weekend at President George W. Bush's ranch in Texas for a discussion on the situation in the Middle East. It is thought that Blair will attempt to persuade Bush to hold off on taking action on Iraq until things in Afghanistan have stabilized.

At the Movies: *Panic Room* at Marcus South Shore

On the Radio: "Oops (Oh My)" by Tweet featuring Missy Elliot

After an off-season filled with promise and hype and the debut of their long-anticipated retractable-roof stadium, the 2001 Brewers were one of the worst team in baseball. Expected to be the team's ace, Jeff D'Amico staggered through 10 starts, posting a 6.08 ERA before being lost for the year. Jeffrey Hammonds, given the biggest contract in team history, missed more than 100 games due to injury and, even when healthy, was mostly a non-factor. Five regulars in the starting lineup spent time on the DL. The only member of the starting rotation not to miss time was Jamey Wright, who finished with an ERA of 4.90. The Brewers were now the only team in baseball to have gotten worse each of the past five seasons. But with the season delayed by a week after the attacks of 9/11, it hardly even seemed to matter.[25]

But on the balance sheet, Miller Park had apparently done what it was supposed to do. With a franchise-record season attendance of 2.8 million, the Brewers were, by the unique bookkeeping of sporting franchises, one of just five MLB teams to turn a profit in 2001. But yet, the team announced they had no plans to increase payroll, which ranked 23rd in the league for 2001. Indeed, the only significant free agent addition the Brewers made that winter—signing veteran second baseman Eric Young to a two-year deal worth $4 million—was only possible when the Brewers secured a trade for Jeromy Burnitz and the $10 million he was owed for 2002.

It was another off-season of rumors and uncertainty for Burnitz, who posted a fourth-straight 30-homer season in 2001. But he'd also struck out 150 times, part of an overall team effort that yielded nearly 1,400 whiffs—easily the highest single-season club total in MLB history. In January, a three-team trade sent Burnitz, D'Amico and two others to the Mets, with pitcher Glendon Rush of the Mets and Alex Ochoa of the Rockies highlighting the return for the Brewers. The Mets billed Burnitz as the final piece to a pennant-winner. "I'd be lying if I told you I didn't think this was a good thing for me," Burnitz said on heading to New York. "I feel pretty danged good about it."[26]

As the Brewers opened camp in Arizona, it was hard to find anyone excited about the team who was not drawing a paycheck from the club. "I do think there are a lot of reasons for optimism," team president Wendy Selig-Prieb told the press. "We worked very hard this offseason to improve this club."[27]

Matt Stairs, a 34-year-old outfielder who'd joined the team on a one-year, $500,000 deal, said the team had a goal of winning 85–90 games. "Do we have a good enough team to win the division?" he asked himself aloud. "That's hard to say."[28]

Aside from a relatively injury-free camp, the only encouraging story to emerge from Arizona that year was that of Alex Sanchez. Sanchez had debuted for the Brewers at the end of 2001 when the rosters expanded, but his gutsy and all-out play in camp elevated him from a fringe prospect to the starting lineup. While Hammonds missed time with an aching shoulder, Sanchez batted .400, stole eight bases, and legged out an inside-the-park homer. At 18 years old, Sanchez, along with 11 others, attempted to sail from his native Cuba to the U.S. on a raft made of wooden planks and held together with rope and inner tubes. After three days at sea, the group was picked up by the U.S. Coast Guard and taken to Guantanamo Bay, where Sanchez spent the next 16 months before being permitted to settle in Miami. When the Brewers opened the season in Houston, Sanchez—who had been waived by Tampa Bay just a year before—started in center field, collecting two hits and scoring three runs with a stolen base in the Brewers 9–3 win.[29]

After dropping the next two in Houston, the Brewers returned to Milwaukee for the home opener against the world champion Diamondbacks. While the opener had already sold out, overall tickets sales were down nearly 25 percent from 2001. And that included a boost in season ticket packages that included access to seats for that summer's All-Star game, which would be played at Miller Park.[30]

It was another Friday night opener for the Brewers and the pregame scene in the parking lots was subdued. One telling scene reported by the *Journal Sentinel* had a group huddled around a space heater and a portable DVD player showing *Field of Dreams*. Just a few years removed from a home opener immersed in nostalgia, the only way to find it now was on a tiny screen perched on a car bumper.[31]

To hype the coming All-Star Game, Gene Conley, Johnny Logan, Larry Hisle, and Gorman Thomas—all former Milwaukee All-Stars— threw out the first pitches. And for the second straight home opener, Robin Yount was on hand, although now it was as the first base coach for the Diamondbacks. "I think Opening Days were probably the most nerve-racking days of the whole season," he said before the game. "Here it's like a cult day."[32]

Fans were also greeted by a video message from George W. Bush. Lest anyone miss the significance of Bush's video visit, more than 200 members of the armed forces were involved in the pregame festivities. It was a changed world, and the National Pastime could let no one forget it.[33]

Lefty Glendon Rusch started for Milwaukee. They key return in the Burnitz deal, Rusch was years past the prospect stage, but the Brewers felt he still had the potential to be a mid-rotation starter. While the Brewers struggled to capitalize against Arizona's Rick Helling—Sanchez singled in the first, but was caught stealing and the Brewers stranded runners in scoring position in the second and third—Rusch retired the first 10 batters he faced. He'd barely broken a sweat by the time Alex Ochoa belted a solo homer in the bottom of the fourth inning to put the Brewers on top.

In the fifth, Rusch worked around a hit-by-pitch for another quick and scoreless inning. In the bottom half, Jose Hernandez led off with a single and moved to second on an error. A batter later, Rusch strode to the plate, expecting to—as he'd already done once that evening—lay down a sacrifice bunt. In 125 career plate appearances, Rusch had collected just six hits—all singles—for a batting average of .055. But Rusch was given permission to swing away. With one strike, he whiffed badly on a curveball. Two pitches later, Helling went back to the bender, but this time, it didn't bend. With a big leg kick and a swing from his heels, Rusch connected with the flailing pitch and sent it soaring into the right field bleachers. It was the first time Rusch had homered since high school.[34]

The Brewers tacked on two more in the sixth when Hernandez drilled a two-out, two-run homer to right and picked up another an inning later when Eric Young scored on a wild pitch. The Diamondbacks finally got to Rusch in the seventh with a solo homer from Luis Gonzalez, but the champs still had just two hits heading into the ninth inning. Another solo homer, this one with two outs, was all the champs could muster. A few minutes later, Rusch got Gonzalez to ground out to finish up one of the most unlikely all-around Opening Day performances in Brewers history.

"It was Glendon Rusch's night," said Davey Lopes after the game. "Hopefully, it's a sign of good things to come."[35]

"It was a total storybook-type night for me," said Rusch, who received three standing ovations on the evening. Asked about the homer, he could only shake his head. "That's a blur to me."[36]

The home opener was the high point for the 2002 Brewers. After losing 10 of their next 11, Davey Lopes was fired. Dean Taylor hung on until August, when he was similarly dismissed. They finished with a 56–106 record, the worst in franchise history by a wide margin.

2003

Friday, April 4, 2003: Giants 7, Brewers 5 (42,570 attendance)
In the News: CDC officials say it is too early to tell if SARS, the highly-contagious respiratory illness, will become a pandemic, although they are noting an increasing number of cases worldwide.
At the Movies: *Chicago*, Oriental Theater
On the Radio: "In Da Club" by 50 Cent

Not even the sunniest-eyed diehard could consider the 2002 season anything but an unmitigated disaster. On their way to a franchise-worst 106 loses and the first last-place finish in a decade, manager Davey Lopes and GM Dean Taylor were fired and veterans Tyler Houston, Alex Ochoa, Jamey Wright, and Mark Loretta were jettisoned for low-level minor leaguers. For a sixth straight season, the Brewers failed to improve their record from the previous year. The franchise-record attendance of 2001 fell by nearly one million and the All-Star game—Milwaukee's chance to showcase their new ballpark to the sporting world—ended in an embarrassing tie.

Just before the end of the season, the shake-up in team leadership grew even more dramatic when Wendy Selig-Prieb, on the job for just more than four years, stepped aside as team president. Taking over day-to-day operations of team were new General Manager Doug Melvin and Milwaukee lawyer and former Marquette basketball star Ulice Payne, who was named team president. Selig-Prieb, who had remained so far from the spotlight in 2002 that the *Journal Sentinel*'s Michael Hunt compared her to Howard Hughes, said the decision had to do with wanting to spend more time with her family and had nothing to do with the team's struggles. Rumors had it that Bud Selig had convinced her to step aside.[37]

"I don't believe in rebuilding plans," Melvin told the press at his introductory press conference. "I want people to be a part of this process to get where we want to go." He said that he considered Ben Sheets, Geoff Jenkins, and Richie Sexson to be "mostly" untouchable, but ruled out nothing else in remaking the roster. Asking about free agency, Melvin took a dualistic approach. He said he wouldn't spend just for the sake of spending, nor would he use budget restraints as an excuse.[38]

A month into his tenure, Melvin announced the surprise hire of Braves coach Ned Yost as manager. Yost hadn't been among the initial pool of interviewees, but a strong endorsement from Braves skipper Bobby Cox piqued Melvin's interest and, after his top choice Ken Macha chose to join the Athletics, Melvin made Yost the offer. A former Brewers back-up catcher whose career highlight was a late-season game-winning homer at Fenway Park in 1982, Yost promised a hard-working club that would stress the fundamentals.[39]

After hiring Yost, Melvin began remaking the roster. Jose Hernandez, Lenny Harris, and Matt Stairs were each free agents and were each shown the door. Ronnie Belliard, who'd hit .211 in 2002 with a .257 on-base percentage, was non-tendered. Ray King, a talented situational lefty who was more valuable to a winner than an up-and-comer, was sent to Atlanta for Wes Helms, who was immediately named starting third baseman. Combing the waiver wire, Melvin picked up outfielders Brady Clark and Scott Podsednik for nothing more than a transaction fee and added veterans Eddie Perez, John Vander Wal, and Royce Clayton on short-term, low-dollar deals.

But Melvin's boldest move of the winter was signing former top prospect Brooks Kieschnick to a minor league deal. Kieschnick, long past his days as a prized outfielder, had reinvented himself as a two-way player: DHing and pitching in relief in the minors and independent leagues. The move was a rare stroke of thinking outside of the box in Milwaukee and generated the most national interest in the Brewers spring camp since they'd traded for Henry Aaron. Working with a good curve and a looping change-up—and with power at the plate—Kieschnick remained enough of a curiosity that he needed to defend himself against charges of being a mere novelty act. "I'm not just doing this for attention," he said, with *Sports Illustrated* printing a weekly "Kieschometer" to gauge the likelihood that Kieschnick would make the team and become baseball's first regular two-way player since the 1950s. "I just love to play this game."[40]

But clean innings and base hits in Arizona from Brooks Kieschnick were not translating into ticket sales in Milwaukee. With ticket sales 17 percent behind the disastrous total from 2002, team president Payne announced a free pre-season exhibition game at Miller Park and encouraged fans to make their complaints about the team known. "I'd rather you holler at me, because it shows you care," Payne said. "I'll take those hits."[41]

Kieschnick was optioned to AAA at the end of camp, but another off-season addition had played his way onto the roster. Picked up off waivers from the Mariners in October, outfielder Scott Podsednik was a 10-year minor league veteran with just 31 big league plate appearances. But he impressed the Brewers brass with his speed and ability to put the bat on the ball. With Jenkins opening the season on the DL with a wrist injury, Podsednik would have a chance to show what he could do.[42]

As the Brewers headed to St. Louis to open the season, they were a younger and hungrier bunch than had slogged through the 2002 schedule. Yost's enthusiasm was infectious and the holdovers on the roster noted a much better attitude in the clubhouse than in years past. Enthusiasm and good vibes aside, however, the team was still near-universally regarded as one of the worst in baseball. Perhaps the most obvious advantage this bunch had over the '02 team was in expectations. The bar had been set so low they couldn't possibly disappoint. The Brewers were swept in St. Louis, allowing 24 runs in three games, before returning home to face the NL champion Giants.[43]

The Payne era saw a number of in-house changes at Miller Park. Live organ music was back and fireworks—with each homer and win—were introduced. There were more activities for kids on the concourses and more stuff for the casual adult fan—including a rock-climbing wall and a hot tub in the outfield area and speed-dating nights. Under a season theme of "It's All Coming Together," fan access to the players was featured with weekly photo and autograph nights.[44]

In a pregame ceremony, Payne honored Bob Uecker, who would join the broadcasters' wing of the Baseball Hall of Fame that summer. After a first pitch from Uecker, Payne remained on the field for team introductions, standing beside Yost near home plate. While the game was declared a sell-out, thousands of seats remained empty. From the just-above-freezing conditions in the stadium lots to the dour atmosphere inside the stadium, it was clear that the Brewers' new ways had yet to infect the fanbase. The *Journal Sentinel* called the atmosphere "as flat and unexceptional ... a home opener as any in recent memory."[45]

Todd Ritchie, another low-risk Melvin pickup, started for the Brewers. After allowing a lead-off single to Ray Durham, a hard sinker to Jose Cruz caught Keith Osik's shin guard and ricocheted so far away that Durham advanced all the way to third. The home crowd booed. It was the seventh pitch of the game. A batter later, Durham scored on a sac fly.[46]

Alex Sanchez, who'd stolen 37 bases and received Rookie of the Year votes in '02, led off the Brewers half with a single, but was promptly erased on a caught stealing. The Giants threatened in the second, collecting two hits and a walk against the laboring Ritchie, but could not score. In the bottom half, John Vander Wal—a 13-year veteran with 81 career homers who was as unlikely an Opening Day clean-up hitter as the Brewers had ever had—stroked a homer into the right field gap to tie the game, 1–1, and inaugurate Miller Park's new fireworks policy. But Ritchie still couldn't

Cheerleaders were one of a number of new features introduced in 2003 to try to liven up the gameday experience (Jeramey Jannene).

figure out the Giants and, in the third, a walk and a hit-by-pitch set the stage for a two-run single by J.T. Snow. Mid-inning, the agitated crowd booed in-game host Sandy Maxx when she appeared on the scoreboard. The host was another new feature for '03.[47]

The Brewers pulled within a run in the fourth when the suddenly heavy-hitting Vander Wal smacked a double and was brought home by a Wes Helms single. In the top of the fourth, Barry Bonds, who'd won his fifth MVP award in 2003, hit a laser-beam homer toward the center field hot tub to make it 4–2. It was the last time the Giants got to Richie, who was done after six innings, the Brewers still in it despite allowing eight hits and four walks, hitting two batters, and throwing two wild pitches.

In the bottom of the sixth, Sexson led off with a solo homer off Giants starter Ryan Jensen before Jeffrey Hammond and Helms hit back-to-back jacks to put the Brewers up 5–4 and chase Jensen. The crowd was back to life and, for the first time all afternoon, it felt like Opening Day. Lefty John Foster came on in the seventh and worked around a single to deliver things to the Brewers set-up/closer combo of Luis Vizcaino and Mike DeJean. The duo had served the team well in '02, with Vizcaino posting a 2.99 ERA and DeJean saving 27 games.

But with one out in the eight, Cruz ripped a flailing slider from Vizcaino for a game-tying homer and Rich Aurilia followed with a single to bring up Bonds. In a move that violated every known aspect of traditional baseball logic (but had become commonplace in this stage of Bonds' career), Yost ordered that Bonds be intentionally walked, pushing the go-ahead run into scoring position. But Vizcaino lost the plate after the free pass and walked Edgardo Alfonzo to load the bases. With Shane Nance on for Vizcaino, J.T. Snow hit a full-count bouncer to Royce Clayton at short. Clayton jumped for the knuckling ball, but it went in and out of his glove. With everyone moving on the pitch, Aurilia scored easily and Bonds lumbered home just ahead of Clayton's throw.[48]

The Brewers made a stand in the ninth when Podsednik lined a pinch-hit single with one away. Clayton followed with what appeared to be an infield hit, dribbled down the third base line. But a conference from the umpires determined that the ball had hit Clayton's bat twice, resulting in a foul ball. ("I felt it," Clayton said after the game. "I was hoping nobody else noticed.") Clayton returned to the plate and popped out. Keith Ginter followed with a three-pitch strikeout to end the game.[49]

"It's no fun starting 0–4," Yost said afterward. "But we're not going to roll over and die."[50]

The Brewers seemed bound for another 100-loss season in 2003 when a 10-game winning streak in late August helped them to a 68–94 finish.

Although their 12-game improvement was their best since 1987, attendance fell to just 1.7 million—less than they'd drawn in 1999 at County Stadium.

2004

Friday, April 9, 2004: Astros 13, Brewers 7 (44,405 attendance)
In the News: A recount will begin today in the recent election for mayor of South Milwaukee. The initial tally resulted in a 2,783–2,783 tie.
At the Movies: *The Passion of the Christ*, Prospect Mall Cinema
On the Radio: "Dirt Off Your Shoulder" by Jay-Z

Brewers fans should have felt pretty good heading into the 2003 off-season. Although the team lost 94 games, they hadn't quit late in the season and had seen several of Doug Melvin's low-risk moves pay off. Scott Podsednik took over in center field when Alex Sanchez sulked his way into a trade and nearly won the National League Rookie of the Year award with a .316 average and 43 steals. Dan Kolb, signed just before the season opened, took over the closer's role and registered a 1.96 ERA. In a season that saw the team release high-dollar free agent signee Jeffrey Hammonds, the Melvin method had acquired the team's standout position player and best pitcher from baseball's discount bin. With the prizes of a replenished farm system—including Rickie Weeks, J.J. Hardy, Corey Hart, and Bill Hall—all progressing on schedule through the farm system, there was reason for genuine hope in Milwaukee.

But in early November, the team's board of directors announced that the payroll for 2004 would be cut by 25 percent, an amount that would almost certainly leave the Brewers with the lowest payroll in baseball. Whatever profits the team had made at Miller Park had been overwhelmed by the club's various debts. Richie Sexson, who'd tied his own club record with 45 homers in 2003, had been negotiating an extension, but would now likely be traded. Geoff Jenkins, with Sexson the team's largest projected earner for 2004, might also be dealt. Ulice Payne came out against the payroll cuts and, after weeks of rumors of about his term as president being beset by feuds and power struggles with the Seligs, resigned his position in late November.[51]

The political reaction to the payroll cut was quick and severe. Lawmakers demanded that the Brewers open their books for review, with one state legislator saying, "The Seligs just scammed the living dickens out of the people of this state." Former governor Tommy Thompson, the most dedicated political backer the stadium project had, said "The Brewers need to put an end to the games. They need to invest in a winning team."

Milwaukee mayor John Norquist said that the Brewers had "an ownership problem."[52]

By mid–November, there were calls for Selig to sell the team. "The fans," wrote the *Journal Sentinel*'s Dale Hoffman, "have been swindled."[53]

On December 1, in a move that Melvin insisted had nothing to do with payroll, the Brewers traded Sexson to Arizona for six players. The huge return included two young starters in Chris Capuano and Jorge De La Rosa and a pair of infielders, shortstop Craig Counsell and first baseman Lyle Overbay, who would be stop-gaps for two of the team's top prospects, Hardy and Prince Fielder. The return was rich enough that Melvin's stance was defensible from a baseball standpoint. But it was still another star player traded away for cheaper talent. And it was not space on the payroll that would be spent elsewhere. With a free agent haul headlined by fringe players like Ben Grieve and Dave Burba, the Brewers' payroll for 2004 was projected to be about $27.5 million—one-third less than 2003 and the lowest in Major League Baseball.[54]

On January 17, in a Friday afternoon press conference with little advance notice given to the media, Wendy Selig-Prieb announced that the team was being put up for sale. "I believe the legacy of the ownership group will in fact be its commitment to securing this franchise to our community," she said. "Despite that stability, however, the board and the owners have concluded that a change of ownership at this time is clearly in the long-term best interests of baseball here in Milwaukee." She denied that the decision had anything to do with the backlash from the previous fall.[55]

Speculation emerged that the group might already have a buyer interested in the team. Just the year before, Senator Herb Kohl had put his Milwaukee Bucks on the market, only to be unable to find a local buyer and pull the team back. Reports emerged that Selig had wanted to sell the team for some time, so perhaps the theatrics of the announcement indicated a buyer was waiting in the wings. Two months later, as the Brewers broke camp with a team that was yet again projected to be one of the worst in baseball, it was clear that such speculation was unfounded. They had found "significant" interest in the team nationally, but no local group was had yet considered a bid. Although the team reportedly had an "ironclad" lease at Miller Park that would prevent relocation, concerns about the future of the Brewers in Milwaukee were too familiar to most fans to dismiss completely.[56]

With just six players back from the Opening Day roster of 2002 and 11 players making their Brewers debuts, the Brewers opened in St. Louis and won three of four from the division rival Cardinals. Arriving back in Milwaukee in first place, the Brewers opened against the Astros in a rare Good Friday opener. The holiday, meant to be a day of quiet reflection for Catholics, required the devoted to fast and abstain from eating meat. After consulting with local church leaders, the team decided on a 3:05 p.m. start time for the game to permit fans to attend morning services before heading out for their theoretically-meatless tailgate parties.[57]

One of the new Brewers that afternoon was shortstop Craig Counsell, who'd grown up in Whitefish Bay and whose father, John, had worked for the Brewers for many years. Counsell's first home opener was in 1980 when Sixto Lezcano beat Boston with a walk-off grand slam. "I have great memories of coming to County Stadium for Opening Day," he said before the game. "More so than actually being in a Brewers uniform, I think it's those memories of being here on Opening Day that makes it special."[58]

A moment of silence was held before the game to honor three giants of Milwaukee baseball who'd passed away over the winter: Hall of Famer Warren Spahn, long-time Braves announcer Earl Gillespe, and two-time Brewers skipper George Bamberger. Badgers basketball star and Milwaukee native Devin Harris, expected to the one of the top picks in the upcoming NBA draft, threw out the first pitch.[59]

Righty Wes Obermueller and Houston's Wade Miller traded zeroes in the first before Houston tagged Obermueller for a run on a groundout in the second. They got to him again in the first when lead-off man Craig Biggio worked a walk, moved up on a sac bunt, and was driven home on a base hit by Jeff Bagwell. Meanwhile, Miller—who was 11–1 lifetime against the Brewers and had an incredible 1.08 ERA at Miller Park—set down the first nine batters he faced.

But in the fourth, the Brewers played some small ball of their own. Podsednik opened with a bunt single and stole second. He moved to third on a sac fly by Counsell and scored on a Jenkins base hit to make it 2–1. Lyle Overbay—who didn't project as a home run hitter, but was said to have a good swing for doubles—followed with a two-bagger to tie the game.

The Brewers tried to manufacture another run in the fourth. After Obermueller hit a two-out single, Yost tried to execute a hit and run. But Podsednik fouled the pitch off. Through a six-pitch at-bat, Obermueller, who'd played shortstop in the minors, went through a number of stops and starts before Podsednik flew out. Heading back out for the sixth, he felt more gassed than his pitch count indicated. He began laboring and leaving the ball up. Bagwell doubled and Lance Berkman drew a walk before Richard Hidalgo lined a ball that just eluded a leaping Wes Helms for a two-run double. Now trailing 4–2, Obermueller was done for the day.[60]

In for Obermueller was Ben Ford, back in the majors after four years since a handful of appearances with the Yankees in 2000. He had no answers for the Astros. He walked the lead-off man, then allowed run-scoring hits to Brad Ausmus, Miller, and Biggio. He walked Adam Everett to load the bases before being pulled for Brooks Kieschnick.

Kieschnick had been one of the more interesting storylines for the Brewers in 2003. Called up in late April, he primarily pitched and pinch hit, but also started seven games at DH and in the outfield. He had become the first player ever to hit home runs as a pitcher, pinch hitter, and DH. After a solid spring, he made the Opening Day roster. With the Brewers already down 7–2, he worked Bagwell to a 2–2 count before the first baseman crushed a fastball into the bleachers above the Brewers bullpen for a grand slam. Kieschnick pitched around a couple of hits to end the inning and threw a clean seventh. He ended his afternoon with a meaningless RBI single in the bottom half.

The Astros tacked on two more in the eighth, but Yost's Brewers wouldn't give in. In the bottom of the eighth, trailing 13–4, Overbay popped a solo homer and catcher Gary Bennett added a two-run bomb to set the 13–7 final score. Over their first five games, the Brewers had scored 37 runs—and surrendered 38.

Asked for his thoughts on the game, Yost said plainly, "This day's over and we come back tomorrow." His team had battled, and that was all he could ask of them. "If they can do that, we'll take whatever the result is, because you can't ask for any more than that. Give the fans their money's worth, play your best, play your hardest, and whatever comes from that we take."

The 2004 Brewers played winning baseball into the second half, and were just 2.5 games out of the Wild Card spot at the break. But a brutal 6–21 mark in August dashed any hopes of a break-out season and the team again finished with 94 losses. In September Selig agreed to sell the team to a group headed by Los Angeles investor Mark Attanasio for $223 million.

2005

Monday, April 11, 2005: Brewers 6, Pirates 2 (42,458 attendance)

In the News: The *Journal Sentinel* has revealed multiple violations of protocol by the MPD in the investigation into the beating of Frank Jude, an African American man, by several off-duty Milwaukee police officers.

At the Movies: *Hitch*, Showtime Cinemas

On the Radio: "Rich Girl" by Gwen Stefani featuring Eve

In late September 2004—with the Brewers mired in a dreadful 22–53 post–All-Star break slump—word leaked that Bud Selig and company had finally found a buyer for the Brewers. Unable to find a local group to take over the club, they entertained a number of bidders nation-wide. The top offer, originally reported as being around $200 million, came from 46-year-old Mark Attanasio, a partner in a Los Angeles money management firm.[61]

Selig, who had turned his tiny initial ownership stake and team president title into a principal share of just under 30 percent, claimed that with all the money he had put back into the team over the years, he would more or less break even once the sale went through. Two audits of the team's financials, one by the state and the other by the City of Milwaukee, were done to investigate allegations that Selig and company had pushed the stadium through for the purpose of inflating the value of the team for an eventual sale. But they found no purposeful misdeeds, only terrible management practices. Selig's claim on breaking even was true.[62]

Just after the season ended, Attanasio gave his first interview with local media. He had long-term goals for the team in Milwaukee and spoke of the "very rich tradition of baseball" in the city. He wanted to head a team that was a winner for both the investors and the fans. "I'm a fan just like they are," he said. "And in that way, I'm no different from anyone in the park. And I'm going to be passionate about the team winning, just like they are." He declined to get into specifics on the team's payroll—presently the lowest in baseball and about one-third of that of the thriftiest National League playoff team—but said he anticipated it would increase.[63]

In late November, the payroll got a bump when the Brewers signed Damien Miller, a Wisconsin native and former All-Star, to a three-year deal worth about $10 million. Two weeks later, the team swung a mini-blockbuster trade with the White Sox, sending Scott Podsednik—who'd regressed offensively in 2004, but led all of baseball with 70 steals—and reliever Luis Vizcaino to the south side for outfielder Carlos Lee, a veteran slugger coming off back-to-back 30-homer seasons. The trade added another $7 million to the Milwaukee payroll and provided an instant upgrade to an offense that struggled mightily during the 2004 collapse.[64]

After the sale was approved in mid–January, Attanasio joined his team at spring training, as eager as any player to participate in the ritual start to the season. Prior to the first spring game, he walked around the infield, taking everything in and personally introducing himself to each player. "I get such a thrill out of this," he told the press.[65]

Attanasio was not the only significant newcomer in camp that spring. Third baseman Jeff Cirillo had rejoined the team, signing as a free agent after being released by the Padres. Three years removed from his last productive season, Cirillo was hoping to rediscover his swing in the city that still considered him a fan favorite. He was set to split time at third with Russell Branyan, another bargain-bin find who had either hit a homer, struck out, or walked in 54 percent of his plate appearances with Milwaukee in 2004. Also drawing the eye that spring was a 22-year-old shortstop named J.J. Hardy. The readiest of a wave of young talent that now had the

Brewers' farm system ranked as baseball's best, Hardy showed incredible range in the field and projected as an above-average hitter. In late March, he was named the team's starting shortstop, the first rookie to earn the job since Kiki Diaz in 1990.[66]

Even if most baseball observers were not sold on the Brewers as a contender, the local buzz over the team (and a payroll increased by 45 percent) was tremendous. On the day single-game tickets went on sale, the club sold more than 90,000, a new franchise record and nearly double the best single-day total in Miller Park history. Riding a pace that nearly tripled that of a year before, more than one million seats had been sold by the season's open, something done only four other times in franchise history.[67]

After opening with a two-game sweep in Pittsburgh and taking one of three from the Cubs at Wrigley, the Brewers came home to a swell of optimism. As temperatures climbed into the high 40s, a party atmosphere returned to the pregame tailgates as grills sizzled and taps flowed with more a sense of hope than ritual. The *Journal Sentinel* talked to several groups of fans that morning who had never seen a game at Miller Park—former loyalists soured on the bad vibes of the late Selig years, but glad to have a reason to celebrate baseball again.[68]

After pregame introductions, Milwaukee got a chance to meet the Attanasio family as they joined Mark on the field for the national anthem, performed by none other than Mark's father, Joe. Despite having never sung in public before, Joe—according to Mark—"chose himself" for the honor. He delivered a faithful, if not operatic, rendition to the delight of the crowd.[69]

Starting for the Brewers against the Pirates was lefty Doug Davis, another Doug Melvin find, who had been picked up after being released by the Rangers in mid-2003 only to start 34 games for the Brewers in 2004 and post baseball's sixth-best ERA among lefthanders. Starting a home opener just a year and half removed from thinking his career might be over, Davis tried hard to control his nerves through the opening innings. Stepping off the mound to take breaths and prowling around the bump between hitters to calm himself, he worked around a walk in each of the first two innings.[70]

In the bottom of the second, Damian Miller introduced himself with a ringing double to right before Branyan dug in against Pittsburgh's Kip Wells. After working a full count, Branyan obliterated a Wells fastball off the scoreboard in center field, nearly hitting his name in the Brewers' lineup, to give Milwaukee a 2–0 lead. The ball traveled an estimated 465 feet.[71]

Davis worked around another walk in the third, but ran into trouble in the fourth. Walking the lead-off batter, he allowed a triple to Tike

Redman and a single to Ty Wigginton to tie the score 2–2 before working out of trouble. In the bottom half, Geoff Jenkins opened with a base hit and, after a Miller pop-out, Branyan once again faced off against Wells. Although the book on Branyan was to bust him inside, Wells had not been hitting his spots on that half of the plate. Once again, he pitched him away, and once again, Branyan crushed it, sending the 2–0 curveball onto the left field concourse 400 feet away. After rounding the bases, "Russell the Muscle"—who had been traded or released four times in the previous three years—was coaxed out of the dugout for the ever-rare Opening Day curtain call.[72]

Leading off the bottom of the fifth, Brady Clark—plucked off of waivers before the 2003 season and now the starting center fielder—tagged Wells for another homer to make it 5–2 Brewers. Davis, gutting his way through with troublesome command, worked through the sixth and seventh allowing only a pair of hits. Reliever Matt Wise came on for the eighth and kept the Pirates off the board. Wells, with a pitch count now over 100, came back out for the bottom of the eighth but was chased after a Carlos Lee walk. Facing Ryan Vogelsong, Miller singled and Branyan—getting another standing ovation—whiffed. Hardy, 0 for 3 on the day, followed with a pop to short right that second baseman Freddy Sanchez dropped, permitting Lee to streak home and set the 6–2 final.[73]

After a nice ovation for the heads-up play by Lee, the giddy home crowd was able to officially welcome back Jeff Cirillo, who followed pinch-hitting for Wise. Cirillo walked, but Clark followed with a flyout. In the top of the ninth, Mike Adams—one a handful of pitchers competing for the Brewers' yet-undecided closer role—pitched around a walk to seal the win.[74]

In his seat just beside the Brewers dugout, Attanasio received a series of hugs, high fives, and pats on the back. "It is a special day here," he said later. "The whole culture here around baseball and our way of celebrating baseball here. It's engaging and charming and it's really why I fell in love with the community and the team."[75]

While never really contending for a playoff spot, the 2005 Brewers surprised everyone by finishing with an even 81-81 mark—the team's first non-losing season in 13 years and an improvement of 14 wins over 2004.

2006

In the News: Secretary of State Condoleezza Rice has made a surprise visit to Iraq to meet with the leaders of the Iraqi parliament. The feuding among rival political blocs there has virtually paralyzed the government and has left the position of prime minister unoccupied since last December.

At the Movies: *Larry the Cable Guy: Health Inspector*, Mayfair Mall 18
On the Radio: "I'm n Luv (Wit a Stripper)" by T-Pain feat. Mike Jones
Monday, April 3, 2006: Brewers 5, Pirates 2 (45,023 attendance)

When Mark Attanasio took over the Brewers, he said that he felt they could be a contender within three years. By the time he had finished his first season as owner, the Brewers felt like they were already on the cusp. Hitting the .500 mark for the first time since 1992, the 2005 Brewers improved their offensive output by more than 90 runs and—with the emergence of Chris Capuano as an 18-game-winner and the continued progress of Doug Davis and Ben Sheets—established a 1-2-3 in their starting rotation not matched since Chris Bosio was still in town. And anchoring the bullpen was the latest Doug Melvin waiver-wire find turned fan favorite in Derrick Turnbow. Dumped by the Angels after the '04 season, Turnbow won the closer's job in mid–April and, featuring a blistering fastball and a slacker's mop of shaggy brown hair, put together one of the more dominant seasons for a closer in team history.[76]

From their fertile farm system, prospects J.J. Hardy, Rickie Weeks, Prince Fielder, Corey Hart, and David Krynzel had all seen time with the big league club in 2005. By season's end, Weeks and Hardy had already taken over the middle infield positions, and Fielder and Hart seemed poised to see regular time in 2006. The ascension of Prince to his throne was made official in early December when the Brewers dealt first baseman Lyle Overbay—who'd batted .289 with a .376 OBP and 87 doubles over two seasons in Milwaukee—to the Blue Jays for outfielder Gabe Gross and pitchers Zach Jackson and Dave Bush.

GM Doug Melvin's turn-around on the Brewers had been so quick and thorough that he was drawing interest from both the Red Sox and Dodgers for their open GM positions. But with a year remaining on his contract, and with work still to be done in Milwaukee, he signed an extension in November that would keep him with the Brewers through the end of 2009. Melvin had proven himself a shrewd judge of under-the-radar talent, but it was skipper Ned Yost who hauled in the Brewers' biggest prize of the winter when he convinced his good friend Robin Yount to sign on as bench coach.[77]

But Robin Yount and optimism were not the only things the Brewers were bringing back from the team's 1980s heyday. At the annual winter warm-up event, the team unveiled a new alternate jersey set for "Retro Sunday" home games. The new look was straight out of the Cecil Cooper era with pinstripes, block lettering and the much-missed "ball and glove" logo. The club also announced the right field wall at Miller Park would be moved in slightly to accommodate a new ground-level party section and that an LED ribbon display board would be added to the face of the club-level seating.[78]

In early January, the Brewers made a second trade with Toronto, this one for third baseman Corey Koskie. Robbed of his spot in the lineup when the Jays acquired All-Star third baseman Troy Glaus, Koskie was had for a low-level minor leaguer and Toronto agreed to cover a portion of the $12 million remaining over the final two years of Koskie's contract. A lifetime .277 hitter who got on base at .396 clip, Koskie was the kind of solid pick-up that would have been unthinkable during the salary-constrained times of just a few years prior. Koskie at third would keep Bill Hall—who'd batted .291 with 17 homers in '05—in his utility role, shoring up depth in the infield and outfield.[79]

For the second straight season, the Brewers broke the franchise mark for tickets sold in a single day, with some waiting in line overnight for single-game tickets to go on sale at the Miller Park box office. The team reported that season ticket sales were also at a record pace and virtually no existing season seat holders had canceled their plans for 2006. With Koskie in the fold and the $38.5 million extension signed by ace Ben Sheets kicking in, the team payroll took another spike, reaching a franchise-high $53 million—nearly double what it was when Attanasio bought the team. At the opening of spring training, the team announced an extension for Yost, keeping him under contract until 2008 with a team option for 2009. Reflecting on his first year on the job, Attanasio said the work had been "more fun than I ever dreamed it would be."[80]

And finally, people outside of Brewers nation began to take notice. In their 2006 baseball preview issue, *Sports Illustrated* named Attanasio one of its 30 baseball figures to watch in '06 and picked the team to finished second in the NL Central. Sheets, the magazine wrote, had the ability to dominate in any start and the Brewers' pitching was "possibly the division's deepest." Sheets, however, had missed the last six weeks of the 2005 season with a muscle tear. His health would be paramount to the Brewers' hopes for '06. "If Sheets is healthy," *SI* declared, "Milwaukee could make a push for the postseason."[81]

But Sheets would not be ready for the open of the '06 campaign. He had strained a muscle in his back in training camp and was set back far enough that he had to stay behind in Arizona to rehab when the team headed north to open at Miller Park against the Pirates. But Sheets and the team expressed optimism that he would only miss one or two starts before being ready to go.[82]

Despite the overcast weather, the thousands who set up in the Miller Park parking lots just past dawn on April 3 could see nothing but sunny days ahead for their home team. "Something feels different about this team," one of them told the *Journal Sentinel*. It was a widely-shared sentiment. Inside, Joe Attanasio once again sang the national anthem as the building hummed with anticipation. The biggest pre-game cheer was saved for bench coach Robin Yount, back in his familiar #19. "It's a pretty big deal. It's going to be exciting," Yount said before the game. "I don't remember one that wasn't, even though I played 20 years. Opening days are special."[83]

With Sheets missing his first season-opener start in five years, Doug Davis took honors for the Brewers. After center fielder Chris Duffy led off with a single, Davis got Jack Wilson to ground to third for an around-the-horn double play, with Prince Fielder making a nice scoop at first on Rickie Weeks' relay. Sean Casey followed with a fly to left that Carlos Lee lost in the glare of the roof panels. The ball glanced off Lee's hands and Casey made it to second base, where Davis would leave him stranded. In the bottom half, J.J. Hardy cracked a one-out solo homer off Pittsburgh ace Oliver Perez to give Milwaukee a quick 1–0 lead. But the Pirates got it right back in the second when second baseman Jose Castillo doubled and Perez, flailing away at the plate with two outs, managed to slap a Davis pitch into center to score the run. In 192 career plate appearances, it was just his eighth career RBI.[84]

Leading off the bottom of the second, Weeks lined a hit to left and, as the ball drifted away from outfielder Jason Bay, took a big turn for second, where Bay's throw beat him by a step. It would be the closest the Brewers would get to reaching second base against Perez for the rest of the afternoon. Getting Brewers hitters to chase his high fastball, Perez rang up nine strikeouts, including four on rookie Prince Fielder. For five innings, Davis matched Perez in scoreless innings, albeit in a less artful fashion, as he kept Pittsburgh off balance and allowed mostly weak contact.[85]

In the Pittsburgh sixth, with runners on second and third, Davis gave Castillo a free pass to load the bases for the light-hitting catcher Humberto Cota. On an 0–1 pitch, Cota hit a roller up the middle. Weeks backhanded it and, his momentum carrying him away from the play, flipped the ball behind his back to Hardy at second base. The throw pulled Hardy, who grabbed it on a bounce, off the base, but he appeared to get his toe back to the bag in time for the force out to end the inning. But umpire Mark Carlson called Castillo safe, permitted a run to score to break the tie. As 45,000 voiced their disapproval, Davis fanned Perez to end the inning.[86]

The score held at 2–1 until the bottom of the seventh. Facing Solomon Torres, Weeks opened with a walk and stole second. Bill Hall, starting at third, worked a full count before drawing his own free pass. Damian Miller followed and showed bunt, trying to lay it down the third base line to advance the runners. But the ball caught too much of the bat and bounced right back to Torres for what would have been an easy double play, but Torres bobbled it. He scrambled to get Miller at first, but the Brewers now had two in scoring position with one out. With lefty Damaso Marte on for Torres, Jeff Cirillo—who'd revived his career in '05 with a .281 average—was called on to pinch hit in the pitcher's spot. With adrenaline surging and the crowd roaring for one of the team's last connections to the County Stadium era, Cirillo forced himself to hold back and wait on his pitch. Sitting on a slider, he got it on 1–1 and rolled it through the hole on the left side to score Weeks and Hall and put the Brewers on top, 3–2. In a rare show of emotion, Cirillo pumped his arms as he ran to first.[87]

An inning later, the Brewers tacked on two more when Carlos Lee followed a Geoff Jenkins base hit with a booming homer to left to put the Brewers up 5–2. And in the top of the ninth, the Brewers faithful let loose with another big noise for the newest Milwaukee phenomenon: the Derrick Turnbow Show. Just having signed a three-year, $6.5 million extension and trotting in to "Fuel" by Metallica, Turnbow blew away Castillo with two fastballs and a knee-buckling curve before allowing a soft base hit to Nate McLouth. With two strikes on Freddy Sanchez and Miller Park as loud as it had ever been, Turnbow got his ground ball, which Weeks, Hardy, and Fielder rolled into a picture-perfect game-ending double play.[88]

"It's official," said Matt Wise, set-up man and close friend to Milwaukee's ninth-inning hero, "Turnbow is a rock star."[89]

If health was the key to success in 2006 for the Brewers, it was easy to lay the blame for their 75–87 finish. Hardy, Weeks, Koskie, and Sheets all missed significant time with injuries and inconsistent pitching—including a full-on meltdown by closer Turnbow at mid-season—which doomed even their modest goal of a winning season.

2007

Monday, April 2, 2007: Brewers 7, Dodgers 1 (45,341 attendance)

In the News: Senate majority leader Harry Reid has backed Senator Russ Feingold's plan to cut off funding for the war in Iraqi beginning March 2008.

At the Movies: *Wild Hogs*, Showtime Cinema

On the Radio: "Girlfriend" by Avril Lavigne

Two thousand and six was a strange year for the Brewers. While they never really felt like a contender—and suffered through a season-long string of injuries—they were near enough to contention in late July to swing a deadline deal that returned ready-to-contribute players for free-agent-to-be Carlos Lee. One of those players, closer Francisco Cordero, turned out to be one of the team's bright spots for '06, dominating in the second half after taking over closing duties from Derrick Turnbow, whose mid-season meltdown (punctuated by a 21.32 ERA for the month of July) ended the city's bout with Turnbow-mania.

Another '06 standout was Bill Hall, the would-be third baseman displaced by Corey Koskie to a utility role who moved to shortstop after J.J. Hardy was lost for the year. Hall socked 35 homers and batted .270 while showing himself more than adequate with the glove at short. Despite being named the team's MVP, his role for 2007 was still not clear. Shortstop was Hardy's position and the team's depth in the outfield was further complicated by GM Doug Melvin's interest in free agent center fielders Dave Roberts and Juan Pierre.[90]

The team still preferred Corey Koskie at third base, but it was unclear when—or if—he would be able to play again. In an early July game against the Reds in Milwaukee, Koskie fell awkwardly while chasing a foul pop, tipping backward and hitting his head on the turf. Koskie finished the game, but would not play again that year as the aftereffects of the concussion soon became overwhelming. He had bouts of dizziness and exhaustion so bad that he had trouble getting out of bed. He found himself unable to concentrate on others while they spoke and had difficulty speaking himself. He tried watching games with his team from the dugout, but was unable to follow the action. He occasionally found his coordination so bad that he was unable to even to reach out and pick up an object.[91]

Catcher was also an issue for the Brewers in the second half and, in late November, Melvin dealt Doug Davis—who'd posted a 4.91 ERA in '06—to the pitching-starved Diamondbacks for catcher Johnny Estrada. Estrada had batted over .300 in '06 and was an immediate upgrade over Damien Miller. But the trade also left a hole in the Brewers' rotation that Melvin sought to cure by moving Hall back to center field and dealing either Mench or Geoff Jenkins to open a spot for either Corey Hart or Gabe Gross. But Melvin found no worthwhile offers on the pair and shifted his attention to the free agent pool.[92]

It was an odd off-season for the Brewers, in that they had money to spend—Mark Attanasio had authorized a payroll of more than $60 million, a stunning 50 percent increase from '06—but the market was so rich that Melvin couldn't find any useful way to spend the money. In December, rumors began linking the team to former Cardinals pitcher Jeff Suppan. One of a number of mid-rotation starters on the market, Suppan had been a steady presence with the Cards for three seasons, with above-average ERA and high win totals. But for the growing number of baseball observers using "advanced stats" to analyze player performance, the book on

Chapter Four. The Aughts

Suppan showed a mediocre talent. Tim Dierkes, writing for MLBtraderumors.com, said "Suppan is primed to be one of the worst signing this winter," predicting that he'd land a four-year contract worth $30 million.[93]

It would actually take the Brewers $40 million over four years to land Suppan, who made up his mind after a five-hour dinner with Melvin and Attanasio at Attanasio's Los Angeles home. It was the biggest contract the Brewers had ever given out. Melvin touted him as a "big game pitcher," the type of player that a contending club needed. Jeff Sackmann, writing for the Brewers blog Brewcrewball.com, using an analytical approach, was less enthusiastic about the deal, noting that Suppan likely benefited greatly in St. Louis from an excellent defense and that his sterling earned run averages would have been mediocre at best had he been pitching in front of the Brewers' less-polished defense.[94]

As the Brewers opened camp, the only real weak spot in the lineup was at third. With Koskie still not ready for game action, Yost had settled on a platoon of Tony Graffanino and Craig Counsell—who had signed as a free agent after two years back in Arizona. But also on the radar that spring was 23-year-old Ryan Braun, now ranked as the team's top prospect. Braun had just finished tearing up the Arizona Fall League and was thought to have a nearly Major League–ready bat. But even as he bashed his way to a .353 spring average with a team-high five homers, his glovework at third (he'd made 44 errors there in just 154 minor league games) kept him out of the Brewers' Opening Day plans.[95]

Optimism was once again high as the Brewers headed north. "We expect this to be a winning team this year," manager Ned Yost said. "I think it's different. Last year, we kept talking about raised expectations. At least for me, it was more hopeful. Now, it really is more quiet confidence." For the second straight year, the Brewers were a dark-horse preseason playoff pick. But once again, the consensus was that health—particularly the health of ace Ben Sheets—was key.[96]

With the Dodgers in town for the opener, Milwaukee felt a little bit of the Southern California warmth as temperatures reached the mid–50s with clear and sunny skies. But the Miller Park roof would remain closed regardless of the weather as a $15 million project to repair the mechanisms that moved the panels was still ongoing. Facing off against LA's Derek Lowe was Ben Sheets, making his fifth season-opening start for the Brewers in six years. Now two years removed from his last injury-free season, Sheets was eager to get going in '07 and make up for the let-down of 2006. He took the mound in the first buzzing with nervous energy. As he set down the Dodgers in order, he said, "[It felt like] I had a sumo wrestler wrestling in my belly."[97]

Rickie Weeks opened the season for the Brewers with a dribbler that

Lowe couldn't handle. Hardy followed with a broken-bat single and Weeks streaked to third. After a Prince Fielder strikeout, Bill Hall—getting a hero's welcome—grounded to second to score Weeks and put Milwaukee up 1–0. In the second, the Dodgers tied it when Jeff Kent crushed a 3–1 fastball from Sheets over the center field fence. But after the homer, the wrestler in Sheets' belly calmed down, and Sheets set down the next three Dodgers hitters.[98]

Corey Hart, who'd won the right field job in spring, opened the bottom half with a double and, two outs later, made a bold steal of third with Weeks batting. After Weeks walked, Hardy rolled a base hit past Nomar Garciaparra at shortstop to score Hart and make it 2–1 Brewers. That would be all Ben Sheets needed. It took just 13 pitches in the top of the third to retire the side, and only eight in the top of the fourth, with Milwaukee now up 3–1 after a Craig Counsell sacrifice fly. In the bottom half, Hardy continued to baffle Lowe, drawing a one-out walk and scoring after singles by Fielder and Estrada. With two away, Geoff Jenkins lofted a high fly ball to left that Luis Gonzalez seemed to have tracked. But with the midday sun blasting through the glass panels of Miller Park's roof, Gonzalez lost the ball and it fell in for a hustle two-run double to bump the lead to 6–1.[99]

Bill Hall launches a home run during the 2007 opener against the Dodgers. A year later, he'd belt two Opening Day homers (Alex Voerman).

Now down five, the Dodgers looked hopeless again in the fifth as Sheets needed just nine pitches to retire the side. In the sixth, he needed only seven. In the bottom of the sixth, Hall—who had signed a four-year, $24 million extension before spring training (the advanced stat crowd declared it to be a great deal for the Brewers)—drilled a solo homer off reliever Mark Hendrickson to make it 7–1. With the Dodgers unable to hold back or make solid contact, Sheets cruised through the seventh and eighth—needing just 10 pitches apiece—to complete a run of 22 straight batters retired since Kent's second-inning homer. When he led off the Brewers' half of the eighth, the home crowd gave him a noisy standing ovation.[100]

When Sheets came back out for the ninth, he had a chance for the Brewers' first complete game one-hitter since Ted Higuera in 1987 and just the sixth in franchise history. But with one out, Brady Clark, traded by the Brewers to the Dodgers just a week before, blooped a double down the left field line. With a man on base for the first time all afternoon, Sheet coaxed a pair of pop flies to end it. Striking out just three, Sheets needed only 104 pitches to complete his gem.

After the game, when asked how he felt about his performance, Sheets flashed his low-key sense of humor. "It feels good. I'd love to go 0 for 4 every game," he said, referring to his 0 for 4 at the plate, which included three whiffs. "I'm getting my strikeouts in, making sure I set the record."[101]

Fifteen years of frustration ended in 2007, as the Brewers finally broke the .500 mark, finishing at 83-79. The Brewers spent 121 days in first place in the NL Central—and held a piece of first as late as mid-September—but a brutal 9-18 August allowed the Cubs to overtake them. The Brewers finished just two games back, the nearest they'd been to a postseason berth in 19 years.

2008

Friday, April 4, 2008: Brewers 13, Giants 4 (45,212 attendance)

In the News: Bus Cook, Brett Favre's long-time agent, says there is no truth to the *LA Times* report that he had been quietly gauging interest for a possible trade for his recently-retired client.

At the Movies: *Superhero Movie*, Ipic Bayshore

On the Radio: "Don't Stop the Music" by Rihanna

The so-called experts had staked the Brewers' hopes for the playoffs in 2007 on the health of Ben Sheets. And indeed they were right. The Brewers were 53–40, 3.5 games up on the Cubs and the best team in the National League when Sheets went on the DL in mid–July. When he returned six weeks later, they were in third place, a game under .500 and 2.5 games back. Beyond Sheets, the only starter to prevent runs at a rate above the league average was 21-year-old Yovani Gallardo.

On the other side of things, the 2007 Brewers bashed 231 homers—tops in the Majors—with Prince Fielder leading the way with 50. Rookie of the Year Ryan Braun, not even called up until late May, hit 34 along with a .324 batting average and league-leading .634 slugging percentage. Corey Hart had his own break-out, slugging 24 homers to go with 23 steals, and J.J. Hardy exceeded all expectations with 26-homers and an All-Star nod.

Heading into the off-season, Doug Melvin and company made re-signing closer Francisco Cordero their top priority. Also looking to add pitching, the team was quietly surprised when free agent Curt Schilling listed the Brewers as one of 12 teams he was interested in signing with for 2008. Coming off a World Series–winning season in Boston, Schilling would be 41 years old in '08 but could still show flashes of dominance. "It's nice to see we're on the baseball map," Melvin said, adding that he had reached out to Schilling's agent. The matter ended up moot, however, when Schilling opted for retirement.[102]

In a move to try to improve their pitching by proxy, the Brewers signed veteran catcher Jason Kendall in late November. Lauded for his ability to call a game and manage pitchers, as well as his ability to get on base, Kendall was seen as a clear step up over Johnny Estrada, who never managed to find a good fit with the Brewers and drew just 12 walks over 120 games in 2007.[103]

Just days after landing Kendall, after weeks of rumors and genuine hope that the Brewers might be able—for one of the few times in franchise history—to retain a key player after he'd entered the free agent market, Francisco Cordero jumped to the Reds for $46 million over four years—just $4 million more than he'd been offered by the Brewers. With a big hole to fill, the Brewers turned to a player they had tried to acquire via trade at the deadline in 2007: Eric Gagne. Between 2002 and 2004, Gagne had been a dominant closer for the Dodgers, even winning a Cy Young Award. After being derailed by injuries, he had rediscovered the old magic in Texas, where he'd saved 16 games in '07 before being traded to Boston, who had outbid Milwaukee to install Gagne as a set-up man. Despite a terrible 20-game run in Boston, the Brewers felt confident enough that he would return to form to give him $10 million for the '08 season.[104]

In another bid to improve their pitching without adding pitchers, the Brewers signed center fielder Mike Cameron to a one-year deal with an option for '09 in mid-January. One of the top defensive center fielders in baseball, Cameron would not only improve the outfield defense but would also force Bill Hall back to third base and allow Braun—who was still dreadful defensively at the hot corner—to take over for the departed Geoff Jenkins in left field. Although the Brewers would need to wait on Cameron, who had to serve a 25-game suspension for testing positive for a banned stimulant late in the '07 season.[105]

Cameron would be allowed to play in spring training games but, unfortunately, he would not be the only player in camp facing scrutiny for involvement with banned substances. Just days after the Gagne signing, the long-awaited report on steroids in baseball prepared by former senator George Mitchell was made public. Gagne was one of several high-profile players the report named as recipients of illegal performance-enhancing drugs. While he would not face discipline from the league, the report cast a pall over his arrival with the team. At the open of camp, Gagne read a statement (in English and in French, as Gagne was a native of Montreal) apologizing for the "distraction," but admitting to nothing. "I'm just here to help the Milwaukee Brewers get to the World Series," he said. "That's all I really care about."[106]

Also drawing attention that spring was Prince Fielder, who showed up sporting a headful of short dreadlocks and a new-found vegetarianism. A book about factory farming, a gift from his wife, had prompted the new lifestyle. "After reading that, [meat] just doesn't sound good to me anymore," he said. "It grossed me out a little bit. It's not a diet thing or anything like that. I don't miss it at all."[107]

With the payroll topping $80 million, the Brewers were projected to be in the top half of spenders for the first time since 1992. And the Brewers were still trying to lock up Fielder and Braun into long-term deals. With Braun appearing on the cover of the *Sports Illustrated* season preview issue, the buzz in Milwaukee was unprecedented. Ticket sales outpaced the 2007's record-setting totals as the club set a goal of three million for '08. Even as the national pundits mostly picked the Brewers to finish behind the Cubs, the Brewers had their sights set squarely on the division title and a World Series.[108]

The Brewers opened in Chicago and took two of three from the Cubs in an opening series that already had a playoff feel. They returned home to host the Giants and, with gameday temperatures in the low 50s, actually found a little too much enthusiasm for pregame tailgating. The expected turnout of tailgaters who did have game tickets was so great that the team announced that tailgaters without game tickets would be asked to leave the lots so that everyone with tickets would be able to park.[109]

But the *Journal Sentinel* reported that the threats—and actual warnings from sheriff's deputies patrolling the lots—did little to change anyone's plans. Nor did it encourage fans who had tickets but preferred to keep the party going—like the group who brought along a custom-built 12-person beer bong—from heading inside. The always-problematic bathroom

Brewers fans Shane Rismeyer (left) and Brian Head enjoy some tailgating staples before the 2008 opener (Jeramey Jannene).

situation in the lots was aided a bit, however, by a number of fans bringing along their own make-shift toilets. Some even offered their facilities (which were, in most cases, a five-gallon bucket with a shower curtain surround) on a pay-per-use basis. The "going rate" ranged from $1 to $3 while a "day pass" for a genuine porta-potty, bought in on a flatbed trailer, ran $10.[110]

Inside the stadium, Carlos Villanueva was as eager as many of those stuck at the far end of a bathroom line. The 24-year-old had made just 12 Major League starts and was only in the rotation while Yovani Gallardo recovered from a knee injury. "You're always nervous," he said of his debut on the big stage. "I even get a little nervous when I pitch in intersquad games. I think it's a good thing for me. If I don't feel that way, I'm not excited."[111]

Villanueva showed no nerves in the first, working around a walk. Rickie Weeks went to work right away on the Giants, leading off with a single and stealing second before Prince Fielder laced a single to bring him home. It was Weeks' 17th straight game with a run scored—which tied an NL record. After Braun struck out, Bill Hall dug in. Hall had seen his power numbers sag in 2007 and had a miserable opening series. On the bus ride home from Chicago, he'd pored over his old at-bats on a portable DVD player, trying to find his lost swing. And on a 1–1 pitch from Jonathan Sanchez, he found it, launching a two-run homer to left-center field to put the Brewers up 3–0.[112]

For the next three innings, Sanchez and Villanueva traded hard-earned zeroes, with each pitcher working around base runners and minor scoring threats. In the bottom of the fifth, Kendall, batting ninth behind the pitcher, led off with a single followed by a Weeks walk. With Miller Park coming to life, Gabe Kapler, lured out of retirement by the Brewers that off-season and part of a platoon while Cameron served his suspension, and Fielder slapped back-to-back run-scoring singles. Both men were still on base when Hall came to bat with one out. Facing reliever Keiichi Yabu, Hall crushed a hanging curve for a 436-foot three-run blast to stretch the Brewers' lead to 8–0. Having fallen out of favor after his big extension and down year in '07, Hall was now greeted with a curtain call.[113]

The Giants finally got to Villanueva in the sixth, collecting four straight hits and scoring twice to chase the righty. Although he left to a standing ovation, he was unhappy with his performance. He'd wanted to go deeper into the game and take some of the load off an already-taxed bullpen. Brian Shouse, a sidearming lefty, finished off the inning with no further damage.[114]

Not content with an 8–2 lead, the Brewers broke the game wide open in the sixth. After Gabe Gross led off with a walk, six of the next seven Brewers batters got hits—the only exception being Braun, who'd finish 0 for 5 on the day. The barrage scored five more runs, including the sixth driven in by Hall. Solomon Torres, picked up in a little-noticed December trade, came on for Milwaukee to complete the rare three-inning save, his only blemish being a two-run homer allowed to catcher Bengie Molina. Torres was surprised by the long outing. "We have a tradition where the pitching coach comes out and shakes your hand when you're done," he said after the game. "I kept waiting for him to come shake my hand and he never came."[115]

The 13–4 win was the Brewers' fourth straight Opening Day win and their 12th in 15 tries. Their 13 runs was the most ever for a home opener and the nine-run margin of victory matched an opener record.

Riding mid-season pick-up CC Sabathia on perhaps the greatest run of starting pitching in team history, the Brewers fought off an early-September lull that cost Ned Yost his job to clinch the NL Wild Card spot on the final day of the season and break the franchise's 26-year playoff drought. Along the way, they set a new team attendance record of more than three million. The Brewers lost in the NLDS to the Phillies, 3 games to 1.

2009

Friday, April 10, 2009: Brewers 4, Cubs 3 (45,455 attendance)
In the News: CIA director Leon Panetta has announced that,

breaking with the Bush administration's policies, the CIA will no longer permit private contractors to interrogate suspected terrorists and that the Obama administration will seek to close secret, U.S.-run overseas prisons.

At the Movies: *Hannah Montana: The Movie*, Southgate Cinemas

On the Radio: "Poker Face" by Lady Gaga

When the Brewers broke their 26-year playoff drought on the last day of the 2008 season—even having to wait until after their victory over the Cubs for a Mets loss to clinch the spot—it was as much an act of survival as one of triumph. A four-and-a-half game lead on the Mets for the Wild Card on September 1 turned into a one-game deficit in just two weeks. Manager Ned Yost was fired and CC Sabathia—picked up in an attention-grabbing mid-season trade—started four games of the Brewers' final 12 games, posting a 1.88 ERA and virtually dragging the team across the finish line.

With a four-game loss to the eventual world champion Phillies dismissed in the midst of postseason euphoria, the Brewers faced steep goals for the 2009 season and, for the first time in the Attanasio era, the team seemed almost certain to take a step backward. The most obvious need was a permanent manager. Dale Sveum, elevated after Yost's firing, had as much of a connection with the young club as any internal candidate for the job, but was dismissed early on in the process when the team announced they would seek an "experienced" candidate. "Basically, my heart was ripped out of my chest," Sveum said upon hearing he would not be a candidate for the job.[116]

The three final candidates for the job were Bob Brenly, Willie Randolph, and Ken Macha—who had been the team's top choice in 2003 when they'd hired Yost. After a week of interviews, the team hired Macha, who had won two division titles in a four-year run with the A's before being fired in 2006. For all the winning he'd done in Oakland, Macha was not a popular figure among fans or players. There was a locker room disconnect between him and his players and an overall lack of communication that made him a difficult man to play for. But the Brewers dismissed that as hearsay and Macha promised that he would always have an "open door" to his players in Milwaukee.[117]

But even more pressing for the Brewers was their starting rotation. Ben Sheets, now four years removed from his last healthy season, had been brilliant in '08, but only threw four innings after September 11. He was now a free agent and the Brewers were not expected to offer him a contract. CC Sabathia, so dominant in his 17 starts as a Brewer that he got NL Cy Young *and* MVP votes, was also a free agent and no one expected the Brewers to able to afford his asking price. The two established closers the Brewers had going into '08 had both pitched poorly—Eric Gagne ran his ERA over 6.00

before losing the closer's job and Derrick Turnbow walked 13 in six nightmare innings before being sent to AAA—and neither were expected back for '09. Neither would Salomon Torres, who finished with 28 saves and announced his retirement.

While Sheets searched in vain for a multi-year deal, the market on Sabathia was similarly slow to develop. In early November, the Brewers made him an offer reportedly in the range of $100 million over four years. Although the offer seemed little more than a good faith gesture—both to the fans and Sabathia—Doug Melvin insisted that it was legit. Moving into the holiday season, the Sabathia rumor mill had it that the Yankees had made an offer topping $140 million, but nothing had yet been heard from CC's preferred destination of the Los Angeles Dodgers. In early December, a report from a San Francisco newspaper had it that Sabathia was leaning toward accepting the Brewers' offer. The thought of not only retaining the game's best pitcher—but outbidding the Yankees to do so—turned out to be a passing one for Brewers fans. Just a day after the report, Sabathia agreed in principle to a seven-year, $161 million mega-deal with the Yankees.[118]

The money the Brewers had offered to Sabathia, Melvin said, would not be rolled over to other free agents. Indeed, a trade with the Yankees—one that would have sent Mike Cameron to the Bronx in exchange for the younger, cheaper center fielder Melky Cabrera—was scuttled when the Yankees asked the Brewers to pick up part of the tab on Cameron's remaining contract. Looking to fill the holes in their rotation, Melvin went bargain hunting. After briefly being connected with 45-year-old Randy Johnson, the Brewers added Braden Looper, a mediocre innings-eater formerly of the Cardinals. For the back end of the bullpen, they signed Trevor Hoffman—the long-time all-world closer of the San Diego Padres—to an incentive-heavy one-year deal. Hoffman was undeniably one of the greatest closers of all time, but was about to be 41 years old and had just posted his highest ERA since 1995. The 2009 payroll projected to be just under what it had been in 2008.[119]

While these developments kept the Cubs as the NL Central favorites among the national pundits, they did nothing to dampen the local excitement for 2009. Once again, the team set a new record for single-day ticket sales, with more than 104,000 sold online and in person as more than 1,000 fans camped out overnight at the Miller Park box office. Six games sold out that first day, and by the open of the season, 1.75 million tickets had already been sold—a total that by itself was greater than half of the Brewers' single-season attendance totals. And with the run on playoff-branded gear, Brewers merchandise sales had tripled since the start of '08.[120]

The Brewers opened in San Francisco, dropping two of three before returning home in the early morning hours on the day of their Good Friday opener against the Cubs. Macha permitted the team to report to the park later than usual for the 3 p.m. game, but this landed several players in the middle of an especially bad Opening Day traffic snarl. Corey Hart was stuck in traffic for two hours. Third baseman Casey McGehee was one of several players fellow motorists screamed at as they tried to inch toward the stadium. More than one saw obscene gestures from fans assuming they were trying to cut in line to secure a good tailgating spot.[121]

The late start was to permit Catholic fans to attend morning services before the game and indeed many tailgaters served up meat-free options (fish tacos were especially popular), but the high-energy match-up with the ultra-rival Cubs ensured that Miller Park would hardly be a place of quiet reflection and fellowship that afternoon. After Branden Looper—given the start because of his experience facing the Cubs in St. Louis—shut down Chicago in the first, Rickie Weeks played the sparkplug role perfectly: advancing to second after shortstop Ryan Theriot airmailed a throw on a routine grounder. He moved to third on a sac bunt by Corey Hart and trotted home when Ryan Braun collected his first-ever home opener base hit. The Brewers portion of the Miller Park crowd roared in approval.[122]

After Chicago's Rich Harden struck out the side in the second, Hart connected for a solo homer to right field to make it 2–0. Leading off the fourth, Milton Bradley smoked Looper's 61st pitch of the afternoon just over the fence in right to make it 2–1. Mike Fontenot followed with a single, but was cut down in a rare caught stealing from catcher Jason Kendall. After a walk, already Looper's fourth of the game, catcher Koyie Hill fanned to end the inning.[123]

In the bottom half, Prince Fielder drew a lead-off walk and, two outs later, Bill Hall appeared to hit an inning-ending pop-up. But with the midday sun blasting through the Miller Park roof panels, neither Theriot nor left fielder Alfonso Soriano could find the ball, and it dropped in for a double. With runners on second and third, Harden intentionally walked Kendall to bring up Looper. After working a 2–1 count, Looper hit a liner off Harden's foot, but the ball bounced right to Theriot, who tossed to first to end the threat. In the top of the fifth, a gassed Looper worked two singles and a hard liner from Soriano that Braun snared on the run in left. Seth McClung relieved Looper for the sixth and, after getting his first two hitters, allowed a base hit to Theriot and then served up a meatball to career .191 hitter Hill, who mashed it for a two-run homer to left-center field to put the Cubs on top, 3–2.[124]

Both teams threatened in the seventh, the Cubs with a one-out double from Kosuke Fukudome and the Brewers loading the bases with two out for Ryan Braun. But Fukudome was stranded and Braun—facing the

Cubs' fireballer Carlos Marmol—flied out harmlessly. In the eighth, Todd Coffey came on for the Brewers and gave up a lead-off double to Fontenot, who moved up on a groundout. After plunking Hill, he faced pinch hitter Aaron Miles with runners on the corners and one out. But Coffey got under Miles' bat with his sinker and worked an inning-ended double play.¹²⁵

The 3–2 score held into the bottom of the ninth. After Kendall opened with a strikeout against Cubs closer Kevin Gregg, pinch-hitter Chris Duffy worked a six-pitch walk to bring up Rickie Weeks. The #2 overall draft pick in 2003, Weeks was in his fifth year as the Brewers' regular second baseman. He'd struggled with injuries and inconsistency, often drawing the ire of the home fans. He'd begun the '08 season as the lead-off hitter but late in the season was reduced to a platoon role and batting in the seven spot. On a 2-1 pitch from Gregg, Weeks hammered a line drive to left. Soriano took a few steps forward before correcting and rushing back as the ball kept carrying. It zipped over his head and Duffy scored easily as Weeks trotted into second. With the game tied, Miller Park vibrated with noise.¹²⁶

Gregg was rattled. On a 2-2 pitch to Corey Hart, he skipped one past

Rickie Weeks bats during the 2008 opener. Weeks was among the most productive Brewers of all-time in home openers and played hero in the '09 lid-lifter (Myles Jaeschke).

Hill and Weeks scooted into third. Gregg tossed two wide of Hart to set up an inning-ending double play. On a 1–2 pitch, with the split-partisanship crowd on their feet and very loud, Ryan Braun slapped a grounder to short and Weeks broke for home. Braun had not hit the ball overly hard and, with Braun's speed, Theriot made the snap decision to skip the double play attempt and fired a one-hopper to Hill, who had tried to position himself to block the plate. Charging down the line, Weeks dove head-first and snuck his left hand around Hill's leg, touching the plate just before Hill applied the tag. Home plate umpire Jim Reynolds threw his arms out to call "safe" and Weeks jumped up and spiked his helmet to the ground as his teammates rushed out of the dugout.[127]

"You can't ask for anything more than Rickie gives," McClung said after the game. "He gets here early and works so hard. Nobody deserves it more."[128]

Taking advantage of a sluggish division, the 2009 Brewers held a piece of first as late as July 4, despite being just five games over .500. But pitching struggles led to a mid-summer swoon that made the team a non-factor on their way to an 80–82 finish.

Chapter Five

The Teens

2010

Monday, April 5, 2010: Rockies 5, Brewers 3 (45,808 attendance)
In the News: Observers feel that, after the contentious battle to get Obamacare passed, it is unlikely the president will be able to do much more before the upcoming midterm elections. It is thought that all of Obama's political capital was expended in the matter.
At the Movies: *Shutter Island*, Oriental Theater
On the Radio: "Tik Tok" by Ke$ha

A year removed from having two legit aces anchoring their rotation, the 2009 Brewers had just one starting pitcher—23-year-old Yovani Gallardo—post an ERA under 5.20. Braden Looper, brought in to eat innings, indeed led the team with 194 of them, but allowed 39 homers and led the league in earned runs allowed. Macha declared that only Gallardo and lefty Manny Parra, who'd had an ERA of 6.36 in 27 starts in '09, were locks for the 2010 rotation. Doug Melvin wanted to add a pitcher via free agency, but with no increase in team payroll expected for 2010, he would need to get creative.[1]

This "creativity" had actually begun in August. Shortstop J.J. Hardy had been mired in a season-long slump when the Brewers made the somewhat shocking decision to demote him to AAA Nashville. For a 26-year-old former All-Star in his fifth season as the Brewers' starting shortstop, this was a very unusual move. When Hardy spent a total of 20 days in the minors before being called back to Milwaukee, the team's motivation became clear. The stint in AAA would keep Hardy's service time low enough to push his free agency back by a full year, making him a more attractive trade chip in the off-season.

Hardy had known what was happening from the moment he'd been demoted and knew that his time in Milwaukee was over. Just after declaring that they would not be bringing back center fielder Mike Cameron, the Brewers dealt Hardy to the Twins for Carlos Gomez. Once the prize of the

Mets' system, Gomez was a high-energy outfielder who had yet to do much in the majors, but whose potential was tantalizing. With Alcides Escobar ready to take over at short and Gomez slated for center, the Brewers had jettisoned $15 million in contract obligations from 2009 and replaced them with two low-dollar, high-ceiling players.[2]

The team was also looking to move Corey Hart, another former All-Star who'd struggled in 2009. Rumors ran all winter about Hart being dealt for pitching. Meanwhile, Melvin zeroed in on mid-rotation free agent starters, eventually settling on lefty Randy Wolf. Despite still facing the last year of Jeff Suppan's disastrous big money deal, Melvin secured Wolf for $30 million over three years. Chris Capuano, who'd missed all of '09, and Doug Davis, coming off three decent years with the Diamondbacks, were also added with low-risk contracts. In January, the Brewers added another veteran, luring four-time All-Star and eight-time Gold Glove winner Jim Edmonds out of retirement.

Despite the many questions about the rotation, the most anticipated moment of spring training was the Brewers Cactus League opener with the San Francisco Giants. The reason was the now-infamous "bowling ball" celebration at home plate at Miller Park after Prince Fielder beat the Giants with a walk-off homer in the final meeting between the two teams in 2009. After Fielder's blast left the yard, his teammates gathered around home and toppled backward as Fielder emphatically leapt onto the plate. It was the most artful of the Brewers' post-win flourishes that dated to the 2008 campaign. The first was their habit of untucking their jersey shirts after a win—a trend started by Mike Cameron as a tribute to his working-class father, who untucked his work shirt at the end of a shift. These bits of fun rubbed some opponents the wrong way, in particular the division-rival Cardinals, whose complaints prompted Bill Hall to orchestrate a "run-off" after one last at-bat win against the St. Louis. After the winning run scored, the team fled the field at full speed for the clubhouse, saving the dear Cardinals from witnessing even a moment of celebration from an opponent.[3]

When Fielder stepped in for his first at-bat of the meaningless game, Giants starter Barry Zito, as expected, drilled Fielder in the back with his first pitch. Fielder, unimpressed, picked up the ball and tossed it back toward the mound. The Giants' message—delivered six months after the offending celebration—might as well have been marked "return to sender." Macha had already ordered a stop to any excessive celebrating, counting himself among the old-school set who wanted the game to be played "the right way." With Cameron and Hall, who had also designed the bowling ball celebration, no longer with the team, players like Ryan Braun and Corey Hart offered tepid support for the new policy. "We don't want to give the other teams reason not to like us," Hart said. "There's a lot of old-school guys out there that might look at things differently."[4]

"We are all in favor" of the change, Macha announced. "I'm ok with guys having fun, but there's a way to have fun and still respect the other team."[5]

The Brewers opened the season at home against the Rockies. After fielding virtually the same starting eight for the '08 and '09 openers, the Brewers opened their 40th anniversary season with Brewers Opening Day first-timers Carlos Gomez and Jim Edmonds in the outfield, Gregg Zaun behind the plate, rookie Escobar at short, and Casey McGehee—a Melvin waiver-wire find who batted .301 in '09 and won a handful of Rookie of the Year votes—batting fifth and playing third base.

On the mound for his first Opening Day start was Yovani Gallardo, who was quietly developing into one of the best young pitchers in the National League. A native of Penjamillo, Mexico, Ted Higuera had been one of Gallardo's idols as a boy and, with the Brewers, he chose to wear Higuera's old #49. "I'm honored to do this and be from Mexico," he said before the game. "You know for sure that you'll have those people behind you, and that's one thing I know I'll always be proud of." Back in Penjamillo, a little town of about 3,000 residents, his grandparents watched each of his starts at a restaurant near their home. "They know what it means," he said of the honor. "Opening day is opening day."[6]

This Opening Day, however, was unlike any other in Miller Park history. With temperatures in the low 70s and the sun shining, the game was played with roof open—the earliest date of any Miller Park game to played in the open air. And to celebrate the team's 40th anniversary, the original Opening Day battery of Lew Krausse and Jerry McNerty completed the game's ceremonial first pitch.[7]

Facing Ubaldo Jimenez, himself one of the best young starters in the league, Gallardo ran into trouble in the second inning. After a one-out ground rule double by Brad Hawpe, Gallardo got Chris Iannetta to pop out. But down on Ian Stewart 2–0, Gallardo bounced a pitch in front of Zaun that caromed off his shin guard to the Colorado dugout. Zaun leapt up but had lost track of the ball. Gallardo, covering home, tried to point him to the dugout, but Zaun couldn't find it. Meanwhile, Hawpe rounded third and scored easily. The count now at 3–0, Gallardo threw a Stewart a lifeless, middle of the plate fastball, assuming he would be taking all the way. Stewart wasn't, and he launched a towering home run that hit the scoreboard in center field to make it 2–0 Rockies.[8]

Gallardo and Jimenez traded zeroes until the top of the fourth, when Todd Helton reached on an error by McGehee, moved to third after a pair of walks, and scored on a sac fly by Stewart. After Jimenez handcuffed the Brewers in the bottom half, the Rockies did more damage against the struggling Gallardo. A pair of singles gave the Rockies runners on first and second with two outs. On Gallardo's 80th pitch of the afternoon, Troy Tulowitzki stroked an RBI single to make it 4–0 Rockies. Surprisingly, Macha let Gallardo lead off in the bottom of the fifth. Both he and Weeks fanned, followed by Gomez's first hit as a Brewer. Gomez, who had once stolen 64 bases in a single season in the minors, broke for second with a 2–1 count on Braun and took the bag easily. Two pitches later, Braun ripped a double off the left field wall to make it 4–1.[9]

Despite being without his best stuff, Gallardo set down the next six in order and, in the bottom of the seventh, Gomez kept up his happy hello to Milwaukee as he crushed an 0–2 curveball off reliever Matt Belisle into the second deck in left field. He even added a little bat flip as he began his trot around the bases. Chris Narveson took over the eighth and worked around a double to keep it 4–2. Riding an unofficial scoreless streak that ran back through spring training, Narveson's luck ran in the top of the ninth when Ryan Spillorghs followed a Carlos Gonzalez double with an RBI single.[10]

Down three heading into the bottom of the ninth and facing Franklin Morales, covering closing duties while All-Star Huston Street was on the DL, the Brewers got right to work. Weeks, down 0–2, got clipped as

Ryan Braun made his Opening Day debut in 2008 and would, for reasons not always related to his play on the field, be among the most loudly cheered players during the ceremonial opener introductions (Ian D'Andrea).

Morales tried to come inside and took first base. He skipped the next pitch past the catcher Iannetta and Weeks moved to second. After feigning a bunt, Gomez dropped the bat on a 1–1 offering and looped it into right field. Weeks moved to third and held while Gomez, who'd come blazing out of the box, moved to second when Hawpe couldn't field the ball cleanly. It was two on and nobody out for Braun, but all he could manage was a fly out that scored Weeks to put the Brewers within two. Fielder followed by smoking a ball up the middle, but the shortstop Tulowitzki had shifted to shallow center and made a leaping grab that sucked the wind of the home crowd. Edmonds followed with another hard-hit ball, but right at Clint Barmes at second. As quickly as it had started, the Brewers' rally was over and the Rockies held on for a 5–3 win.[11]

"It's hard to get too upset," said Craig Counsell, who'd gone 0–2 on the afternoon after taking over the McGehee at third. "We have the other team's closer on the ropes and you hit a couple of line drives. That's the game of baseball."[12]

Even if Ken Macha hadn't told the team to tone things down, there wouldn't have been much for the Brewers to celebrate in 2010. The team held a winning record for just one day all season and, while never really falling apart, languished in mediocrity throughout the 77–85 campaign.

2011

Monday, April 4, 2011: Braves 2, Brewers 1 (46,017 attendance)

In the News: At least 20 have been injured and one killed in protests in Afghanistan over the public burning of a Quran by a Florida pastor.

At the Movies: *Win Win*, Downer Theater

On the Radio: "Just Can't Get Enough" by the Black Eyed Peas

When the Brewers took on the Reds, who'd already clinched the division title, on the final day of the 2010 season, it was already known that Ken Macha would not be back for 2011. All the issues that had dogged him in Oakland—the disconnect with players, the lack of communication, his old-school ways and ill fit with younger players—had poisoned his time in Milwaukee. He'd lost his team early and never won it back. In the third inning of that meaningless game, Ryan Braun popped out to Joey Votto at first and didn't bother running to first. Macha pulled him from the game. Afterward, a handful of players thanked Macha for his time with the team. Many others did not.[13]

In his last session with the Milwaukee media, Macha laid blame on Braun and Prince Fielder. "Those are the two [problematic] guys," he said. "But the rest of the guys it was all positive." On Braun, he said, "I talked a lot to Ryan, almost every day, but he does his own thing. He's going to do what he wants to do." On Fielder, "I don't know if there were any guys on the staff that talked a whole lot to him this year."[14]

Braun had been an All-Star that year and got a few stray MVP votes. Fielder led the team in homers and on-base percentage. Rickie Weeks and Corey Hart had both posted the best numbers of their careers and Casey McGehee clubbed 23 homers to go with an .800 OPS to show that 2009 had been no fluke. But once again, a lack of pitching had killed any chance of contention. The lone bright spot of the staff was John Axford, who—just a year and a half after spending an off-season working as a bartender in his native Canada—took over the closer's role from an out-of-gas Trevor Hoffman and posted a 2.48 ERA with 24 saves.

The Brewers needed a leader and they needed arms. From a field that included Bob Melvin, Joey Cora, and Bobby Valentine, Doug Melvin and company hired Angels bench roach Ron Roenicke. In contrast to Macha, Roenicke was excellent at managing the various personalities within a clubhouse, and in return, his players had a deep loyalty to and respect for him as a coach. He was personally reserved, but preferred an aggressive style on the field. He'd let his players play, but he'd get them to play as one.[15]

After two years of less-than-sterling relations between Ken Macha and his star players, the Brewers brought in Angels bench coach Ron Roenicke for the 2011 season (Jeramey Jannene).

With one year left until Fielder became a free agent—and with him having rebuffed all attempts to work out an extension—Doug Melvin saw 2011 as the Brewers' last best chance to make a deep playoff run. In early December, he struck a deal with the Blue Jays, sending Brett Lawrie—the Brewers' top-ranked prospect—north in exchange for pitcher Sean Marcum. Coming back from Tommy John surgery in 2010, Marcum started 31 games while posting a 3.64 ERA and striking out nearly four times as many hitters as he walked. The advanced statistics on him showed that he'd been significantly better than any Brewers starter had been in '10.[16]

Two weeks later, Melvin made a true blockbuster, landing former Cy Young Award winner Zack Greinke from Kansas City for a package of young talent headlined by Alcides Escobar and Lorenzo Cain. After being nearly unhittable in 2009, Greinke had slid back in 2010 and, sick of the Royals' constant losing, demanded a trade. Greinke was also one of the game's true personalities. Diagnosed with anxiety disorder after nearly leaving baseball in 2006, Greinke had a sharp intellect and could be quite witty, but his unique way of engaging with others often made him seem aloof. Introduced to the Milwaukee media, he expressed excitement for joining the team, albeit with a blank face. "[Hearing of the trade], I was probably the happiest I've been ... since I was drafted in baseball," he said. After a searching moment, he added, "I was happy when I got married too."[17]

"This is what I call a 'now' trade," Melvin said of the deal. He had been after Greinke since the end of the World Series and had upped his offer to the Royals more than once. It also took some convincing of Greinke himself, who had to waive a no-trade clause. Part of selling the trade involved invoking Milwaukee as the ideal place for him to work and live. The small town vibe that had undoubtedly kept other players away sealed the deal for Greinke. "There's more people to ignore in New York or Boston than there are in Milwaukee," he said. "But I'll still ignore them, probably."[18]

With most of the starting lineup and starting rotation spots settled, the Brewers headed into spring training with the singular goal of staying healthy. But that proved difficult. Jonathan Lucroy, who'd established himself as the primary catcher in 2010, broke his pinky finger early in camp and would open the season on the DL, as would Corey Hart, who strained a muscle in his back and needed more time to get ready. But the biggest blow came when, after two poor spring outings, Greinke learned that he'd broken a rib at the start of camp. The injury was an unusual one for a pitcher and Greinke initially refused to say what had happened, only that it was "something stupid." Eventually, he admitted that he'd been playing pick-up basketball and had fallen on his side going for a rebound. "I had a lot of fun doing it," he said. "But it wasn't worth it." He was expected to miss all of April.[19]

Just as the team was about to head north, Melvin made a minor trade with the Nationals, sending them a minor leaguer for disgruntled reserve outfielder Nyjer Morgan. A rangy defender and a slap hitter with speed, Morgan was best known around baseball for the number of on-field fights he'd been involved in. But Melvin dismissed that and was convinced that he'd landed a solid fourth outfielder and not a troublemaker. "I think he's a player with a lot of fire in him and a lot of energy," Melvin said, dropping him into the middle of a clubhouse that would no longer be on pins and needles. "He's not the only guy we have with fire and emotions."[20]

The day Morgan arrived in Brewers camp, Roenicke asked the outfielder to introduce himself to the team. Braun and Fielder, both feeling loose under the team's new leadership, had each already greeted Morgan. "We want you to be yourself," they'd told him. With the whole team watching, Morgan flexed his arms and scowled.

"What's up, fuckers?" he shouted.[21]

The Brewers opened in Cincinnati, dropping three in a row to the Reds before heading home. It was Miller Park's tenth anniversary and the club celebrated with a new, $11 million scoreboard that featured more than 6,000 square feet of high-definition video screen. To help stoke the city's title fever, 11 members of the recently-crowned world champion Green Bay Packers threw out the ceremonial first pitches. For the real thing, Roenicke handed the ball to 29-year-old lefty Chris Narveson. Both Narveson and Atlanta's Brandon Beachy worked around baserunners in the first and Beachy tiptoed past a lead-off double in the second to leave the game scoreless into the bottom of the third. Rickie Weeks, who'd hit two homers in the opening series in Cincinnati, led off with another bomb, this one a line-drive rocket over the fence in left-center.[22]

Narveson was hitting his spots and keeping Braves batters off balance with his looping curve. He kept the Braves off the board in the fourth and, after the Brewers could make nothing of two baserunners in their half, did the same in the fifth. After his fourth inning jam, Beachy settled in and retired nine Brewers in a row. Both clubs went to their bullpens in the seventh, the Brewers clinging to a 1–0 lead. Kameron Loe tossed a scoreless frame and, after advancing Morgan to second with just one out, Peter Moylan did the same to the Brewers.

Into the eight, Roenicke went to his set-up man, off-season free-agent pick up Takashi Saito. Once an All-Star closer with the Dodgers, Saito had a career ERA of just 2.19. Facing Martin Prado leading off, Saito ran the count full before Prado caught enough of one to poke it over the left field fence to tie the game. Saito then fanned Nate McClouth and got Chipper Jones to ground out before Dan Uggla popped one to left that bounced off the top of the fence and out for a go-ahead homer. It was the first time in Saito's Major League career that he'd allowed two homers in a single inning.

In the bottom half, Ryan Braun laced a one-out single to bring up Prince Fielder as the potential go-ahead run. But, facing lefty Johnny Venters, Fielder grounded weakly into the shift for an inning-ending double play. Down to their last chance in the bottom of ninth and facing rookie fireballer Craig Kimbrel, the Brewers didn't even manage to put the ball in ball in play. In a 15-pitch inning, Kimbrel struck out the side and the Brewers' opening skid ran to four games.

But in the clubhouse after the game, the atmosphere was not that of a team struggling to win their first game. "When you look at this team, you don't see anybody frustrated," said Carlos Gomez. "We know we're a good team. We've got to think about tomorrow and how to win tomorrow. It's going to come. You're going to see that team that scares everybody."[23]

Six games under .500 in early May, the Brewers took off after Greinke's return and took over first place for good in late July. Their 96–66 record tied for the best in franchise history and they ultimately ended up just two wins short of a trip to the World Series.

2012

Friday, April 6, 2012: Cardinals 11, Brewers 5 (46,086 attendance)

In the News: Google has announced that they will soon introduce a head-mounted device that will function like a hybrid of a smart phone and a pair of reading glasses.

At the Movies: *The Turin House*, UWM Union Theater

On the Radio: "Starships" by Nicki Minaj

The 2011 edition of the Brewers was destined to be a franchise classic. With legit MVP candidates in both Ryan Braun and Prince Fielder, a deep starting rotation and knock-out bullpen, and a trash-talking sparkplug in Nyjer Morgan, the team was one of the Brewers' best ever. But looking ahead to 2012, they were almost certain to lose a cog of their machine. Fielder had turned down several extension offers from the Brewers and would now be on the open market. While the Brewers vowed to make him a serious offer, it was all but assured he would be offered more money elsewhere.

The heartbreak of the NLCS loss was tempered somewhat when Ryan Braun won the NL MVP award (Fielder placed third) after putting together one of the most impressive all-around performances in franchise history. As Braun basked in the glow of his win, the Brewers took an aggressive stance on the free agent market. They were rumored to be willing to go as high as $120 million over six years to keep Fielder and were linked to infielders Jose Reyes and Aramis Ramirez.[24]

And then, on December 10, came the bombshell. ESPN's *Outside the Lines* reported that, during the playoffs, Braun had failed a league-administered test for performance enhancing drugs. He was currently appealing the result but, if it stood, he faced a 50-game suspension to open the 2012 season. The news came from a leak within the league. The result of the test—per the league's agreement on testing with the players' union—should not have been made public until after the appeal process. But that hardly mattered now. Braun insisted that he would be vindicated.[25]

Meanwhile, the Brewers signed third baseman Aramis Ramirez, formerly of the Cubs, to a deal worth $46 million over four years. One of the best-hitting third basemen in the game, Ramirez was an immediate upgrade to a hot corner situation in Milwaukee that had little production in 2011 and he would be a big part of the team's efforts to replicate the offensive output now certain to be lost with Fielder. With no good external options, first base duties would be split between Corey Hart and Mat Gamel—a one-time top prospect who had yet to find his swing, or consistent health, at the big league level.[26]

All the while, the Braun drama played on. A report, the source of which was unclear, spread that Braun had flunked the test due to elevated levels of testosterone. "Insanely high," per the report, twice as high as anyone had ever shown, a suggestion that something had to have gone wrong with the test. A celebrity gossip website reported that the result had nothing to do with PEDs and was instead the result of medication Braun was taking for a "private medical condition." Braun's camp, working full time to help him beat the rap, cited numerous "highly unusual" aspects to the test. The team, his teammates, and the fans cautiously rallied to his defense, while those outside of the Brewers' bubble branded him a cheater and a fraud.[27]

Braun's appeal hearing, which was supposed to be a tightly-guarded secret, was held in late January, at the same time Braun was in New York to accept his MVP plaque. "Sometimes in life we all deal with challenges we never expected to endure," he said in his acceptance speech to the baseball writers. "I've chosen to view every challenge I've ever faced as an opportunity and this will be no different. I've always believed that a person's character is revealed through the way they deal with those moments of adversity."[28]

A month after his appeal, a three-person panel voted 2–1 with Braun, ruling that the urine sample that triggered the positive test had not been properly handled. The sample, which should have been shipped to the

Chapter Five. The Teens

testing lab the same day it was collected, had stayed in the home of the collector for two days before being shipped. While not an explicit violation of the rules, it was enough to cast doubt and Braun was cleared.[29]

The ruling came the day before Braun was to report to training camp and his arrival was treated as the Brewers' first big win of 2012. The MVP was overjoyed, the cloud had lifted, and the Brewers would be at full-strength all season. "It's like we won the lottery," said Jonathan Lucroy. "When I heard," said Nyjer Morgan, "I was as happy as a pig in slop." To a man, his teammates expressed nothing but full support for Braun's version of events.[30]

The next day, Braun gave a press conference with the entire team in attendance. He took an aggressive stance, clearly angry over the way he'd been treated throughout the process. "The system in the way it was applied to me in this case was fatally flawed," he said. Then he went on about the time between the collection of his sample and its delivery to the testing facility. "What could have possibly happened in that 44-hour period?" he asked. "There were a lot of things that we learned about the collector, about the collection process, about the way that the entire thing worked that made us very concerned and very suspicious about what could have actually happened." He cited unnamed experts that said it would be "easy" to tamper with a sample if one were so motivated. He said he understood the gravity of what he was alleging could have happened and he would not make such statements lightly. "I know what it's like to be wrongly accused of something. For me to wrongly accuse somebody else of something wouldn't help anybody."[31]

Certain to face hostile crowds all season long on the road, Braun and the Brewers were happy to open the 2012 campaign in Milwaukee against the reigning world champion Cardinals, minus Brewers-killer Albert Pujols—who had jumped to the Angels that off-season as a free agent. For the Brewers, it would again be Yovani Gallardo on the hill to start the season. After he worked around a pair of walks in the first, Rickie Weeks led off the bottom half with a sharp base hit to center. Carlos Gomez, still yet to find his swing in the bigs, continued his home opener hot streak with by lacing one down the left field line and motoring into third for a triple. The roar for the run-scoring hit grew even louder as Braun strode to the plate. A second standing ovation—he'd gotten the treatment during pregame intros, too—and chants of "MVP! MVP! MVP!" culminated with a line-out to short. Aramis Ramirez then received his welcome to Milwaukee and responded with a run-scoring groundout to make it 2–0 Brewers.[32]

The Cards got one back in the second on a solo homer by Yadier Molina. It was the only tally of the inning, but Gallardo was struggling to hit his spots. An inning later, the Cards had no trouble squaring him up. Carlos Beltran and Matt Holliday opened the frame by homering on back-to-back pitches. Lance Berkman followed with a walk and David Freese, the MVP of the 2011 World Series, obliterated a lifeless Gallardo pitch to make it 5–2. By the time Gallardo finally worked out of the inning, he'd already thrown 67 pitches on the afternoon. After a clean third from Jaime Garcia, Freese burned the Brewers again with an RBI single in the top of the fourth. Gallardo's afternoon was over after seven hits, five walks, and six earned runs. "Today I just sucked," he told reporters after the game. "That's all you can say."[33]

The Brewers finally seemed to have something going in the fifth when Gamel, getting the start at first base, and Lucroy slapped singles to start the inning. Nori Aoki—purchased by the Brewers from Yakult of the Japanese League—got his own standing ovation as a welcome to the Majors, but struck out. Weeks followed with a bouncer to second that caused a collision in which Lucroy was called out for interference and Gomez ended the threat with a fly out.

The Cardinals added runs in the sixth and seventh and the home fans began to get bored and restless. The lines at the concession stands grew and the idle chatter of the grandstands turned to anything but what happening on the field. In the top of the ninth, with the score 8–2 and fans streaming toward the exits, sidearmer Tim Dillard labored through his second inning, absorbing four hits, a walk, and three more runs in an effort to save the bullpen for the next day's game. In the bottom half, backup catcher George Kottaras slugged a three-run homer to bring the remaining fans to their feet and cut the margin to six. Three batters later, the tally was St. Louis 11, Milwaukee 5, and the long afternoon was finally over.

It was an ugly loss, but it counted in the standings just the same as any other. And the Brewers faithful certainly preferred an Opening Day dud with the MVP in uniform over a win with him banished. "It was great, man," Braun said of his reception. "I truly appreciate it from the bottom of my heart."[34]

The Brewers struggled out of the gate in 2012 and were nine games under .500 when they dealt the free-agent-to-be Greinke in late July. Although they far out of the division race, a second-half surge brought them within striking distance of the newly-added second Wild Card. They ended up at 83–79, five games out of a playoff spot.

2013

Monday, April 1, 2013: Brewers 5, Rockies 4 (10 innings) (45,781 attendance)

In the News: Twitter has announced a plan to start charging users $5 per month to use vowels in tweets, or so says one of a number of April Fools' Day "news" items that have gone viral.

At the Movies: *In Your Dreams: Stevie Nicks*, Oriental Theater

On the Radio: "Started from the Bottom" by Drake

Just as it had been prior to their 2011 breakout, pitching held the Brewers back in 2012. On the offensive side, the Brewers posted a fearsome lineup that saw a major breakout by Jonathan Lucroy, a solid debut season from Nori Aoki, a 30-homer campaign from Corey Hart, and a top-10 finish in the MVP voting from Aramis Ramirez—not to mention the object of every other NL city's derision in Ryan Braun, who had a season just as good as his MVP campaign, earning him a second place finish for the 2012 award.

On the other side, however, a cobbled-together but decent rotation was tanked by an all-around meltdown in the bullpen. Only one reliever who totaled more than 35 innings posted an ERA under 4.00. An early-season offer of a five-year, $100 million extension to Greinke was turned down, leading the Brewers to deal him to the Angels just before the deadline. With the contracts of Randy Wolf (who was released in August) and Sean Marcum (who spent July and August on the DL) also coming off the books, the Brewers planned a significant payroll reduction for 2013. Doug Melvin insisted that they had enough potential pitching talent already in the organization to make it work.[35]

Indeed, the 2012–13 off-season had mostly been a series of departures for the Brewers (Nyjer Morgan, Marcum, Francisco Rodriguez, Claudio Vargas, and Manny Parra) and a handful of low-profile free agent signings (Tom Gorzelanny, Mike Gonzalez). The team also brought back Alex Gonzalez—who'd posted mediocre numbers in a handful of games at shortstop in 2012—as a candidate for the wide-open job at first base. And then, for the second straight winter, a Ryan Braun bombshell dropped.

Just before the open of spring training, Yahoo! Sports reported that Braun was among the more than one dozen Major League players whose names were found in paperwork from the Miami-area Biogenesis anti-aging clinic. The records listed regimens of human growth hormone, synthetic testosterone, and other performance-enhancing drugs forbidden by Major League Baseball. Although there was no drug listed with Braun's name—unlike players such as Yasmani Grandal, Gio Gonzalez, Bartolo Colon, and Alex Rodriguez, who were all listed with specific means of doping—his was listed on a sheet of clients who owed money, indicated as $20–30,000.[36]

The lack of a PED listed with Braun's name held him out of the original reporting on the documents. When his inclusion was reported a few days later, he was ready with an explanation. The money was owed for work that he contracted to the clinic's operator, Anthony Bosch, to help with the appeal of his initial failed test the year before. The consultation from Bosch provided nothing useful, Braun said, which led to a dispute over compensation and thus his name on clinic documents.[37]

As suspicious as they were of his claims of "vindication" over this overturned positive test, most national observers found his latest story nearly impossible to believe. "It's hard to find somebody who is less qualified or less credible [than Bosch]," ESPN's T.J. Quinn wrote of the saga. "[He] doesn't have a medical license, although he tells people he is a doctor, [and] he was connected to [Manny Ramirez], who was suspended for PED use four years ago.... The idea that anyone would go to him as a credible witness is astounding." Furthermore, it was disclosed that Bosch was not listed as a consultant in Braun's appeal paperwork. Additional disclosures from the clinic files revealed a mention of the "Braun advantage" in reference to Melky Cabrera, who had been suspended for 50 games in 2012 after testing positive for synthetic testosterone—the same substance that Braun's overturned test had allegedly turned up. Cabrera admitted using PEDs and even declined to accept the 2012 NL batting title—despite having the highest eligible batting average in the league.[38]

Other bits of Brewers news managed to break the constant chatter about Braun that spring. After an uptick in his offensive numbers in 2012, the Brewers gave Carlos Gomez a three-year extension worth $24 million. Mat Gamel, expected to compete with Gonzalez for time at first, needed knee surgery and would miss the entire season. And, in late March, the Brewers made a somewhat desperate attempt to shore up their starting pitching by signing free agent Kyle Lohse to a three-year deal that would cost them $33 million and their first-round draft choice in 2013.[39]

But all eyes were on Braun, and not just those of the fans and media. *USA Today* reported that Braun was now MLB's "Public Enemy #1." The league, still furious over Braun beating his initial failed test, was going all-in on the outfielder, interviewing friends, associates, and other players. While MLB had no real power over anyone outside of the game, they were empowered to suspend anyone who did not cooperate with their inquiries. It was widely thought that a suspension of at least 50 games could come at any time.[40]

Once again, the Brewers opened the season at home, hosting the Colorado Rockies. Braun was still warmly received by the hometown fans, but the warmth felt more labored and less joyful. There were no MVP chants when Braun struck out in the first inning, no standing ovation to rub his "vindication" in everyone else's face. The cheers for Braun felt hollow.

Nor was the Milwaukee faithful overly impressed with Yovani Gallardo, who was having his now-familiar home opener struggles. The

Ryan Braun and his teammates stand for the national anthem before the 2013 opener against Colorado. It was widely expected that Braun would be suspended at some point during the coming season (Matthew J. Prigge).

Rockies left a pair of runners on in each of the first two innings before getting to Gallardo in the third, when Carlos Gonzalez singled and Troy Tulowitzki followed by mashing a fastball up in the zone over the fence in right-center field. The Brewers got one of those back in the bottom half when Nori Aoki—Ron Roenicke's anointed lead-off hitter for 2013—popped a solo homer off Colorado's Jhoulys Chacin. After another labor-intensive but scoreless frame in the fourth, Gallardo again left a fastball up to a dangerous hitter—this time Gonzalez, who drove it into the Rockies' bullpen to make 3–1 Colorado.[41]

Gallardo gave way to Aldredo Figaro, making his Brewers debut. He swapped scoreless frames with Chacin in the sixth and seventh. In the eighth, Burke Badenhop—another newcomer—took over for Figaro and set the Rockies down in order. Then, facing Wilton Lopez, the Brewers bats finally managed to get things going. Shortstop Jean Segura, the main piece in the return for Zack Greinke, led off with a single but was erased when Aoki grounded into a fielder's choice. Weeks followed with a single to move Aoki to third and Braun drove him in with an infield single to put the Brewers within a run.

By this point in the afternoon, the dreaded Miller Park shadows had moved across the infield. With the mid-afternoon sun streaming through the glass panels of the roof, it was typical for a handful of middle-inning at-bats to feature a batter bathed in sunshine while the pitcher was semi-hidden in shadow. Tracking a pitch moving from the shadows to the light was exceedingly difficult and Aramis Ramirez, now batting with the tying and go-ahead runs on base, was not looking forward to it. "I was looking for a cloud to come through right there," Ramirez said after the game. And, in a stroke of luck that the Brewers must have felt they were due, a patch of cloud blotted out the sunshine just long enough for Ramirez to lash a 2–2 pitch from Lopez into the left field corner for a two-run double that put the Brewers up, 4–3.[42]

That brought on John Axford to close things out. Eager to move past a season that saw his ERA from 2011 more than double, Axford ran full counts on each of the first two hitters he faced before getting them on swinging strikes. Now facing Dexter Fowler, Axford tossed a first-pitch meatball, a 95-mph fastball right down the middle, and Fowler tattooed it into the right field bleachers to tie the game.[43]

Unable to do anything with a two-out single in the bottom of the ninth, the Brewers turned to Jim Henderson—one of the lone success

Elvis was in the building for the 2013 opener, part of a long tradition of fans donning costumes for the big game (Chris Zantow).

stories of the 2012 bullpen—to keep the Rockies off the board in the tenth. In the bottom half, Weeks drew a one-out hit-by-pitch and, with Braun batting, stole second. After Colorado's Adam Ottavino walked Braun intentionally, Ramirez worked an unintentional base-on-balls to bring up Lucroy with one out and the winning run 90 feet away. After taking strike one, Lucroy got a slider, waited back on it, and skied it deep to center. Fowler made the catch, but his throw home had no hope as Weeks sped in with the winning run.

"You can't ever get down too much because weird things happen," Roenicke said after the game. "A lot of time, luck is involved in it. Sometimes when you play hard and stay after it, you get some breaks."[44]

The Brewers didn't get many breaks in 2013. After finishing April with a 14–11 record, they struggled through a putrid 6–22 May and never recovered. Braun missed nearly six weeks in June and July with a nerve injury in his hand and had returned to action when he was suspended for the remainder of the season. In accepting the penalty, Braun finally admitted to using PEDs. The Brewers finished with a 74–88 record, their worst since 2004.

2014

Monday, March 31, 2014: Brewers 2, Braves 0 (45,691 attendance)
In the News: North and South Korea are shelling each other's parts of the Yellow Sea. The exchange started with a military exercise by the North, who notified the South via fax. The South responded with its own volley of water-bound missiles.
At the Movies: *Grand Budapest Hotel*, Oriental Theater
On the Radio: "Happy" by Pharrell Williams

For Ryan Braun and the Brewers, 2011 had been the triumph, 2012 the repudiation, and 2013 the reckoning. After being nailed with a 65-game suspension—in the midst of the season that was already mostly lost to injury—Braun finally came clean, admitting that he'd used synthetic testosterone in the form of both lozenges and a topical cream. He said that he'd used them to help recover from the various aches and pains of everyday play. He broke his media silence just before Thanksgiving, when he spoke to reporters during the team's annual Thanksgiving food drive. "I wish I had the ability to go back and change things and do things a lot differently, but unfortunately, I can't," he said. "I don't anticipate being able to earn back everybody's support, but I certainly intend to do everything in my power to do that and I won't stop trying." Asked about his now infamous press conference from before the 2012 season, he replied, "That was a big mistake."[45]

Since his suspension, Braun and his fiancé, Larissa, had been invited to dinner by the sample collector whom Braun had once suggested had been responsible for his positive test. After dining with the man and his family, Braun and the collector had a "productive and positive" conversation, per Braun. Braun said that he'd made no monetary payment to the man, but that they'd made a kind of peace. "We've made amends," Braun said. The collector, as he had throughout the ordeal, made no public comment.[46]

In Braun's absence, 25-year-old fringe prospect Khris Davis suddenly found himself as the Brewers' regular right fielder and responded by crushing his way to a .596 slugging percentage over 56 games. Willing to grant Davis a full-time job in '14, the Brewers dealt Nori Aoki to the Royals for lefty starter Will Smith. The team also made inquiries to free agent starter Ryan Dempster, attempting to overhaul an uninspiring rotation. The Brewers also sought to upgrade at first base, a position that saw little production in 2013 after Corey Hart—who was now a free agent—was lost for the season to a knee injury.[47]

After weeks of rumors linking the team to the Mets' Ike Davis fizzled out when the Brewers were unwilling to part with useful pitching, the team made a run at former Dodger James Loney but were outbid by the Tampa Bay Rays. Finally, in late January, GM Doug Melvin found his starter. With a four-year deal worth $52 million, the Brewers landed 30-year-old Matt Garza. With moderately above-average numbers and having missed significant time each of two previous seasons to injury, Garza was a familiar type of high-dollar newcomer to the Milwaukee staff. He would join Yovanni Gallardo and Kyle Loshe at the top of the rotation, while unprovens like Smith, Tyler Thornburg, and Jimmy Nelson fought to fill out the bottom.[48]

With Garza as the lone off-season addition of even a moderate profile and the lingering unease of the Braun situation dominating the spring narrative, the Brewers could not have found a better preseason friend than the ragged little dog who wandered into their training facility one afternoon in February. Third base coach Ed Seder first noticed the pup, who was malnourished and wore a grease stain on his fur that suggested he'd been hit by a car. Sedar, who had a rescue dog of his own at home, cleaned him up and fed him eggs and sausage from the clubhouse buffet. The dog—soon to be dubbed "Hank" in honor of Hank Aaron—stuck close by Sedar at first, but was quickly embraced by the entire team. While a search was undertaken for his owner, players took turns bringing him home at night. But during the day, hanging out with the team as they ran drills and worked out, Hank became a sudden internet celebrity. *People Magazine*, *Good Morning America*, the *Today Show*, and the *Tonight Show* all took time to profile Hank, who was now thought to have been a stray. Yovani Gallardo, who'd gotten especially close to the dog, considered him a part of the team. "I think he's going to fit right in," Gallardo said. "He's laid back, has fun, enjoys coming out here every day taking care of business. He's a good guy. He'll talk to everybody."[49]

And so it was fluffy little Hank, who had gone from 11 to 14 pounds since showing up in camp, who was the team's star attraction when they headed home for Opening Day against the Braves in Milwaukee. With Hank shirts, caps, and plush toys in high demand (with 20 percent of sales going to the Humane Society), *ABC World News* sent a crew to Miller Park to document Hank's homecoming as the *Milwaukee Journal Sentinel* ran a daily "Hank Watch" feature. Although the Brewers had signed him to a "lifetime contract," he would soon officially retire from full-time duty with the Brewers after the opener and move in with a team employee.[50]

In the midst of all of this, the Brewers had actually assembled a team that some saw as a dark horse contender. With a mix of young and proven veteran pitching, a healthy Ryan Braun, and Carlos Gomez coming off a break-out season, the Brewers had a chance in the middling NL Central. For the fifth straight season opener, Gallardo got the ball and once again worked himself into quick trouble. After a lead-off seeing-eye single from Jason Heyward, Gallardo went 3–0 on B.J. Upton before coaxing him into a groundout and closing out the inning with a pair of pop-outs. In the bottom half, Gomez led off with a rocket into left field that Justin Upton muffed. Gomez moved to second easily and, while Upton feigned a throw in from the outfield, Gomez inexplicably broke for third. Upton lobbed the ball to Chris Johnson, covering the base, and he tagged out Gomez 10 feet shy of the bag.[51]

After Jean Segura grounded out, Braun stepped in and was—for the third straight home opener—welcomed back with a standing ovation. With a few stray scattered boos, Braun flied out. "I kind of allowed the adrenaline and the emotion of the moment to take over and had a pretty horrendous at-bat," he said later, "but something that I'm very thankful for and appreciative of."[52]

Gallardo and Atlanta's Julio Teheran each worked around a pair of baserunners in the second before trading 1-2-3 innings though the top of the fourth. In the bottom half, Segura led off with a walk before Braun poked a broken bat single into left that moved Segura to third. With Aramis Ramirez up, Braun stole second and, two pitches later, Ramirez ripped a double to left that cleared the bases and put the Brewers up 2–0.

Gallardo labored through the fifth and sixth, but managed to keep the Braves off the board. In the bottom of the sixth, a bit of baseball history happened when, after Braun appeared to beat out an infield hit, Atlanta manager Fredi Gonzalez challenged the call. Major League Baseball had instituted instant replay for the 2014 season and, after a 58-second deliberation by the replay umpires in New York, the ruling on the field was overturned for the first ever successful replay challenge in MLB history.[53]

Brandon Kintzler came on for the Brewers in the seventh and, with the help of a diving stab of an Andrelton Simmons scorcher by Ramirez at third, set the Braves down in order. The Brewers, still unable to get much together offensively, went quietly in the bottom half, and Will Smith, moved to the bullpen during spring training, retired the Braves in the eighth to supposedly set the stage for closer Jim Henderson.

Like John Axford before him, Henderson was a tall righty, a native of Canada, and a late bloomer on the mound. Breaking in with the Brewers in 2012 after a decade in the minors, Henderson emerged as a stopper in 2013, saving 28 games and posting a 2.70 ERA. But Henderson hadn't been looking right all spring. Looking to seal the Brewers' first home opener shutout since 1979, Ron Roenicke made a gut-feeling move and called for Francisco Rodriguez—back for his fourth stint with the Brewers—to warm up for the ninth.

Rodriguez had had his own troubles in the spring, actually posting a higher ERA than Henderson and missing time after stepping barefoot on a cactus. After a harmless Brewers half of the eighth, Rodriguez fanned the lead-off batter Johnson before Justin Upton laced a single to left. Dan Uggla followed with a liner up the middle that, with the Brewers infield shifted to the left side, would have made for an easy double play ball for second baseman Scooter Gennett. But the ball caromed off Rodriguez's glove, slowing it enough that Gennett could only get Upton at second. With the Evan Gattis at the plate as the tying run, Rodriguez worked him to a full count before getting him to flail at a change-up out of the zone to end the game.[54]

"We threw the ball well as a team," Ramirez said after the game. Despite his double accounting for the afternoon's only runs, Ramirez deflected the focus to Gallardo, who'd finally earned an Opening Day win. "'Yo' gave us six strong innings and the bullpen did the rest. 'Yo' worked hard and he's out there every fifth day, so it's nice to see."[55]

The 2014 Brewers spent 159 days in first place in the NL Central, a team record that still stands, but a second-half collapse doomed them to obscurity. Still holding first on August 30, they were eight games back just four weeks later. They finished at 82–80.

2015

Monday, April 6, 2015: Rockies 10, Brewers 0 (46,032 attendance)
In the News: The Wisconsin Badgers men's basketball team has not

lingered too long on celebrating their upset of undefeated Kentucky in the Final Four, instead focusing on preparing for their national title match-up with Duke.

At the Movies: *Furious 7*, Avalon Theater
On the Radio: "Uptown Funk!" by Mark Ronson feat. Bruno Mars

For the first half of the 2014 season, the Brewers played the role of world-beater. They had surprised everyone as baseball's most electric team and seemed to be on their way to winning a second division title in four years. And then they stopped hitting. The team that averaged a healthy 4.4 runs per game before the break averaged 3.4 runs per game after and the team's collective OPS fell by 50 points. During a brutal 14-game stretch from late August to early September, they won just one game and managed to score more than four runs just twice. They were in first place at the start of that stretch, 1.5 games up on St. Louis. By the end of it, they were in third place, six games back.

After a post-season "internal assessment" of what had gone wrong, hitting coach Johnny Narron and first base coach Garth Irog were dismissed. Manager Ron Roenicke would be back in 2015, but all reports indicated he would be on a very short leash. Meanwhile, former manager Ned Yost was in the midst of an amazing playoff run that saw his underdog Royals win eight straight games to clinch the pennant and then nearly upset the favored Giants in the final moments of Game Seven of the World Series.[56]

The Brewers' next move of the off-season was to decline their $14 million option on second baseman Rickie Weeks. The move was an obvious one, given that Weeks had not played a full season since 2012, but it was still a sad good-bye to the Brewers' longest-tenured player. While there was a lingering feeling that he'd never lived up to his potential, he was among the NL's best second basemen between 2007 and 2011. And in home openers, he was among the team's all-time elite: only Robin Yount had collected more hits or been on base more times in Brewers lid-lifters.

On the opposite side of the offensive collapse in 2014 was a surprisingly solid pitching staff. Four starters registered ERAs of under 3.70 and an unlikely ace emerged in second-year Wily Peralta, who won 17 games. In early November, the Brewers dealt swingman Marco Estrada to Toronto for slugger Adam Lind, who would be next in line in the rotation of mostly underwhelming post–Prince Fielder Brewers first basemen. The Brewers were also reportedly listening on Yovani Gallardo and Kyle Loshe, both of whom had been solid in 2014 and both of whom would be free agents after the '15 season.[57]

And then, for almost two months, nothing happened. Even the rumor mill on the Brewers had gone quiet. Brewcrewball.com called it "the most boring offseason in Brewers history." The team had veteran talent, valuable pieces that had, nonetheless, not yet resulted in consistent winning. They could sell these players off and start a rebuild or keep making win-now moves in the hopes that the magic of early 2014 could be recaptured. But instead, they remained in a holding pattern until mid–January, when they parted with another long-time star by trading Gallardo to the Texas Rangers for prospects Luis Sardinas and Marcos Diplan and reliever Corey Knebel.[58]

If parting with Gallardo—and saving about $9 million in the process—indicated that they were heading for a rebuild, matters were confused by rumors that soon followed connecting the Brewers to high-dollar free agent pitchers James Shields and Max Scherzer. There was also talk of a trade with Philadelphia involving malcontent closer Justin Papelbon—whose huge contract the Phillies wanted to dump. But the Papelbon deal fell apart and the only high-profile starter the Brewers added was Dontrelle Willis, who hadn't pitched in the majors since 2011 (he wouldn't make the team). The team did make a late-winter signing, however, once again bringing back closer Francisco Rodriguez, who'd been unable to find a long-term deal and settled with a two-year pact for just under $7 million.[59]

And once again, there was springtime Ryan Braun news out of Arizona, and, for once, it was devoid of any controversy. Braun had struggled in 2014 with nerve pain in his thumb. He was limited to just 135 games and faded in the latter half of the year, with his slugging percentage falling by 140 points and his batting average dropping by more than 70. Using a form of cryotherapy, doctors numbed pain sensors near this right thumb. The procedure was not guaranteed to work, but as Braun tore through Cactus League pitching—batting over .400 with three homers—he felt optimistic about a return to his All-Star form. "It feels good to be in a place where

Miller Park slowly begins to fill before the 2015 opener against Colorado, although most of the buzz among the fans that day was reserved for that night's Wisconsin-Duke NCAA National Championship basketball game (Matthew J. Prigge).

I'm healthy and can take a regular swing," he said. "Anytime you can deal with adversity it can make you stronger. It's something that I will be able to learn from and grow from."[60]

But even as the Brewers headed north to open the season, the focus of the Wisconsin sports world was on the UW men's basketball team, who were in the process of storming their way through the western bracket of the NCAA tournament. When they knocked off Kentucky on April 4, it set up a national championship date with Duke on April 6, just a few hours after the Brewers hosted the Rockies in the opener. With temps in the 40s outside Miller Park and fans huddled around grills, the buzz was all about the Badgers. And it would mostly stay all about the Badgers.

After a pregame ceremony to honor Joe Attanasio, who had passed over the winter, a video of him singing the national anthem from 2014 was played to honor the country and a man who'd become as much a part of Opening Day in Milwaukee as any Brewers player. With "JOE" stenciled in the dirt behind home plate, Kyle Loshe took the hill and imminently lost the feel on his fastball. Carlos Gonzalez and Troy Tulowitzki mashed back-to-back doubles and, after getting Justin Morneau to pop out, Nolan Arenado ripped a fastball for another double and Cory Dickerson mashed a limp heater for a two-run homer.[61]

Down 4–0 before even having a turn at-bat, the Brewers did little to suggest such an offensive assault was necessary. They went in order in the first and made nothing out of two singles and a hit-by-pitch in the second. Tulowitzki opened the third with another double and, two batters later, Arenado hit a towering homer into the left field bleachers. As he trotted around the bases, the home crowd booed loudly. Down 6–0, Roenicke sent Loshe back out for the fourth and opposing pitcher Kyle Kendrick tagged his second pitch for Colorado's fifth double of the afternoon. He moved to third on a wild pitch and jogged home when Gonzalez ripped a single to mercifully end Loshe's day.

Michael Blazek took over for Loshe and made his own mess, allowing singles to Tulowitzki and Arenado to make it 8–0. Dickerson followed with a fly to left-center that just eluded a sliding Carlos Gomez and bounced over the fence for a two-run ground rule double. The top half of the fourth inning was not yet over and both Arenado and Dickerson had tied their career highs for RBI in a single game with four apiece. In the bottom half, the Brewers strung together a couple of singles to put runners on first and third for Scooter Gennett. Gennett struck out and the Brewers would not threaten for the rest of the afternoon.

With most of the 46,000-plus checked out or headed for the parking lot, Neal Cotts, Will Smith, and Jeremy Jeffress handled the Rockies without incident for the rest of the day. The lone bright spot for the Brewers was newly-acquired first baseman Adam Lind, who collected three meaningless singles. To add to overall gloom of the outings, the Brewers made three errors and Braun was removed from the game after the fifth inning when he tweaked his side making a diving catch. Past the opening introductions, the only true moment of joy for the home crowd came in the middle of the eighth inning, when a scoreboard tribute to the Badgers was accompanied by House of Pain's "Jump Around," the longtime staple of Badgers' sporting events.[62]

When it was all over, the 10–0 pounding was the worst Brewers Opening Day loss since the 12–0 beating they'd taken in the very first game in franchise history. But the team was eager to dismiss it as just "one of those days." "I don't put any more pressure on myself because it was opening day or be any more disappointed because it was opening day," said Loshe, whose eight earned runs were the most charged to any Brewers pitchers in a single Opening Day appearance. "It's disappointing to have a game like that. I've been around long enough [to know] that it's going to happen again, I'm sure."[63]

After the Badgers lost the title game to Duke that evening, the Brewers slopped their way to one of the worst starts in franchise history, opening at 2-13. In early May, Roenicke was fired and replaced by assistant to the general manager Craig Counsell. The team's fortunes improved under Counsell, but they still finished with 94 losses, their worst showing in a decade.

2016

Monday, April 4, 2016: Giants 12, Brewers 3 (44,318 attendance)
In the News: Donald Trump's presidential campaign will reportedly scale back the public role of campaign manager Corey Lewandowski after he was arrested and charged with battery for forcibly grabbing a female reporter's arm at a campaign event.

At the Movies: *My Big, Fat Greek Wedding 2*, Downer Theater

On the Radio: "My House" by Flo Rida

If the Brewers had appeared on the fence about a rebuild heading into the 2015 season, it quickly became apparent that they had simply been waiting to pull the trigger. When it was clear that the team would not contend in '15, they dumped Ron Roenicke for a ready-made replacement in Craig Counsell. A special assistant to GM Doug Melvin since his retirement as a player in 2011, Counsell had actually interviewed for the manager's job in Tampa before the 2015 season, but removed himself from the running after he'd advanced in the process. In an unusual move for an in-season manager switch, the Brewers did not add the "interim" tag to Counsell's title and immediately gave him a three-year contract.⁶⁴

In the lead-up to the trade deadline, the Brewers held two prized trade chips in catcher Jonathan Lucroy and center fielder Carlos Gomez. After a reported deal with Mets fell through, Gomez was dealt to Houston with pitcher Mike Fiers for prospects Adrian Houser, Brett Phillips, Domingo Santana, and Josh Hader. A day later, fourth outfielder Gerardo Parra was sent to Baltimore for 22-year-old pitcher Zach Davies.

As it was, these would be the final personnel moves for GM Doug Melvin, who had been with the team since 2002. After Melvin was moved into an advisory position in the front office, 30-year-old David Stearns was hired from a field of 44 candidates as the Brewers' new general manager. Most recently an assistant GM in Houston, Stearns fit the mold of the new way of imaging a baseball executive. A Harvard graduate who had gone directly into baseball after college, he'd been a key part of the Astros' recent rebuild, which saw them go from 111 losses in 2013 to a playoff berth two years later. Even Stearns' hiring was analytical—the Brewers had hired a recruitment company to rank each candidate with 40 sets of data points. But in the end, Mark Attanasio said, Stearns "just felt right."⁶⁵

After the season ended, Stearns set to work remaking the Brewers. His first move was to claim 31-year-old pitcher Junior Guerra off waivers from the White Sox. He then cleared out the coaching staff, dismissing five coaches and clearing the way for Cousell to build his own staff. After a host of Brewers filed for free agency, he brought back just one: utility man Hernan Perez, a mid-season waiver pick-up by Melvin who'd batted .270 in limited action in 2015. A few days later, he dealt closer Francisco Rodriguez, an All-Star in 2015, to Detroit for package including a young catcher named Manny Pina. A day later, he got speedy shortstop Jonathan Villar from Houston for a low-level minor leaguer. In early December, he traded Adam Lind, the team's 2015 leader in wins above replacement (WAR), to Seattle for a package of minor leaguers that included 20-year-old pitcher Freddy Peralta. Ten days after that, he shipped back-up first baseman Jason Rodgers to Pittsburgh for outfielder Keon Broxton.

Stearns had made it known that there was no one on the roster was untouchable and Lucroy remained the attractive trade chip. While the team had a ton of money coming off of the books, with Gomez and Aramis Ramirez already traded away and Kyle Loshe having filed for free agency, the only significant signing Stearns made was to add big first baseman Chris Carter on a one-year deal for $2.5 million. The Brewers payroll, which had recently topped $100 million, was now on track to be the lowest in baseball.⁶⁶

Most Brewers fans seemed to recognize the logic in shedding payroll as a part of a rebuild, but some in the media accused the team of "tanking"—a practice previously limited mostly to professional basketball that had recently gained some traction in baseball. Perhaps the most egregious of cases was that of Stearns' old Astros, who'd stripped the roster bare while saving money and racking up prospects via top spots in the amateur draft. In a piece by Jayson Stark on ESPN.com, an unnamed AL executive said, "I think Milwaukee is tanking. They're basically trying the Houston approach. They spent a lot of money trying to win. It didn't work. So now they're prepared to go through three or four years of losing."[67]

Stearns dismissed such claims, but one of the few recognizable names left on his team was not so sure. "I want to win and I don't see us winning in the foreseeable future," Jonathan Lucroy said in January. "I want to go to a World Series. That's what all players want. Rebuilding is not a lot of fun for any veteran guy." Lucroy had hoped to stay in Milwaukee long-term, even approaching the team about an extension early in the 2015 season. But the team was no longer interested in a long-term commitment.[68]

Meanwhile, Stearns kept making trades. Shortstop Jean Segura, on alert ever since Villar was brought in, was sent to Arizona at the end of January for a package headlined by pitcher Chase Anderson. Khris Davis, coming off a 27-homer season, was sent to Oakland two weeks later for pair of minor leaguers. By the time training camp opened, five of the eight regular position players from 2015 were no longer with the team, along with two members of the starting rotation and the closer. At the same time, the Brewers farm system—ranked 29th overall by Baseball America the year before—was now ranked in the top 10.[69]

By the time the team headed north, Villar had beaten out top prospect Orlando Arcia for the job at shortstop and Broxton—who'd been among the most impressive newcomers in camp—had won a spot in center field. Zach Davies, riding a string of good starts to close the '15 season, won a slot in the starting rotation. Jeremy Jeffress would start the season as the team's closer while Corey Knebel and Will Smith both opened on the DL. It was an especially rewarding honor for Jeffress, a former first-round draft choice who'd been traded away in the Zack Greinke deal. Unable to find his groove with Kansas City or Toronto, he returned to Milwaukee as a little-desired free agent in 2014 and emerged in 2015 as a legit late-inning ace, posting a 2.65 ERA.

Opening in Milwaukee against the Giants—winners of three of the last six World Series—the Brewers returned just 10 players from last year's Opening Day roster, featured a payroll that had been cut by nearly 50 percent, and were expected to be among the league's worst teams. Jonathan Lucroy, reflecting the team's comfort with being the underdog (and possibly trying to laugh away his comments from January), gave the media a declaration before the game. "We're going to win some games," he said with a grin. "We're not going to go 0–162."[70]

As a steady snow fell outside, Mark Attanasio's sons, Dan and Mike, sang the national anthem (a tribute to "Pop-pop," they said) and James Beckum, a former Negro League player and founder of Milwaukee's Beckum-Stapleton Little League, threw out the game's first pitch.[71]

Facing off against San Francisco ace Madison Bumgarner was Wily Peralta. Peralta looked sharp in the first inning, touching 98 with his fastball and setting the Giants down in order. In the bottom half, Bumgarner—who was dealing with the flu—struggled with his command. After Domingo Santana led off with a single, Bumgarner walked Villar and Lucroy to load the bases for Chris Carter, who'd hit 61 homers over the previous two seasons with Houston. Carter worked a five-pitch walk to force in a run before Bumgarner got Aaron Hill to roll into a double play.

Peralta ran into trouble in the second. After Carter booted a throw at first to allow Hunter Pence to reach, Brandon Belt followed with a double and Matt Duffy knocked them both in with a single to give the Giants a 2–1 lead. Peralta worked out of trouble and, in the bottom half, Scooter Gennett drilled a lifeless Bumgarner fastball halfway up the second deck in right field for his first career home run off a left-handed pitcher. The Giants broke the tie in the top of the third on an RBI single by Denard Span as Peralta labored through a 32-pitch inning. But once again, the Brewers struck back with a lead-off homer, this one off the bat of Villar, putting the score at 4–3 San Francisco. A few batters later, the Brewers threatened with Braun and Carter on base and one out with Hill batting, but Carter was thrown out trying to advance on a passed ball and Hill fanned to end the inning. It would be the last real threat the Brewers would mount that afternoon.

The Giants got to Peralta again in the fourth. After he walked Bumgarner, a double moved him to third and Span brought him home with a sac fly. In the fifth, now facing Carlos Torres, Duffy struck again with a two-run bomb that hit just above the "1982 AL Champions" flag in left. The homer made it 7–3 and an all-too-familiar feeling set in at Miller Park. As the Brewers foundered at the plate against a settled-in Bumgarner, the lines at the concession stands grew long and the idle chatter in the grandstands turned to other subjects. The only bit of excitement was the return of Chris Capuano, an off-season pickup, who came in for a clean sixth inning.[72]

Things went from bad to nuclear in the eighth when, facing Ariel Pena, Span came to bat with two on and two out. With the count full, Span poked one into the right field bleachers for a three-run homer to give him a five–RBI afternoon in his Giants debut. Joe Panik, who had just nine career homers in 173 games, followed with a towering home run of his own. On the very next pitch, former MVP Buster Posey crushed a third straight homer, this one nearly hitting the center field scoreboard. Those fans who remained on hand opened up with loud booing. The 12–3 score would end up as the final, giving the Brewers back-to-back Opening Day floggings. "This is day one," Counsell said after the game. "They are going to learn every day they are here. It is important that they learn from every day."[73]

Despite all the sour prognostications, the 2016 Brewers never allowed themselves to play the role of whipping boy. Aside from a poor showing in April and a dreadful swoon in August, they played right around .500 baseball in the season's other four months and ended the season on a 17–13 run.

2017

Monday, April 3, 2017: Rockies 7, Brewers 5 (43,336 attendance)

In the News: Giannis Antetokounmpo has been named the NBA's Eastern Conference Player of the Month for March. He led the Bucks to a 14–3 record in March, their best single month since the 1971 championship season.

At the Movies: *Power Rangers*, AMC Bayshore

On the Radio: "I Feel It Coming" by the Weekend feat. Daft Punk

Rarely in Brewers history had a 73-win team given fans so much to be happy about. Chris Carter won the NL home run title with 41 bombs. Ryan Braun had a mostly healthy season, his most productive since 2012. Jonathan Villar, picked up for a lightly-regarded minor leaguer, got on base at a .369 clip and led the NL with 62 steals. Junior Guerra, who'd opened the season in AAA, emerged as a team ace, with a 2.81 ERA over 20 starts. And when Jonathan Lucroy was finally traded (along with closer Jeremy Jeffress) to Texas at the trade deadline, the return was headlined by one of baseball's top prospects in Lewis Brinson.

Just after the season, the Brewers extended Craig Counsell's contract through the end of 2020 season. "This was probably the easiest decision I've to make over the last year," said GM David Stearns.

"I want to be here through this process," Counsell said at the press conference announcing the deal. "I want to be part of October baseball in Milwaukee and this is the only place where I want to be a part of October baseball."[74]

Both Stearns and Counsell said that, despite the losing record, their incremental goals for 2016 had all been met. The team led the league in stolen bases and, despite their offense ranking near the bottom of the NL, they'd seen a big increase in walks and ranked second in the league in pitches seen per plate appearance. Looking ahead to 2017, the Brewers only had two players eligible for free agency, Chris Capuano and Blaine Boyer, neither of whom the team planned on bringing back. In the longer term, only Ryan Braun and Matt Garza were secured with multi-year contracts. Stearns' club was young, hungry, and cheap, with a phalanx of highly-regarded prospects nearing Major League readiness.[75]

Given the manic pace of Stearns' first off-season, there were expectations that his trading spree would continue into 2017. One of the most persistent rumors involved Braun and the Los Angeles Dodgers. A Braun-for-Yasiel-Puig swap had reportedly been in the works throughout the 2016 season, with talks going right down the deadline. One report had it that Braun would "likely" be dealt to the Dodgers over the off-season, although the matter had been complicated by the Dodgers' recent sale and MLB's insistence that the new ownership tend to the franchise's massive debt—which likely precluded adding payroll.[76]

In a surprising move, the team declined to tender a contract to first baseman Chris Carter, who would likely be due a payday of $8–10 million. While standard baseball logic would have made retaining the league's home run leader—one that had been picked off the scrap heap, no less— would have been a no-brainer, Stearns and his team looked past a singular statistic and saw a player with extreme defensive limitations who did little with the bat besides hit homers. And if the Carter move was a surprise, his replacement—introduced just days later—was a true stunner.[77]

Eric Thames didn't have much of a Major League résumé—two seasons of part-time play with a career on-base percentage of under .300— but when he'd joined the NC Dinos of the Korean Baseball Organization in 2014, he found his stroke. For three seasons, Thames destroyed KBO pitching. In 2015 alone, he hit 42 homers and batted .381 while stealing 40 bases. He won the league's MVP award that year and became something of a national sensation. He had a song written about him and was nicknamed "God" by his fans—although he didn't particularly care for the moniker. His fame grew so immense that he had trouble even leaving his apartment to dine out or go on a date. Stearns had been keeping tabs on him since his brief stint in the Astros' system. When his contract with NC was up, he began shopping his services to American teams. Stearns landed him with a three-year deal worth $15 million. It was his first major free agent signing.[78]

Thames was perhaps the Brewers' most intriguing signing since they gave a chance to Japanese League legend Yutaka Enatsu. There was the obvious interest in how his huge KBO numbers would translate to the

With a wrestler's build and an easy-going personality, Eric Thames arrived in Milwaukee from the Korean Baseball Organization and immediately won over fans with a record-setting April power spree (Taysomhillfan).

Majors (most considered the KBO to have a talent level comparable to that of AAA) but there was also Thames himself. With a bushy beard and a bodybuilder's physique, Thames certainly stood out in a crowd. He read a lot, studying everything from professional wrestling to Zen philosophy. He'd even taught himself a remedial kind of Korean in his spare time. But he was glad to be returning to the States, and especially happy to have landed with the Brewers. "I came to Milwaukee before I signed, checked it out, and after an hour I knew it was where I wanted to be," he said before the 2017 season. "I love the Midwest. I love the hospitality of people. And Milwaukee has great beer. I love beer."[79]

A week after signing Thames, Stearns shored up the other side of the infield by trading reliever Tyler Thornburg to Boston for 27-year-old Travis Shaw, a late-blooming third baseman who was about to be displaced by top prospect Rafael Devers. Informed of the trade, Shaw had to Google Thornburg's name—despite his having pitched in the Majors since 2012. Seeing his 2016 stat line—a 2.15 ERA and 13 saves—Shaw was satisfied. "It's a pretty good guy to be traded for, I guess," he later said.[80]

Although Stearns added some low-risk free agents into the mix before camp opened—including infielder Eric Sogard and pitchers Joba Chamberlain, Tommy Milone, and former All-Star Neftali Feliz, who would be named the team's closer—there were far fewer positional battles than there

Chapter Five. The Teens

had been the year before. With Orlando Arcia ready to take over at short, Villar moved to second base. Newcomers Thames and Shaw would play the corners with Braun, Keon Broxton, and Domingo Santana returning in the outfield. There were questions on the pitching staff, but the potential ran deep, as did the list of Brewers farmhands among the various top prospects lists published before the season. So deep were the 2017 Brewers that Scooter Gennett—their starting second baseman for the last three seasons—was cut in the final week of camp to make way for Jesus Aguilar, a waiver-wire addition who had tremendous minor league stats, but had never been able to find regular Major League playing time.

For the sixth straight year, the Brewers opened the season at home, once again facing the Colorado Rockies. Bud Selig, who had been elected to the Baseball Hall of Fame over the winter, threw out the first pitch and Junior Guerra—just two years removed from thinking his career might be over—was given the honors for the Brewers. Guerra opened strong, setting down the Rockies in order in the first. Jon Gray, coming off a solid rookie season, then did the same to Milwaukee. In the top of the second, after plunking lead-off man Nolan Arenado, Guerra fanned a pair and had former Brewer Mark Reynolds on a 2–2 count when he hung a ball that Reynolds sent into the Brewers' bullpen.

The score held at 2–0 into the bottom of the third when the rookie Arcia led off with a single. Guerra followed by laying down a sac bunt, but just a few feet out of the batter's box, he pulled up, clutching his leg. After taking a few hops and being tagged out, he grimaced as he walked gingerly back to the dugout. His afternoon was over and, in the top of the fourth, the Rockies wasted no time in getting to reliever Tommy Milone. Arenado popped a single that Thames could not run down in shallow right and Trevor Story rifled a double to left. Then, a pair of former Brewers knocked in runs, with Gerardo Parra lining a single to center and Reynolds grounding into a force-out at second.

With the score 4–0 and the Brewers unable to solve Gray, it felt like another Opening Day dud. But in the bottom of the fifth, the Crew came roaring back. Catcher Jett Bandy opened with a single and Arcia and Aguilar, pinch hitting for Milone, both reached to load the bases for Villar. Villar corked Gray's first pitch into center, where Charlie Blackmon misplayed it, allowing Villar to scoot to second as two runs scored. Thames followed with a double to right to tie the game, 4–4. As the home crowd came to life, Thames gestured to his teammates in the dugout with his hands opened wide. Righty Scott Oberg relieved Gray and fanned Braun for the first out, but then it was Travis Shaw's turn to say hello to the Brewers faithful as he smoked a double into the right-center gap to put the Brewers on top.

It was still 5–4 in the top of the seventh when Milwaukee's Jhan

Marinez, hoping to get the game to Counsell's back-end combination of Corey Knebel and Feliz, ran into a mess. Parra led off with a bunt single and Reynolds followed with a double to left. Parra never stopped running and, with a bullet relay from Arcia in shallow left, Bandy tagged him out at home. But Marinez continued to labor, allowing a single and a walk to load the bases and end his afternoon.

Knebel came in to face Blackmon and got him to ground sharply to short. It was a tailor-made, jam-escaping double play ball, but Villar, after taking the toss from Arcia, bobbled the transfer. Reynolds scored to tie the game. With D.J. LeMahieu batting, Blackmon broke for second. Bandy's throw was on target, but Villar had forgotten to cover second base. He got to the bag just in time to deflect the ball from heading into center field, but the runner, seeing what was developing, had already broken for home. He scored without a throw to give the Rockies a 6–5 lead.[81]

Dispirited but not broken, the Brewers had a chance to take things back in the eighth. Facing Adam Ottavino, Keon Broxton and Santana drew a pair of walks to open the inning. With Bandy at bat, the Brewers executed a perfect double steal to put runners on second and third with no one out. But, facing a stream of nasty breaking balls from Ottavino, Bandy, Arcia, and pinch hitter Hernan Perez each struck out, with Arcia and Perez flailing badly on pitches far off the plate.[82]

Colorado picked up an insurance run in the eighth, but the Brewers had nothing left. A game-ending double play with Braun at bat was challenged by Counsell, which gave the Crew a brief reprieve, but a few minutes later, the call was upheld and the Brewers took their sixth home opener loss in eight tries. As had become custom at Miller Park following a Brewers loss, "Three Little Birds" by Bob Marley and the Wailers played as the fans filed from the stadium. *Don't worry about a thing / 'Cause every little thing gonna be all right....*

After a record-setting April from Eric Thames, the Brewers surged to top of the NL Central standings in May and entered the All-Star break with a stunning 5.5 game lead on the field. A rough patch after the break cost them the division lead, but they bounced back and ended up at 86–76, just one game out of the final Wild Card spot.

2018

Monday, April 2, 2018: Cardinals 8, Brewers 4 (45,393 attendance)

In the News: After a years-long debate on the matter, the dam on the Milwaukee River in Estabrook Park—built in the 1930s, but non-functional for more than a decade—is finally being demolished.

At the Movies: *Isle of Dogs*, Oriental Theater
On the Radio: "Perfect" by Ed Sheeran

As heartbreaking as it might have been to finish just a game away from their first postseason berth in seven years, it was a heartbreak that no one could have expected at the start of the season. Three question marks in the starting lineup heading into the season had emerged as All-Star caliber players: Domingo Santana, Travis Shaw, and Eric Thames—who had each hit 30 or more homers and drawn 60-plus walks. Rookie Orlando Arcia hit .277 with 15 homers of his own while showing fantastic potential with his glove. Keon Broxton had been similarly impressive in center. And, despite a number of injuries, the pitching staff boasted impressive turns by Chase Anderson (2.79 ERA), Zach Davies (17 wins), Jimmy Nelson (10.2 Ks per nine innings), and Corey Knebel (39 saves and a 3.7 WAR). Two thousand seventeen also saw the debuts of two of the team's most highly-regarded prospects in Lewis Brinson and Josh Hader. In short, the rebuild was over. The future had arrived.

No team in baseball had spent less on payroll over the past two seasons as the Brewers. And with Matt Garza's $12.5 million annual pay about to come off the books, observers expected the Brewers to be among the off-season's biggest spenders. Most expected that money to be spent on the starting rotation. While Davies and Anderson were locks for 2018, the Brewers would be missing a huge piece in Nelson, who had suffered a catastrophic shoulder injury while diving into a base in a September game in Chicago. Surgeons essentially needed to rebuild the shoulder, and there was not even a timeline yet for his return. And even with the tantalizing prospect of moving Hader and his wipeout slider and explosive fastball into the rotation (he had worked almost exclusively as a starter before being called up in June) and slotting Brent Suter, the soft-tossing over-achiever from Harvard, into the back end, that still left an open spot in the rotation with few impressive internal options to fill it.

Two names that the Brewers were immediately linked to were Jake Arrieta, the former Cy Young award winner late of the Cubs, and Yu Darvish, the four-time All-Star who'd just helped the Dodgers win a pennant. They were the top two pitchers available on the market and would each command a contract far larger than anything the Brewers had ever given out. It was expected that the Brewers could add $25 million or more to the 2018 payroll.[83]

Trade rumors buzzed around Brewers camp as well. With Brinson and Brett Phillips expected to be ready for full-time play in 2018, a glut of outfielders seemed to be the most obvious source of trade bait. Teams made inquiries on both Santana and Broxton and the years-old Braun-to-LA rumors popped up yet again. With Braun now holding 5-and-10 trade-veto rights, he needed to approve of any trade he was involved in. He'd said in the past that the only team he'd even consider moving to was his hometown LA Dodgers. Meanwhile, the Brewers were reportedly asking about pitchers Matt Harvey of the Mets, Chris Archer of the Rays, and Gerrit Cole of the Pirates.[84]

The Brewers' first significant move of the off-season was to secure Jeremy Jeffress for 2018. Jeffress, who had twice been traded away by the Brewers, was brought back for a second time at the trade deadline in 2017 in a minor swap with Texas. His time in Texas had been marred by a drunk driving arrest that had forced him into treatment for alcoholism. He'd previously entered rehab for issues with marijuana stemming from an undiagnosed case of juvenile epilepsy that caused seizures, for which he had been using pot to self-medicate. Back in Milwaukee, sober and with a new focus on his well-being, he returned to form in the second half of 2017, shaving nearly two runs off his ERA.[85]

Several weeks of hot stove buzz later, the Brewers signed journeyman pitcher Jhoulys Chacin, a nine-year veteran who projected more as an innings-eater than an impact starter. Entering the new year, the Brewers still seemed to be in wait-and-see mode as the free agent market was slow to develop. "We're always looking to get better," said GM David Stearns in early January. "We remain interested if the right opportunities are presented to us. But I am comfortable with our group, as is, if that's how we head into spring training."[86]

Two weeks later, when rumors had it that the Brewers had made official offers to both Arrieta and Darvish—a sensational claim that would have likely meant a spending spree of $200 million or more—Brewers nation was on high alert for any breaking news. A few days later, news broke and it took everyone by surprise.[87]

On January 25, reports emerged nearly simultaneously that the Brewers had signed free agent center fielder Lorenzo Cain and traded for Miami outfielder Christian Yelich. Cain had been part of the package in the Zack Greinke trade in 2011 and had helped the Royals to two pennants and a World Series win as one of the AL's best center fielders. He was lured in with $80 million over five years—the richest free agent contract in team history. Yelich was lesser known, but even more talented. Hidden away on perpetually lousy Marlins teams, he was a toolsy corner outfielder who was expected to boost his power numbers at Miller Park. Just 26 years old and signed to a team-friendly contract, he cost the Brewers a quartet of prospects, headlined by Brinson. With Ryan Braun now expected to see some time at first base, the Brewers had essentially assembled a four-man rotation of starter-quality outfielders, while still leaving Broxton or Santana as possible trade candidates.[88]

And while rumors still buzzed about the Brewers signing Darvish, they instead opted for 31-year-old junk baller Wade Miley, who hadn't posted an ERA under 4.00 since 2013. The Brewers opened camp confident that they were serious World Series contenders. More than a few observers questioned the logic of their off-season spree, but no one doubted that they were a team worth watching. MLB.com's Richard Justice even made the somewhat bold declaration that Yelich was a "darkhorse" MVP candidate in the NL.[89]

The Brewers opened the 2018 season in San Diego, winning the opener in extra innings and stealing game two with a dramatic five-run ninth. They completed the sweep on Saturday night with a five-hit outburst from Yelich. Two days later, they hosted the Cardinals for the home opener, Zach Davies facing off against Miles Mikolas, who had just returned from a three-year stint in Japan. Both pitchers were sharp out of the gate; the highlight of the first inning and half was a sensational spinning throw from Arcia to nail Jose Martinez on a close play at first. Many Pina, a member of MLB's All-Rookie team in '17, opened scoring in the second with a solo homer into the Cardinal bullpen.

The Cardinals struck back in the third, with Paul DeJong leading off with a single and coming around to score on a Jedd Gyorko double. Gyorko moved to third when Davies threw a pick-off attempt into center field and scored moments later when Dexter Fowler dumped a base hit into shallow center to put the Cards up 2–1. In the bottom half, the Brewers tied it when Cain squared up a hanging breaking ball from Mikolas and sent it soaring over the Brewers bullpen, leaning way back on his follow through as was his trademark style. As Cain rounded the bases, the Brewers bullpen broke into a coordinated and exaggerated clapping motion as Jeffress did the viral "floss dance."

The 2–2 score held into the top of the fifth. With two away, Davies plunked Gyorko to bring up the pitcher Mikolas. Hitless for his career, Mikolas was just looking to put the ball in play, but when Davies left a 1–1 cutter over the heart of the plate, Mikolas swung hard and did not miss. In left field, Braun could only watch as the ball bounced off the Club Goodwill sign for a two-run homer. An inning later, the Cards struck again. Davies allowed three straight singles to open the inning (one was cut down on a caught stealing), followed by a sac fly from Martinez to make it 5–3 and another single by Yadier Molia to put runners at the corners for DeJong. Brandon Woodruff, a 25-year-old who'd made the roster as a swingman, spelled Davies and got way too much of the plate with his second pitch. DeJong crushed it for a no-doubt three-run homer. With the score now 8–2, a few stray boos were heard from home crowd, more likely directed at the smattering of Cardinals fans in attendance than at the Brewers.[90]

But the Brewers were not ready to roll over just yet. In the bottom of the sixth, Shaw reached on a single and Eric Thames—author of a 10-homer April in 2017—obliterated a Mikolas offering into the second deck in right. The Brewers put two more runners on in the inning to chase Mikolas but couldn't capitalize. Although Woodruff and Oliver Drake kept St. Louis off the board the rest of the way, the Brewers fared no better against Bud Norris, Tyler Lyons, and Jordan Hicks. A Thames double in the eighth was all that would bring the crowd back to life that afternoon. With the fans mostly checked out and the score 8–4 Cardinals, pinch-hitter Jesus Aguilar bounced into a double play in the bottom of the ninth to end it and push Milwaukee's home opener losing streak to four—their longest stretch of lid-lifter futility since a six-game skid from 1988 to 1993.

"Obviously, we're all disappointed, a little bit," Thames said afterward. "But you can't get too caught up in it. It's not the postseason. We have a lot more of these games left."[91]

The Brewers did indeed have a lot of regular season games left—162, in fact. In prime contention for a playoff spot, but five games behind the front-running Cubs at the start of September, the Brewers caught fire and tied Chicago on the second to last day of the season. They beat the Cubs in a tie-breaker game in Chicago and rode a franchise-record 12-game winning streak into the NLCS against the Dodgers, where they came up just one win short of a pennant.

2019

Thursday, March 28, 2019: Brewers 5, Cardinals 4 (45,304 attendance)

In the News: The avowed neo-Nazi who killed a woman when he sped his car into a crowd of protestors at a white supremacist march in Charlottesville, Virginia, has plead guilty to federal hate crime charges. The plea is part of a deal that will spare him the death penalty.

At the Movies: *Us*, Oriental Theater

On the Radio: "Shallow" by Lady Gaga and Bradley Cooper

Just one season removed from fielding a team with absolutely no expectations, the Brewers in 2018 came heartbreakingly close to just their second trip to the World Series in franchise history. The off-season moves by David Stearns had paid off immensely. Christian Yelich nearly won the NL triple crown and won the league's MVP award in a landslide. Lorenzo Cain was exactly what the team needed in the lead-off spot, made the All-Star team, and placed seventh in MVP voting. And Wade Miley and Jhoulys Chacin, the lightly-regarded starting pitching upgrades, combined to post a WAR of 3.4—while Yu Darvish and Jake Arrieta, playing for the Cubs and Phillies, respectively, for a total of $55 million in 2018, combined for a WAR of 2.8.

The 2018 Brewers had been a team of many moving pieces. Craig Counsell saw 50 different players see game action and used 30 different pitchers throughout the season—both franchise records (by contrast, the 1982 team used just 33 different players and just 15 pitchers). The pitching staff was an especially unique coalition of talent. Jeremy Jeffress, used mostly as a one-inning man, led the staff in WAR with 3.4. Only one pitcher (Chacin) won more than 10 games. Three pitchers recorded 10 or more saves. Seven pitchers started 10 or more games, but only Chacin remained in the rotation the entire season. And their most dominating pitcher was Josh Hader, the minor league starter with the closer's stuff who had emerged as a multi-inning throwback to the days of the "fireman" reliever from the 1980s. Counsell had begun referring to his pitchers less in terms of individual roles and more often as "out-getters" who could be tasked with anything at any time.

A few key members of the out-getters filed for free agency after the season, including Miley, Dan Jennings, and trade deadline addition Gio Gonzalez. Other in-season pickups like Mike Moustakas and Curtis Granderson filed as well and were not expected to return. For a second straight off-season, rumors had the Brewers connected to several high-profile pitchers, both free agents and trade candidates: Dallas Keuchel, Sonny Gray, J.A. Happ, and Nathan Evoldi. None were franchise-shifting talents and all would likely command an expenditure that history had shown Stearns to be unwilling to spend on pitching. There were also trade rumors linking Milwaukee to Noah Syndergaard and Madison Bumgarner—pitchers now more famous than productive—but everything seemed to be more smoke than fire.[92]

On the offensive side, most positions appeared to be settled, with top prospect Keston Hiura—recently named the MVP of the Arizona Fall League—slated to take over at second base at some point in 2019. One weak point offensively was catcher, with fan-favorite Manny Pina offering little value with his bat. The top backstop on the market was the Marlins' J.T. Realmuto, who was about to get too expensive for Miami's shrinking budget. Meanwhile, the lingering effects of the Brewers' playoff run and the big name rumor hype of the off-season had pushed Brewers fever to a pitch not seen since the early 1980s. In January, Brewers on Deck, a winter event where players signed autographs and the team sold off discounted merchandise, sold out for the first time ever.[93]

While fans gathered downtown, the Brewers off-season—indeed, the entire MLB off-season as a whole—had been very slow to develop. A few weeks later, the Brewers took advantage of the slow market and made a stunning addition by signing former Dodgers catcher Yasmani Grandal. Originally expected to seek a multi-year deal worth $60 million-plus, Grandal took a one-year deal with the Brewers for $18 million. A month later, the Brewers made another surprise deal when they brought back Moustakas—who'd also been expected to sign a multi-year pact—on a one-year deal worth $10 million.[94]

It was all part of an increasingly upsetting off-season for the Major League Players' Association. The off-season's two best available free agents—indeed maybe the greatest pair of single-year free agents ever—26-year-olds Bryce Harper and Manny Machado both remained unsigned as did the market's top pitchers, Keuchel and dominant closer Craig Kimbrel. One-year deals by Grandal and Moutakas seemed to be indications of panic on the part of players, an attempt to find a decent yearly pay for '19 and retest the market in a year. The union suspected collusion by the owners, adding to an already troubling list of grievances with the league over the growing practices of tanking and service-time manipulation of young players. Harper and Machado eventually signed contracts each worth about $100 million less than expected and neither Keuchel nor Kimbrel—who'd both be linked to the Brewers throughout training camp—would find new teams before the middle of the season.[95]

With Grandal and Moutakas, the Brewers' payroll now projected near $125 million, another franchise high and up nearly $25 million from 2018. "The money sort of all came together at once," said Mark Attanasio. "That wasn't part of the plan. You can't sequence this. So, I had to make a decision are we going to sequence it or do everything at once. We did everything at once.... All the chips are all in now. We'll find the money at mid-season if we need to."[96]

By the time the Brewers packed for Milwaukee, there was already trouble in the bullpen. Corey Knebel needed Tommy John surgery and would miss the entire season. Jeffress was experiencing arm weakness and would open on the newly-rechristened "injured list," as would swingman Brent Suter. Jimmy Nelson, who'd had a breakout year as a starter in 2017 but would likely work out of the pen upon his return from having his wrecked shoulder rebuilt, was still not ready for game action. With their unconventional approach to "out-getting" and the injuries, most national observers did not expect them to repeat as division champs. A few saw them a Wild Card team. Nearly all of them expected a significant backslide.[97]

The Brewers opened the season at home, again hosting the Cardinals and facing Miles Mikolas. Chacin got the ball for the Brewers, following a ceremonial quartet of first pitches from Brewers MVPs Yelich, Ryan Braun, Robin Yount, and Rollie Fingers. Chacin struck out the side in the first, but ran into big trouble in the second. With two away and no

Chapter Five. The Teens 213

Longtime fans (left to right) Rachel Vaselenak, Amanda Mann, Lauren Nastachowski, Jessica Burch, and Angela Andre share their traditional season-opening champagne toast before the 2019 opener (courtesy Jessica Burch).

one out, he walked Dexter Fowler and on back-to-back pitches gave up home runs to Kolten Wong and Harrison Bader to give the Cards a 3–0 lead. Both homers were no-doubt bombs, an odd rough patch for a pitcher who'd given up just 18 homers in 2018 over nearly 200 innings.

The Brewers got one back in the bottom half when Moustakas, with "Moooose!" cheers from the home crowd, blasted a solo homer that landed just under the center field scoreboard. Chacin looked sharp again in the third, needing just 13 pitches to retire the Cards and, in the bottom half, it was Milwaukee's turn for a big inning. With one away, Mikolas worked Chacin to a 1–2 count before the pitcher slapped a single between third and short. On an 0–2 count, Cain followed with a single up the middle. Taking his place on first base, he raised his hands to the home dugout and twinkled his fingers, asking his teammates to "show [him] some love."[98]

With a chance to put his team on top, Yelich strode to the plate. After having spent the last two and half months of the 2018 season as the greatest ballplayer on earth, the MVP belted the first pitch he saw into center field; it just brushed the top of Bader's mitt as it dropped over the fence to put the Brewers up 4–3. An inning later, Chacin stepped in again and again Mikolas worked him to a two-strike count. Chacin had, early on in spring when discussing his hitting with Counsell, declared that he wanted to hit a home run in 2019. He'd only hit one in his career, six years earlier with the Rockies. Standing in against the Cardinals' ace, he was just trying not to strike out. But when Mikolas threw a hanging slider, Chacin got all of it and dumped it into the Brewers' bullpen for his second hit of the game.[99]

Former MVP award winners Rollie Fingers (1981, second from left) and Robin Yount (1982, 1989, third from left) joined Ryan Braun (2011 NL MVP, left) and Christian Yelich (2018 NL MVP) for first-pitch ceremonies before the 2019 home opener (Steve Schar).

In the seventh, with Junior Guerra having taken over for Chacin, Wong struck again, homering into the St. Louis bullpen to cut the Brewers' lead to one. Guerra finished the inning cleanly to hand it to Hader for a two-inning save attempt. With the Brewers unable to put anything together against the Cardinals bullpen, Hader dissected the heart of the Cardinals lineup, fanning Paul Goldschmidt, Paul DeJong, and Marcell Ozuna in order on just 11 pitches. All 11 were fastballs, all in the high 90s, and each man went down swinging.[100]

The 5–4 score held into the top of the ninth. The Cardinals finally made contact against Hader when Yadier Molina led off by flying to center. Hader then worked Fowler to a 1–2 count before blowing him away on an unhittable high fastball. With only power-hitting Jose Martinez standing in the way of a rousing Opening Day win, Hader opened with a ball wide of the plate. He shot for the outside edge on his second offering, but Martinez lunged for it and didn't miss. The crowd, already on its feet, gasped as the ball arched dangerously toward the outfield wall. In center field, Cain jogged toward the right-center gap, eyes upward. A couple members of the Cardinals bullpen held up their arms, anticipating a game-tying homer. Nearing the wall, Cain leapt, arm extended. With his glove arched just over the cusp of the fence, he flicked his wrist and pulled the ball back. His jump was so precise, he barely touched the padding of the wall as he landed. Yelich, tracking the play from his spot in right, bounced past Cain and shouted, "Not today!" as the center fielder fired the ball into the air. Cain bounded toward the infield, shaking his head as the Miller Park crowd went wild.

Counsell admitted that he'd thought the ball was gone. "Yeah, I said a bad word," he said later. "I hope the kids don't see it."[101]

"I tried to time it," Cain said after the game. "I was talking to the baseball, telling it to come down. I timed it well and was able to bring it back."[102]

"This game showed us we still have that magic," Chacin said afterward. "The way we played at the end of the season, we still have that magic."[103]

The most magical part of the 2019 season came when the Brewers needed it most. On September 10 in Miami, with the Brewers two games out of a playoff spot, Yelich—on pace for another MVP award—broke his kneecap and was lost for the year. Improbably, the Brewers won 14 of their next 16, easily claiming a Wild Card spot and nearly winning the division. The magic ran out during in the Wild Card game against the eventual world champion Nationals, when the Nats stunned the Brewers with three runs off Hader in the eighth inning for a comeback win.

CHAPTER SIX

The Twenties

2020

Monday, August 3, 2020: White Sox 6, Brewers 4 (0 attendance)
In the News: President Trump called a statement by the White House's coronavirus coordinator suggesting the United States could be entering a "new phase" of widespread infection "pathetic." More than 150,000 Americans have died from COVID-19 so far.
At the Movies: *All city theaters closed*
On the Radio: "Watermelon Sugar" by Harry Styles

It was hard to see the end of the Brewers' 2019 season as anything but heartbreaking. Playing for their injured star after Christian Yelich was lost with a broken kneecap, the Brewers were the hottest team on the planet as they clinched their first back-to-back playoff berths since 1981–82. They had been four outs away from upsetting the Nationals and moving into a five-game NLDS where anything was possible. Once again, the Brewers had needed many moving pieces to make it work. They released Jhoulys Chacin, their Opening Day starter, and Jeremy Jeffress, their 2018 bullpen ace, during the season as both struggled. In-season additions Jordan Lyles and Drew Pomeranz picked up the slack, both emerging from nowhere to become the team's top starter and reliever down the stretch. Brent Suter, unsure if he'd be able to play at all in 2019, came back from injury and recorded a minuscule 0.49 ERA over 18 innings. On the other side, Keston Hiura took over at second base, batting .303 with 19 homers in a half-season's action.

But a free agent exodus seemed to indicate that the team's payroll would roll back for 2020. Grandal and Moustakas both sought multi-year deals and were both dismissed as too expensive to retain. Pomeranz and Lyles both filed for free agency and found little interest from the Brewers on open market. Travis Shaw, who'd slumped his way onto the bench in mid-season, was not offered a contract. The team option on Eric Thames, who'd taken over for Jesus Aguilar (who himself was eventually traded) and hit 25 homers, was declined.

Chapter Six. The Twenties 217

The 2020 Brewers' new look would extend past the roster. In mid-November in a ceremony at Miller Park, a remade uniform set and logo were unveiled. Calling back to the Brewers' look of the 1970s and 1980s, a modified "ball and glove" returned as the team's primary logo and set of block-letter blue-and-gold uniforms were cast as the home and away costuming. Also unveiled was an emblem commemorating the team's 50th anniversary. A slate of celebratory events and giveaways were planned for the 2020 season as well.

Shortly after the unveiling, it was confirmed that the Brewers would cut payroll. Reports also said that everyone on the roster except for Yelich—who'd placed second in the NL MVP voting—was a possible trade candidate. The biggest trade piece was Josh Hader, who was arbitration eligible and certain to reap a huge salary boost. The first big move of the off-season was a trade with San Diego that sent Zach Davies, the Brewers' top starter in '19, and Trent Grisham, a rookie outfielder who'd taken over for Yelich at season's end, to the Padres in exchange for pitcher Eric Lauer and shortstop Luis Urias. Both players returned in the deal were young and cheap.[1]

Another trade yielded slugging catcher Omar Narvaez and former All-Star outfielder Avisail Garcia was signed to a two-year, $18 million free agent contract. The moves maintained a plus-hitter behind the plate and an overloaded outfield that had served them well in the past, but the new payroll constrictions gave the team fewer overall options and an even tighter margin of error. At the Brewers on Deck event, Mark Attanasio urged fans to "trust the process" and claimed that the Brewers had operated at a loss during the 2019 season. Observers were quick to note, however, that "operating at a loss" did not necessarily mean that the team was losing money and needed to cut expenses.[2]

On March 3, however, the Brewers made headlines across baseball when they announced a nine-year, $215 million extension for superstar Christian Yelich, essentially making one of the best players in baseball a Brewer for life. "I've only been here for two years, but it's felt like a lot longer," Yelich said in a press conference announcing the deal. "Ever since I came here it felt like a natural fit. As a player, that's what you want, a chance to win, something that feels organic, and it felt right to me. And I didn't really have aspirations to play anywhere else, and fortunately we were able to work that out where we don't have to worry about that anymore."[3]

In other news that day, the first U.S. death from the rapidly-spreading respiratory infection known as COVID-19 was confirmed by health officials. Just days earlier, the World Health Organization had elevated the threat level from COVID to "very high." Five days after Yelich signed his deal, MLB announced that spring training clubhouse access would be restricted for non-players. On March 11, Rudy Gobert of the Utah Jazz tested positive for COVID and, later that day, the NBA made the stunning decision to suspend the season indefinitely. The next day, the Brewers lost to the Dodgers in a rain-shortened game. Shortly after they left the field, MLB announced that spring activities would be suspended imminently and the start of the season would be delayed by at least two weeks. Three days later, a Yankees player tested positive, the first confirmed case in either spring league. A day after that, the open of the season was pushed back to mid–May. At the earliest.[4]

In the run-up to what would have been Opening Day, widespread uncertainty clouded baseball and pretty much every other aspect of life in America. Stay-at-home orders were issued in Wisconsin and thousands of businesses closed with no clear idea of when it might be safe to reopen. In late March, the players and owners agreed to a deal that would pay the players the pro-rated portion of their salary based on how many regular season games were able to be played. There was talk about starting the regular season in spring training stadiums, to limit travel and avoid the web of state and local restrictions on gatherings. In May, teams began to cautiously reopen training camps, leading to a spree of COVID outbreaks across baseball. Several players expressed concerns about playing the season at all.[5]

But quickly enough, the long-simmering feud between the players and owners became just as much a threat to the season as COVID. The owners wanted to go back on their agreement from March and asked that the players take additional cuts to their pro-rated pay to offset their losses from being unable to sell tickets. The players balked. After weeks of fruitless negotiations, commissioner Rob Manfred imposed a 60-game season, the shortest allowed under the March agreement. The league claimed it was for safety's sake. The players saw it as a way to keep payrolls as low as possible.

In late June, the players agreed to the 60-game schedule. Teams would only play opponents from their region to limit travel. Players would be tested every other day. There would be a universal designated hitter, seven-inning double headers, and a runner on second base to start each inning in extras. Sixteen teams would qualify for a kind-of postseason World Series tournament. No fans would be allowed to attend.[6]

After a quick "summer camp" to get into playing shape, the Brewers opened their season in Chicago against the Cubs. After a 3–3 opening road trip, they returned home to an empty Miller Park to face the Cardinals. There had already been an outbreak severe enough on the Marlins to force the first COVID-related cancelation of games. Heading home, Ryan

Braun admitted that he was "day to day" on whether he wanted to keep playing. Players had the right to "opt out" of the 2020 season and several players had already done so. "There's a real fear and anxiety for all of us," said Braun, who had a newborn son at home. "I don't feel comfortable with where we're at. It makes it really difficult to concentrate on baseball."[7]

The opener, set for July 31, was canceled when multiple Cardinals players tested positive. Any hope for a home opener double-header of seven-inning games—as strange an Opening Day as anyone could have ever imagined—was dashed when a full-blown outbreak hit the Cards. The entire opening series was called off, three of 33 MLB games canceled that weekend. In the wake of all this, Lorenzo Cain officially opted out. "I wish all of my great teammates the best of luck this season and look forward to getting back on the field in 2021," he said in a statement. "Please stay safe."[8]

Over that same weekend, Braun ended up in the hospital when an injured finger became infected and bench coach Pat Murphy suffered a mild heart attack while the team ran drills. When the White Sox arrived in Milwaukee on August 3, healthy enough to open the home season, no one could be blamed for wondering if such games even mattered.[9]

Brett Anderson, starting for the Brewers, ran into trouble right

Miller Park sits empty for the 2020 home opener. After a weekend of canceled games and COVID-19 outbreaks, many thought the season might not last much longer (Jay Saeger).

away, suffering from the same rust that had hampered pitchers across the league. He allowed a single and double to open the game, and then let both score on a pair of sacrifices. The Brewers struck back in the bottom half when Yelich doubled and Avisail Garcia ripped a double just past the glove of third baseman Yoan Moncada to bring him home. Sox starter Carlos Rodón was finished after two innings and Anderson gave way after the third. Corbin Burnes and Matt Foster traded gutsy zeroes into the fifth when the Brewers loaded the bases and Garcia brought home two with a line-drive single to put the Brewers up 3–2. An inning later, the Brewers slopped together another run after Justin Smoak, signed as a low-cost replacement for Thames at first, stroked a single. He moved to second when Manny Pina was hit by a pitch, to third when Arcia rolled into a double play, and then home on a base hit by Ben Gamel. The players applauded and mimicked high-fives while wearing masks in the dugout, now up 4–2, as their cheers and shouts echoed among the empty seats.

The Brewers still led 4–2 in the top of the seventh when, with Luis Robert on second, Burnes faced slugger Jose Abreu. Burnes had been cruising and had just fanned Moncada on a series of nasty cutters. But Abreu had gotten a good look at Burnes the inning before, during an 11-pitch battle that Burnes had won with a strikeout. With David Phelps ready to go in the bullpen, Counsell considered making a move, but went with his gut and let Burnes try to finish off the inning. Burnes nibbled, working the count to 3–0, and then Abreu struck, crushing the fourth pitch to the batter's eye in center field to tie the game.[10]

Phelps came on and, an inning later, allowed the go-ahead run to score on a wild pitch with two out. In the top of the ninth, Moncada crushed a solo homer off Corey Knebel to make it 6–4. In the bottom of the ninth, after Huira hit a two-out double, Yelich came to bat as the potential tying run. After working a full count, he grounded out weakly to second base to end the game.[11]

"It's all right to be a little afraid right now. It's all right to wonder what's going on," Counsell said after the game in comments that had nothing to do with his team's slow start. "We try to come to work and do the one thing we love, which is play baseball and compete. We do love to do those things, absolutely. [But] there's other stuff going on and it's real and it affects you." Still, despite everything that had happened over the weekend and the tenuous grasp baseball seemed to have on its 2020 season, Counsell felt the team had a good reason to keep playing. "That's when we get to do what we love to do. It's the best time of the day."[12]

Never once above .500 and rarely showing the spark that had made them such a force over the past two seasons, the Brewers sputtered to a 29–31 finish, unremarkable, but still good enough to clinch the eighth seed in the National League, their third straight playoff appearance. In the best-of-three first round, they were swept by the eventual world champion LA Dodgers.

2021

Thursday, April 1, 2021: Brewers 6, Twins 5 (10 innings) (11,740 attendance)

In the News: According to figures just released by the CDC, COVID-19 was the third-leading cause of death in the United States in 2020, with 385,000 killed by the virus. It was the primary cause of a 16 percent spike in the national death rate.

At the Movies: *Godzilla vs. King Kong*, Avalon Theater

On the Radio: "Up" by Cardi B

Baseball had survived in 2020. Despite dozens of canceled games and a spree of positive tests and team-wide outbreaks, the 60-game season and expanded playoff tournament had made it through to the conclusion of a World Series winner. The Brewers were, technically speaking, a factor in this. Along with Houston, they made history by being the first losing teams to earn a postseason berth. But little about the 2020 Brewers felt like a triumph. There were bright spots: a star turn from Corbin Burnes, who nearly won the ERA title and received Cy Young votes, and a Rookie of the Year award for Devin Williams, who turned in an impossibly low 0.33 ERA over 27 innings. But the offense was lost all season and what had been a solid 1 through 8 lineup just a few years earlier was now full of holes.

The first significant bit of off-season news was long expected. Just after the season, Ryan Braun became a free agent for the first time in his career. He had not yet decided if he would return to play in 2021, but signs seemed to indicate that the Brewers were ready to move on. Also in transition that fall was long-time third base coach Ed Sedar. A popular figure both in the clubhouse and with fans, he'd become known for his mini home run celebrations as players passed third—a leaping high five with Braun, a "dab" with Orlando Arica—as well as his double-handed wave to the crowd during Opening Day introductions. Sedar had been on the coaching staff since 2007, but would shift into an advisory role for 2021.[13]

As had become his trademark, David Stearns' off-season got off to a slow start. His first move came in early December when he traded Corey Knebel, who'd missed all of 2019 and pitched poorly in 2020, to the Dodgers for a player to be named. Indeed, the biggest news involving Stearns of the early winter involved his own status with the Brewers. For the past year, Stearns had held the titles of general manager and president of baseball operations. With a number of teams interested in assistant GM Matt Arnold, the team officially separated Stearns' roles, leaving him as the president of baseball ops and promoting Arnold to the role of GM. The move was in part to retain Arnold, who would have otherwise been permitted to leave for a GM job elsewhere. Stearns himself was in demand by the New York Mets, but the Brewers denied a request by the team to interview Stearns for their vacant GM position.[14]

Topping any news about front office shuffling or minor league signings in mid–December was the roll out of the first COVID-19 vaccines. With the hope that the vaccine would finally curtail the now year-old pandemic, it was expected that fans would be able to return to stadiums for 2021. But there were still questions about whether the season would be able to begin on time. The owners wanted staff and players to be vaccinated before they opened their camps. Given the expected pace of the vaccine roll out, this would mean a delayed spring training and, most likely, a delayed season. The players saw this as another attempt by the owners to cut costs.[15]

In mid–January, the league announced a set of safety protocols for the coming season. There would be no vaccine mandate for players or fans, but "pod" seating formats would be preferred and masks required. While no decision on the Major League season had yet been made, the minor league season would be pushed back to limit the number of players in spring camp.[16]

And then, on January 22, the baseball world and many worlds beyond it mourned the passing of Henry Aaron, a towering figure in both sports and Civil Rights. Aaron's passing hit Milwaukee especially hard. He'd been a key figure in putting the city on the baseball map, not only as an MVP with the Braves but also as an elder statesman on the Brewers. In a spontaneous show of love, fans laid flowers and mementos at Aaron's statue outside Miller Park in the days after his passing. The Brewers later unveiled a "44" patch that would be worn on their sleeves throughout the season.

In early February, the Brewers finally made an off-season move of note when they signed free agent second baseman Kolten Wong to a two-year deal. Wong, a long-time Brewers nemesis as a career Cardinal, would displace Keston Hiura, who had regressed in 2020 but still factored heavily into the team's 2021 plans. Huira would likely now move to first base, filling the unsettled situation there while limiting the liability of Huira's problematic defense.

Meanwhile, there was still no consensus on how many of the COVID-related features of the 2020 season would carry over to 2021. The owners wanted a truncated season, with a universal DH and expanded playoffs. Their proposal to the players' union would have pushed the season back by a month and given commissioner Rob Manfred the power to suspend operations under certain COVID-related circumstances. The union rejected the deal, still certain that ownership was trying to gain concessions in the lead-up to what was certain to be a contentious battle over the soon-to-expire labor agreement.[17]

Back home, the Brewers prepared a 350-page proposal to city health officials detailing a plan to allow for 35 percent capacity at home games. The city had just approved a plan to permit for 10 percent capacity at Milwaukee Bucks games. The city eventually permitted a 25 percent capacity plan that included pod seating, a ban on tailgating, and an agreement from the team to be more liberal in opening the stadium's retractable roof.[18]

"Miller Park" was another part of Brewers lore that transitioned for the 2021 season. Under a deal finalized the year before, the naming rights for the park shifted to American Family Insurance, and shortly after the new year, signage for "American Family Field" went up at the now 20-year-old ballpark. Meanwhile, the city made it known that the capacity limits at the stadium were all part of the ever-fluid COVID situation. While state and city case numbers had been declining since the vaccine roll out (about 10 percent of city residents were fully vaccinated), a spike in cases due to a possible variant of the virus would lead to another summer of fan-less baseball.[19]

Just after the team arrived in Milwaukee from Arizona for the April 1 season opener against the Twins, a false positive on a routine test briefly put the entire team into isolation protocols. Once the matter was cleared up, Christian Yelich used it as an opportunity to urge Brewers fans to get vaccinated and confirmed that he would be getting his shot when all state residents became eligible on April 5.[20]

With fewer than 12,000 masked fans scattered throughout the park and no tailgating permitted, there was an alien feel to the afternoon. But in the top of the first, when Luis Urias made a diving stab to retire Twins lead-off man Luis Arráez, a real cheer filled the ballpark and everything felt just a little bit closer to normal. Woodruff and Minnesota's Kenta Maeda traded zeroes into the bottom of the third when, after a one-out walk and two-out base hit, Woodruff uncorked a wild pitch that scored a run. A pitch later, Max Kepler dumped a single into center field—where Lorenzo Cain was playing while masked—to score another.

Maeda labored in the bottom half of the third, giving up singles to Wong and Avisail Garcia and plunking Yelich to load the bases for Travis Shaw—who'd rejoined the Brewers as a free agent over the winter. With two away and a full count, Maeda missed wide to push a run across and make it 2–1, but the Brewers could do no more damage. The Twins got the

For the first time in 18 months, fans begin to fill seats for a home Brewers game. Even with pod seating and mandatory masking, the 2021 opener gave the players a feel of "real baseball" again (C. Beine).

run back in the fourth when Arráez stroked an RBI single. Freddy Peralta, slated for a spot in the starting rotation, spelled Woodruff in the fifth and—despite allowing a pair of runners—recorded three swinging strikeouts.

The Brewers chased Maeda in the bottom of the fifth, when Yelich singled and Shaw reached on an error. After Cain singled off reliever Tyler Duffy to load the bases, Omar Narvaez blooped a base hit to left. Yelich scored easily, but Shaw—waved home by new third base coach Jason Lane—was thrown out by 10 feet. Peralta returned for a rocky sixth in which he loaded the bases but—once again—struck out the side. In the top of the seventh, the Twins pushed their lead to 5–2 when Byron Buxton crushed a 456-foot two-run homer off side-arm reliever Eric Yardley. The score held into the bottom of the ninth.[21]

Down to their last chance, Wong earned first with a one-out hit-by-pitch and Hiura reached when Minnesota closer Alex Colome bungled the throw to first on a dribbler back to the mound. Yelich came to bat as the tying run and ripped a drive to right that brought everyone to their feet. Kepler, racing back, leapt for the ball at the warning track, but it went in and out of his glove for a loud base hit. Wong scored, but Hiura was forced to settle for second. A ground out by Garcia moved both runners up, but left the Brewers down to their final out. Travis Shaw, who'd played his way back onto the team in spring, followed and lined the first pitch he saw into the gap to the tie the game.[22]

Josh Hader took over for the Brewers in the 10th and, in the excitement of the moment, forgot all about the extra-inning format that had carried over from 2020. Andrelton Simmons, the final Twins out of the ninth, was posted on second base as Hader warmed up. When Narvaez came out to go over the signs with Hader, the pitcher was confused until Narvaez reminded him of the automatic runner. Not that it mattered much anyway, as Hader tore through the three men he faced, striking out each swinging with gas that touched 100 miles per hour.[23]

In the bottom of the 10th, with Cain taking second base, Narvaez blooped a single that moved him to third and brought up Orlando Arcia, who had entered the game as a defensive replacement in the sixth. Arcia hacked at the first pitch and hit a lazy chopper just to the right of the mound. Playing Arcia in and to pull, second baseman Jorge Polanco darted across the infield grass as Cain sprinted home. Polanco made a clean pick and threw a perfect dart to the plate, but Cain dove in just ahead of Mitch Garver's tag to win it and—for the first time in a year and a half—send real-life Brewers fans home happy.

"You know, that's the one thing about this team, man, we never quit," Hader said after the game. "Obviously having the fans there to bring that extra juice, I think that's what you love."[24]

Hader was not the only Brewer to acknowledge the rush from having fans in attendance. Nearly everyone commented on it and they were all glad to see it. But Luis Urias probably summed it up best. "It actually felt like baseball, you know?" he said. "Omar [Narvaez] and I were walking in from the bullpen before the game and he was like, 'Man, this feels like baseball.' I said, 'Yeah, it does.'"[25]

It wasn't just the fans in stands that made it feel like pre-pandemic Brewers baseball in 2021. After a mid–May scuffle, the Brewers took hold of first place in late June and never let it go, clinching the flag on the last home date of the season before a full house. But when the offense that had been inconsistent all season dried up in October, the Brewers were bounced from the playoffs in the first round by the eventual world champion Atlanta Braves.

2022

Thursday, April 14, 2022: Brewers 5, Cardinals 1 (42,794 attendance)
In the News: Fifty days into the Russian invasion of Ukraine, reports say that the Ukrainian resistance is beginning to weaken Russian forces.

Ukraine has claimed to have struck a key Russian warship with cruise missiles, although Russia claims that the ship was evacuated because of an accidental fire.

At the Movies: *You Won't be Alone*, Downer Theater

On the Radio: "As It Was" by Harry Styles

By mid–September, it seemed like the 2021 Brewers could be a team of destiny, up by 15 games on the rival Cardinals and on pace for the best record in team history. But the Brewers won just four times in the season's final 14 games as their offense—problematic most of the year—went AWOL. Although the Brewers were never really in danger of losing the division lead, a 17-game winning streak by St. Louis trimmed their final margin for the NL Central to just five games. In the NLDS, the Brewers caught a hot Braves team and managed just six runs in a 3–1 series loss.

And if the end to the 2021 season put Brewers fans in a gloomy mood, the forecast for the winter did nothing to raise their spirits. It was widely expected that owners would institute a lockout once the collective bargaining agreement between expired on December 1. Both sides remained far apart on several key issues and signs of progress toward a preemptive deal were not to be found. So, upon the conclusion of the World Series, the Brewers went cautiously to their off-season work. The team stood likely to lose a handful of 2021 regulars via free agency, including starter Brett Anderson, outfielder Avisail Garcia, and mid-season pick-up Eduardo Escobar.[26]

In late November, team ace Corbin Burnes, who'd led the NL in ERA and a handful of other categories, was voted the 2021 NL Cy Young Award winner. It was a sensational turn-around for Burnes, who'd pitched himself back into the minor leagues just two years prior with an ERA of nearly 9.00. "For me it wasn't really a goal until really my 2019 season," he said after winning the prize. "When you get kicked in the teeth like that, to try to come back to the best in the league is the goal."[27]

On December 1, with the CBA just hours away from expiring, the Brewers traded Jackie Bradley, Jr.—a free agent signing prior to the '21 season who'd underperformed mightily as a Brewer—back to the Red Sox in exchange for Hunter Renfroe. Renfroe had hit 31 homers in '21 and was penciled in as a regular for the Brewers' '22 outfield. The following day, the owners officially locked the players out, freezing all Major League transactions and barring players from using any team facilities. The players wanted an increase in the pool of money used for bonuses to pre-arbitration players and modifications made to revenue sharing with an increase in the cap for the payroll luxury tax. The owners wanted to base free agency eligibility on age rather than service time. It would be two weeks before the two sides would meet to negotiate and after a month it was reported that "little progress" made been made.[28]

Just before the scheduled start of spring training, the owners finally made a counter-proposal to the players. Finding it "underwhelming," the players rejected the offer and, three days later, spring training was officially delayed. Days later, a meeting between the sides lasted just 15 minutes, and the next day, the owners canceled the first week of spring games. In late February, a deadline to avoid a delay of the regular season was set and then reset as the players accused the owners of operating in bad faith and making too few concessions in order to secure a deal. On March 1, Commissioner Rob Manfred announced that the first week of the regular season would be canceled and not made up. On March 9, Manfred canceled another week of games. Observers expressed little optimism that a deal would be reached without significant damage to the season schedule.[29]

But the next day, a surprise deal was reached between the players and owners that addressed the lingering financial matters and also implement an expanded postseason and a universal designated hitter rule. The season would open on April 7 and the Brewers' home opener, originally scheduled for March 31 against the Diamondbacks, was now set for April 14—a local holiday known as "Milwaukee Day" for its representation of the city's 414 area code—against the Cardinals. In a break from their previous assertions, the owners even found a way to make up the games lost from the first week of the schedule.[30]

In a rush to make up for the three lost months of the off-season, the Brewers were connected to a flurry of free agents, most notably veteran slugger Nelson Cruz, who'd broken in with the Brewers in 2005. A week after the end of the lockout, they landed former MVP outfielder Andrew McCutchen with a one-year, $8.5 million deal to be the Brewers' first regular designated hitter since Kevin Seitzer.[31]

As a truncated spring training got underway in Arizona, the Brewers were in the rare position of being considered a consensus favorite for a division title and, using the various stat-based mathematical predictions for the coming year, were projected as one of the top teams in baseball. "I can tell you, 1,000 percent, that this is the best group of athletes we've had in 18 years," principal owner Mark Attanasio told reporters in Arizona. "We have a lot of hope this year with our club."[32]

Back home, a public still upset over the lockout was greeted with news that the Brewers could soon be asking for yet more taxpayer support for their home park. With the long-controversial regional sales tax having just been retired, it was reported that the Brewers would soon commission a report on the status of American Family Field and its sustainability as a Major League venue. A clause in a team's lease—which ran through

2030—stipulated that the facility must remain among the league's top 25 percent of stadiums in various quality metrics. It was widely suspected that the report the team had commissioned—which would be due out sometime over the summer—would find that the stadium was not up to that standard and that publicly-funded upgrades would be needed. Once again there were rumblings that, if the city and state could not help to fund a proper venue, the Brewers might consider relocation.[33]

After a 3–3 opening road trip, the Brewers returned to Milwaukee for the first full-capacity Opening Day since 2019. The game was scheduled for a 4:14 start, and fans began to stream into the parking lots shortly after noon for the first Opening Day tailgating in three years. They were met with sunshine and high-40s temperatures, but also with winds so severe that a piece of a window from the downtown Chase Tower was torn away and sent crashing to the street below. Although the team advised against setting up tents or canopies, thousands toughed it out, working hard to light grills without much complaint. They were just happy to finally be back.[34]

After an emotional first pitch by Tucker Sparks—a 12-year-old whose younger brother was among those killed when a car sped through the Waukesha Christmas parade the previous November—Brandon Woodruff took the hill for the Brewers and welcomed himself home with a three-up, three-down first. Facing his 40-year-old former teammate Adam Wainwright, Milwaukee lead-off man Kolton Wong ripped the second pitch he saw into the right field corner for an easy triple. Two batters later, McCutchen laced a single up the middle to allow Wong to trot home and give the Brewers a lead they would not surrender.

With one away in the second, the home crowd booed loudly as 42-year-old Albert Pujols—now among the all-time leaders in a half-dozen offensive stats—came to the plate for his first appearance in Milwaukee as a Cardinal since he'd torched the Brewers with a .478 batting average in the 2011 NLCS. With the noise as much a sign of angsty respect as anything else, Pujols hit a sharp grounder that Wong snagged in shallow center field, but his rushed throw to first went into the dugout and Pujols was credited with his 3,305th hit and awarded second base. A few pitches later, Pujols inexplicably broke for third base ahead of Woodruff's delivery. Woodruff stepped off and easily threw him out at third, much to the delight of home faithful.

With one away in the bottom of the inning, Omar Narvaez caught all of a Wainwright fastball and crushed it into the Cardinals' bullpen to make it 2–0 Brewers. The Cardinals threatened in the next frame when Harrison Bader and Yadier Molina collected back-to-back singles. But after a sac bunt and a groundout, Woodruff worked slugger Paul Goldschmidt to a

1–2 count. A change-up from Woodruff appeared to catch the plate, but umpire Lance Barrett called ball two. Woody came back with a slider that looked even better, but once again Barrett called a ball. Steaming on the mound, Woodruff coaxed a groundball, but Goldschmidt was given first base on a catcher's interference call. Facing a bases loaded situation and still agitated by being squeezed at the plate, Woodruff took a breath. An often fiery competitor who had once been ejected from a game for arguing balls and strikes, Woodruff found a new calm at the onset of his sixth Major League season. *Clear it out, reset, and worry about the next pitch*, he told himself. He did and got Tyler O'Neill to fly out harmlessly to end the inning. On his way back to the Brewers dugout, however, Woodruff glared at Barrett and held up two fingers to indicate the number of strikes he'd been denied.[35]

In the bottom half, the Brewers—struggling so far in '22 with runners on—got back-to-back hits with two men on, including a booming run-scoring double from Narvaez, to take a 4–0 lead. Woodruff permitted nothing more than a two-out walk over the next two innings before giving way to off-season pick-up Trevor Gott, a 29-year-old journeyman from Kentucky. Gott cruised through a pair of scoreless innings as the Brewers tacked on another run in the sixth when Jace Peterson walked, stole second, and came around on a base hit by Wong. Gott gave way to Jandel Gustave, a similarly-traveled righthander, for the eighth. Leadoff man Tommy Edman crushed Gustave's fifth pitch of the afternoon for a solo homer to center, but his spark found no fuel and the Cardinals went quietly the rest of the way.

In the ninth, those still on hand stood as Gustave dispatched long-time home opener menace Nolan Arenado and Pujols. The official attendance of 42,794 was the lowest reported full-capacity opener tally since 2005 and thousands of seats in the upper bowl remained empty all afternoon, perhaps a reality of the "new normal" in the wake of the now-two-year-old COVID pandemic. Facing Paul DeJong, Gustave worked quickly and sealed the win with a swinging strikeout.

"Nice getting a win," manager Craig Counsell said after the game. "You wanted a full house and to get them a win. That makes it a good day. That's what I'd say."[36]

"The fans are amazing," said Kolton Wong, who finished with two hits and a stolen base. "You can tell there's a little bit of alcohol in there, they're a little rowdy. But it's so fun." It had been among the cleanest and easiest Opening Day wins in team history and it officially pushed the franchise into winning territory among openers with a 27–26 all-time mark. But, just like any other home opener, it was just a single game, no more important to the final standings than any other lone game over the course

The author and his sister, Angela Yamashita, are all smiles after the Brewers topped the Cardinals, 5–1, in the 2022 opener (Jessica Burch).

of the long season. But it was—more so than any other lid-lifter since the vans containing all the worldly possessions of the Seattle Pilots were ordered to head east from Provo instead of west—a return home for baseball in Milwaukee and for all the emotions and love that people connect to and express through this otherwise meaningless little game.[37]

"That's what we were missing for a while," Wong continued. "Now that things are starting to feel back to normal, you can feed off that. This crowd, every single time they're out here, you feed off that energy they're bringing—that liquid courage. I love it. Keep it coming."[38]

After the best 50-game start to a season in franchise history, injuries and inconsistency smothered the progress of the 2022 Brewers. Still in first place at the All-Star break, the team stunningly traded away all-world closer Josh Hader—a move that brought about a late-season bullpen collapse that left them out of the playoffs for the first time in five seasons.

Appendix: The Opening Day All-Timers

Catcher: The Brewers have had some pretty solid catchers over the years, with Hall of Famer Ted Simmons and All-Stars Jonathan Lucroy, Darrell Porter, and B.J. Surhoff all getting multiple Opening Day starts. But **Mike Matheny** outslugged them all. In three Opening Day starts, Matheny hit a homer and two doubles with a .444 batting average. Only three other Brewers with as many home opener plate appearances have a higher OPS (on base plus slugging) than Matheny's 1.444.

First Base: While Prince Fielder, Cecil Cooper, and George Scott are easily the three best first-sackers in team history—and combined for 19 Opening Day starts at the position—**Eric Thames** was lethal in his two starts, going four for nine with a pair of doubles and a homer. He matches Matheny's .444 home opener average and tops his OPS with a 1.500 mark.

Second Base: Among the 13 Brewers with 25 or more home opener plate appearances, no one—at any position—comes near the numbers **Rickie Weeks** put up in eight starts at second base. He collected 12 hits (second only to Yount all-time) and got on base at .487 clip (aided by three hit-by-pitches). In the 2009 opener, his bottom-of-the-ninth double tied the game and his daring dash home on a groundball won it.

Third Base: Only Don Money (six) and Paul Molitor (five) got more Opening Day nods at third than **Aramis Ramirez** (four), but neither did the lid-lifter damage that Ramirez did. Am-Ram collected six hits and a walk in 15 plate appearances with two doubles and five driven in. Bill Hall deserves an honorable mention here as one of the biggest opener bats in team history, but he split his time between third and the outfield.

Shortstop: While Robin Yount made nine starts at short between 1974 and 1984, he collected just three hits. J.J. Hardy and Orlando Arica, the two next most frequent starters there during home openers, didn't fare much better. But in four starts between 1995 and 1998, **Jose Valentin** swung a very hot bat, slugging two homers and batting .313.

Outfield: Even a die-hard Brewers fan might have forgotten that **Turner Ward** started in the outfield in three straight home openers (1994–1996) and certainly few knew that in home opener games Ward has the highest OPS in team history among players with five or more plate appearances. In those three games,

Ward went three for nine with five walks, a double and two homers. Tied with Hall for most opener homers with three are **Jeromy Burnitz** and **Sixto Lezcano**. Lezcano had one of the most memorable hits in opener history with his 1980 walk-off grand slam (his second opener slam) and he also ranks tops in team history in opener RBI. Burnitz was perhaps the toughest Opening Day out in team history, going five for 13 with eight walks.

Starting Pitcher: No Brewer with multiple home opener starts can compare to Iron **Mike Caldwell**, who recorded a 0.53 ERA over his 1979 and 1981 opener starts. He tossed the only complete-game shutout in opener history in 1979 and lost a heartbreaker in '81 when he allowed just one run over eight innings.

Relief Pitcher: In terms of pure dominance, no one can match **Josh Hader**. With appearances in 2019 and 2021, he had thrown three perfect Opening Day innings, allowing just two balls to be put into play.

Opening Day statistics compiled by Jason Lebeck.

Chapter Notes

Chapter One

1. Chris Zantow, *Building the Brewers: Bud Selig and the Return of Major League Baseball to Milwaukee*, McFarland, 2019, 77, 83.
2. Ibid., 83, 89.
3. Ibid., 95, 96, 99.
4. Ibid., 92.
5. "Brewers Jubilant at News of Shift," *Milwaukee Sentinel*, April 1, 1970.
6. Ibid.
7. Zantow, *Building the Brewers*, 100; "Brewers Jubilant at News of Shift."
8. "Brewers Boast Solid Infield," *Milwaukee Sentinel*, April 1, 1970.
9. "Brewers Make Uniform Adjustments," *Milwaukee Journal*, April 2, 1970.
10. "Stadium Clean-up Nears D-Day," *Milwaukee Sentinel*, April 2, 1970.
11. "Fans Find Promised Land Jammed in Low Rent District," *Milwaukee Sentinel*, April 8, 1970.
12. David E. Skelton, "Lew Krausse," SABR Biography Project, https://sabr.org/bioproj/person/lew-krausse-2/; "37,237 See Angels Jar Brewers," *Milwaukee Sentinel*, April 8, 1970.
13. "Facts of Life," *Milwaukee Journal*, April 8, 1970.
14. "Fans Find Promised Land Jammed in Low Rent District," *Milwaukee Sentinel*, April 8, 1970; "4 Youths Get $100 Fines for Misconduct at Stadium," *Milwaukee Journal*, April 8, 1970.
15. *Building the Brewers*, 111.
16. Ibid., 122.
17. "Lane was Selig's Man in December," *Milwaukee Sentinel*, January 26, 1971.
18. "Pattin Decides to Get Serious," *Milwaukee Journal*, March 28, 1971.
19. "Kuenn Takes Over as Brewers' Batting Instructor," *Milwaukee Sentinel*, March 29, 1971.
20. "Brewers Eye Million Attendance," *Milwaukee Journal*, April 4, 1971.
21. "Lockwood Realizes Ambition by Starting Brewers' Opener," *Milwaukee Journal*, April 9, 1971.
22. "Brewers Expect Huge Crowd," *Milwaukee Journal*, April 9, 1971; "Food Sales Depend on Score," *Milwaukee Sentinel*, April 10, 1971.
23. "Home Opener New Thrill for Lockwood," *Milwaukee Sentinel*, April 9, 1971.
24. Bill Nowlin, "Skip Lockwood," SABR Biography Project, https://sabr.org/bioproj/person/skip-lockwood/.
25. "Home Opener New Thrill for Lockwood."
26. "Overweight Doyne Ready for 1st Pitch," *Milwaukee Journal*, April 9, 1971.
27. "A Good Day Made Great," *Milwaukee Journal*, April 11, 1971.
28. Ibid.
29. "Pena Waits for a Walk," *Milwaukee Journal*, April 11, 1971.
30. Ibid.
31. "Brewers Trade for 6 Bosox," *Milwaukee Sentinel*, October 11, 1971.
32. "Lane Seeks Power Boost in Big Trade," *Milwaukee Journal*, October 11, 1971.
33. Ron Anderson, "George Scott Biography," SABR Biography Project, https://sabr.org/bioproj/person/george-scott/; "Scott Finds New Life with Brewers," *Milwaukee Sentinel*, March 1, 1972.
34. "Scott Finds New Life with Brewers," *Milwaukee Sentinel*, March 1, 1972.
35. "1972: Labor Pains," The Great

Game Online Book of Baseball, https://thisgreatgame.com/1972-baseball-history/.
36. "Brewers Break Camp and Scatter," *Milwaukee Journal*, April 3, 1972.
37. Ibid.
38. "No Fun for Heartbroken Homer," *Milwaukee Journal*, April 2, 1972.
39. "Brewers Postpone Home Opener Friday," *Milwaukee Journal*, April 6, 1972; "Won't Play Until Strike Ends: Lonborg," *Milwaukee Sentinel*, April 8, 1972.
40. "1972: Labor Pains."
41. "Brewers Battle Tigers in Debut," *Milwaukee Sentinel*, April 21, 1972.
42. "Brewers were Rebuffed on Daylight Opener," *Milwaukee Journal*, April 21, 1972.
43. "Play Ball! Kids Had All the Fun," *Milwaukee Journal*, April 23, 1972.
44. "Bristol Thinks it Through," *Milwaukee Journal*, April 23, 1972.
45. "Tigers Ruin Opener for Brewers, 8-2," *Milwaukee Journal*, April 23, 1972.
46. Ibid.
47. "Telling Year for Brewers," *Milwaukee Sentinel*, February 9, 1973.
48. "Telling Year for Brewers"; "Time to Frolic at Stadium," *Milwaukee Sentinel*, April 10, 1973.
49. "Time to Frolic at Stadium."
50. "Money to Pay Off—Crandall," *Milwaukee Sentinel*, November 1, 1972; "Money: Let Me Alone, I'll Hit," *Milwaukee Sentinel*, November 1, 1972.
51. "Early Spring Drills Delayed," *Milwaukee Sentinel*, February 9, 1973; Tracy Ringolsby, "The Previous 11 Times The MLB Season was Interrupted," *Baseball America*, March 23, 2020, https://www.baseballamerica.com/stories/ringolsby-the-11-previous-times-the-mlb-season-was-interrupted/.
52. "A Day at the Old Ball Game in Sun City," *Milwaukee Journal* April 2, 1973; "Thomas, Garcia Will Start for Brewers," *Milwaukee Journal*, April 5, 1973.
53. "Brewers Home Opener Anyone's Guess," *Milwaukee Sentinel*, April 10, 1973.
54. "Brewers Home Opener Anyone's Guess"; "Garcia Wakes Up to Snowy Surprise," *Milwaukee Journal*, April 10, 1973.
55. "Garcia Wakes Up to Snowy Surprise."
56. Ibid.
57. "Brewers Will Field Shovelers," *Milwaukee Sentinel*, April 10, 1973.
58. "Brewers Ready to Go—Finally," *Milwaukee Sentinel*, April 13, 1973; "Brewers Must Wait for Home Opener," *Milwaukee Journal*, April 9, 1973; "Parsons' No Hitter Exits with a Groan," *Milwaukee Journal*, April 14, 1973.
59. "Pasons Chills Orioles on 1 Hit," *Milwaukee Sentinel*, April 14, 1973; "Parsons' No Hitter Exits with a Groan," *Milwaukee Journal*, April 14, 1973; "Green Beret on the Beam, So Are the Groundskeepers," *Milwaukee Journal*, April 14, 1973.
60. "Pasons Chills Orioles on 1 Hit"; "Parsons' No Hitter Exits with a Groan."
61. "Everyone Impressed by Parsons But Parsons," *Milwaukee Sentinel*, April 14, 1973.
62. "Boomer Joins Century Club," *Milwaukee Sentinel*, December 21, 1973.
63. "From Cotton Picker to Gold Digger," *Milwaukee Sentinel*, March 13, 1974.
64. "Cubs Contenders? Jury Remains Out," *Milwaukee Journal*, March 15, 1974; "Brewers Give Shot to Kid Shortstop," *Milwaukee Journal*, March 12, 1974.
65. "Brewers Give Shot to Kid Shortstop."
66. "Yount to Open Season for Brewers," *Milwaukee Sentinel*, March 28, 1974.
67. "Brewers Cash In on Youth," *Milwaukee Journal*, March 31, 1974.
68. "Brewer Weather Watch," *Milwaukee Journal*, April 4, 1974.
69. "The Ordeal of a Rookie Shortstop Named Yount," *Milwaukee Sentinel*, April 6, 1974.
70. Ibid.
71. "So Brewers Fell? Nobody's Perfect," *Milwaukee Journal*, April 6, 1974; "Opening Day, A Running Report," *Milwaukee Journal*, April 6, 1974; "Fans Find Nothing So Rare as Opening Day," *Milwaukee Sentinel*, April 6, 1974.
72. "So Brewers Fell? Nobody's Perfect."
73. "Bosox Blunder By Brewers," *Milwaukee Sentinel*, April 6, 1974; "The Ordeal of a Rookie Shortstop Named Yount."
74. "The Ordeal of a Rookie Shortstop Named Yount."
75. Matthew J. Prigge, "Welcome Home, Henry," *Shepherd Express*, February 8, 2016.

76. "Aaron Signs 2 Year Pact," *Milwaukee Sentinel*, November 15, 1974.
77. "Porter Insists He'll Play Out Contract," *Milwaukee Sentinel*, February 12, 1975.
78. Ibid.
79. "Brewers Show 4th in Ratings," *Milwaukee Sentinel*, April 7, 1975; "Kobel to See Arm specialist," *Milwaukee Sentinel*, April 2, 1975.
80. "Aaron Rediscovers Homer Trot," *Milwaukee Journal*, April 3, 1975.
81. Ibid.
82. "Opener is Virtual Sellout," *Milwaukee Sentinel*, April 10, 1975.
83. "Looking Swell, Henry!" *Milwaukee Journal*, April 12, 1975; Fallon Acker, "The Surprising History of the American Tailgate," Spoon University, https://spoonuniversity.com/lifestyle/surprisingly-great-food-combos-more-shocking-than-the-patriot-win; "Everybody Off for a Stadium Tailgate Party," *Milwaukee Journal*, August 9, 1974.
84. "Brewers, Hank Warm Chilly Fans," *Milwaukee Sentinel*, April 12, 1975.
85. "Brewers, Hank Warm Chilly Fans"; "Looking Swell, Henry!"
86. "It's Like Old Times at County Stadium," *Milwaukee Sentinel*, April 12, 1975; "It's a Happy Return for Aaron," *Milwaukee Sentinel*, April 12, 1975.
87. "It's a Happy Return for Aaron."
88. "Champion Just That for Brewers," *Milwaukee Journal*, April 12, 1975.
89. "It's Like Old Times at County Stadium."
90. "Aaron Tell His Story and Tells it… And," *Milwaukee Journal*, April 12, 1975.
91. Ibid.
92. "Grammas Would Like the Brewers to Trade," *Milwaukee Sentinel*, January 26, 1976.
93. "Money on Market, Bidders Are Aplenty," *Milwaukee Journal*, December 10, 1975; "Brewers Back Home with Same Look," *Milwaukee Journal*, December 14, 1975.
94. "Porter Gets Cut—But Only in Barber Chair," *Milwaukee Sentinel*, February 3, 1976.
95. "Brewers Have Reason to Fret," *Milwaukee Sentinel*, February 27, 1976.
96. "Yount May Play Out his Option," *Milwaukee Sentinel*, March 12, 1976; "Yount Wants Multiyear Pact," *Milwaukee Sentinel*, March 31, 1976.
97. "Baseball Players Get Jobless Aid," *Milwaukee Sentinel*, March 9, 1976; "Oh, Those Poor Players," *Milwaukee Journal*, March 11, 1976.
98. "The Customers Always Write," *Milwaukee Sentinel*, March 23, 1976.
99. "Opener No Big Deal—Martin," *Milwaukee Sentinel*, April 8, 1976; "This Could Be the year of Decision for Slaton," *Milwaukee Sentinel*, April 6, 1976.
100. "Young Stand Out in Brewers Crowd," *Milwaukee Sentinel*, April 9, 1976; "That Was the Old Ballgame," *Milwaukee Journal*, April 9, 1976.
101. "Aaron, Slaton Open Up Big," *Milwaukee Sentinel*, April 9, 1976.
102. "Opening Day was Aaron's Dish," *Milwaukee Sentinel*, April 9, 1976.
103. Ibid.
104. "Mound's Indescribably Bad to Yanks," *Milwaukee Journal*, April 9, 1976.
105. "Brewers Select Bando in Draft," *Milwaukee Journal*, November 4, 1976.
106. "Brewers Shine in Money Game," *Milwaukee Journal*, January 30, 1977: "Brewers Say Picks will Sign," *Milwaukee Sentinel*, November 5, 1976.
107. "Scott Loves Deal, But…," *Milwaukee Sentinel*, December 7, 1976: "Brewers Say Picks will Sign."
108. "Sal Joins the Family," *Milwaukee Journal*, November 20, 1976.
109. "Porter Wanted to Go to KC," *Milwaukee Sentinel*, December 7, 1976; "Scott Loves Deal, But…."
110. "Frisella's Death a Shocker," *Milwaukee Journal*, January 3, 1977; "Brewers' Honor to Frisella," *Milwaukee Journal*, April 7, 1977.
111. "Brewers Expect Bando to Become Captain," *Milwaukee Sentinel*, March 19, 1977; "First Base Not Same," *Milwaukee Journal*, March 8, 1977; Eric Aron, "Cecil Cooper Biography," SABR Biography Project, https://sabr.org/bioproj/person/cecil-cooper; "First Base Not Same," *Milwaukee Journal*, March 8, 1977.
112. "With Spirits Riding High, Brewers Set Sail," *Milwaukee Journal*, April 6, 1977; "Brewers' Honor to Frisella."
113. "With Spirits Riding High, Brewers Set Sail."
114. "Brewers' Motto: Think Win," *Milwaukee Sentinel*, April 5, 1977.

115. "Fans Put Braves Days to Rest," *Milwaukee Sentinel*, April 13, 1977.
116. "Palmer Spoils a Grand Opener," *Milwaukee Sentinel*, April 13, 1977.
117. "Seats Full, Bases Empty at Brewer Opener," *Milwaukee Journal*, April 13, 1977.
118. "Grammas' 9th Inning Move Backfires," *Milwaukee Journal*, April 13, 1977.
119. Ibid.
120. "Brewers on the Brink of Something Big," *Milwaukee Journal*, April 13, 1977.
121. Matthew J. Prigge, "When Robin Yount Almost Quit," *Shepherd Express*, December 14, 2015.
122. "Dalton New Brewers GM," *Milwaukee Sentinel*, November 21, 1977; Dale Voiss, "Harry Dalton," SABR Biography Project, https://sabr.org/bioproj/person/harry-dalton/.
123. "Hisle a Brewer for Almost $3 Million," *Milwaukee Sentinel*, November 19, 1977.
124. "Dalton's Aim: Rid Brewers of 'Losers,'" *Milwaukee Sentinel*, November 22, 1977.
125. "Exit Slaton, Enter Oglivie," *Milwaukee Journal*, December 10 1977.
126. "Orioles Bamberger to Manage Brewers," *Milwaukee Journal*, January 20, 1978; "Bamberger: Candid Start," *Milwaukee Journal*, January 20, 1978.
127. Dennis Degenhardt, "Gorman Thomas," SABR Biography Project, https://sabr.org/bioproj/person/gorman-thomas/.
128. "Bamberger Burns as Brewers Show up Late for Practice," *Milwaukee Sentinel*, March 7, 1978.
129. "When Robin Yount Almost Quit."
130. "Molitor May Be Ahead of Schedule," *Milwaukee Sentinel*, March 9, 1978; "Enthusiasm Up: So Are Ticket, Parking Costs," *Milwaukee Sentinel*, April 6, 1978.
131. "Brewers Feel More Sure with New Boss," *Milwaukee Sentinel*, March 13, 1978; "Hisle Making His Mark as a Nice Guy," *Milwaukee Journal*, April 2, 1978; "Enthusiasm Up: So Are Ticket, Parking Costs."
132. "When Robin Yount Almost Quit."
133. "Brewers Try New Suits," *Milwaukee Journal*, April 7, 1978; "Brewers Rise to Occasion—Perfectly," *Milwaukee Sentinel*, April 8, 1978.
134. "Brewers Rise to Occasion—Perfectly."
135. "Molitor Shows Class, Cool," *Milwaukee Journal*, April 8, 1978.
136. "When Robin Yount Almost Quit."
137. "Hisle's Opener Swell," *Milwaukee Journal*," April 8, 1978; "Brewers Get in Licks," *Milwaukee Sentinel*, April 8, 1978.
138. "Brewers Get in Licks."
139. "Pitchers Pleased by Punch," *Milwaukee Journal*, April 8, 1978.
140. "Hisle High, Molitor Cool in Opening Win," *Milwaukee Sentinel*, April 8, 1978.
141. Ibid.
142. "Molitor Looks to New Fields, Drills as Outfielder," *Milwaukee Sentinel*, February 13, 1979.
143. "Why Me, Lord?" *Milwaukee Journal*, February 9, 1979; "Brewers do Well on Game Show," *Milwaukee Journal*, March 2, 1979.
144. "Smooth Camp Suits Dalton Just Fine," *Milwaukee Sentinel*, March 6, 1979.
145. "Gorman: '78 Was no Fluke," *Milwaukee Sentinel*, March 2, 1979; "Spring Training Has Light Moments for Brewers," *Milwaukee Sentinel*, March 21, 1979.
146. "Spring Training Has Light Moments for Brewers," *Milwaukee Sentinel*, March 21, 1979.
147. Ibid.
148. "Selig Proceeds With Caution," *Milwaukee Journal*, April 3, 1979; "Report: Yankees Won't Re-hire Martin," *Milwaukee Sentinel*, April 4, 1979.
149. Issac Buttke, "Mike Caldwell," SABR Biography Project, https://sabr.org/bioproj/person/mike-caldwell/.
150. "Caldwell Puts Bosox Bats on Ice," *Milwaukee Sentinel*, April 11, 1979.
151. "Caldwell's Proof is in his Pitching," *Milwaukee Journal*, April 10, 1979.
152. "Brewers Say Rookie Umpire's Call Was Off Base," *Milwaukee Journal*, April 11, 1979.
153. "Sorensen is Caldwell's Image Man," *Milwaukee Journal*, April 11, 1979.
154. "Brewers Say Rookie Umpire's Call Was Off Base."

Chapter Two

1. "Dalton Laughs off Cosell's Big Trade," *Milwaukee Journal*, October 11, 1979.
2. "Who is Lezcano?" *Milwaukee Journal*, April 3, 1980.

3. "Draft to Fill Free Agent Fantasies?" *Milwaukee Journal*, October 30, 1979.

4. "Spring Training is Basically Kid Stuff," *Milwaukee Journal*, March 2, 1980; Daniel Okrent, *Nine Innings: The Anatomy of Baseball as Seen Through the Playing of a Single Game*, McGraw-Hill, 1985, 155; "Gorman Already Stormin' in Midseason Form," *Milwaukee Journal*, March 5, 1980.

5. "Martinez Says Brewers Will Vote for Strike," *Milwaukee Sentinel*, March 6, 1980; "Loss of Leg Not About to Limit Kuenn's Role on Brewer Staff," *Milwaukee Sentinel*, March 10, 1980.

6. "Bamberger to be out for Two Months," *Milwaukee Journal*, March 10, 1980; "Bamberger Stable After Operation," *Milwaukee Journal*, March 27, 1980.

7. "He'll Manage," *Milwaukee Journal*, March 11, 1980; "Brewers Think Strike is Right," *Milwaukee Sentinel*, April 2, 1980.

8. "Brewers Spring Statistics," *Milwaukee Journal*, April 10, 1980; "Brewers Home Opener Sold Out," *Milwaukee Sentinel*, February 29, 1980; "A Slam-Bang Way to Open the Season," *Milwaukee Sentinel*, April 11, 1980.

9. "Bambi, In Lights, Turned 'Em On," *Milwaukee Sentinel*, April 11, 1980.

10. Ibid.

11. "Old Man Yaz Lauds Slaton and Lezcano," *Milwaukee Sentinel*, April 11, 1980.

12. Okrent, *Nine Innings*, 21, 244; "Brewers Grand Opening is a Real Blast," *Milwaukee Journal*, April 11, 1980.

13. "Bambi, In Lights, Turned 'Em On."

14. "Brewers Open in Grand Style," *Milwaukee Sentinel*, April 11, 1980.

15. "Buck's Buckaroos Still Bambi's Bombers," *Milwaukee Journal*, April 11, 1980; "Brewers Open in Grand Style."

16. "Bambi, In Lights, Turned 'Em On," *Milwaukee Sentinel*, April 11, 1980; "Brewers Grand Opening is a Real Blast," *Milwaukee Journal*, April 11, 1980.

17. "Bamberger to Step Down After Sunday," *Milwaukee Sentinel*, September 6, 1980.

18. "Such a Deal!" *Milwaukee Journal*, December 5, 1980.

19. "Will Brewers Big Deal Bring Them a Pennant?" *Milwaukee Journal*, December 13, 1980.

20. Ibid.

21. "Brewers Looking for a Leader," *Milwaukee Sentinel*, February 19, 1981; "Reserved Seats Sold out for Brewers' Opener," *Milwaukee Journal*, January 25, 1981; "Brewers are Proving to be Very Apt Pupils," *Milwaukee Sentinel*, March 10, 1981.

22. Okrent, *Nine Innings*, 97; "Rodgers at Camp, Walking Around Slowly," *Milwaukee Journal*, March 2, 1981.

23. "Selig, Martinez agree on Fans, Not Issues," *Milwaukee Sentinel*, February 26, 1981.

24. "Tailgater Class of '81 Slurps Up Opening Day Tradition," *Milwaukee Journal*, April 16, 1981.

25. "Tailgater Class of '81 Slurps Up Opening Day Tradition"; "Fans Celebrate the Rites of Summer," *Milwaukee Journal*, April 17, 1981.

26. "Fans Toast Season of Baseball, Beer," *Milwaukee Sentinel*, April 17, 1981.

27. Okrent, *Nine Innings*, 111; "All Bets Off! Brewers Shut Out," *Milwaukee Sentinel*, April 17, 1981.

28. "All Bets Off! Brewers Shut Out."

29. "Protest Earns Tribe's Hargrove a Fast Ejection," *Milwaukee Sentinel*, April 17, 1981.

30. "All Bets Off! Brewers Shut Out"; "Fans Celebrate the Rites of Summer."

31. "All Bets Off!"

32. "Nothing's Brewing in Home Opener," *Milwaukee Journal*, April 17, 1981.

33. Ibid.

34. "Rodgers Grades Himself a C+ or B- for the Season," *Milwaukee Sentinel*, October 16, 1981.

35. Okrent, *Nine Innings*, 14, 111; "Respect," *Milwaukee Sentinel*, April 6, 1982; "Rodgers Grades Himself a C+ or B- for the Season."

36. Gorgon Gattie, "Pete Ladd," SABR Biography Project, https://sabr.org/bioproj/person/pete-ladd/; "Money Making Another Switch," *Sporting News*, February 20, 1982; "Phils Disgusted, Deals Collapse," *Sporting News*, January 2, 1982.

37. "Fingers' Injury Gives Brewers a Scare," *Sporting News*, April 3, 1982; Okrent, *Nine Innings*, 255; "Fingers Eyes Quick Recovery," *Milwaukee Sentinel*, March 15, 1982.

38. "Sno Fooling: Brewers in Houston," *Milwaukee Journal*, April 7, 1982.

39. "Rangers Rain on Brewers Parade in

Home Opener," *Milwaukee Sentinel*, April 17, 1982.

40. Dennis Degenhardt, "Moose Haas," SABR Biography Project, https://sabr.org/bioproj/person/moose-haas/#_edn1; "Milwaukee Brewer Right-Hander Moose Haas is an Amateur Magician," UPI, March 25, 1981, https://www.upi.com/Archives/1981/03/25/Milwaukee-Brewer-right-hander-Moose-Haas-is-an-amateur-magician/9110354344400/; "Brewers are Best, Says Hurler Haas," *Sporting News*, March 13, 1982; "Rangers Rain on Brewers Parade in Home Opener," *Milwaukee Sentinel*, April 17, 1982.

41. "Fingers Loses His Touch in Clutch," *Milwaukee Sentinel*, April 17, 1982.

42. "Moore is Fourth Injured Brewer," *Milwaukee Sentinel*, April 17, 1982.

43. "Fingers Loses His Touch in Clutch"; "Rangers Rain on Brewers Parade in Home Opener," *Milwaukee Sentinel*, April 17, 1982.

44. "Rangers Rain on Brewers Parade in Home Opener."

45. "Brewers Sign Kuenn to 1-Year Pact," *Milwaukee Sentinel*, October 26, 1983; Matthew J. Prigge, "The 1983 Brewers are Easily the Most Disappointing Team in Franchise History," *Shepherd Express*, July 24, 2017.

46. "Who's Excited? Not MVP Robin," *Sporting News*, November 22, 1983.

47. "Brewers in Demand All Over Wisconsin," *Sporting News*, January 10, 1983; "Reds Won't Goose Step for Russ," *Sporting News*, March 14, 1983; "Brewers Kept Chill Out of Winter," *Milwaukee Journal*, January 2, 1983.

48. "Brewers Kept Chill Out of Winter," *Milwaukee Journal*, January 2, 1983.

49. "If McClure Leaves, Brewers May Deal," *Sporting News*, December 6, 1982; "Brewers Fret Over Fingers," *Sporting News*, January 3, 1983; "Outlook Bleak for Vuckovich," *Sporting News*, March 28, 1983; "Molitor Signs with Brewers for Five Years," *Milwaukee Journal*, February 17, 1983; "Writers See Expo-Brewer World Series," *Sporting News*, April 4, 1982.

50. "Vuckovich Not Joking This Time," *Milwaukee Journal*, March 17, 1983; Rory Costello, "Pete Vuckovich," SABR Biography Project, https://sabr.org/bioproj/person/pete-vuckovich/.

51. "Vuckovich Not Joking This Time."

52. "Ladd and Gibson Fill Fingers' Role," *Sporting News*, April 11, 1983; "48% Positive Brewers Will Take World Series," *Milwaukee Sentinel*, April 15, 1983; "Barbecuers Pick Yount as Most Popular Invitee," *Milwaukee Sentinel*, April 16, 1983.

53. "Brewers Left Cold in Home Opener," *Milwaukee Journal*, April 16, 1983.

54. "Play Ball! Tailgaters Gather Early," *Milwaukee Journal*, April 15, 1982; "Baseball's Back!" *Milwaukee Journal*, April 15, 1983.

55. "Kuenn Move Fails, Royals Trip Brewers," *Milwaukee Sentinel*, April 16, 1983.

56. Ibid.

57. "McClure Loses Feel on Sinker," *Milwaukee Sentinel*, April 16, 1983.

58. "Kuenn Move Fails, Royals Trip Brewers," *Milwaukee Sentinel*, April 16, 1983.

59. Ibid.

60. Ibid.

61. "Once Again, Gura Masters the Brewers." *Milwaukee Journal*, April 16, 1983.

62. "Lachemann Will Get Brewer Job Monday," *Milwaukee Journal*, October 2, 1983; Norm King, "Rene Lachemann," SABR Biography Project, https://sabr.org/bioproj/person/rene-lachemann/.

63. "Brewers Take No Risks in Sundberg Deal," *Milwaukee Journal*, December 9, 1983.

64. "Vuckovich is Cautiously Optimistic," *Sporting News*, February 27, 1984.

65. "Simmons Relishes New DH Role," *Sporting News*, January 30, 1984.

66. "Important Test for Fingers' Arm to Come This Week," *Milwaukee Journal*, March 25, 1984; "Augustine, Fingers, Make the Opening Day Roster," *Milwaukee Journal*, April 3, 1984.

67. "Hurts Hamper Molitor, Vucko," *Sporting News*, April 9, 1984.

68. Matthew J. Prigge, "The Rise and Fall of Sportsvue," *Shepherd Express*, August 28, 2017.

69. "Victory, Cold Weather, Perfect Match for Latch," *Milwaukee Journal*, April 18, 1984; "Lacheman Relishes Home Debut," *Milwaukee Sentinel*, April 18, 1984.

70. "Mother Nature Taunts Fans at

Opener," *Milwaukee Sentinel*, April 18, 1984.
71. "Notes and Quotes," *Milwaukee Sentinel*, April 17, 1984.
72. "Mets Plan for Strawberry Sunday," *Sporting News*, January 23, 1984; "Lacheman Relishes Home Debut."
73. "Brewers Heat Up Cold Opener," *Milwaukee Sentinel*, April 18, 1984; "Relishes Home Debut," *Milwaukee Sentinel*, April 18, 1984.
74. "Notes and Quotes," *Milwaukee Sentinel*, April 18, 1984.
75. "Lacheman Relishes Home Debut"; "Notes and Quotes," *Milwaukee Sentinel*, April 18, 1984.
76. "Victory, Cold Weather, Perfect Match for Latch," *Milwaukee Journal*, April 18, 1984; "Lacheman Relishes Home Debut."
77. "This Guy Ready Can Really Hit," *Milwaukee Journal*, April 18, 1984.
78. "Yount Undergoes Shoulder Surgery," *Sporting News*, November 26, 1984.
79. Ibid.
80. "Bambi's Back," *Milwaukee Sentinel*, September 28, 1984.
81. "Brewers' Outfield is Crowded," *Sporting News*, February 25, 1985; "Giles is Rewarding Bamberger's Faith," *Sporting News*, April 1, 1985.
82. "Yount Undergoes Shoulder Surgery," *Sporting News*, November 26, 1984; "Yount in Leftfield for Trial Saturday," *Milwaukee Sentinel*, March 23, 1985.
83. Matthew J. Prigge, "A Japanese Legend in Brewers Blue," *Shepherd Express*, May 15, 2017.
84. "Brewers Ready, Winding Up for a Better Sales Pitch in '85," *Milwaukee Journal*, April 8, 1985.
85. "Giles Reportedly Busted for Drugs," *Sporting News*, December 31, 1984; "Hope Rekindled by a Kid's Game," *Milwaukee Sentinel*, April 10, 1985; "Tailgates Down, Spirits Up," *Milwaukee Journal*, April 9, 1985.
86. "Out at the Cold Ball Game," *Milwaukee Journal*, April 10, 1985; "After All This Time, Seaver is Still Terrific," *Milwaukee Journal*, April 10, 1985.
87. "After All This Time, Seaver is Still Terrific."
88. "Bumbling Brewers Spoil Bambi's Return," *Milwaukee Journal*, April 10, 1985.
89. "Bumbling Brewers Spoil Bambi's Return."
90. "Out at the Cold Ball Game," *Milwaukee Journal*, April 10, 1985.
91. "Brewers Delighted with Green Deal," *Sporting News*, December 16, 1985; "Moore: Brewers Days Near End," *Milwaukee Sentinel*, February 12, 1986.
92. "Brewers," *Sporting News*, February 24, 1986.
93. "Brewers Take Green Gamble," *Milwaukee Journal*, December 16, 1985; "For '86 Starters, Put Tigers No. 1," *Sporting News*, January 6, 1986.
94. Craig Brown, "Collusion and the No-Risk Free Agents of 1988," *The Hardball Times*, February 29, 2008, https://tht.fangraphs.com/collusion-and-the-no-risk-free-agents-of-1988.
95. "At $710,000, First Sackers Can Drive Cadillacs," *Sporting News*, February 10, 1986.
96. Matthew J. Prigge, "We're Really Lucky Nobody Got Killed," *Shepherd Express*, February 28, 2017.
97. "Simmons Bids a Quiet Exit," *Milwaukee Journal*, March 6, 1986.
98. "Brewers Are Eager for Opener," *Milwaukee Sentinel*, April 14, 1986.
99. "Play Ball! And Party!" *Milwaukee Journal*, April 14, 1986.
100. "Only the Texas Rangers Bloomed in Our April Showers," *Milwaukee Journal*, April 15, 1986.
101. "Cold, Wet Crowd Finds Ways to Take Chill Off Opening Day," *Milwaukee Sentinel*, April 15, 1986; "Opening Day Down the Drain," *Milwaukee Journal*, April 15, 1986; "Brewers Play a Washout," *Milwaukee Journal*, April 15, 1986.
102. "For Brewers, Opening Day Magic Doused," *Milwaukee Sentinel*, April 15, 1986.
103. "Brewers Flop in Home Opener," *Milwaukee Sentinel*, April 15, 1986.
104. "Opening Day Down the Drain"; "Brewers Play a Washout."
105. "Orioles Tap Cal Ripken," *Sporting News*, October 13, 1986.
106. "Who's on First? How About Yount?" *Milwaukee Journal*, December 7, 1986; "Brewers," *Sporting News*, March 2, 1987.
107. "Oglivie Japan Bound," *Sporting News*, February 9, 1987; "Moore Brewer No More," *Sporting News*, December 22,

Notes—Chapter Two

1986; "Brewers," *Sporting News*, November 3, 1986.

108. "Brewers," *Sporting News*, December 22, 1986; Jeff Barto, "1986 Winter Meetings: A Rigged Market," *SABR Research Journal*, https://sabr.org/journal/article/1986-winter-meetings-a-rigged-market-collusion-ii/.

109. "Baseball Owners Ordered to Pay Players $102 Million," *Washington Post*, September 18, 1990.

110. "Brewers," *Sporting News*, March 16, 1987.

111. "Vuckovich Finds Life in Arm, Hope in Heart," *Sporting News*, March 16, 1987.

112. "Higuera Jeopardizing Status," *Milwaukee Sentinel*, March 7, 1987; "Brewers," *Sporting News*, March 30, 1987; "Vuckovich Retires," *Milwaukee Journal*, April 2, 1987.

113. "Brewers Enter Phase II in Rebuilding Process," *Milwaukee Journal*, April 5, 1987; "Magazines Give Brewers Little Respect," *Milwaukee Journal*, April 5, 1987; "A Love Affair," *Milwaukee Journal*, April 6, 1987.

114. "Brewers Wives Calmly Soak Up Festivities of Opening Day," *Milwaukee Sentinel*, April 7, 1987.

115. "News and Notes," *Milwaukee Sentinel*, April 7, 1987; "As Openers Go, it was a Beauty," *Milwaukee Sentinel*, April 7, 1987; "Stanley, Sox Unable to Remove Winter's Chill," *Milwaukee Journal*, April 7, 1987.

116. "Brewers' Old Guard Leads Way," *Milwaukee Sentinel*, April 7, 1987; "Yount's Plans Uncertain, but Team Hopeful," *Milwaukee Journal*, November 7, 1986.

117. "Brewers Review," *Milwaukee Journal*, April 7, 1987; "As Openers Go, it was a Beauty."

118. "161 Is Brewers Magic Number," *Milwaukee Journal*, April 7, 1987.

119. "Brewers Review," *Milwaukee Journal*, April 7, 1987.

120. "Brewers Review," *Milwaukee Journal*, April 7, 1987; "Higuera in Top Form After a Forgettable Spring," *Milwaukee Sentinel*, April 7, 1987.

121. "Brewers' Old Guard Leads Way."

122. "Brewers Finally Let Cooper Go," *Milwaukee Sentinel*, January 13, 1988.

123. "Brewers," *Sporting News*, February 15, 1988; Craig Brown, "Brewers Gambling that '87 Wasn't a Mirage," *Sporting News*, March 14, 1988; Craig Brown, "Collusion and the No-Risk Free Agents of 1988," *The Hardball Times*, February 29, 2008, https://tht.fangraphs.com/collusion-and-the-no-risk-free-agents-of-1988; Ron Simon, *The Game Behind the Game: Negotiating in the Big Leagues*, Stillwater: Voyageur Press, 1993, 162.

124. "Higuera Agrees to 1 Year Contact," *Milwaukee Sentinel*, February 9, 1988.

125. Matthew J. Prigge, "The Loss of a Milwaukee Boy," *Shepherd Express*, February 29, 2016, https://shepherdexpress.com/sports/brew-crew-confidential/loss-milwaukee-boy-28-years-ago-harvey-kuenn-passed-away/.

126. "At The Gate," *Milwaukee Journal*, April 15, 1988; "Brewers Partying Lives up to Billing," *Milwaukee Sentinel*, April 16, 1988.

127. "Weather Doesn't Put a Chill on Tailgaters," *Milwaukee Sentinel*, April 16, 1988.

128. "Weather Doesn't Put a Chill on Tailgaters"; "Gantner's Injury Causes Shuffling," *Milwaukee Journal*, April 16, 1988; "Brewers Partying Lives up to Billing"; "Higuera Will Miss Home Opener," *Milwaukee Journal*, April 14, 1988.

129. "Higuera Will Miss Home Opener"; "Brewers Opening Isn't Very Grand," *Milwaukee Journal*, April 16, 1988.

130. "Brewers Opening Isn't Very Grand."

131. "Will 1988 Be the Year of the Balk in the NL?" *Sporting News*, March 21, 1988; "Balks Unkind to Fans, Game," *Milwaukee Journal*, April 16, 1988.

132. "7th Loss Ruins Brewer Home Opener," *Milwaukee Sentinel*, April 16, 1988.

133. "All This Balking is a Bore," *Milwaukee Sentinel*, April 16, 1988.

134. "Balks Unkind to Fans, Game."

135. "7th Loss Ruins Brewer Home Opener," *Milwaukee Sentinel*, April 16, 1988.

136. Ibid.

137. "Overlooked Evans Building Hall of Fame Case," *Sporting News*, January 30, 1989.

138. "Brewers," *Sporting News*, December 12, 1988.

139. "Brewers Stuck in a Money Pit," *Milwaukee Journal*, December 21, 1988; "Public Ownership is Considered," *Milwaukee Journal*, August 30, 1990; "Signals on Stadium Mixed, Schultz Says," *Milwaukee Journal*, November 30, 1988.
140. "Brewers Gets Some Good News on Bad Teddy," *Sporting News*, February 6, 1989; "Mr. Baseball Stricken," *Sporting News*, February 27, 1989.
141. "Insiders Say," *Sporting News*, March 20, 1989.
142. "Brewers," *Sporting News*, April 10, 1989; "How the Experts are Picking 'Em," *Milwaukee Journal*, April 2, 1989.
143. "Revelry Judged Winner, but Game Ends in Loss," *Milwaukee Sentinel*, April 11, 1989.
144. "Revelry Judged Winner, but Game Ends in Loss"; "Giamatti's Outlook is Sunny At Opener," *Milwaukee Sentinel*, April 11, 1989.
145. "Valentine's Maneuvers Spell Relief," *Milwaukee Sentinel*, April 11, 1989; "For Shivering Rangers, It was Mind Over Matter," *Milwaukee Sentinel*, April 11, 1989.
146. "Brewers Shell Hough, Lose Anyway," *Milwaukee Journal*, April 11, 1989.
147. Ibid.
148. Ibid.
149. "Yount Offers No Excuses," *Milwaukee Journal*, April 11, 1989.

Chapter Three

1. "Brewers Shakeup Begins," *Sporting News*, October 9, 1989.
2. "Selig's Support Boosts Site for New Stadium," *Milwaukee Journal*, February 13, 1990.
3. "Brewers," *Sporting News*, November 20, 1989; "Brewers," *Sporting News*, November 27, 1989.
4. "Parker Signs 2-Year Pact with Brewers," *Milwaukee Sentinel*, December 4, 1989.
5. "Angels," *Sporting News*, December 18, 1989; "Selig Helps Keep Yount a Brewer," *Milwaukee Sentinel*, December 20, 1989.
6. Simon, *The Game Behind the Game*, 176–177.
7. Paul Staudohar, "Baseball Labor Relations: The Lockout of 1990," *Monthly Labor Review*, October 1990, pp. 32–36.
8. "Instant Replay: Molitor on DL Again," *Sporting News*, April 16, 1990.
9. "Fans Make Opening Day One Big Party," *Milwaukee Journal*, April 11, 1990; Dave Parker, "Missing Chapters from Baseball Legend Dave Parker's Memoir," MLBBRO.com, https://mlbbro.com/2021/05/31/exclusive-missing-chapters-from-baseball-legend-dave-parkers-memoir-cobra-a-life-of-baseball-and-brotherhood-part-3/.
10. "Brewers a No-show against Sox," *Milwaukee Sentinel*, April 11, 1990.
11. "Fans Make Opening Day One Big Party," *Milwaukee Journal*, April 11, 1990; "Opening Day Bleacherites Support their Local Deputy," *Milwaukee Sentinel*, April 11, 1990.
12. "He Manages Under Stress," *Milwaukee Journal*, April 11, 1990.
13. "Chicago's Ventura Walks to a Key Role," *Milwaukee Journal*, April 11, 1990.
14. "Milwaukee Has No Alibi in 5-3 Loss," *Milwaukee Sentinel*, April 11, 1990.
15. "Milwaukee Has No Alibi in 5-3 Loss"; "Brewers a No-show against Sox," *Milwaukee Sentinel*, April 11, 1990.
16. "Happier Clubhouse is Trebelhorn's Goal," *Sporting News*, February 4, 1991; "Is that Cliquing Sound Coming from the Clubhouse?" *Milwaukee Journal*, April 7, 1991.
17. "Happier Clubhouse is Trebelhorn's Goal," *Sporting News*, February 4, 1991; "Imperfect Fit," *Milwaukee Journal*, April 7, 1991.
18. "If Higuera Returns, It's for 4 More Years," *Sporting News*, December 3, 1990.
19. "Players See Brewers Moving in Right Direction," *Milwaukee Sentinel*, December 7, 1990.
20. "New Stadium is Needed, but Not a Miracle Cure," *Milwaukee Journal*, December 30, 1990.
21. "Old Stadium May Go, But Debt Will Linger until 2006," *Milwaukee Journal*, November 18, 1990; "Danger Signals in Stadium Flap," *Milwaukee Sentinel*, November 9, 1990; "Who Will Pay for What at Stadium?" *Milwaukee Journal*, December 2, 1990.
22. "Hopes for Higuera Affect Move to DL," *Milwaukee Journal*, March 31, 1991.
23. "Brewers Out to Bounce Back from Surprises," *Milwaukee Sentinel*, March

16, 1991; "Milwaukee Brewers," *Sporting News*, April 1, 1991.
24. "Sheffield and Club Attempting to put a Lid on it," *Milwaukee Journal*, April 6, 1991.
25. "Bosio Sees Better Days Ahead," *Milwaukee Sentinel*, April 16, 1991.
26. "Here's a Survival Kit for the Home Opener," *Milwaukee Journal*, April 14, 1991.
27. Ibid.
28. "Surhoff Finally Ends his 0-18 Slump," *Milwaukee Journal*, April 16, 1991.
29. "Homers Grand for Baltimore," *Milwaukee Journal*, April 16, 1991.
30. "Homers Grand for Baltimore"; "Brewers Facing a Hard Sell," *Milwaukee Sentinel*, April 16, 1991.
31. "Surhoff Finally Ends his 0-18 Slump," *Milwaukee Journal*, April 16, 1991.
32. "Brewers: Dalton Out, Bando In," *Milwaukee Sentinel*, October 9, 1991.
33. "Torborg May Have Left With Less Than White Sox's Blessing," *Sporting News*, October 21, 1991.
34. Michael Clair, "Scouting Ballplayers in 1980s Playgirl," Baseball Prospectus, May 21, 2013, https://www.baseballprospectus.com/news/article/20639/baseball-proguestus-dollar-sign-on-the-glistening-muscle-scouting-ballplayers-in-1980s-playgirl/; "Brewers Name Astros' Garner Next Manager," *Milwaukee Journal*, October 30, 1991.
35. "Shea-Zam," *Sporting News*, December 16, 1991.
36. "Stadium Aid Advances but Foes Promise Fight," *Milwaukee Journal*, October 18, 1991; "Minus a New Stadium, Baseball Dies Here: Selig," *Milwaukee Journal*, November 3, 1991.
37. "Has Sheffield Taken it Too Far?" *Milwaukee Journal*, March 13, 1992; "Sheffield Still Miffed at Organization," *Milwaukee Sentinel*, March 13, 1992.
38. "Logic Paints this Trade as a Good One," *Milwaukee Journal*, March 29, 1992.
39. "Marketing Steps to the Plate," *Milwaukee Sentinel*, February 18, 1992.
40. "Stubbs Wins Back Fans with Impressive Start," *Milwaukee Sentinel*, April 7, 1992.
41. "Quayle Pitches for Brewers, Bush," *Milwaukee Sentinel*, April 7, 1992; "Closer to Home," *Milwaukee Journal*, April 7, 1992.
42. "Closer to Home"; "Little Guys Come off Looking Very Big," *Milwaukee Sentinel*, April 7, 1992.
43. Paul Hoffman, "Kevin Seitzer," SABR Biography Project, https://sabr.org/bioproj/person/kevin-seitzer/.
44. "Garner Picks Him, then he's Picked On," *Milwaukee Journal*, April 7, 1992.
45. "Stubbs Wins Back Fans with Impressive Start," *Milwaukee Sentinel*, April 7, 1992.
46. Ibid.
47. Ibid.
48. "Milwaukee Brewers," *Sporting News*, November 23, 1992.
49. Matthew J. Prigge, "The Messy Divorce of the Brewers and Paul Molitor," *Shepherd Express*, November 3, 2016, https://shepherdexpress.com/sports/brew-crew-confidential/messy-divorce-brewers-paul-molitor/.
50. "Stadium Options Discussed Committee," *Milwaukee Sentinel*, June 30, 1992; "Brewers' Ballpark: Echoes of Ebbets," *Milwaukee Journal*, July 12, 1992; "Skybox Leases Moving Quickly," *Milwaukee Journal*, October 2, 1992.
51. "The Messy Divorce of the Brewers and Paul Molitor."
52. "Money plays Role in Yount's Return," *Milwaukee Sentinel*, March 31, 1993.
53. "Brewer Budget Already at Limit," *Milwaukee Sentinel*, February 8, 1993; "Milwaukee Brewers," *Sporting News*, March 22, 1993; "Milwaukee Brewers," *Sporting News*, April 12, 1993.
54. "Milwaukee Brewers," *Sporting News*, November 29, 1993.
55. "Milwaukee Marks 20 Years Since Cryptosporidium Outbreak," *Milwaukee Journal Sentinel*, April 6, 2013.
56. "Devoted Brewers Fans Overcome Obstacles to Attend Home Opener," *Milwaukee Journal*, April 12, 1993.
57. "The Lone Opener," *Milwaukee Journal*, April 13, 1993.
58. "Drinking in a Queasy Performance," *Milwaukee Journal*, April 13, 1993.
59. "Tonsillitis Keeps Jaha on Bench," *Milwaukee Sentinel*, April 13, 1993.
60. "Pitching Performance a Nightmare," *Milwaukee Sentinel*, April 13, 1993.
61. "Brewers Stick to Stadium Plan,

Plan to stay here," *Milwaukee Journal*, May 13, 1993; "Brewers Must Vent Methane," *Milwaukee Journal*, June 17, 1993; "Norquist Says Brewers Need More Help to Build Stadium," *Milwaukee Journal*, August 13, 1993.

62. "Milwaukee Brewers," *Sporting News*, November 15, 1993.

63. "An Awful Offseason," *Sporting News*, December 6, 1993.

64. "Milwaukee Brewers," *Sporting News*, December 20, 1993.

65. "Brewers Plan Old-Time Look to Bring in Big-Time Money," *Milwaukee Journal*, November 1993.

66. Matthew J. Prigge, "Ugly Times: The Much-Maligned Brewers Make-Over of 1994," *Shepherd Express*, March 13, 2017, https://shepherdexpress.com/sports/-brew-crew-confidential/ugly-times-much-maligned-brewers-make-over-1994/.

67. "Yount Caps Stellar Career," *Milwaukee Journal*, February 11, 1994.

68. "Opening Day," *Milwaukee Journal*, April 4, 1994; "Box Lunch," *Milwaukee Journal*, April 3, 1994.

69. "Party On," *Milwaukee Journal*, April 5, 1994; "Most of the Action was Off of the Field," *Milwaukee Journal*, April 6, 1994.

70. "Brewers are Kings of the Road," *Milwaukee Journal*, April 5, 1994; "Vaughn Make Strong Statement with Fashion," *Milwaukee Journal*, April 6, 1994.

71. "Key Play is Twice as Nice," *Milwaukee Journal*, April 6, 1994.

72. "Brewers get A's for Persistence," *Milwaukee Sentinel*, April 6, 1994.

73. Ibid.

74. "Key Play is Twice as Nice," *Milwaukee Journal*, April 6, 1994.

75. "Brewers get A's for Persistence."

76. Ibid.

77. "Changes in Economy Affect Stadium Plans," *Milwaukee Journal*, April 19, 1994; "Pack Won't be Back," *Milwaukee Sentinel*, October 13, 1994; "Sports Lottery Goes to Ballot for April Vote," *Milwaukee Journal*, February 16, 1995.

78. "Baseball Owners Impose Salary Cap," *Milwaukee Sentinel*, December 23, 1994.

79. "Coaches Feeling Heat to Honor Strike," *Milwaukee Sentinel*, January 16, 1995.

80. Matthew J. Prigge, "Brewers to Hold Replacement Tryouts," *Milwaukee Sentinel*, January 19, 1995; "Ladies and Gentlemen, Your 1995 Replacement Brewers (almost)," *Shepherd Express*, April 6, 2015, https://shepherdexpress.com/culture/milwaukee-history/ladies-gentlemen-1995-replacement-milwaukee-brewers-almost/.

81. "Thompson Vows Stadium Plan," *Milwaukee Journal Sentinel*, April 12, 1995.

82. "Looking for Bright Spots," *Milwaukee Journal Sentinel*, April 26, 1995.

83. "Major League," *Milwaukee Journal Sentinel*, April 25, 1995; "Brewers Opening Day by the Numbers," *Milwaukee Journal Sentinel*, April 27, 1995.

84. "Opening Onslaught is a Good Start," *Milwaukee Journal Sentinel*, April 27, 1995; "Opening Day Fans Expect Brewers to Win Them Back," *Milwaukee Journal Sentinel*, April 27, 1995.

85. "Premiere is a Smash," *Milwaukee Journal Sentinel*, April 27, 1995.

86. "Devereaux Would Rather Forget About Opening Day," *Milwaukee Journal Sentinel*, April 27, 1995.

87. Ibid.

88. "Brewers Opening Day by the Numbers," *Milwaukee Journal Sentinel*, April 27, 1995.

89. "Opening Onslaught is a Good Start," *Milwaukee Journal Sentinel*, April 27, 1995.

90. "Stadium Supporters Keep Their Hopes Alive," *Milwaukee Journal Sentinel*, October 6, 1995; Senate's Wild Night Yields 'Yes' Vote," *Milwaukee Journal Sentinel*, October 7, 1995.

91. "Around the Bases," *Sporting News*, October 30, 1995.

92. "Milwaukee Brewers," *Sporting News*, December 18, 1995; "Milwaukee Brewers," *Sporting News*, January 6, 1996.

93. Matthew J. Prigge, "Paul Molitor Goes Home," *Shepherd Express*, December 12, 2016, https://shepherdexpress.com/sports/brew-crew-confidential/paul-molitor-goes-home-brewers-miss-ignitor-part-ii/.

94. "Paul Molitor Goes Home."

95. "Hamilton Rips Brewers' Tactics," *Milwaukee Journal Sentinel*, March 12, 1996.

96. "Brewers Finally Reel in McDonald," *Milwaukee Journal Sentinel*, January 21, 1996.

97. "McDonald Farms Out Gators," *South Florida Sun-Sentinel*, March 27, 1990; "McDonald Settles into Quieter Life," *Milwaukee Journal Sentinel*, April 9, 1996.
98. "Garner Isn't About to Give up Hope," *Milwaukee Journal Sentinel*, March 31, 1996; "Brewers Tickets Get Dusty," *Milwaukee Journal Sentinel*, March 28, 1996; "Trouble Snowballs for Team," *Milwaukee Journal Sentinel*, April 9, 1996; "Stadium Tax to Continue," *Milwaukee Journal Sentinel*, April 16, 1996.
99. "Cheers, Fears at Opener," *Milwaukee Journal Sentinel*, April 10, 1996.
100. "Brewers Report," *Milwaukee Journal Sentinel*, April 10, 1996; "The Game Lifts Selig's Spirits," *Milwaukee Journal Sentinel*, April 10, 1996.
101. "Cheers, Fears at Opener," *Milwaukee Journal Sentinel*, April 10, 1996.
102. "Cheers, Fears at Opener"; "SportsDay," *Milwaukee Journal Sentinel*, April 10, 1996.
103. "Brewers Report," *Milwaukee Journal Sentinel*, April 10, 1996.
104. "The Game Lifts Selig's Spirits," *Milwaukee Journal Sentinel*, April 10, 1996.
105. "Milwaukee Brewers," *Sporting News*, December 30, 1996.
106. "CBA History," Cot's Contracts, https://legacy.baseballprospectus.com/compensation/cots/league-info/cba-history/; "From Confrontation to Cooperation," *Sporting News*, November 4, 1996.
107. "Home Opener No longer Sells Out," *Milwaukee Journal Sentinel*, April 7, 1997; "Play Ball," *Milwaukee Journal Sentinel*, April 7, 1997.
108. "Tosa Man Killed Trying to Move Wire," *Milwaukee Journal Sentinel*, April 7, 1997; "Worst Opening Day," *Milwaukee Journal Sentinel*, April 8, 1997.
109. "Worst Opening Day."
110. "Eldred, Relievers Save Day," *Milwaukee Journal Sentinel*, April 8, 1997.
111. "Worst Opening Day"; "Eldred Just Rolling with the Punches," *Milwaukee Journal Sentinel*, April 8, 1997.
112. "Fans Nearly Force Forfeit of Game," *Milwaukee Journal Sentinel*, April 8, 1997; "Eldred Just Rolling with the Punches."
113. "Worst Opening Day."
114. "Worst Opening Day"; "Eldred Just Rolling with the Punches."
115. "Worst Opening Day."
116. "Worst Opening Day"; "Eldred Just Rolling with the Punches."
117. "Fans Nearly Force Forfeit of Game"; "Worst Opening Day."
118. "Worst Opening Day," *Milwaukee Journal Sentinel*, April 8, 1997.
119. "A New League on Life," *Milwaukee Journal Sentinel*, November 7, 1997.
120. Matthew J. Prigge, "When the Brewers Made a Play for Kenny Lofton," *Shepherd Express*, December 5, 2016, https://shepherdexpress.com/sports/brewcrew-confidential/brewers-made-play-kenny-lofton/.
121. "Brewers," *Sporting News*, December 29, 1997.
122. "Brewers," *Sporting News*, February 9, 1998.
123. "Brewers Expect Miller Time to Bring a Flow of Revenue," *Sporting News*, February 2, 1998; "Brewers," *Sporting News*, February 9, 1998.
124. "Brewers Back to National League Future," *Milwaukee Journal Sentinel*, April 8, 1998; "Brewers Fans Forgive, Forget, and Party," *Milwaukee Journal Sentinel*, April 8, 1998; "Fans can Take Look at Stadium of Future," *Milwaukee Journal Sentinel*, April 7, 1998.
125. "For Aaron, Many Happy Returns," *Milwaukee Journal Sentinel*, April 7, 1998; "Brewers Report," *Milwaukee Journal Sentinel*, April 8, 1998.
126. "Pounding the Point Across," *Milwaukee Journal Sentinel*, April 8, 1998.
127. "Leading off With Patience," *Milwaukee Journal Sentinel*, April 8, 1998.
128. "Reliever Fox Takes a Walk on the Wild side," *Milwaukee Journal Sentinel*, April 8, 1998.
129. "Brewers Back to National League Future."
130. "Selig Takes Reins," *Milwaukee Journal Sentinel*, July 10, 1998.
131. "Selig-Prieb Ready to Run the Show," *Milwaukee Journal Sentinel*, July 9, 1998.
132. "Pitcher Abbott Agrees to One-Year Deal With Brewers," *Milwaukee Journal Sentinel*, January 28, 1999.
133. "Brewers Keep Vina—For Now," *Milwaukee Journal Sentinel*, April 5, 1999.
134. "Atlanta," *Sporting News*, November 16, 1998; "St. Louis," *Sporting News*, December 21, 1998.

135. "Milwaukee," *Sporting News*, February 22, 1999; "Molitor Stays With Twins," *Milwaukee Journal Sentinel*, February 12, 1999.
136. "Numbers Game," *Sporting News*, April 1, 1996.
137. "Milwaukee," *Sporting News*, February 22, 1999; "Stadium Work Said to Be Back On Track," *Milwaukee Journal Sentinel*, February 13, 1999.
138. "Brewers Hit 10,000 Mark in Season Ticket Sales," *Milwaukee Journal Sentinel*, April 2, 1999; "Ballpark Gave Selig the Thrills of a Lifetime," *Milwaukee Journal Sentinel*, April 16, 1999.
139. "Brewers Keep Vina—For Now"; "County Stadium Stands Tall in its Final Opener," *Milwaukee Journal Sentinel*, April 17, 1999.
140. "Feeling Cover all the Bases," *Milwaukee Journal Sentinel*, April 16, 1999.
141. "Brewers Expect Third-Largest Crowd Ever Today at County Stadium," *Milwaukee Journal Sentinel*, April 16, 1999; "Brewers Report," *Milwaukee Journal Sentinel*, April 17, 1999.
142. "Cubs Hitters Have a Feast," *Milwaukee Journal Sentinel*, April 17, 1999.
143. "Triple Play Doesn't Turn Tide," *Milwaukee Journal Sentinel*, April 17, 1999.
144. Ibid.
145. "Cubs Hitters Have a Feast," *Milwaukee Journal Sentinel*, April 17, 1999.
146. "Fans' Behavior Commendable," *Milwaukee Journal Sentinel*, April 17, 1999.

Chapter Four

1. "Selig-Prieb Pulls the Trigger," *Milwaukee Journal Sentinel*, August 13, 1999.
2. "The Dean Taylor Era Begins," *Milwaukee Journal Sentinel*, September 22, 1999.
3. "Lopes is Facing a Huge Challenge with Brewers," *Milwaukee Journal Sentinel*, November 5, 1999.
4. "A Rebuilding Blockbuster," *Milwaukee Journal Sentinel*, December 14, 1999.
5. "Acevedo's Place Isn't Quite Clear," *Milwaukee Journal Sentinel*, December 20, 1999.
6. "Change is in the Script," *Milwaukee Journal Sentinel*, November 10, 1999.
7. "Miller Park Project gets a Lift," *Milwaukee Journal Sentinel*, January 22, 2000.
8. "Brewers Put Down New Roots," *Milwaukee Journal Sentinel*, April 2, 2000.
9. "Brewers See Home Opener as Part of New Era," *Milwaukee Journal Sentinel*, April 10, 2000; "What's Baseball Without a Few Snowflakes in the Outfield," *Milwaukee Journal Sentinel*, April 10, 2000.
10. "Brewers See Home Opener as Part of New Era"; "Fans Bundle Up for Ice Cold Beer, Ice Cold Baseball," *Milwaukee Journal Sentinel*, April 11, 2000; "SportsDay," *Milwaukee Journal Sentinel*, April 11, 2000.
11. "What's Baseball Without a Few Snowflakes in the Outfield"; "SportsDay," *Milwaukee Journal Sentinel*, April 11, 2000; "Inside Pitch," *Milwaukee Journal Sentinel*, April 11, 2000.
12. "Haynes Pitches Positive Attitude," *Milwaukee Journal Sentinel*, April 11, 2000.
13. "Fans Bundle Up for Ice Cold Beer, Ice Cold Baseball," *Milwaukee Journal Sentinel*, April 11, 2000; "Another Chilly Reception," *Milwaukee Journal Sentinel*, April 11, 2000.
14. "Lopes is Exorcizing the Ghosts of Losing Past," *Milwaukee Journal Sentinel*, April 11, 2000.
15. "Rich Brew," *Milwaukee Journal Sentinel*, December 23, 2000.
16. "Milwaukee," *Sporting News*, December 11, 2000.
17. "Bleach Boys," *Sports Illustrated*, April 2, 2001.
18. "Brewers Fly Home on Wings of Confidence," *Milwaukee Journal Sentinel*, March 29, 2001; "Scary Prospect," *Sporting News*, March 5, 2001.
19. "Quick Hits from Opener," *Milwaukee Journal Sentinel*, April 7, 2001.
20. "A Grand Opening," *Milwaukee Journal Sentinel*, April 7, 2001; "A First Time for Everything," *Milwaukee Journal Sentinel*, April 7, 2001; "Wows Galore from a Star-Studded Gallery," *Milwaukee Journal Sentinel*, April 7, 2001.
21. "A First Time for Everything."
22. "Hernandez Unloads Bases, Offense," *Milwaukee Journal Sentinel*, April 7, 2001.
23. "Closed for Business," *Milwaukee Journal Sentinel*, April 7, 2001.
24. "A First Time for Everything."
25. "Homers Don't Offset the Injuries—or strikeouts," *Sporting News*, October 15, 2001.

26. "Burnitz Apple of Mets' Eye," *Milwaukee Journal Sentinel*, January 22, 2002; "Burnitz Glad the Waiting is Over," *Milwaukee Journal Sentinel*, January 22, 2002.
27. "Is it Next Year Yet?" *Milwaukee Journal Sentinel*, April 5, 2002.
28. Ibid.
29. "Hot Spring by Sanchez Turns Heads," *Milwaukee Journal Sentinel*, March 29, 2002; "Hope Floats," *Milwaukee Journal Sentinel*, April 5, 2002.
30. "Sales of Season Tickets Plunge," *Milwaukee Journal Sentinel*, April 5, 2002.
31. "Victory Helps Thaw a Big Chill," *Milwaukee Journal Sentinel*, April 6, 2002.
32. "Robin Returns to Old Nest," *Milwaukee Journal Sentinel*, April 6, 2002.
33. "Sore Elbow Sidelines King," *Milwaukee Journal Sentinel*, April 6, 2002; "Victory Helps Thaw a Big Chill," *Milwaukee Journal Sentinel*, April 6, 2002.
34. "Rusch Hour," *Milwaukee Journal Sentinel*, April 6, 2002.
35. Ibid.
36. Ibid.
37. "Selig-Prieb Makes Right Move by Taking One for the Team," *Milwaukee Journal Sentinel*, September 26, 2002; "Brewers Fans Can Start Dreaming Again," *Milwaukee Journal Sentinel*, September 26, 2002.
38. "Brewers Take Positive Steps," *Sporting News*, October 7, 2002.
39. "Proving Ground," *Milwaukee Journal Sentinel*, October 30, 2002.
40. "Kieschnick Takes a Two-Way Road," *Sporting News*, March 3, 2003.
41. "First 25,000 get in Free," *Milwaukee Journal Sentinel*, February 28, 2003.
42. "Spring Bad, But Over," *Milwaukee Journal Sentinel*, March 30, 2003; "Milwaukee Brewers," *Sporting News*, March 31, 2003.
43. "Spring Bad, But Over"; "A Full Plate," *Milwaukee Journal Sentinel*, March 30, 2003.
44. "More Than A Game at the Old Ballpark," *Milwaukee Journal Sentinel*, March 30, 2003; "Peanuts, Cracker Jack, and Much Much More," *Milwaukee Journal Sentinel*, April 5, 2003; "Brewers Level With Fans," *Milwaukee Journal Sentinel*, January 31, 2003.
45. "Hard Work, Not Gimmicks the Key," *Milwaukee Journal Sentinel*, April 5, 2003; "Conference Call Helps Avoid Foul-Up," *Milwaukee Journal Sentinel*, April 5, 2003.
46. "Hard Work, Not Gimmicks the Key."
47. "Peanuts, Cracker Jack, and Much Much More."
48. "Looking Good Until the Last Drop," *Milwaukee Journal Sentinel*, April 5, 2003.
49. Ibid.
50. Ibid.
51. "Cuts May Imperil Brewers on Field," *Milwaukee Journal Sentinel*, November 9, 2003; "Cuts Give Brewers a Murky Future," *Milwaukee Journal Sentinel*, November 11, 2003; "End Runs, Hits, and Errors," *Milwaukee Journal Sentinel*, November 16, 2003.
52. "Legislators Wants to Audit Brewers," *Milwaukee Journal Sentinel*, November 13, 2003.
53. "Let's Find Someone to Rescue the Brewers," *Milwaukee Journal Sentinel*, November 12, 2003.
54. "Home Improvement," *Milwaukee Journal Sentinel*, December 2, 2003.
55. "Brewers Put Team Up for Sale," *Milwaukee Journal Sentinel*, January 17, 2004.
56. "Brewers Put Team Up for Sale"; "Locals Not Swinging at Brewers Pitch," *Milwaukee Journal Sentinel*, March 24, 2004.
57. "Devout Fans," *Milwaukee Journal Sentinel*, April 9, 2004.
58. "Ballclub's makeup Excites Jenkins," *Milwaukee Journal Sentinel*, April 10, 2004.
59. "Ballclub's makeup Excites Jenkins"; "Making a Pitch," *Milwaukee Journal Sentinel*, April 10, 2004.
60. "Miller Allows Four Hits, Two Runs in Win," ESPN, April 9, 2004, https://www.espn.com/mlb/recap/_/gameId/240409108.
61. "Brewers Accept Money From LA Investor," *Milwaukee Journal Sentinel*, September 28, 2004.
62. "Brewers Accept Money From LA Investor"; "A 26 Year Guarantee," *Milwaukee Journal Sentinel*, September 30, 2004.
63. "Attanasio Wants Brewers to be a Winning Team Here," *Milwaukee Journal Sentinel*, October 5, 2004.

64. "Brewers Trade for White Sox Slugger," *Milwaukee Journal Sentinel*, December 14, 2004.
65. "Attanasio the Fan Show up for Spring Opener," *Milwaukee Journal Sentinel*, March 5, 2005.
66. "Off to the Right Start," *Milwaukee Journal Sentinel*, March 28, 2005.
67. "Brewers Set One-Day Mark," *Milwaukee Journal Sentinel*, February 27, 2005; "New-Look Offense Ready to Hit Town," *Milwaukee Journal Sentinel*, April 11, 2005.
68. "Inside Pitch," *Milwaukee Journal Sentinel*, April 12, 2005.
69. "Feeling Right at Home," *Milwaukee Journal Sentinel*, April 12, 2005.
70. "Davis Steels Nerves to Pick Up Victory," *Milwaukee Journal Sentinel*, April 12, 2005.
71. "Home Opener," *Milwaukee Journal Sentinel*, April 12, 2005.
72. "Home Opener"; "In My Opinion," *Milwaukee Journal Sentinel*, April 12, 2005; "Wells Mind Goes Soft," *Milwaukee Journal Sentinel*, April 12, 2005.
73. "Davis Steels Nerves to Pick Up Victory," *Milwaukee Journal Sentinel*, April 12, 2005.
74. "In My Opinion," *Milwaukee Journal Sentinel*, April 12, 2005.
75. "Feeling Right at Home," *Milwaukee Journal Sentinel*, April 12, 2005.
76. "Owner Isn't Skipping a Step," *Milwaukee Journal Sentinel*, April 12, 2005.
77. "Melvin, Brewers Seal the Deal," *Milwaukee Journal Sentinel*, November 6, 2005; "Brewers Bring Back Big Wheel in Yount," *Milwaukee Journal Sentinel*, November 4, 2005.
78. "Old is New Again," *Milwaukee Journal Sentinel*, December 2, 2005; "Attanasio Sets Sights on Brewers' Future," *Milwaukee Journal Sentinel*, November 18, 2005.
79. "Brewers Solidify Third Base," *Milwaukee Journal Sentinel*, January 7, 2006.
80. "For Brewers, It's Game Reset," *Milwaukee Journal Sentinel*, January 13, 2006; "A Whole New Ballgame," *Milwaukee Journal Sentinel*, February 26, 2006; "Camp Report," *Milwaukee Journal Sentinel*, February 26, 2006.
81. "Milwaukee Brewers," *Sports Illustrated*, April 3, 2006.
82. Jeff Sackmann, "Great Ben Sheets News," Brew Crew Ball, April 1, 2006, https://www.brewcrewball.com/2006/4/1/15659/93894.
83. "How's This for a Start?" *Milwaukee Journal Sentinel*, April 4, 2006; "Brewers Notes," *Milwaukee Journal Sentinel*, April 3, 2006.
84. "Brewers Send Fans Home Happy," *Milwaukee Journal Sentinel*, April 4, 2006; "Brewers Notes," *Milwaukee Journal Sentinel*, April 4, 2006.
85. "How's This for a Start?"
86. "Opening Gambit," *Milwaukee Journal Sentinel*, April 4, 2006.
87. "Tracey Hopes Pirates Can Step Up With Brewers," *Milwaukee Journal Sentinel*, April 4, 2006.
88. "It's Official, Turnbow is a Rockstar," *Milwaukee Journal Sentinel*, April 4, 2006.
89. Ibid.
90. "Brewers on a Budget Plan," *Milwaukee Journal Sentinel*, November 26, 2006.
91. "Third Base," *Milwaukee Journal Sentinel*, February 23, 2007.
92. "All Talk and No Action," *Milwaukee Journal Sentinel*, December 8, 2006.
93. "Suppan, Brewers Agree to Four-Year Contract," *Milwaukee Journal Sentinel*, December 25, 2006; Tim Dierkes, "2007 Top 50 Baseball Free Agents," MLB Trade Rumors, https://www.mlbtraderumors.com/2006/11/2007-top-50-bas.html, November 2, 2006.
94. "Suppan, Brewers Agree to Four-Year Contract," *Milwaukee Journal Sentinel*, December 25, 2006; Jeff Sackmann, "What We Can Look for from Suppan," Brew Crew Ball, December 29, 2006, https://www.brewcrewball.com/2006/12/29/182534/30.
95. "Brewers Notes," *Milwaukee Journal Sentinel*, February 20, 2007.
96. "Brewers Notes," *Milwaukee Journal Sentinel*, February 25, 2007; "Sheets Music," *Milwaukee Journal Sentinel*, April 3, 2007.
97. "Sheets Music."
98. "Back with a Bang," *Milwaukee Journal Sentinel*, April 3, 2007; "Lowe Lacks Luster," *Milwaukee Journal Sentinel*, April 3, 2007.
99. "Sheets Music."
100. Jeff Sackmann, "Yes!!!!!!" Brew Crew Ball, February 5, 2007, https://www.

brewcrewball.com/2007/2/5/163911/1412; "Sheets Music."
101. "Sheets Music."
102. "Schilling Interest Flattering," *Milwaukee Journal Sentinel*, November 2, 2007.
103. "Brewers Strike Deal with Kendall," *Milwaukee Journal Sentinel*, November 22, 2007.
104. "Cordero Signs With Reds," *Milwaukee Journal Sentinel*, November 24, 2007.
105. "Dollars and Change," *Milwaukee Journal Sentinel*, January 12, 2008.
106. "Brewers Notes," *Milwaukee Journal Sentinel*, February 19, 2008.
107. "First Base," *Milwaukee Journal Sentinel*, February 21, 2008.
108. "Is this the Year?" *Milwaukee Journal Sentinel*, February 17, 2008; Roguejim, "Long Term Offers out to Braun, Fielder," Brew Crew Ball, March 30, 2008, https://www.brewcrewball.com/2008/3/29/185615/455; "Division Lines are Drawn," *Milwaukee Journal Sentinel*, April 4, 2008.
109. "Brewers Crack Down on All-Day Parking Lot Parties," *Milwaukee Journal Sentinel*, April 5, 2008.
110. Ibid.
111. "Brewers Notes," *Milwaukee Journal Sentinel*, April 4, 2008.
112. "Milwaukee Romps in Home Opener," *Milwaukee Journal Sentinel*, April 5, 2008.
113. "Here's Lookin' at You, Kid," *Milwaukee Journal Sentinel*, April 5, 2008.
114. "Pitching In," *Milwaukee Journal Sentinel*, April 5, 2008.
115. Ibid.
116. "Sveum Strikes Out," *Milwaukee Journal Sentinel*, October 18, 2008.
117. "Brewers Hire Ken Macha," *Milwaukee Journal Sentinel*, October 31, 2008.
118. "Pitchers Don't Accept Offers," *Milwaukee Journal Sentinel*, December 8, 2008; Cwyers, "Brewers Frontrunner for Sabathia," Brew Crew Ball, December 9, 2008, https://www.brewcrewball.com/2008/12/9/687856/brewers-frontrunner-for-sa; "Compensation Deterioration," *Milwaukee Journal Sentinel*, December 25, 2008.
119. Kyle Lobner, "Cameron Trade Hits Snag," Brew Crew Ball, December 11, 2008, https://www.brewcrewball.com/2008/12/11/689611/cameron-trade-hits-snag.
120. Kyle Lobner, "On Waiting Until the Last Minute," Brew Crew Ball, April 6, 2009, https://www.brewcrewball.com/2009/4/6/824831/on-waiting-until-the-last-minute; "Cold, Windy Camps, Hot Tickets," *Milwaukee Journal Sentinel*, March 1, 2009; "Attanasio Happy for Brewer Baseball," JS Online Brewers Blog, April 10, 2009.
121. "Brewers Rally in 9th to Clip Cubs," JS Online Brewers Blog, April 10, 2009; "Brewers have Trouble Getting to Miller Park," JS Online Brewers Blog, April 10, 2009.
122. "Religious Brewers Fans Face Sacrifice Situation," *Milwaukee Journal Sentinel*, April 10, 2009; "Game Updates," *Milwaukee Journal Sentinel* Brewers blog, April 10, 2009.
123. "Game Updates."
124. Ibid.
125. Ibid.
126. Ibid.
127. "The Player Fans Love to Hate," JS Online Brewers Blog, April 10, 2009.
128. "The Long Way Home," *Milwaukee Journal Sentinel*, April 11, 2009.

Chapter Five

1. "Macha: Gallardo and Parra the only "locks" for the rotation," Brew Crew Ball, December 8, 2009, https://www.brewcrewball.com/2009/12/8/1192461/-macha-gallardo-parra-the-only.
2. "Creating Arm Room," *Milwaukee Journal Sentinel*, November 7, 2009.
3. Jon Heyman, "Brewers May Be Young, but They're Ditching the Youthful Exuberance," si.com, https://www.si.com/more-sports/2010/03/10/youthful-brewers, March 10, 2010.
4. Ibid.
5. Ibid.
6. "Gallardo Proud of His Heritage," *Milwaukee Journal Sentinel*, April 5, 2010.
7. "Come Down From Your Ledges, Brewers Fans," *Milwaukee Journal Sentinel* Web Edition, April 5, 2010.
8. "Brewers Fall to Colorado on Opening Day," *Milwaukee Journal Sentinel* Web Edition, April 5, 2010; "Brewers vs.

Rockies, Game 1," JS Online Brewers Blog, April 5, 2010.

9. "Brewers vs. Rockies, Game 10."

10. Ibid.

11. "Brewers vs. Rockies, Game 1"; "Come Down From Your Ledges, Brewers Fans."

12. "An Out of Synch Day," JS Online Brewers Blog, April 5, 2010.

13. "Macha Struggled to Forge Bonds," *Milwaukee Journal Sentinel*, October 5, 2010.

14. Ibid.

15. "Meeting the Demands," *Milwaukee Journal Sentinel*, November 3, 2010.

16. Jordan Mader, "The Brett Lawrie for Shaun Marcum Trade," Brew Crew Ball, December 6, 2010, https://www.brewcrewball.com/2010/12/6/1859068/-the-brett-lawrie-for-shaun-marcum-trade.

17. "Greinke Highly Regarded," *Milwaukee Journal Sentinel*, December 20, 2010; "Quotes from Zack Greinke's Introductory Press Conference," Brew Crew Ball, December 20, 2010, https://www.brewcrewball.com/2010/12/20/1887917/-quotes-from-zack-greinkes-introductory-press-conference.

18. "Brewers Pay High Price to Nab Pitcher Greinke," *Milwaukee Journal Sentinel*, December 20, 2010; "Greinke Man of Few Words, But Speaks His Mind," *Milwaukee Journal Sentinel*, February 22, 2011.

19. "Greinke Heads to Disabled List," *Milwaukee Journal Sentinel*, March 9, 2011.

20. "Gomez Still the Guy, Melvin Says," *Milwaukee Journal Sentinel*, March 28, 2011.

21. Lee Jenkins, "Strange Brew (But It's Working)," *Sports Illustrated*, August 29, 2011.

22. "Brewers New Scoreboard Clearly a Hit With Fans," *Milwaukee Journal Sentinel* Web Edition, April 2, 2011; "Game Blog: Braves 2, Brewers 1," JS Online Brewers Blog, April 4, 2011.

23. "Brewers Insist They're Not Frustrated," JS Online Brewers Blog, April 4, 2011.

24. Mark Polishuk, "Brewers Could Offer Fielder Six Years, $120MM," MLB Trade Rumors, https://www.mlbtraderumors.com/2011/12/brewers-could-offer-fielder-six-years-120mm.html, December 1, 2011.

25. "Braun Drug Test Positive," *Milwaukee Journal Sentinel*, December 11, 2011.

26. "Melvin: Corey Hart will be Asked to Play Some First Base," Brew Crew Ball, January 16, 2012, https://www.brewcrewball.com/2012/1/16/2712228/-melvin-corey-hart-will-be-asked-to-play-some-first-base.

27. Kyle Lobner, "Ryan Braun and the Five Stages of Grief: Anger," Brew Crew Ball, December 13, 2011, https://www.brewcrewball.com/2011/12/13/2633106/-ryan-braun-and-the-five-stages-of-grief-anger; "Medication to Blame for Dirty Banned Substances Test," TMZ, December 19, 2011, https://www.tmz.com/2011/12/19/ryan-braun-medication-baseball-steroids/#.Tu8491b4KXI; "Brewers' Ryan Braun, NL MVP, Pleads Case," *Daily News*, January 20, 2012, https://www.nydailynews.com/sports/baseball/national-league-mvp-ryan-braun-milwaukee-brewers-pleads-case-special-panel-avoid-50-game-suspension-failing-drug-test-elevated-testosterone-level-article-1.1008968.

28. "Braun's Entire Speech," JS Online Brewers Blog, January 21, 2012.

29. "Braun Cleared," *Milwaukee Journal Sentinel*, February 24, 2012.

30. "News Buoys the Brewers," *Milwaukee Journal Sentinel*, February 25, 2012.

31. "Braun Comes out Swinging," *Milwaukee Journal Sentinel*, February 26, 2012.

32. "Game Blog: Cardinals at Brewers, Opening Day Edition," JS Online Brewers Blog, April 6, 2012.

33. "Win or Lose, It's a Party," *Milwaukee Journal Sentinel*, April 7, 2012.

34. "Greeted with Initial Cheers," *Milwaukee Journal Sentinel*, April 7, 2012.

35. "Various Factors Lead Brewers to Tighten Team Salary," *Milwaukee Journal Sentinel*, January 21, 2013.

36. "Ryan Braun Attributes PED link to Research for 2011 Drug Appeal," *Milwaukee Journal Sentinel* Web Edition, February 5, 2013.

37. Ibid.

38. "Reactions to Ryan Braun's Second PED Chapter Range from Agnostic to Skeptic," JS Online Brewers Blog, February

6, 2013; Kyle Lobner, "Ryan Braun Biogenesis Link," Brew Crew Ball, February 6, 2013, https://www.brewcrewball.com/2013/2/6/3959036/ny-daily-news-ryan-braun-biogenesis; NPetrashek, "The Braun Advantage," Brew Crew Ball, February 8, 2013, https://www.brewcrewball.com/2013/2/8/3965868/the-braun-advantage.

39. "Mat Gamel Injury," Brew Crew Ball, February 18, 2013, https://www.brewcrewball.com/2013/2/18/4001672/-mat-gamel-injury-significant-right-knee-injury-will-keep-him-out-for; Kyle Lobner, "Carlos Gomez Contract," Brew Crew Ball, March 13, 2013, https://www.brewcrewball.com/2013/3/13/4100652/-carlos-gomez-contract-brewers-set-to-extend-center-fielder-for-four.

40. "MLB Sets Sights on Braun, A-Rod," *USA Today*, March 19, 2013.

41. "More Opening Day Woes for Yovani Gallardo," JS Online Brewers Blog, April 1, 2013.

42. "Late to the Festivities," *Milwaukee Journal Sentinel*, April 2, 2013.

43. Ibid.

44. Ibid.

45. "Silence Broken," *Milwaukee Journal Sentinel*, November 28, 2013.

46. "Ryan Braun, Dino Laurenzi Jr., and Dinner," JS Online Brewers Blog, November 27, 2013.

47. NoahCJ, "Brewers Trade Rumors," Brew Crew Ball, November 11, 2013, https://www.brewcrewball.com/2013/11/11/5088682/brewers-red-sox-ryan-dempster-trade-rumors; NoahCJ, "Brewers Appear Unwilling to Give Up Pitching in Trades," Brew Crew Ball, January 6, 2014, https://www.brewcrewball.com/2014/1/6/5280106/ike-davis-brewers-mets-trade-rumors.

48. "Brewers Appear Unwilling to Give Up Pitching in Trades"; NoahCJ, "Matt Garza, Brewers Agree to 4-year Contract," Brew Crew Ball, January 23, 2014, https://www.brewcrewball.com/2014/1/23/5338482/matt-garza-brewers-free-agent-signing.

49. Danielle Mauldin, "From Stray to Stardom," TieBreaker, August 1, 2018, https://www.tiebreaker.com/hank-mlb-milwaukee-brewers-ballpark-pup/?post_diff=14809,&utm_content=&utm_source.

50. "Lots to Dig on Opening Day," *Milwaukee Journal Sentinel*, April 1, 2014.

51. "Game Report," *Milwaukee Journal Sentinel*, April 1, 2014.

52. "Braun's Focus Takes Hit After Warm Reception," *Milwaukee Journal Sentinel*, April 1, 2014.

53. Ibid.

54. "In-Game Blog," JS Online Brewers Blog, March 31, 2014.

55. "A Kiss Goodbye," *Milwaukee Journal Sentinel*, April 1, 2014.

56. "Ron Roenicke will Remain," Brew Crew Ball, October 10, 2014.

57. NoahCJ, "Brewers Trade Rumors," Brew Crew Ball, November 24, 2014, https://www.brewcrewball.com/2014/11/24/7275889/brewers-trade-rumors-yovani-gallardo-kyle-lohse.

58. NoahCJ, "The Most Boring Offseason in Brewers History," Brew Crew Ball, January 14, 2015, https://www.brewcrewball.com/2015/1/14/7545297/-Brewers-offseason-rumors-trades-signings.

59. Derek Harvey, "Brewers in Serious Talks to Acquire Jonathan Papelbon," Brew Crew Ball, January 23, 2015, https://www.brewcrewball.com/2015/1/23/7876873/-brewers-in-serious-talks-to-acquire-jonathan-papelpon; NoahCJ, "James Shields Could be Falling Right into Brewers' Price Range," Brew Crew Ball, February 3, 2015, https://www.brewcrewball.com/2015/2/3/7968751/james-shields-rumors-signing-brewers.

60. "Braun Gives Spring a Thumb's Up," *Milwaukee Journal Sentinel*, April 6, 2015.

61. "Opener Offers Tribute to Attanasio's Father," *Milwaukee Journal Sentinel*, April 7, 2015; "Season Starts with a Pratfall," *Milwaukee Journal Sentinel*, April 7, 2015.

62. "Season Starts with a Pratfall."

63. Ibid.

64. "Brewers Give Counsell Three-Year Deal," JS Online Brewers Blog, May 4, 2015.

65. "More Than a General Sense," *Milwaukee Journal*, September 22, 2015.

66. Kyle Lesniewski, "Brewers Trade Rumors," Brew Crew Ball, October 26, 2015, https://www.brewcrewball.com/2015/10/26/9614402/report-brewers-willing-to-listen-to-offers-on-anybody.

67. Jayson Stark, "The Odd and

Notes—Chapter Five

Troubling State of the National League," ESPN.com, January 14, 2016, https://www.espn.com/mlb/story/_/id/14568028/odd-troubling-state-national-league.

68. Kyle Lesniewski, "Jonathan Lucroy Admits Trade Best for Both Sides," Brew Crew Ball, January 20, 2016, https://www.brewcrewball.com/2016/1/20/10796900/-jonathan-lucroy-admits-hed-rather-get-traded.

69. Kyle Lesniewski, "Brewers Farm System Ranked 9th by Baseball America," Brew Crew Ball, February 12, 2016, https://www.brewcrewball.com/2016/2/12/10977652/milwaukee-brewers-farm-system-ranked-9th-by-baseball-america.

70. "Stumbling Out of the Gate," *Milwaukee Journal Sentinel*, April 4, 2016.

71. "Brewers Fans Brave Cold for Tailgating Fun," *Milwaukee Journal Sentinel* Web Edition, April 4, 2016.

72. Ibid.

73. "Stumbling Out of the Gate," *Milwaukee Journal Sentinel*, April 4, 2016.

74. Jaymes L, "Brewers Extend Craig Counsell's Contract Through 2020," Brew Crew Ball, November 11, 2016, https://www.brewcrewball.com/2016/11/11/13599208/brewers-craig-counsell-manager-extension.

75. "Brewers Extend Craig Counsell's Contract Through 2020."

76. Kyle Lesniewski, "Dodgers Debt Problems Could Complicate Potential Ryan Braun Trade," Brew Crew Ball, November 28, 2016, https://www.brewcrewball.com/2016/11/28/13762394/-dodgers-debt-problems-could-complicate-potential-ryan-braun-trade.

77. Kyle Lesniewski, "Brewers Sign 1B/OF Eric Thames to 3 Year Deal," Brew Crew Ball, November 29, 2016, https://www.brewcrewball.com/2016/11/29/13775078/milwaukee-brewers-sign-1b-of-eric-thames-to-3-year-deal.

78. "From Bust to 'God' and Back," *USA Today*, April 18, 2017; "Brewers Sign 1B/OF Eric Thames to 3 Year Deal."

79. "From Bust to "God" and Back."

80. Jaymes L, "Travis Shaw had to Google Tyler Thornburg After Trade," Brew Crew Ball, December 20, 2016, https://www.brewcrewball.com/2016/12/20/14029372/travis-shaw-google-tyler-thornburg-trade.

81. "Signs of Trouble Are Quick to Emerge," *Milwaukee Journal Sentinel*, April 4, 2017.

82. Ibid.

83. Kyle Lesniewski, "Milwaukee Brewers May be Setting Their Sights on Jake Arrieta," Brew Crew Ball, November 12, 2017, https://www.brewcrewball.com/2017/11/12/16640216/milwaukee-brewers-may-be-setting-their-sights-on-jake-arrieta-per-report.

84. JP, "Milwaukee Brewers Outfielders are Drawing Trade Interest," Brew Crew Ball, December 8, 2017, https://www.brewcrewball.com/2017/12/8/16754694/-milwaukee-brewers-outfielders-domingo-santana-trade-interest-ryan-braun-brett-phillips-lewis-brinson; Kyle Lesniewski, "Report: Milwaukee Brewers Among Teams Exploring Chris Archer Trade," Brew Crew Ball, December 11, 2017, https://www.brewcrewball.com/2017/12/11/16765090/-report-milwaukee-brewers-among-teams-exploring-chris-archer-trade; JP, "Milwaukee Brewers Talking with Pirates About Gerrit Cole, Josh Harrison," Brew Crew Ball, December 12, 2017, https://www.brewcrewball.com/2017/12/12/16769852/milwaukee-brewers-talking-with-pirates-about-gerrit-cole-josh-harrison.

85. Ryan Fagan, "Brewers' Jeremy Jeffress Talks About Epilepsy, Rehab Realizations, and his Dog," *Sporting News*, April 18, 2019, https://www.sportingnews.com/us/mlb/news/brewers-jeremy-jeffress-talks-about-epilepsy-rehab-realizations-and-his-dog/fbze5ql8fc0a140sbwls795mg.

86. "In a Quiet Winter for Baseball Industry, Brewers Continue to Explore Personnel Moves," *Milwaukee Journal Sentinel*, January 6, 2018.

87. Kyle Lesniewski, "Milwaukee Brewers have Submitted an Offer to Yu Darvish, per Report," Brew Crew Ball, January 21, 2018, https://www.brewcrewball.com/2018/1/21/16917498/milwaukee-brewers-have-submitted-an-offer-to-yu-darvish-per-report.

88. "Stearns Knocks Two out of the Park," *Milwaukee Journal Sentinel*, January 26, 2018.

89. Kyle Lesniewski, "Milwaukee Brewers Have Made a Nine-Figure Offer to Yu

Darvish, Per Report," Brew Crew Ball, February 8, 2018, https://www.brewcrewball.com/2018/2/8/16993438/milwaukee-brewers-have-made-a-nine-figure-offer-to-yu-darvish-per-report; "Travis Shaw, Christian Yelich Listed as Dark Horse MVP Candidates by MLB.com," Brew Crew Ball, February 5, 2018, https://www.brewcrewball.com/2018/2/5/16974028/travis-shaw-christian-yelich-listed-as-dark-horse-mvp-candidates-by-mlb-com.

90. "Little-Known Pitcher Miles Mikolas Ruins Brewers Home Opener with His Bat," *Milwaukee Journal Sentinel* Web Edition, April 2, 2018.

91. "Cardinals Have A Knack for Spoiling Brewers' Parties," *Milwaukee Journal Sentinel* Web Edition, April 2, 2018.

92. Kyle Lesniewski, "Milwaukee Brewers Interested in JA Happ, Per Report," Brew Crew Ball, November 23, 2018, https://www.brewcrewball.com/2018/11/23/18108655/milwaukee-brewers-among-those-interested-ja-happ-per-report-astros-yankees-blue-jays-angels-phillies; Kyle Lesniewski, "Milwaukee Brewers Interested in trading for Madison Bumgarner, Per Report," Brew Crew Ball, November 27, 2018, https://www.brewcrewball.com/2018/11/27/18114137/milwaukee-brewers-interested-in-trading-for-madison-bumgarner-per-report-san-francisco-giants; Brad Ford, "Milwaukee Brewers Interested in trading for Noah Syndergaard, Per Report," Brew Crew Ball, November 29, 2018, https://www.brewcrewball.com/2018/11/29/18117444/milwaukee-brewers-showing-interest-in-acquiring-noah-syndergaard-per-report-new-york-mets.

93. "Brewers' Annual 'On Deck' Event Sells Out," *Milwaukee Journal Sentinel* Web Edition, January 7, 2019.

94. "2018-19 Top 50 MLB Free Agents," MLB Trade Rumors, November 3, 2018, https://www.mlbtraderumors.com/2018/11/mlb-free-agent-predictions-2019.html.

95. "2018-19 Top 50 MLB Free Agents," MLB Trade Rumors, November 3, 2018, https://www.mlbtraderumors.com/2018/11/mlb-free-agent-predictions-2019.html; Eric Stephen, "Tony Clark's Statement on Collusion was a Necessary Stand Against MLB," SB Nation, November 7, 2019, https://www.sbnation.com/mlb/2019/11/7/20953616/tony-clark-mlbpa-statement-collusion-mlb-labor-war; Kyle Lesniewski, "Talks Between Milwaukee, Craig Kimbrell, are 'Pretty Serious,' Per Report," Brew Crew Ball, March 20, 2019, https://www.brewcrewball.com/2019/3/20/18275066/talks-between-milwaukee-brewers-craig-kimbrel-are-pretty-serious-per-report.

96. Kyle Lesniewski, "The Chips Are All In Now, Says the Owner of the Milwaukee Brewers," Brew Crew Ball, February 22, 2019, https://www.brewcrewball.com/2019/2/22/18235927/milwaukee-brewers-mark-attanasio-the-chips-are-all-in-now-says-the-owner.

97. "National Writers Predict Where the Brewers Will Finish in 2019," *Milwaukee Journal Sentinel* Web Edition, March 27, 2019.

98. "When Lorenzo Cain and the Brewers Put their Hands Up in Celebration, They're Just Looking for a Little Love," *Milwaukee Journal Sentinel*, June 14, 2018.

99. "It was just One Game Out of 162, But Brewers Provided Wow Factor in Season Opener," *Milwaukee Journal Sentinel* Web Edition, March 28, 2019; "Brewers 5, Cardinals 4," *Milwaukee Journal Sentinel* Web Edition, March 28, 2019.

100. "Brewers 5, Cardinals 4," *Milwaukee Journal Sentinel* Web Edition, March 28, 2019.

101. "It was just One Game Out of 162, But Brewers Provided Wow Factor in Season Opener."

102. Ibid.

103. "Brewers 5, Cardinals 4," *Milwaukee Journal Sentinel* Web Edition, March 28, 2019.

Chapter Six

1. David Gibson, "Lorenzo Cain, Keston Hiura, Josh Hader," Brew Crew Ball, December 3, 2019, https://www.brewcrewball.com/2019/12/3/20993436/milwaukee-brewers-lorenzo-cain-keston-hiura-josh-hader-available-for-trade.

2. Jaymes L, "Brewers On Deck," Brew Crew Ball, January 26, 2020, https://www.brewcrewball.com/2020/1/26/21082670/brewers-on-deck-payroll-mark-attanasio;

Kyle Lesniwski, "Owner Mark Attanasio Says Milwaukee Brewers Operated "at a loss" Last Year," Brew Crew Ball, February 19, 2020, https://www.brewcrewball.com/2020/2/19/21143687/milwaukee-brewers-owner-mark-attanasio-operated-at-a-loss-last-year.

3. Jaymes L, "Christian Yelich Gives First Comments Since Signing Historic Contract Extension," Brew Crew Ball March 6, 2020, https://www.brewcrewball.com/2020/3/6/21168200/christian-yelich-milwaukee-brewers-extension-press-conference-comments.

4. Dayn Perry, Katherine Acquavalla, and R.J. Anderson, "Timeline of How COVID-19 Pandemic has Impacted the 2020 MLB Season," CBS Sports, July 29, 2020, https://www.cbssports.com/mlb/news/timeline-of-how-the-covid-19-pandemic-has-impacted-the-2020-major-league-baseball-season/.

5. "Timeline of How COVID-19 Pandemic has Impacted the 2020 MLB Season."

6. "MLB Players Agree to 60-Game Regular Season, will Report to Training Camp on July 1," Brew Crew Ball, June 23, 2020, https://www.brewcrewball.com/2020/6/23/21299907/mlb-players-agree-to-60-game-regular-season-will-report-to-training-camp-on-july-1st.

7. Kyle Lesniwski, "Ryan Braun Day-to-Day," Brew Crew Ball, July 28, 2020, https://www.brewcrewball.com/2020/7/28/21345625/milwaukee-brewers-ryan-braun-opt-out-coronavirus.

8. Jaymes L, "Lorenzo Cain Issues Statement After Opting out of 2020 Season," Brew Crew Ball, August 1, 2020, https://www.brewcrewball.com/2020/8/1/21351033/milwaukee-brewers-lorenzo-cain-opt-out-2020-season-statement.

9. "The Count Goes Against Them," *Milwaukee Journal Sentinel*, August 4, 2020; David Gibson, "Milwaukee Brewers Bench Coach Pat Murphy Suffers Heart Attack," Brew Crew Ball, August 2, 2020, https://www.brewcrewball.com/2020/8/2/21352086/milwaukee-brewers-bench-coach-pat-murphy-suffers-heart-attack.

10. "With a Fateful 3-0 pitch, The Night Turned Sour for Corbin Burnes and the Brewers," *Milwaukee Journal Sentinel* Web Edition, August 4, 2020.

11. "With a Fateful 3-0 pitch, The Night Turned Sour for Corbin Burnes and the Brewers."

12. "The Count Goes Against Them," *Milwaukee Journal Sentinel*, August 4, 2020.

13. Kyle Lesniwski, "Milwaukee Brewers Announce Coaching Staff for 2021," Brew Crew Ball, November 4, 2020, https://www.brewcrewball.com/2020/11/4/21550003/milwaukee-brewers-announce-coaching-staff-for-2021-ed-sedar-moves-to-advisory-role.

14. "Brewers Promote Matt Arnold," *Milwaukee Journal Sentinel*, November 19, 2020; Jaymes L, "Reports: Brewers Reject Mets' Request to Interview David Stearns," Brew Crew Ball, November 17, 2020, https://www.brewcrewball.com/2020/11/17/21571256/reports-brewers-reject-mets-request-to-interview-david-stearns.

15. JP, "Reports: Start of MLB 2021 Season Could be Delayed," Brew Crew Ball, December 17, 2020, https://www.brewcrewball.com/2020/12/17/22180012/-report-start-of-mlb-2021-season-could-be-delayed.

16. David Gibson, "No Requirement for COVID-19 Testing or Vaccinations for Fans," Brew Crew Ball, January 12, 2021, https://www.brewcrewball.com/2021/1/12/22226807/-no-requirement-for-covid-19-testing-or-vaccinations-for-fans-attending-mlb-games-in-2021; JP, "Report: MLB to Delay Start of AA and A Minor League Seasons," Brew Crew Ball, January 6, 2021, https://www.brewcrewball.com/2021/1/6/22215885/report-mlb-to-delay-start-of-double-a-and-class-a-minor-league-seasons.

17. David Gibson, "Union Rejects League's Latest Proposal," Brew Crew Ball, February 2, 2021, https://www.brewcrewball.com/2021/2/2/22262191/union-rejects-latest-proposal-spring-training-162-game-mlb-regular-season-expected-to-begin-on-time.

18. Jaymes L, "Brewers Ask Health Officials to Allow 35% Capacity at American Family Field," Brew Crew Ball, February 18, 2020, https://www.brewcrewball.com/2021/2/18/22290456/brewers-ask-health-officials-to-allow-35-capacity-at-american-family-field.

19. "Milwaukee Could Reinstate COVID Restrictions if Cases Don't Ease," *Milwaukee Journal Sentinel*, Mach 31, 2021.

20. Kyle Lesniwski, "On the Eve of Opening Day, Milwaukee Brewers Endure a False Positive COVID-19 Scare," Brew Crew Ball, March 31, 2021, https://www.brewcrewball.com/2021/3/31/22361372/on-the-eve-of-opening-day-milwaukee-brewers-endure-a-false-positive-covid-19-scare.

21. "Long Wait for Brewers' Fans Well Worth It," *Milwaukee Journal Sentinel*, April 2, 2021.

22. "Brewers 6, Twins 5 (10 Innings)," *Milwaukee Journal Sentinel*, April 2, 2021.

23. "Long Wait for Brewers' Fans Well Worth It."

24. "Brewers 6, Twins 5 (10 Innings)."

25. "After a Season in Which so Much Felt Wrong, Brewers and Their Fans are Eager for Fresh Start," *Milwaukee Journal Sentinel* Web Edition, March 31, 2021.

26. Kyle Lesniewski, "Matt Arnold Withdraws Name from Consideration for Mets' Job," Brew Crew Ball, October 27, 2021, https://www.brewcrewball.com/2021/10/27/22748383/-matt-arnold-withdraws-name-from-consideration-for-mets-job-will-get-extension-with-brewers; Kyle Lesniewski, "Matt Arnold Withdraws Name from Consideration for Mets' Job," Brew Crew Ball, October 27, 2021, https://www.brewcrewball.com/2021/10/27/22748383/matt-arnold-withdraws-name-from-consideration-for-mets-job-will-get-extension-with-brewers.

27. "Brewers Ace Corbin Burnes Wins National League Cy Young Award," *Milwaukee Journal Sentinel*, November 17, 2021.

28. Ethan Sanabria and Ben Morse, "MLB Lockout: What we Know—a Timeline," CNN.com, March 10, 2022, https://www.cnn.com/2022/02/28/sport/-mlb-lockout-explainer-spt-intl/index.html; Tim Stebbins, "Lockout Timeline," NBC Sports, February 24, 2022, https://www.nbcsports.com/chicago/cubs/mlb-lockout-timeline-another-day-little-progress-talks.

29. Sanabria and Morse, "MLB Lockout: What we Know—a Timeline."

30. Jacob Lev and David Close, "MLB Reaches Labor Agreement with Players," CNN.com, March 10, 2022, https://www.cnn.com/2022/03/10/sport/mlb-labor-deal-spt/index.html.

31. JP, "Brewers Have Shown Interest in Nelson Cruz, per Report," Brew Crew Ball, March 13, 2022, https://www.brewcrewball.com/2022/3/13/22975207/-brewers-have-shown-interest-in-nelson-cruz-per-report.

32. Will Sammon, "The Brewers Look Like Contenders Once Again," The Athletic, March 24, 2022, https://theathletic.com/3208287/2022/03/24/the-brewers-look-like-contenders-once-again-but-will-they-end-up-one-big-move-short-of-a-title/.

33. Bruce Murphy, "Brewers Want $100m Tax Subsidy?" Urban Milwaukee, March 14, 2022, https://urbanmilwaukee.com/2022/03/14/back-in-the-news-brewers-want-100-million-tax-subsidy/; Bruce Murphy, "Brewers Seek More Taxpayer Dollars," Urban Milwaukee, February 14, 2022; "Here's How the Milwaukee Brewers Might Seek $100 million in New Public Money," *Milwaukee Journal Sentinel*, March 11, 2022.

34. "Sidewalks Below Chase Tower Closed," *Milwaukee Journal Sentinel*, April 15, 2022.

35. "Brandon Woodruff is Sharp V. Cardinals," *Milwaukee Journal Sentinel*, April 14, 2022; Will Sammon, "Brewers' Woodruff Takes Out His Frustration on the Cardinals," The Athletic, April 14, 2022, https://theathletic.com/3251258/2022/04/14/brewers-brandon-woodruff-takes-out-his-frustration-on-the-cardinals-not-the-umpire-this-time/.

36. "Brandon Woodruff is Sharp V. Cardinals," *Milwaukee Journal Sentinel*, April 14, 2022.

37. Ibid.

38. Ibid.

Bibliography

Books

Okrent, Daniel. *Nine Innings: The Anatomy of Baseball as Seen Through the Playing of a Single Game*. New York: McGraw-Hill, 1985.

Simon, Ron. *The Game Behind the Game: Negotiating in the Big Leagues*. Stillwater, MN: Voyageur, 1993.

Zantow, Chris. *Building the Brewers: Bud Selig and the Return of Major League Baseball to Milwaukee*. Jefferson, NC: McFarland, 2019.

Periodicals

Milwaukee Journal
Milwaukee Journal-Sentinel
Milwaukee Sentinel
New York Daily News
Shepherd Express (Milwaukee)
Sporting News
Sports Illustrated

Websites

Baseballamerica.com
Baseballprospectus.com
Baseball-reference.com
Brewcrewball.com
ESPN.com
Expressmilwaukee.com
Fangraphs.com
Jsonline.com
Mlbbro.com
Mlbtraderumors.com
Onmilwaukee.com
SABR.org
Si.com
Theathletic.com
Thebaseballcube.com
Thisgreatgame.com
Tiebreaker.com
Tmz.com
Upi.com
Urbanmilwaukee.com

Index

Numbers in **_bold italics_** indicate pages with illustrations

Aaron, Henry **_26_**, 27, 28–29, 30, 34, 127, 222
Abbott, Jim 129
ABC World News 193
American Family Field *see* Miller Park
Aoki, Nori 186, 187, 189
Archer, Chris 208
Arcia, Orlando 205, 207, 221, 225, 231
Arenado, Nolan 197
Arizona Diamondbacks 1, 145–146
Arnold, Matt 221
Arnsberg, Brad 90–91
Arrieta, Jake 207, 208, 210
Atlanta Braves 182–183, 193–194
Attanasio, Joe 156, 160, 197
Attanasio, Mark 154–155, 157, 158, 159, 162, 199, 201, 212, 217, 227
Augustine, Jerry 42, 44, 46, 70, 71
Axford, John 180, 190

Baltimore Oriole 20–21, 37–38, 42–44, 97–99
Bamberger, George 40, 41, 42, 45, 47, 50–51, 52–53, 54, 58, 71, 75, 76, 79, 153
Bando, Sal 35–36, 37, 39, 45, 46, 47, 58, 100, 104–105, 121, 126, 134, 135
Baumer, Jim 27, 37, 39
Baylor, Don 94, 100, 135
Beckum, James 201
Bell, Jerry 24
Bernie Brewer 18–19, 21, 73
Berry, Sean 129
Betts, Bob 52, 132
Birkbeck, Mike 86–87, 88
Blair, Paul 21
Bonds, Barry 150
Bosch, Anthony 188
Bosio, Chris 97–98
Boston Red Sox 23–25, 47–48, 52–53, 82–83
Branyan, Russell 155, 156–157
Braun, Ryan 1, 163, 166, 167, **_178_**, 179–180, 182, 183, 187, 193, 195–196, 202, 203, 207–208, 212, **_213_**, 218–219, 221; PED controversy 184–185, 186, 187–188, 191–192
brewcrewblog.com 163, 195–196
Briggs, John 12, 24, 25, 29–30
Bristol, Dave 6, 10, 17, 111
Brock, Greg 80
Brooks, Robert 119
Brown, Ollie 20, 21
Buckner, Bill 82
Burnes, Corbin 221, 226
Burnitz, Jeromy 121, 125, 126, 128, 131, 132, 140–141, 142, 144, 231
Burris, Ray 71
Bush, George W. 142, 145

Cabrera, Melky 171, 183
Cain, Lorenzo 3, 181, 208, 209, 210, 214, 215, 219, 223
Caldwell, Mike 46–48, 56–57, 58–59, 71, 231
California Angels 8–9, 11–12, 106–107
Cameron, Mike 166–167, 171, 175, 176
Capuano, Chris 152, 158, 176
Carroll, Clay 45
Carter, Chris 199, 202, 203
Chacin, Jhoulys 1, 208, 210, 212–214, 215, 216
Champion. Bill 29
Chapman, Lou 7, 14, 23, 45
Chicago Cubs 131–133, 172–174
Chicago White Sox 69–70, 74–75, 94–95, 115–116, 219–220
Chmura, Mark 138
Cincinnati Reds 141–143
Cirillo, Jeff 133, 136, 155, 157, 161
Clark, Brady 147, 157, 165
Clayton, Royce 147, 150
Clear, Mark 76
Cleveland Indians 28–29, 56–57
Colburn, Jim 23–24, 27, 36
Cole, Gerrit 208
Coleman, Joe 17
Colorado Rockies 177–179, 188–191, 197–198, 205–206

Conley, Gene 145
Cooper, Cecil 1, 24, 36–37, 42, 45, 46, 61, 62, 84
Cordero, Francisco 162, 166
Correa, Ed 77–78
Counsell, Craig *51*, 62, 152, 153, 163, 179, 198–199, 202, 206, 211, 215, 220, 229
Counsell, John 62
COVID-19 217–219, 221, 222–223, 229
Crandall, Del 19, 21, 23, 25, 29, 30–31, 43
Crim, Chuck 91
cryptosporidium 105–106, 108

Dalton, Harry 39, 41, 52–52, 54–55, 59, 62, 63, 66–67, 71, 76, 84, 88–89, 92, 96, 97, 98, 100
D'Amico, Jeff 142, 143
Damon, Johnny 140
Darvish, Yu 207, 208, 210
Darwin, Danny 76
Davis, Dick 71
Davis, Doug 156, 158, 160, 162, 176
Davis, Khris 192, 200
Deer, Rob 76, 79
Dembski, Barbara 57
Dempsey, Rick 38
Detroit Tigers 16–17
Devereaux, Mike 115
Diaz, Kiki 156
Dickerson, Corey 197
Dierkes, Tim 163
Divisional Series 57, 58, 169, 225, 226
Donaldson, John 7
Doyne, John 8, 12, 16
Dwyre, Bill 32

Earl, Tony 73
Edmunds, Jim 176
Eldred, Cal 104, 106–107, 122, 137
Enatsu, Yutaka 72
Estrada, Johnny 162, 166

Fielder, Prince 1, 158, 166, 167, 176, 179–180, 181, 182, 183
Fingers, Rollie 54–55, 56, 58, 59, 60–61, 63, 67, 68, 71, 75, 212, *213*
Fitzgerald, Edmund 17
Fitzgerald, Jim 68, 73
Florida Marlins 138–139
free agency 31, 35, 39–40, 45, 55, 56, 67, 92–93, 96, 100, 104–105, 117, 126, 129, 136, 140, 144, 147, 155, 162, 163, 166, 170–171, 176, 182–183, 188, 192, 196, 208, 211–212, 222, 226, 227; collusion by owners against 76, 80, 89, 93, 96
Freese, David 186
Frisella, Danny 36

Gagne, Eric 166, 167, 170–171
Gallardo, Yovani 175, 177–178, 185–186, 188–189, 193, 194, 195, 196

Gammons, Peter 76
Gantner, Jim 42, 46, 55, 72, 74, 88, 97, 106
Garcia, Pedro 19, 20, 21
Garland, Wayne 56
Garner, Phil 100, 102, 111, 113, 116, 124, 128, 131, 132, 133, 134, 135
Garza, Matt 192
Giamatti, Bart 90
Giles, Brian 72
Gomez, Carlos 175–176, 183, 185, 188, 193, 199
Gomez, Hector 1
Gonzalez, Gio 187, 211
Good Morning America 192
Gossage, Goose 49
Grammas, Alex 30, 34, 35, 38, 39
Grandal, Yasmani 187, 212, 216
Green, David 55, 75–76
Green Bay Packers 7, 11, 94, 112–113, 122, 182
Greer, Rusty 123
Greinke, Zack 181, 183, 186, 187
Grissom, Marquis 126
Guerra, Junior 199, 202, 205

Haas, Moose 60, 69–70, 74
Hader, Josh 3, 199, 211, 215, 225, 230, 231
Hall, Bill 162, *164*, 165, 168–169, 176, 231
Hamilton, Darryl 117, 118
Hammonds, Jeffrey 140, 143, 151
Haney, Larry 76
Hank (dog) 192–193
Hardy, J.J. 155–156, 158, 166, 175–176, 231
Hargrove, Mike 57
Harmon, Merle 28
Harper, Tommy 7, 13
Harris, Devin 153
Hart, Corey 158, 166, 172, 176, 177, 181, 187
Hartenstein, Chuck 87, 92
Harvey, Matt 208
Hegan, Mike 7
Henderson, Jim 194
Henry, Doug 107–108
Hernandez, Jose 136, 147
Higuera, Ted 72, 80–81, 82–83, 84–85, *85*, 88, 89, 96, 105, 177
Hisle, Larry 40, 42, 43, 47, 48, 57, 63, 145
Hiura, Keston 211, 222
Hoffman, Dale 152
Hoffman, Trevor 171, 180
Horn, Sam 99
Hough, Charlie 90
Houston Astros 153–154
Hovley, Steve 8
Howard, Frank 40, 46
Hunt, Michael 147
Hunter, Catfish 34

Infante, Lindy 94

Jackson, Reggie 60
Jaha, John 115, *116*

Index 259

James, Dion 72
Jansen, Dan 86
Jeffress, Jeremy 200, 202, 207, 209, 211, 216
Jenkins, Geoff 137, 140–141, 147, 151
John, Tommy 87
Johnson, Randy 171
Johnson, Tim 22
Jones, Doug 125
Justice, Richard 209

Kansas City Royals 64–66
Karl, Scott 127–128, 136
Kendall, Jason 166
Kieschnick, Brooks 147–148, 153–154
Knebel, Corey 196, 221
Knoblauch, Chuck 102–103
Kobel, Kevin 27
Kohl, Herb 73, 90, 152
Kolb, Dan 151
Kosco, Andy 11
Koskie, Corey 159, 162
Kottaras, George 1
Krausse, Lew 8
Kubiak, Ted 6
Kuenn, Audrey 62, 86
Kuenn, Harvey 10, 50–51, *61*, 62, 65, 66, 85, 86
Kuhn, Bowie 29

labor disputes 14–16, 19, 31–32, 50–51, 55–56, 57, 58, 93, 112–114, 212, 218, 226–227
Lachemann, Rene 66–67, 69, 70, 71
Ladd, Pete 59, 75
Lahoud, Joe 15, 17
Lane, Frank 10–11, 13–14
League Championship Series 61, 183, 210, 228
Lee, Carlos 155, 162
Lerch, Randy 59
Levy, Paul 32
Lezcano, Sixto 29, *43*, 49–50, 52–53, 55, 231
Lind, Adam 195, 199
Listach, Pat 104, 121
Lloyd, Graeme 107, 120, 121
Lockwood, Skip 11–12
Lofton, Kenny 126
Logan, Johnny 145
Lohse, Kyle 188, 195, 197, 198, 199
Lonborg, Jim 14–15
Looper, Braden 171, 172, 175
Lopes, Davey 135–136, 139, 140, 146
Los Angeles Dodgers 163–165
Lucroy, Johnathan 181, 185, 191, 200–201, 202
Lynn, Fred 48

Macha, Ken 147, 170, 176–177, 179–180
Manfred, Rob 218, 223, 227
Manning, Rick 77
Marcum, Sean 181, 187
Martin, Billy 34

Martinez, Jose 3
Mason, Milt 18
Matheny, Mike 124, 231
Maxx, Sandy 150
May, Dave 22
McClung, Seth 174
McClure, Bob 54, 62, 65, 77
McCutchen, Andrew 227
McDonald, Ben 118, 119–120
McGehee, Casey 172, 177, 180
McPhail, Lee 65
Melvin, Doug 147, 152, 158, 162, 166, 171,175, 182, 187, 199
Messersmith, Andy 8–9
Miley, Wade 209, 210
Milkes, Marvin 5, 9–10
Miller, Damien 155
Miller, Wade 153
Miller Park 117, 118–119, 120, 121, 122, 125, 127, 131, *133*, 134, 135, 137, *138*, 141–142, 144, 148, *149*, 151, 156, 158–159, 163, 172, 182, *189*, *195*, *219*, 222; as American Family Field 223, *224*, 227–228
Milwaukee Braves 7, 9, 16, 131
Milwaukee Bucks 68, 73–74
Milwaukee County Stadium 7–8, 11, 16, *18*, 20, 28, 42, 62, *64*, 69, 72–73, *78*, *81*, 83, *98*, 109, *110*, *113*, *119*, 122, 131–132, 133–134, *136*, 137, *138*, 139; need for replacement of 89, 96–97, 101, 104–105, 108, 112–113, 114, 117, 119
Minnesota Twins 102–103, 223–225
Mr. Belvedere 89
MLBtraderumors.com 163
Molitor, Paul 1, *41*, 41–42, 44, 45, 62, 63, 66, 67–68, 69, 71, 72, 82, 84, 92, 93, 101, 104–105, 108, 117, 130–131
Money, Don 19, *33*, 46, 53, 55, 67
Montreal Expos 127–128
Moore, Charlie 46, 59, 75, 80
Morgan, Nyjer 182, 183, 185
Moustakas, Mike 211, 212, 213, 216
Murphy, Pat 219
Muser, Tony 76, 79, 92

Narveson, Chris 182
Nelson, Jimmy 207
New York Yankees 32, 34, 46, 58, 85–87
Newfield, Marc 121
Nilsson, Dave 112
Norquist, John 86, 97, 152
Nunez, Edwin 99, 112

Oakland Athletics 119–120
Oates, Johnny 123
Obermueller, Wes 153
O'Donnell, John 56
Oglivie, Ben 40, 45, 52, 75, 80
Outside the Lines 184–185
Overbay, Lyle 152, 158

Palmer, Jim 37
Parker, Dave 92–93, 94, 97
Parsons, Bill 16, 20–21
Pattin, Marty 10, 11, 14
Payne, Ulice 42, 147, 148, 151
Pena, Roberto 12
People Magazine 192
Peralta, Freddy 199
Peralta, Wily 195
Pettit, Lloyd & Jane 73–74
Pinson, Vada 31
Pittsburgh Pirates 156–157, 160–161
Plesac, Dan 78–79, 83, 98
Podsednik, Scott 147, 148, 151, 155
Porter, Darrell 16, 27, 31, 36, 54, 77
Pujols, Albert 185, 228
Pulsipher, Bill 132

Quayle, Dan 102
Quinn, T.J. 188

Ramirez, Aramis 184, 187, 190, 194, 199, 231
Randolph, Willie 99, 135, 170
Raymonds, Hank 42, 65, 82
Ready, Randy 69–70, 71
replacement players 114
Reyes, Jose 184
Ritchie, Todd 149–150
Robidoux, Billy Jo 78
Robinson, Frank 28–29, 40
Rodgers, Bob "Buck" 50, 54, 55, 57, 58, 59, 61
Rodriguez, Eduardo 27
Rodriguez, Ellie 10, 12
Rodriguez, Francisco 196, 199
Roenicke, Ron *170*, 191, 195, 198
Rollins, Rich 6, 7
Rusch, Glendon 1, 144, 145–146
Ryan, Nolan 50, 89

Sabathia, CC 169, 170–171
Sackmann, Jeff 163
St. Louis Cardinals 3, 54–55, 176, 185–186, 209–210, 212–215, 219, 226, 228–230
Saito, Taskashi 182–183
San Francisco Giants 149–150, 168–169, 176, 200–202
Sanchez, Alex 144–145, 149, 151
Sandburg, Ryne 59
Santana, Domingo 199, 207
sausage race 116, 125
Scherzer, Max 196
Schilling, Curt 166
Schroeder, Bill 72, 82, 88
Schultz, Dale 86
Scott, George *13*, 14, 16, 22, 29, 35, 36, 47–48
Seaver, Tom 69–70, 74
Sedar, Ed 192, 221
Seitzer, Kevin 102–103, 113, 117, 121
Selig, Allen "Bud" 6, 7, 15, 16, 18, 20, 30, 31, 32, 39, 46, 68, 73–74, 90, 93, 96–97, 100, 101, 105, 108, 117, 119, 120, 125, 135, 141–142, 147, 151, 154–155, 205; as MLB commissioner 104, 108–109, 121–122, 129
Selig-Prieb, Wendy 129, 135, 144, 147, 151, 152
Sexson, Richie 140–141, 143, 147, 152
Seattle Pilots 5–6
Shaw, Travis 204, 207, 223
Sheets, Ben 137, 140, 141, 147, 158, 159, 163–165, 170
Sheffield, Gary 88, 94, 95, 97, 98–99, 101
Sick's Stadium 5
Simmons, Ted 54–55, 57, 58, 67, 75, 76–77
Simon, Ron 93
Skibosh, Tom 55
Skube, Bob 64, 65–66
Slaton, Jim 15, 32, 34, 40, 45, 52–53
Sorenson, Lary 48, 55
Sosa, Sammy 132
Spahn, Warren 131, 153
Sport 82
Sporting News 56, 63, 76, 88, 90, 93, 96, 108, 141
Sports Challenge 45
Sports Illustrated 141, 148, 159, 167
Sportsvue *68*, 69, 70
Sprague, Ed 27
Stairs, Matt 144, 147
Stanley, Bob 82–83
Stark, Jayson 200
Stearns, David 199, 200, 202, 210, 221–222
Stubbs, Franklin 96, 103
Sundberg, Jim 67, 71
Suppan, Jeff 162–163
Surhoff, B.J. 80, 112, 117
Suter, Brent 207, 216
Sutton, Don 71
Sveum, Dale 170

tailgating 28, 32, 37, *38*, 51–52, 56, 69, 73, 77, 82, 87, 90, 97, 115, 122, 127, 133–134, 141, 145, 153, 156, 167, *168*, 172, 197, 199, *213*, 228
Taylor, Aaron 122
Taylor, Dean 135, 136, 146
Tellman, Tom 65
Tenace, Gene 35, 36
Texas Rangers 59–61, 77–79, 122–125
Thames, Eric 203, *204*, 205, 206, 207, 210, 216, 231
Thomas, Gorman 1, 19, 40–41, 45, 46, 50, 53, 54, 55, 58, 59, 60, 62, 63, 64, 66, 80, 145
Thompson, Tommy 82, 114, 117, 119, 151
Tiant, Luis 24
Today Show 192
Tonight Show 89, 192
Torres, Solomon 169, 171
trades 8, 10, 13, 19, 22, 27, 36, 40, 55, 71, 76, 80, 88, 97, 101, 121, 126, 136, 137, 140, 144, 147, 152, 155, 158, 159, 161–162, 165, 169, 170, 175–176, 181, 182, 186, 192, 195, 199–200, 202, 204, 208, 211, 217, 221, 226; rumors 31,

40, 49, 54, 59, 84, 130, 140, 151, 171, 176, 192, 195, 203, 207–208, 211, 217
Travers, Billy 37
Trebelhorn, Tom 79–80, 82–83, 86–88, *87*, 95, 96, 97, 100
Tucker, Michael 142
Turnbow, Derrick 158, 161, 162, 171

Uecker, Bob 16, 85, 89–90, 124, 138, 141, 148
uniforms 7, 42, 109, 136–137, 158, 217
University of Wisconsin men's basketball team 138, 196, 197, 198
Urias, Luis 225
USA Today 188

Valentin, Jose 101, 128, 136, 231
Vander Wal, John 147, 149–150
Vaughn, Greg 95, 97, 111, 121
Villanueva, Carlos 168–169
Villar, Jonathan 199
Vina, Fernando 129–130, 132, 136
Vuckovich, Pete 54–55, 58, 62, 63, 67, 71, 77, 81–82, 85

Walton, Danny 12
Ward, Turner 1, 119–120, 231
Weathers, David 143

Weeks, Rickie 158, 160, 168, 172, *173*, 174, 195
Wegman, Bill 100
Wickman, Bob 121, 125, 139, 140
Wild Card Game 215, 216
Williams, Devin 221
Wilson, Jim 19, 20, 22
Wise, Matt 161
Wolf, Randy 176, 187
Wong, Kolton 222, 229–230
Woodruff, Brandon 228–229
World Series 13, 49, 61, 62
Wright, Clyde 11

Yahoo! Sports 187
Yastrzemski, Carl 25, 52, 53
Yelich, Christian 208, 209, 212, *213*, 215, 216, 217, 223
Yost, Ned 147, 148, 150, 154, 158, 169, 170, 195
Young, Dick 37
Young, Eric 144
Yount, Larry 105
Yount, Robin 1, 22–23, *23*, 24, 25, 28, 31–32, 39, 41–43, 44, 45, 46, 47, 48, 50, 54, 62, 63, 65, 72, 77, 82, 91, 92–93, 101, 102, 104, 105, 109–110, 141, 145, 158, 160, 212, *213*, 231

Zito, Barry 176

www.ingramcontent.com/pod-product-compliance
Ingram Content Group UK Ltd.
Pitfield, Milton Keynes, MK11 3LW, UK
UKHW041933140426
5217IPUK00014B/454